AUTHORITARIAN LAUGHTER

AUTHORITARIAN LAUGHTER

Political Humor and Soviet
Dystopia in Lithuania

Neringa Klumbytė

CORNELL UNIVERSITY PRESS   **ITHACA AND LONDON**

First published 2022 by Cornell University Press

Library of Congress Cataloging-in-Publication Data

Names: Klumbytė, Neringa, author.
Title: Authoritarian laughter : political humor and Soviet dystopia in Lithuania / Neringa Klumbytė.
Description: Ithaca, New York : Cornell University Press, 2022. | Includes bibliographical references and index.
Identifiers: LCCN 2022005833 (print) | LCCN 2022005834 (ebook) | ISBN 9781501766688 (hardcover) | ISBN 9781501766695 (paperback) | ISBN 9781501766701 (pdf) | ISBN 9781501766718 (ebook)
Subjects: LCSH: Šluota (Periodical)—Influence. | Political satire, Lithuanian. | Lithuania—Politics and government—20th century—Humor.
Classification: LCC DK505.74 .K585 2022 (print) | LCC DK505.74 (ebook) | DDC 947.93—dc23/eng/20220224
LC record available at https://lccn.loc.gov/2022005833
LC ebook record available at https://lccn.loc.gov/2022005834

For Ieva and Kajus

Contents

Acknowledgments   ix

Relevant Dates   xiii

Note on Transliteration   xv

Introduction: Authoritarian Laughter   1

1. Banality of Soviet Power   28

2. Political Intimacy   47

3. The Soviet Predicament   65

4. Censorial Indistinction   88

5. Political Aesthetics   118

6. Multidirectional Laughter   135

7. Satirical Justice   169

8. Soviet Dystopia   198

Post Scriptum: Revolution and Post-authoritarian Laughter   219

Conclusion: Lost Laughter and Authoritarian Stigma   229

Notes   235

References   263

Index   277

Acknowledgments

Any joke is a story that people tell each other about themselves. I was fascinated by the stories I discovered while exploring the state's attempts to create Soviet laughter in Lithuania and refashion people's emotions, morals, and thoughts. These stories uncovered the limits of authoritarianism and state power as well as the boundlessness of freedom. My gratitude for this journey goes to Lithuanian writers, journalists, and artists as well as my colleagues, friends, and family.

I am grateful to the artists, journalists, writers, and editors who generously shared their memories of their lives in Soviet times. My deepest gratitude goes to Kęstutis Šiaulytis and Dalia Šiaulytienė. I cannot even imagine this book without Kęstas's unwavering support and patience while answering my endless questions. Kęstas introduced me to the *Broom*'s laughter and guided me through its secret world of graphic art. I am grateful for his insights and friendship. As I write in my introduction, this book would not be the same without discovering the personal archive of Juozas Bulota, the longtime *Broom* editor in chief. My deep gratitude goes to his son, Juozas Bulota, for spending weeks with me while I reviewed this archive. Thank you to Donata Bulotienė for welcoming me to her summer home and her past.

I am indebted to Stasė Lukšienė and the late Albertas Lukša for always welcoming me into their beautiful village home. I treasure my memories of country cheese and honey covered in flowers, and I was happy to have met the "big dog" Mika. My gratitude goes to Andrius Cvirka and the late Birutė Cvirkienė for opening to me the worlds of art and deep history. Without them, the pages on artistic opposition in the *Broom* would not have been so interesting. I am also very thankful to the late Romas Palčiauskas and his family. Palčiauskas's comic strips populated the pages of the *Broom* and entertained Lithuanian youth, undermining the ideological goals of Soviet laughter. Alina Samukienė and Arvydas Samukas, the family of *Broom* artist Fridrikas Samukas, kindly shared their memories about Fridrikas Samukas's graphic art.

I was happy to have met Algirdas Radvilavičius and Anelė Radvilavičienė. I am grateful to their grandson Donatas Bartusevičius for keeping in touch. I wish that Radvilavičiai, Albertas Lukša, Romualdas Lankauskas, Andrius Deltuva, Birutė Cvirkienė, Goda Ferensienė, and Romuladas Palčiauskas had lived to see this project completed. They were in my thoughts when I wrote this book, and their memories are part of it, including Lukša's story about his mare Kaštonė that escaped from the Nazis and found her way back after three weeks, and Lankauskas's recollections of his "execution" by means of *Broom* parody. I thank Regina Rudaitytė and the late Romualdas Lankauskas for opening the doors to their world of art and literature for me; Vladimiras Beresniovas for stories about Kaunas's cartoonists; Šarūnas Jakštas, Jonas Lenkutis, and Andrius Gruzdaitis for thoughts about graphic art; and Jonas Varnas for teaching me that any state power is just a joke. Thank you to Vytautas Žeimantas, Domas Šniukas, Česlovas Juršėnas, Adolfas Strakšys, Ona Banadienė, Laima Zurbienė, and Jeronimas Laucius for introducing me to Soviet journalism and sharing their invaluable knowledge. Vytautė Žilinskaitė was one of a few women who wrote satires and feuilletons for the *Broom* as well as *Krokodil*. Her story of receiving a *Krokodil* diploma coated with glue spoke about uneasy gender and nationality relations. Dita Lomsargytė-Pukienė and Elena Kurklietytė-Bubnienė graciously shared their memories of work as journalists in Soviet times. I deeply value Dita Lomsargytė-Pukienė's insights into her life during World War II, which became an entrance to one of the chapters in this book.

For an outsider to the field, anthropological research may seem a strange endeavor—if someone looked at my online browsing history, they would see that I had to look up words on guns because cartoon characters were pictured with them, then searched *Playboy* pages in hope of finding an image published in the *Broom*; explored sites of drunk tanks and rehabilitation centers in search of adequate translations, or CIA websites for words to describe KGB documents. My daughter Ieva has always been a wonderful linguistic mediator and translator. When I asked her to check if my description of drunks lying on the street with wetted pants sounded right in English, I got a concerned message instead: "Mom, what are you writing about?" I never imagined that I would need to know the technical vocabulary of agricultural machinery or construction materials to understand what the *Broom* editors were talking about. Some of this vocabulary will be soon forgotten, since many Soviet realities do not exist anymore. While writing the book, I had to navigate through three different languages: Lithuanian, Russian, and English. I thank Glenn Novak, Sarah Stankorb, and Karyn Keane for editorial assistance. Many thanks to Benjamin Sutcliffe and Masha Stepanova for their assistance with transliteration.

I treasure the community at the Havighurst Center for Russian and Post-Soviet Studies at Miami University and especially the collegiality of Stephen Norris, Benjamin Sutcliffe, Venelin Ganev, Scott Kenworthy, Daniel Prior, and Zara Torlone. I know some of their thoughts have become mine, and I cannot untangle them now. Thanks to Stephen Norris for conversations about the *Broom* and *Krokodil*, for being the first to read my full manuscript, and for encouragement and inspiration. I am in debt to Benjamin Sutcliffe for always reminding me of the relevance of Russian literature. My Department of Anthropology colleagues, Mary Jane Berman, James Bielo, Cameron Hay-Rollins, Linda Marchant, Leighton Peterson, Mark Peterson, and Homayun Sidky, have always been supportive of my academic undertakings, and I deeply thank all of them. I thank my students, and especially Alex Adams and Brady Knox, for discussions on humor. Most of the research for this project was carried out in the summers of the 2010s and during my leave in 2016–17, which I spent in Lithuania. I am in debt to the Department of Anthropology, the Havighurst Center, and the College of Arts and Science at Miami University for the institutional support.

I am grateful to my colleagues and friends who read parts of this manuscript and provided important comments: Maria Galmarini-Kabala, Gediminas Lankauskas, Vasiliki Neofotistos, and Gulnaz Sharafutdinova. I have learned much from them, and sharing this work with them made my writing more meaningful. Rima Praspaliauskienė and I exchanged drafts of our book projects and underwent a publishing journey together. Thank you, Rima, for always being a call away and for your most valuable advice, friendship, stories, and jokes. I deeply thank Bruce Grant, Julie Hemment, and Dovilė Budrytė for reviewing this book. As always, Bruce pushed me to think beyond geographic and theoretical boundaries and reflect on the *Broom* in the context of the broader history of satire. Bruce's work on satire, empire, and peripheries has always been an inspiration. I thank Julie for noticing things I never did myself, for asking me questions about research and writing I never thought of asking, and for encouraging me to think about authoritarian politics in a global context. I am indebted to Dovilė Budrytė for insightfully suggesting that I address the relation between humor and revolution in greater depth. Thanks to Dovilė, I wrote the post scriptum to this book and reflected on perestroika time and post-authoritarian laughter. Martha Lampland generously read the entire manuscript as well. Her critical insights about history, gender, censorship, and humor helped me make some of my arguments more nuanced. My thanks go to Dominic Boyer, Elizabeth Dunn, Jessica Greenberg, Amir Weiner, and Nancy Ries for their support of this project. In the early stages of my work on humor, I learned a lot from Dominic Boyer and Angelique Haugerud and their fascinating work on political satire. I was lucky to work with James Lance at Cornell University, whose support and professional integrity made this book publication a memorable and heartfelt journey. My thanks go to Clare Jones and Karen Laun for overseeing this project at the production stage.

My interest in humor goes back to a conference, "Totalitarian Laughter: Culture of the Comic under Socialism," at Princeton University in 2009, organized by Serguei Oushakine. Discussions with Serguei and his inspiring work on Soviet satire and comedy informed my thinking. That the title of this book resonates with the conference title is something I owe partly to Serguei Oushakine and partly to Robert M. Hayden, whose thoughtful advice helped me choose it. I am thankful to Tomas Matza for inviting me to present my research at Pittsburgh University, my alma mater; to Amir Weiner for giving me an opportunity to present my research on humor at Stanford University; and to Krisztina Fehérváry for inviting me to give a lecture at the University of Michigan. I also thank Philip Gleissner for organizing a KruzhOHk lecture at the Ohio State University, and for valuable discussion on this topic with Epp Annus, Angela Brintlinger, Alexander Burry, Theodora Dragostinova, and other KruzhOHkians.

Dalia Cidzikaitė helped to organize an event devoted to the *Broom*, "Vanished Laughter," on April 28, 2017, at the Martynas Mažvydas National Library of Lithuania, which was filmed by Giedrius Subačius. Daukantė Subačiūtė and Mantas Palaima filmed another event, Bulota's hundredth anniversary at the Lithuanian Writers' Union, when I was not able to arrive in time for it. My deep thanks to all of them. I also thank archivists of the Lithuanian Central State Archive (LCSA), the Lithuanian Archive of Literature and Art (LALA), the Lithuanian Special Archive (LSA), and the librarians of the Martynas Mažvydas National Library of Lithuania. I am grateful to director Juozapas Blažiūnas for always welcoming me at the Lithuanian Archive of Literature and Art and for assistance with archival documents and images. Thank you to Darius Pocevičius for sharing Jonas Jakimavičius's photo with Lenin in Lukiškių Square. I thank Juozas Bulota for letting me publish his father's personal archival photos. I am appreciative of Kęstutis Šiaulytis, Romualdas Palčiauskas, Vladimiras Beresniovas, Andrius Cvirka, the late Andrius Deltuva, and the late Algirdas Radvilavičius for giving permission to use their artwork published in the *Broom*. I thank all artists, writers, and journalists for allowing me to use interview materials in this book. Many cartoons that could not be included in a published version of this book can be found at neringaklumbyte.com.

My family—Virginija Misevičienė, Kęstutis Misevičius, Vaiva Jakienė, Kamilis, Dovydas, Vilis and Gediminas Jakai, Nijolė Petkuvienė, Daiva Jasiulionienė, Valdonė Petrauskaitė, and Danius Jasiulionis—have always been an important part of my life. Gulnaz Sharafutdinova, Oana Godeanu-Kenworthy, and Anne Roma have been my new family since I arrived in Oxford. I am grateful to them for all small and big things that we share. I thank Giedrius Subačius for sharing the life journey and its adventures together. I dedicate this book to Ieva and Kajus. I love them forever and beyond. I hope they will always laugh and laugh together.

Relevant Dates

1795–1915   Most of current Lithuania's territory is part of the Russian Empire
1915–1918   Most of current Lithuania's territory is part of the German Empire
1917   The Bolshevik Revolution
1918   Lithuania is reestablished as an independent democratic state with the capital of Vilnius
1920   Vilnius and its region are occupied by Poland; Lithuania's capital is moved to Kaunas
1922   The USSR is created
1922   *Krokodil* (Crocodile), a pan-Soviet satire and humor journal, is founded
1926   A military coup d'état in Lithuania; Lithuania becomes an authoritarian state
1934   Underground *Broom* is published by Lithuanian artists-revolutionaries
1936   Publication of the *Broom* is discontinued
1939   The Molotov-Ribbentrop Pact, August 23
1939   Beginning of World War II, September 1
1940   The Red Army occupies Lithuania, June 15
1940   Lithuania is proclaimed the Lithuanian Soviet Socialist Republic, July 21
1940–1941   The *Broom* is published legally
1941   First mass deportations of Lithuanian citizens by the Soviet government, June 14
1941   Nazi Germany invades Lithuania, June 22
1941–1944   Lithuanian Holocaust and Nazi occupation
1944–1953   Anti-Soviet guerrilla warfare in Lithuania
1945–1952   Multiple mass deportations of civilians from Lithuania by the Soviet government
1953   The death of Stalin
1953–1964   Nikita Khrushchev is the general secretary of the Communist Party of the USSR
1956   Nikita Khrushchev's "Secret Speech" denouncing Stalin
1956   Reestablishment of the *Broom*
1962   The Manege Affair

1964–1982	Leonid Brezhnev is the general secretary of the Communist Party of the USSR
1968	The Prague Spring
1972	Self-immolation of Romas Kalanta and riots in Kaunas, Lithuania
1985	Mikhail Gorbachev becomes the general secretary of the Communist Party of the USSR
1987	The first unsanctioned pro-independence public protest action in Vilnius
1988	Sąjūdis, the Movement for Reformation, is founded in Lithuania, June 3
1990	Lithuania adopts the Act of the Reestablishment of the State of Lithuania, March 11
1991	Soviet troops kill fourteen civilians during a peaceful protest in Vilnius, January 13
1991	Referendum for Lithuania's independence, February 9
1991	The *Broom* becomes an independent legal entity—*Šluota* Ltd. (*Broom* Ltd.)
1991	Unsuccessful Communist coup in Moscow, August 19–21
1991	The United States recognizes the restoration of Lithuania's independence, September 2
1991	The USSR recognizes Lithuania's independence, September 6
1991	Lithuania becomes a member of the United Nations, September 17
1998	The *Broom* is closed
2001	Sluota.lt (Broom.lt) is published online

Note on Transliteration

I used the Library of Congress transliteration system (without diacritics) for Russian and Ukrainian, except in certain proper names that have widely accepted spelling in English (e.g., Anatoly Lunacharsky). Translations from Lithuanian and Russian are my own, except when cited from English-language or translated sources.

AUTHORITARIAN LAUGHTER

AUTHORITARIAN LAUGHTER

It was a dreary November night in 1980 when Juozas Bulota returned home with an unusually crammed briefcase. His teenage son ran to open the briefcase in search of new magazines his father often stashed within. "Be careful, my head is in there," the elder Bulota warned.

The son saw an ugly, red clay bust with a grotesque version of Bulota's face staring out from inside. Bulota's wife also peeked into the briefcase and told him, "You have to hide it, so nobody can see it." They put it into a cupboard.

"The fun will start," Bulota quipped with amusement, "when I am gone. You will not be able to throw it away or break it since it is my head. You will feel bad about hiding it somewhere since it is a piece of artwork by the famous artist Petrulis. You will plan to take it to our summer house, but you will be afraid it will get stolen. You will see, when I am gone, my head will bother you for the rest of your life."[1]

Indeed, when Bulota passed away fourteen years later, the head was moved from place to place until they finally left it in the corner of the apartment balcony facing the woods and hidden behind a vase. Before what would have been Bulota's hundredth birthday in 2018, his family remembered his "head" and brought it back into their living room (figure 0.1).

Juozas Bulota was the editor in chief of the Lithuanian satire and humor magazine the *Broom* (*Šluota* in Lithuanian), which was founded in 1956.[2] The magazine was instrumental to authoritarian statecraft—laughter had to serve the cause of the Communist Party in building and governing Soviet society in Lithuania. Bulota presided over the magazine for almost three decades (1956–1985). At the

FIGURE 0.1.   The clay head of Juozas Bulota and photos of him in the Bulota family apartment, 2019. Photo by the author.

time he brought his "head" home, five more years remained until his retirement. In this briefcase also traveled censored *Broom* issues, various Communist Party documents, satire and humor magazines from other Soviet socialist republics, and readers' letters. In the mid- and late 1980s, he brought back small unfolded pieces of paper with scribbled questions sent to him by people from the audience during his public lectures.[3] Some of them expressed nationalistic sentiments and were openly anti-Soviet. Bulota's wry smile on the clay head must have testified to the failures of authoritarian statecraft—Soviet laughter ultimately turned against the regime itself.

Authoritarian laughter, the Soviet government's project of satire and humor, was seemingly paradoxical: while it aimed to serve Communist Party ideological agendas and involve editors, artists, writers, journalists, and readers in creating communist society, it encompassed opposition that undermined the government's initiatives.[4] This apparent paradox of authoritarian laughter, integral to the political history of the *Broom*, is the major focus of this book. I argue that authoritarian laughter was multidirectional; it was a communicative exchange among artists and different audiences that was both ideologically correct and oppositional. While all laughter is ambiguous and contextual, the concept of multidirectionality allows me to explicate its circulation and reception and underscore the fact that the same jokes were often meaningful in different ways to different audiences—authorities, censors, and readers. Communist Party ideologists could see the *Broom* artists and writers fighting against unresponsive, inept bureaucrats or the shoddiness of industrial production, while readers could generalize *Broom* criticisms to the socialist system itself. Authorities read depictions of criminals, robbers, homeless people, or sexualized images of women in the West as a critique of "rotten capitalism." Yet these same images aroused some readers' fascination with the West and desire to visit it.

Studies of authoritarianism usually focus on state power, violence, and the abuse of human rights. This book contributes to these studies by exploring intimate commonplace experiences of power—creating cartoons and satires, negotiating with censors, laughing and embracing official popular culture. I show that in the absence of democratic forms of political participation, the Soviet authoritarian state involved citizens in statecraft and provided meaningful forms of engagement through the outlet of a satire and humor magazine.[5] Looking into intimate encounters with authoritarianism through the lens of laughter, I seek to understand how authoritarian regimes become part of everyday experiences of their citizens, involve them in their political projects, and make their ideologies appealing at moral, emotional, and embodied levels—or fail to restructure visions of social and everyday lives.

The *Broom* was an ideological institution of a Soviet authoritarian state.[6] In Lithuania it was regulated by the policies and norms of the Central Committee of the Communist Party (CP CC): only one satire and humor magazine was published in the Lithuania language; the ideological profile of the magazine was set and policed through editorial offices, censors, and the CP CC; and satire and humor were used as forms of disciplining individuals as well as tools of propaganda to serve the regime's interests.

The *Broom*, however, from when it was founded, was an unstable and incomplete project of Soviet laughter. Lithuania was a site of contested Sovietness, owing to its pre-Soviet history of sovereignty, the violence of World War II and of the postwar era, religious and linguistic difference, and proximity to Eastern Bloc countries and Western Europe. These contexts, as well as Lithuanians' minority status in the USSR, shaped Soviet laughter in Lithuania.

This book covers the period from 1956, when the *Broom* was founded, to 1985, when Mikhail Gorbachev, the general secretary of the Communist Party of the Soviet Union, came to power. Juozas Bulota's almost thirty-year leadership of the *Broom* partly explains the relative consistency of the magazine's content from the time of its founding to 1985. Neither after the Prague events of 1968, nor the youth riots of 1972 in Lithuania, did the *Broom* visibly change its course. As

I discuss in my post scriptum, the *Broom* radically changed during perestroika, becoming a revolutionary magazine advocating for Lithuania's independence from the USSR. Although the *Broom* continued to be published in the 1990s, the post-authoritarian *Broom* did not survive long in post-Soviet times, ceasing publication in 1998.[7] Nostalgia for jokes past shows how deeply political humor was rooted in everyday life.

Laughter and Statecraft

While we do not usually think of laughter as a tool of statecraft, the Soviet government did. Laughter was used as a weapon against the enemies of the USSR, a propaganda tool directed at international as well as local audiences. It was a form of regime governance through public criticizing, shaming, and ridicule. The Soviet authorities anticipated that citizens would contribute to the socialist construction of the new society by laughing at drunks and speculators, snobs and loafers, priests, bad managers, and clumsy bureaucrats, all with a view toward getting rid of "enduring shortcomings" from the "bourgeois past" to advance to communism.[8] Soviet laughter thus was also a means for shaping citizens into Soviet subjects.

Laughter as a tool of statecraft had its roots in Bolshevik revolutionary thought. For Lenin, both the press and literature had to fulfill an important mission in educating the people. Lenin advocated that "art must serve propaganda," and laughter had to become "a weapon of class struggle." For Anatoly Lunacharsky, the Bolshevik commissar for enlightenment (1917–1929), art had to organize social thought, to act on emotions and intellect (Gérin 2018, 28).[9] Laughter was a sign of strength of society and a sign of victory (Lunacharsky [1931] 1964, 76, cited in Oushakine 2012, 195). Many diverse thinkers of the Soviet period—Mikhail Koltsov, Boris Efimov, Mikhail Bakhtin, and Sergei Eisenstein, among others—also saw Soviet laughter as a form of power (see Norris 2013; Oushakine 2011). They anticipated, in Lunacharsky's words, the role of laughter to be "as important as ever in our struggle, the last struggle for the emancipation of human beings" (Lunacharskii [1931] 1964, 538, cited in Gérin 2018, 3).

Under Stalin, intellectuals were further engaged in developing common "communist humor language" (Low 1950). Humor was valued "as a corrective, 'scourging,' 'lashing' or otherwise castigating 'relicts of the bourgeois past,' which were impeding the development of the new, healthy socialist society" (Milne 2004, 3). In post-Stalinist years, Nikita Khrushchev claimed that satire was "armed in defense of our Party and the people" with the intention of destroying "everything that hinders our advancement towards communism" (Mesropova and Graham 2008, 2–3).

Officially, Lithuanian satirists after World War II embraced Soviet perspectives on laughter.[10] Juozas Bulota would scribble a note for himself on a newspaper that he might have been reading from the book *Malaia zemlia* (*Small Land*, 1978) by Leonid Brezhnev, general secretary of the Central Committee of the Communist Party of the Soviet Union, echoing Lunacharsky's position: "Laughter is a great force, expressing optimism and spiritual health of people."[11] In one of his lectures, Bulota paraphrased Marx by saying that "laughter is needed so people would separate with the difficult past cheerfully."[12] Journalist Albertas Lukša (1958, 55), reflecting on Marxist beliefs that state coercive institutions will disappear in communism, wrote in his college thesis in 1958 that the power of laughter will be stronger than law. As a *Broom* journalist for thirty-six years, Lukša used the power of laughter to discipline wrongdoers and prevent various transgressions.

The opposition I encountered in the official Soviet satire and humor magazine made me wonder if Soviet theorists of laughter might have been wrong about the functions of laughter as a tool of statecraft. Emil Draitser, a freelance journalist for *Krokodil* (Crocodile) and other print media in the 1960s and early 1970s, captures the paradox of Soviet laughter as both serving and undermining the regime when he notes that Soviet satire may seem an oxymoron. "How could a totalitarian state tolerate public criticism? How could it encourage this criticism by putting professional satirists on its payroll?" Draitser asked (2021, 3). Official media debates in the 1920s and 1930s about the appropriateness of laughter in Soviet Russia illustrate that some Bolshevik ideologists and writers were concerned that critical satire and humor would turn people against the government (Oushakine 2012).[13] They knew that the prominent Russian writers Nikolai Gogol (1809–1852) and Mikhail Saltykov-Shchedrin (1826–1889) built their success on their scathing critique of corrupt, stupid, and lazy bureaucrats, a satirical tradition Soviet Russia inherited (Oushakine 2012). Russian satirical literature, according to Oushakine, "practically creat[ed] a subgenre of anti-governmental satire" (196). In 1923, Bolshevik historian Iakov Shafir argued that "it is not an easy thing to know where exactly a critique of concrete individuals stops and where a critique of the regime starts" (Shafir 1923, 8, cited in Oushakine, 197). In 1929, *Literaturnaia gazeta* (Literary newspaper), a newspaper of the Federation of Soviet writers, published a series of essays on the role and function of socialist satire, including Vladimir Blium's commentary on Soviet satire as an oxymoron (Oushakine 2012, 200). While a majority of writers affirmed that satire could be repurposed for Soviet society, Blium argued that since "satire knows no positive content . . . therefore every attempt to develop satirical forms under socialism would amount to a 'counterrevolutionary' assault, to 'a direct strike against our own statehood and our own public'" (Blium 1929, cited in Oushakine 2012, 200). "The very notion of 'the Soviet satirist,'" Blium suggested, "was an oxymoron, equal to such similarly unimaginable phenomena as 'Soviet banker' or 'Soviet landlord'" (E.G. 1930, cited in Oushakine, 201).

Stalinist-era debates about Soviet laughter did not see criticism itself as dangerous (see Oushakine 2012). The critique itself was founded on Marxist beliefs about art, media, literature, and ideas of historical materialism. Criticism generally—and critical satires or cartoons particularly—were mechanisms of the betterment of society anticipating advancement to communism. Criticism was not an issue as long as it was not directed against the regime and did not contradict Communist Party ideology. Nevertheless, throughout Soviet history, a question of *potential* critique of the regime in satires and cartoons remained a key political and aesthetic issue for Soviet authorities (cf. Oushakine 2012). The theorists of Soviet laughter would aim to resolve the issue by endorsing laughter's propaganda role and disciplining function, by creating realistic satire with an educational purpose, as well as "positive satire" that would provide a constructive alternative (see Oushakine 2012). Satire and humor that merely entertained were rejected because they were seen as bourgeois in nature. Realistic portrayals of Soviet life and disciplining pedagogy allowed Soviet authorities to direct a reader in meaning-making. Oushakine notes that debates about Soviet laughter under Stalin were replaced by the instrumental deployment of laughter for the affirmation of the consolidated regime (205).

By 1933, in the Soviet Union, *Krokodil* was the only major union-wide satirical magazine left, published under the supervision of *Pravda* (Truth), the Communist Party newspaper (see Alaniz 2010, 52). When Lithuania was incorporated into the USSR in 1940, the *Broom* for several months coexisted with another major Lithuanian leftist satirical magazine, *Kuntaplis* (Wooden clog) (see chapter 1). After World War II the *Broom* was the only satire and humor magazine in Lithuania published in the Lithuanian language. Editors' self-censorship, as well as censorship by Glavlit (the Main Directorate on Literature and Presses) and the Central Committee of the Lithuanian Communist Party (LCP CC), had to ensure that satire and humor were appropriate for the newly emerging Soviet society. Among Lithuanian authorities and satirists there was little debate of the established principles of Soviet laughter, although Juozas Bulota, in Moscow in 1972, raised the issue of revisiting comic strips as an acceptable rather than capitalist genre for Soviet society (see chapter 6). Instead of debating, editors, writers, and artists *created* multidirectional laughter. The intrinsic ambiguity of humor, editors' transgressions, the absence of clearly articulated ideological censorship rules, critical audiences, and the changing cultural landscapes in late socialism itself, which became more open to modernist and entertaining humor, shaped the *Broom*'s multidirectional laughter. In late-Soviet times, from the 1960s to the 1980s, *Broom* Soviet laughter, to use Draitser's and Blium's terms, looked more and more like an oxymoron.

The Broomiana

In its first issue of the year 1957, the pan-Soviet magazine *Krokodil* announced to Soviet audiences the birth of the Lithuanian *Broom* and Latvian *Dadzis* (Thistle) (figure 0.2). *Krokodil*'s mascot crocodile was always the biggest and most visible figure, with a status of someone important in graphic portrayals of Soviet satire and humor magazine mascots. Crocodile was depicted with sharp teeth and a pitchfork. Other Soviet satire and humor magazines carried names such as *Wasp*, *Hornet*, *Nettle*, *Thistle*, *Fist*, *Pepper*, or *Hedgehog*, suggesting biting or prickly satire. The name *Broom* referred to sweeping various scum from society, cleansing and purifying.

FIGURE 0.2.   Red Crocodile in a red suit, the mascot of the pan-Soviet satire and humor magazine *Krokodil*, escorts two "newborns"—the Latvian satire and humor magazine mascot *Dadzis* (Thistle) and the Lithuanian satire and humor magazine mascot *Broom*: "In the family of friends—a big joy, for bureaucrats—a new concern, in Riga brother *Dadzis* and in Vilnius sister *Šluota* were born. I wish them health, strength, and sharp wits! *Krokodil*." *Krokodil,* January 1957, no. 1, p. 11.

From its founding in 1956, the *Broom* became the major institution of state-sponsored laughter in Soviet Lithuania. Like *Krokodil* in Soviet Russia (see Etty 2019; Pehowski 1978) or *Perets* (Pepper) in Soviet Ukraine (Yeremieieva 2018), the *Broom* was one of the most popular magazines in Soviet Lithuania.[14] The *Broom* rose from a circulation of twenty thousand copies in 1956 to over one hundred thousand in the 1980s.[15] Thus, at its peak, there was approximately one magazine copy per thirty-six inhabitants in Lithuania, with a population of over 3.5 million.[16] *Broom* artist Kęstutis Šiaulytis argued that every issue of the *Broom* was read by another six to nine people (Milkevičiūtė 2020). Carrying no advertising, the *Broom* was profitable, unlike many other newspapers and magazines, such as the major LCP CC newspapers *Tiesa* (Truth) and *Komjaunimo tiesa* (Communist youth truth).[17] While many Soviet industries were not efficient, the *Broom*'s profits equaled those of a successful collective farm. Juozas Bulota, the editor in chief, counted it in hundreds of thousands of rubles.[18] Popularity and profits seem to indicate that authoritarian statecraft at the everyday level, through the intimacy of laughter, was successful. I would argue that the *Broom* was successful because it advanced multidirectional laughter.

The *Broom* was not only the center of satire and humor in Lithuania but also a public phenomenon that journalist Domas Šniukas (2018) called *broomiana* (Lith. *šluotiana*).[19] Journalist Jonas Bulota, the brother of the editor in chief Juozas, wrote in 1984 that it would probably be easier to name writers, poets, journalists, and artists who *did not* collaborate with the *Broom*, rather than those who did (Jonas Bulota 1984, 9). The *Broom* was at the center of cartoonists' work and community.[20] In 1958, just two years after the *Broom* was founded, around sixty artists—thirty-two professional artists, plus students of the Vilnius Art Institute and nonprofessional artists—were collaborating with the *Broom*.[21] The number of collaborating artists was similar in the 1980s. *Broom* artists hosted cartoon exhibitions and published collections of cartoons, jokes, and postcards. *Broom* editors organized national student humor competitions. The *Broom* was a sponsor of comedy groups (Lith. *agitbrigados*); *Broom* journalists even wrote performance scripts.[22] *Broom* editors participated as judges in competitions for choirs and dance groups. *Broom* satirists gave public lectures at professional union palaces, literary museums, houses of culture in the provinces, universities, schools, and even orphanages.

Before the internet and with limited TV and visual-culture access, cartoons were a very popular visual communication genre.[23] From 1971 to 1981, in addition to the *Broom* magazine, editors regularly published *Šluotos kalendorių* (*Broom* calendar), a collection of *Broom* cartoons and jokes organized monthly (Jonas Bulota 1984).[24] *Broom* artists also published cartoons in other magazines, journals, and newspapers. The *Broom* assisted factories and enterprises by publishing the cartoon series *Į pagalbą sienlaikraščiams* (Help to newspaper walls) every three months. Newspaper walls presented agitation and propaganda materials and often were created by the workers themselves. If a factory lacked skilled artists, it could use *Broom* materials for its newspaper walls, in this way integrating *Broom* art into the factory's public space (see Juozas Bulota 1965, 6).

As this book will show, satire was important in the state's efforts at crime prevention and ensuring justice and order. The *Broom* participated in various inter-institutional campaigns such as youth delinquency prevention, as well as publishing materials on hooliganism, theft, speculation, and drunk driving, based on the Internal Affairs Ministry and People's Courts. The *Broom* set an example to various other newspapers and magazines that published satirical pieces or cartoons. In 1978, literary scholar Vytautas Kubilius wrote that everybody writes ironic aphorisms: "Every regional newspaper has its own humorist. . . . Every year several Lithuanian humor books get published. It does not have a precedent. We are becoming merrier" (Kubilius 1978, 161).

As I was conducting my research, twenty-five years after the collapse of the Soviet Union, everyone I met who came of age in Soviet Lithuania knew the *Broom*. Those readers' memories indicated overarching positive reception of the *Broom*. During the interviews, my questions about the *Broom* were often followed by pleasant smiles and recollections of reading, collecting, purchasing, and sharing the *Broom* with others. Former readers recalled long lines by newsstands that sold the magazine; others remembered subscribing to the *Broom* instead of other mainstream newspapers or magazines to fulfill their workplace-required subscription quotas for Soviet print media.[25] *Broom* readers used the fictional character Kindziulis and some other *Broom* humor to create unofficial jokes, this way blending the distinction between official and unofficial humor. Some of the *Broom* jokes survived to the twenty-first century.[26]

Theoretical Approach and Contributions

This book contributes to studies of Soviet authoritarianism by addressing questions that have long interested region scholars: the relationship between the state and citizens, state power and resistance, state propaganda and popular participation. Studies in the 1950s that advanced the concept of totalitarianism (Friedrich and Brzezinski 1956; Arendt 1951) presented the Soviet state as an institution exercising near total power over society through secret police, propaganda, and centralized control over the economy. In this view, society existed only as a collection of atomized individuals either completely brainwashed or repressed by the mighty state apparatus (see Klumbytė and Sharafutdinova 2012). The revisionists of the 1970s–1980s, including Arch Getty, Sheila Fitzpatrick, Moshe Lewin, and Robert Thurston, all challenged the reigning framework and advanced a social history approach. They provided important explanations for how the Soviet state secured mass support, while also questioning assumptions of the totalitarian model as to the extent to which the state could control society in a top-down fashion.[27] Post-revisionist scholarship, especially Soviet subjectivity studies (Halfin 1999; Hellbeck 2006; Kharkhordin 1999; Kotkin 1995; Naiman and Kiaer 2006; O'Keeffe 2013), promoted a new research agenda, focusing on what it meant to be Soviet, how Soviet values were internalized, how individuals learned to speak Bolshevik (Kotkin 1995), how they self-represented themselves (Hellbeck 2006), and how Soviet citizens emerged in performance of "Sovietness" (O'Keeffe 2013). The focal point for totalitarian approaches, in revisionist and post-revisionist scholarship, was the Stalinist period. Studies on late socialism have focused on liberalization of the regime (Klumbytė and Sharafutdinova 2012; Fainberg and Kalinovsky 2016) and normality of life despite the state (Yurchak 2006; Tsipusky 2016). These studies recognized the repressive state apparatus but drew their attention to social, economic, and political pluralism, relative freedoms, and the ability of citizens to live "normal" lives.[28]

In this book, I introduce new analytics in an attempt to capture complexities of state governance and political participation in the context of the project of Soviet laughter in Lithuania. I show that editors joined the Soviet satire and humor magazine and participated in production of Soviet laughter without deep commitment to the Soviet state and communism. I use the concept of the *banality of power* to capture the everyday commonplace process of participation in the authoritarian milieu (cf. Mbembe 2001, see chapter 1). I also maintain that editors' relation to power can be defined as *banal opposition*, the opposition within the system itself. Their agency, embedded in authoritarian structures and relations of power, I define as *antagonistic complicity*, the disagreeing consensus, which implicates both association with the regime as well as opposition. I also use, following Jacques Rancière, the concept of *dissensus*, reconfiguration of the common experience of the sensible, and a gradual reframing of the sensible field (Rancière 2010) to speak about *Broom* editors' and readers' opposition. While *banal opposition* refers to opposition existing at the structural and institutional level, *dissensus* is a process-oriented term for opposition in action, that is, the ongoing rearticulations of commonsense experience policed by the Communist Party authorities. Another key concept in my approach is *political intimacy*, which entails trust and coexistence within the same political episteme, dialogue, and reciprocity among editors, censors, and authorities. Editors were united by political intimacy grounded in the Soviet predicament, their uneasy relations with Soviet power (see chapter 3), ethnic difference, and minority status in the USSR.

My approach to laughter as *multidirectional* does not distinguish between official and unofficial humor, the distinction prominent in studies on humor. Many such studies of humor focus on unofficial joking and its subversive potential and often follow classic works of Sigmund Freud (1976), Mikhail Bakhtin (1984), and Mary Douglas (1991). They explore the individual's liberation from and transgression of the dominant social structures, power regimes, and official discourses (see, e.g., Adams 2005; Barker 1999; Goldstein 2003). Studies of humor in the former Soviet region relatedly approach laughter through the conceptual lens of resistance and focus on laughter as subversive of state power and a weapon of the relatively powerless (see Adams 2005; Arkhipova and Mel'nichenko 2008; Skradol 2009; Yurchak 1997).[29] Studies of Soviet official satire and humor magazines focus primarily on humor propaganda (see Gérin 2018; Norris 2013) or analyze state control and censorship of the official humor (Yeremieieva 2018; Yekelchyk 2006). John Etty (2019) aptly challenged the divide between official and unofficial humor in the first book-length study devoted to *Krokodil*. He noted that *Krokodil*'s graphic satire should be understood beyond propaganda, while the criticism of cartoons sometimes "bordered on the subversive." The analytical lens of official and unofficial humor is not useful in the case of the *Broom*, since many cartoons and satires contained both ideologically correct and oppositional messages.

Multidirectional laughter is political and transformative. I rely on a broader notion of politics to include not only state-level policy and the ideological discourse of Communist Party slogans, but also mundane experiences of drawing cartoons, writing letters of complaint, or reading and retelling *Broom* jokes, all integral aspects of laughter. My understanding of "political" follows Rancière's formulation of "politics" as irreducible to the exercise of, or struggle for, power.[30] According to Rancière, "it is the configuration of a specific space, the framing of a particular sphere of experience, of objects posited as common and as pertaining to a common decision, of subjects recognized as capable of designating these objects and putting forward arguments about them" (Rancière 2009, 24). I see Rancière's conceptualization of politics akin to what I seek to accomplish: namely, to describe minute circulations and intimate experiences of power. Rancière's political theory highlights democratic moments in politics by making equality central to political struggle. According to Rancière, the fundamental principle of politics is the equality of all individuals (see Deranty 2003). For Rancière, the social field is always defined by hierarchy and domination, and inequality is its basic logic (see Deranty 2003). The police constitute the structure that regulates this field, a partition of the sensible/perceptible. The essence of politics, for Rancière, is disagreement. Political disagreement is a "form of a dispute that takes place when speakers will not or cannot address each other as partners in dialogue" (Russell and Montin 2015, 547). In his perspective, "The confiscation of speech is the beginning of exploitation. The end of exploitation demands that speech be given back to the exploited" (Deranty 2003, 140). According to Rancière's perspective, the exploited express their own experiences, thoughts, and desires for recognition by removing barriers and confronting the authorized forms of speech. In my approach, editors' and readers' communication was delimited by editorial, Glavlit, or CP CC censorship and policed by censors and CP authorities. Editors and readers sought to express their own experiences, thoughts, and desires for recognition by using this discourse and transgressing it. Rancière's methodology did not center on heroic figures of workers or the leaders of the proletariat in nineteenth-century France. He analyzed dreams and thoughts of those workers who expressed their ideas in diaries or literary works by focusing on the moral, aesthetic, and political experiences. In a parallel way, to understand authoritarianism as an everyday experience, I did not look at dissidents, who were the leaders of the anti-Soviet opposition, but writers and artists in charge of communicating state ideology to people and a popular domain of humor that provided for everyday involvement in the public space. Unlike Rancière, I do not find the Marxist concept of "exploitation" or the division between different classes useful in my analysis.

In my approach, laughter is transformative in the sense that it communicates dissensus, reconfiguring the established and authorized common sense and state ideology and order. Unlike Mikhail Bakhtin and his followers, who emphasize that laughter or the carnivalesque is a "temporary suspension of the official system with its prohibitions and hierarchical barriers" (Bakhtin 1984, 89), I claim that laughter is a form of communication integral to political transformations.[31] The *Broom*'s laughter entailed reframing of experience and common sense by systematic critique of some issues, silence, and Aesopian rearticulation—a figurative discourse with subtexts—of others.[32] Dissensus was coproduced and emergent among artists, writers, journalists, and readers. Rancière's analytics of *dissensus* are useful to conceptualize emergent opposition as a form of relation to power, not reducible to resistance to the regime itself. I explore dissensus as emergent, sometimes sporadic, embedded in the *Broom* editors' work and readers' sentiments. It existed in multiple forms, from voicing injustices perpetrated by city-level authorities or collective farm chairmen, dissatisfaction with poor-quality clothing, to (rarely mentioned openly) discontent with the regime itself.

By adapting Rancière's perspective on politics as "the configuration of a specific space, the framing of a particular sphere of experience" (Rancière 2009, 24) and on dissensus as reframing of the sensible field (Rancière 2010), I am able to discuss relations of power irreducible to state/people and power/resistance dichotomies, to see power and opposition as contingent, relational, and emergent realities, and integrate state and everyday levels into analysis. Both concepts are helpful to conceptualize how *Broom*'s laughter was changing everyday sensibilities through adapting official ideological discourse and reconfiguring common sense authorized by this discourse.

Antagonistic Complicity

After World War I, the Russian Empire lost much of its western frontier, as the newly independent states of Lithuania, Latvia, Estonia, Finland, and Poland reemerged. Lithuania was a democratic republic until 1926 and an authoritarian regime from 1926 to 1940. Soviet occupation of Lithuania, Latvia, and Estonia during World War II, from the USSR's perspective, was a reintegration of the former Russian Empire's western territories. In Lithuania, Soviet authorities had to confront national identity anchored in lost sovereignty and linguistic and religious differences from Russia.[33] They also faced an armed anti-Soviet resistance that extended to all of Lithuania and lasted until the early 1950s, when the last leaders of Lithuania's Fight for Freedom Movement were executed.[34]

When the *Broom* was created in 1956, memories of Soviet and Nazi occupations, the Holocaust, deportations to the Gulag, and armed postwar resistance were part of many families' history. The total population loss due to Soviet and Nazi occupation, emigration, and war victims was over 1 million people out of 2.5 million in 1945 (Anušauskas 2012, 279). Nazis and Lithuanian collaborators killed over 95 percent of Lithuanian Jews (see Anušauskas et al. 2005, 222). Close to half a million people, according to Arvydas Anušauskas, were *Soviet* "genocide and terror victims and experienced violence" (2012, 280).[35] This historical context shaped the *Broom* and made it different from many other Soviet satirical magazines.

It is not possible to avoid the question of complicity if you study authoritarian regimes. Western scholars' explorations of complicity often rely on a presupposition of a particular agency of a liberal subject having personal autonomy, capable of knowing oneself and society through the faculty of reason, defining the relationship between the knowing subject and the social order in utilitarian instrumental terms (Krylova 2000, 123–24). In her 2000 article, Anna Krylova argues that in 1950s American scholarship, we encounter either an indoctrinated-believing subject or a cynical subject, complicit with an immoral society (128), while in the 1970s, a "conformist" was the unencumbered, critical subject who accepts a status quo (134). The 1990s gave rise to a "resisting subject," previously found in isolated dissident cases, which became a mass phenomenon (141).

A resisting, collaborating, or victimized subject is prevalent in scholarship on Soviet Lithuania (see, e.g., Girnius 2016). Scholars have approached Soviet power through the lens of imperialism (e.g., Grybkauskas 2016) and postcolonialism (e.g., Kelertas 2006; Annus 2018). "Soviet" has been dissociated from "national" and attributed to state governance and ideological control as well as state institutions (Grybkauskas 2016; Vaiseta 2018; Ramonaitė and Kavaliauskaitė 2011).[36] While post-revisionist scholars ask how citizens were Sovietized, researchers who focus on Lithuania explore various forms of opposition—the prevalence of national identities, negotiations with authorities in Moscow, and the preservation of Lithuanian traditions—which led to proclaiming independence in 1990 (see Ivanauskas 2015; Klumbys 2008; Ramonaitė and Kavaliauskaitė 2011; Ramonaitė 2015a). Moreover, the burgeoning literature focuses on traumatic experiences of World War II and the postwar era (Budrytė 2011; Davoliūtė and Balkelis 2012). Some scholars extend the victimization approach to the entire Soviet period, as in the case of persecution of religious believers (Streikus 2002) or Soviet collectivization and improvement (Lith. *melioracija*) campaigns that displaced villagers and homestead dwellers from the late 1960s to the 1980s (see Davoliūtė 2013).[37]

The questions of agency interconnect with questions of responsibility in post-Soviet Lithuania, where the Communist Party is illegal and the Soviet Union is identified as an occupational regime during which the country experienced moral and material losses still counted in billions by the government.[38] Some *Broom* editors and contributors have been vulnerable to a negative association with "collaborators" of the Soviet government, what I call *authoritarian stigma*, for their work at the Soviet humor propaganda magazine. Half the *Broom* editors were members of the Communist Party, which the right-wing parties in post-Soviet Lithuania have proposed should become recognized as a criminal organization. In chapter 1, I argue that the founding editors of the *Broom* shared, in Michael Rothberg's (2019) terms, "complex implication." The analytics of the *implicated subject*, introduced by Rothberg, acknowledge that nobody is completely innocent. *Broom* editors had a position of power and privilege of cultural elites without being direct agents of harm, and thus were implicated in Soviet history as its associates. The concept of "implicated subject" helps to acknowledge responsibility beyond narrower legalistic categories of guilt or collaboration (Rothberg 2019). In chapter 6, I claim that their agency—*antagonistic complicity*—was embedded in the authoritarian structures and relations of power, not simply manifestations of their will.

The concept of *antagonistic complicity*, the disagreeing consensus, implicates association with the regime as well as opposition to it. "Complicity" in popular usage may imply association, collaboration, collusion, commitment to joint actions, sharing of ideas, or consent to wrongdoing. In authoritarian settings, as I show, complicity could exist without unity and solidary and shared beliefs.

Moreover, it can entail conflict, disagreement, and dissensus. Introducing the concept of *antagonistic complicity* gives a venue to speak about agency that is irreducible to conformity or open resistance against the state punishable by law, and to recognize an alternative form of opposition, neither "weapons of the weak" (Scott 1985), "power of the powerless" (Havel 1978), or dissident resistance. As discussed in chapter 6, *Broom* artists created a Lithuanian graphic art tradition different from that of *Krokodil*, but they were not an antistate underground organization. *Broom* artist Kęstutis Šiaulytis's statement that "it was in fashion to be against" succinctly captures the banality of such opposition.[39] The *banal opposition*, as stated above, is the opposition within the system itself, institutionalized, and accepted or ignored by authorities.[40] As a result, the repercussions that artists faced included reprimands, administrative fines, demotions, or transfers to other jobs, not prison.

Antagonistic complicity was enacted in artists' hesitancy to draw political cartoons that favored the Soviet state as well as caricatures with antireligious and anti-imperialist themes. Moreover, *Broom* graphic art in many cases violated the socialist realist imperative to be explicit about the content and avoid intellectualism and ambiguity; it espoused nationalist sentiments and favored Western modernist traditions, and, in some cases, artists coded their critique of the regime in Aesopian language. Such graphic art created disruptions in ideological visions of the state about building a communist society and Soviet modernity and expressed dissensus shared by artists, writers, and readers. When Soviet power structures no longer enforced complicity, antagonistic complicity disintegrated with glasnost and perestroika. After January 13, 1991, when Soviet troops tried to reclaim power in Lithuania, the *Broom* published a special newsletter, *Red Genocide*, in support of Lithuania's independence (see post scriptum in this book).[41] It is not possible to claim that *Broom* editors advanced ideas of Lithuania's independence during the three decades when the *Broom* was published; they did not. However, their humor rooted in ethnic difference, minority status, and anti-Sovietness, mediated by political intimacy, as discussed below, contributed to making Lithuania's independence in the late 1980s an imaginable future for *Broom* readers (see post scriptum). The movement toward Lithuania's sovereignty in the late 1980s employed the discourse of environmental pollution, injustices of the authorities, Russification and Sovietization of the Lithuanian people, economic stagnation, and lack of freedoms. These themes were present in the pages of the *Broom*, some coded in Aesopian language. Importantly, the *Broom* editors' critique of everyday life, lack of consumer goods, substandard quality of food in canteens and restaurants, unfinished constructions of apartment buildings, or muddy and messy surroundings of new housing districts created dystopian visions of Soviet society and raised hopes and desires for a different future (see chapter 8 and post scriptum). Many of the editors who were in charge of *Broom* Soviet laughter transitioned in the late 1980s to Lithuanian revolutionary laughter and declared that communism was a joke (see post scriptum).

Political Intimacy

Multidirectional laughter that became the hallmark of the *Broom* was shaped by relations of *political intimacy*. Political intimacy entailed trust and coexistence within the same political episteme, dialogue, and reciprocity. Editors, contributors, and even censors often shared banal opposition and protected one another. Artist Jonas Varnas remembered how censors used to inspect an art exhibition before the opening and advise the removal of cartoons that could have been unacceptable "for Moscow."[42] One such cartoon portrayed a worker building a brick wall with a hammer, and, at the bottom, a *kolkhoz* (Rus., collective farm) woman cutting rye with a sickle. Since the hammer and sickle symbolized proletarian solidarity, and the worker and the peasant were the major agents of Soviet history, the cartoon could be seen as mocking state ideological symbols (see Varnas 2017).[43] The artist and the censor, in this case, shared political intimacy, which mediated their actions. Intensities of intimacy differed, and conflicts terminated them (see chapter 2).

Political intimacy integrates recognition and loyalty. Recognition means that editors and censors or journalists and Central Committee instructors accepted each other's status and role in the regime. Loyalty is an associational attachment, a disposition that involves a commitment to secure or at least not jeopardize the interests or well-being of another. Censors trusted editors to deliver ideologically correct cartoons and satire, since they were loyal members of the intellectual elite (chapter 5). In times of conflict, such as when an antisemitic cartoon was published in 1957, Juozas Bulota, the editor in chief, was requested by the Central Committee to exercise stronger vigilance in the future. In a few other cases, Bulota grabbed a briefcase with sausages, smoked eel, and vodka and went to Moscow to settle things down.[44] In the end political intimacy was preserved.

Like cultural intimacy (Herzfeld [1997] 2016), political intimacy can be mobilized when different people use commonly shared social idioms that simultaneously produce a sense of belonging to a political group or community. "Cultural intimacy" in Herzfeld's initial formulation ([1997] 2005) explained nationalist sentiments and people's relations to the nation-state. In his revised edition of 2016, Herzfeld suggested extending this concept to other geopolitical communities, "different organizational structures and to the cultural values associated with them" (Herzfeld [1997] 2016, 56).

Herzfeld reflected on my concept of *political intimacy*, introduced and discussed in "Political Intimacy: Power, Laughter, and Coexistence in Late Soviet Lithuania" (Klumbytė 2011), by stating that it "seems to satisfy a minimalist but process-oriented definition of cultural intimacy and indeed to instantiate the potential for unexpected collusion that is one of its most salient aspects" (Herzfeld [1997] 2016, 58).[45] In my reading of Herzfeld's work the term "cultural" in "cultural intimacy" is suggestive of broader collectives and contexts and is focused on everyday sociality (cf. Neofotistos 2010). My concept of political intimacy refers to a particular form of sociality embedded in Soviet authoritarianism. It designates contingent and intersubjective relations of power. Political intimacy is, thus, about interdependence, loyalties, attachments, trust, and friendships. In the case of the *Broom*, political intimacy was shaped by the editors' ethnic difference and minority status in the USSR, their covert opposition to authorities in Moscow and some Central Committee leaders in Lithuania, and negativity toward Soviet bureaucratic regulations and Communist Party prerogatives. Conceptually, Herzfeld (2005, 13) argued, the nation-state is constructed out of intimacy. Citizens in a nation-state are united by relations of cultural intimacy, but they may or may not share political intimacy.

Another concept related to political intimacy is Alexei Yurchak's *svoi* (Rus., one of us), a sociality of "normal people." Yurchak uses Russian categorizations of themselves as "normal," against dissidents and activists who read the authoritative texts in a literal way (Yurchak 2006). He gives an example of the dissident-like person, who refused to pay his Komsomol dues "out of principle" and caused much irritation among his colleagues, as opposed to a woman, one of the *svoi*, a "normal person," who collected the dues—involuntary but unavoidable payments—simply fulfilling the assignment imposed on her from above (2006, 109). *Svoi* agreed to pay the dues in order not to get into trouble, since not paying them could impede professional promotion, permission to travel abroad, or financial bonuses (108). Yurchak argues that paying and collecting the Komsomol dues was not about ideological allegiance (109). Dale Pesmen notes that *svoi chelovek* (Rus., one of ours) was used in economic and power-related contexts: "'One of ours' was a person with whom one could speak openly without fearing that what one said would be used against one" (Pesmen 2000, 165). Like the category of political intimacy, *svoi* refers to trust, friendships, and togetherness. Yurchak and Pesmen describe *svoi* in a context of horizontal relations in a group opposed to other groups or the state. Political intimacy, in contrast, refers to *both* hierarchical and horizontal relationships.[46]

The analytics of political intimacy can be used to define interdependence among subjects in different regimes. In the case of Soviet authoritarianism, political intimacy was shaped by a preeminence of personal authority and patron-client relations over institutional norms. Political intimacy mediated and reaffirmed hierarchies and statuses, but also provided security and some control over individual actions.[47] Drawing an ambiguous cartoon, artists could expect that censors would let them know if they had overstepped the boundaries of what the regime could accept and tolerate. At the same time censors trusted that artists would not try to publish or draw something that would get them all in trouble. In the case of Soviet Lithuania, political intimacy had an ethnic dimension. Russians, who migrated to Lithuania in Soviet times, and Lithuanian Jews in some cases were excluded from inner circles (see chapters 1 and 2).[48] Artists and journalists, by positioning themselves against Russians and Jewish people, expressed nationalistic and antisemitic sentiments. These sentiments emerge in archival documents, interviews, and memoirs. Any explicit opposition or nationalistic or antisemitic sentiments were carefully censored and, with a few exceptions, did not appear in the *Broom*.

The above discussed concepts of *dissensus, banal opposition, antagonistic complicity*, and *political intimacy* provide a conceptual framework to interpret editors' relations to power and the *Broom*'s multidirectional laughter in Soviet Lithuania.

Historical Ethnography

The research leading to this monograph spans over a decade. I presented my first paper on the *Broom*'s humor at the "Totalitarian Laughter" conference at Princeton University in 2009. After publishing several articles on Soviet and post-Soviet humor between 2011 and 2014, I decided to expand my research into a book project. In the summer of 2015, I was able to locate archives of the *Broom* long considered lost and started systematic research. Although I met with artists, writers, and journalists who worked for the *Broom*, I was not able to find relatives of Juozas Bulota. Calls to women listed in the phone book under the name "Bulotienė" to ask apologetically whether their husband was Juozas Bulota were not fruitful. In 2018, I considered my research complete and planned to focus exclusively on writing, when I discovered that the son of Juozas Bulota was organizing a celebration commemorating what would have been his father's hundredth birthday, at the Lithuanian Writers' Union. Because of a flight delay, my airplane landed in Vilnius several hours after this event. Although I missed the celebration, I still met with Juozas Bulota, who was named after his father, and the editor's widow, ninety-year-old Donata Bulotienė. That summer, I was invited by Bulota's son to study the editor in chief's personal archive and spent several weeks in Bulota's chair at his desk in his apartment, surrounded by mementos and furniture of his time. I reviewed piles of documents, photographs, articles, and greeting cards and materials in his briefcases, unopened for over thirty years since his retirement from the *Broom*. There was his bust with a wry smile on a table. This book would have been different if not for these briefcases and meeting with his family. I would have viewed the role that the editor in chief played in the magazine—a view largely based on *Broom* Communist Party Primary Organization meeting reports—as that of a professional bureaucrat committed to the Communist Party principles. The part of his life reading Western magazines and a booklet on communist crimes in the Soviet Union, listening to the US Voice of America, and avoiding vacationing in the LCP Central Committee resort "not to kneel to the higher authorities" would have remained invisible.

My methodological approach—historical ethnography—incorporates data from various sources, as I elaborate below: different archives and interviews, study of Soviet time materialities, media and literature analysis, and participation in a public event with *Broom* editors.[49] Immersion, distinct to an ethnographic analysis in contemporary settings, was an important methodological imperative in my study. It refers to various encounters with things, objects, ideas, and people, related to the *past* object of study, and seeking understanding of the past through experience mediated by these encounters.

Soviet Materialities

In the 2010s, in Vilnius, I visited the *Broom* headquarters, editors' homes, and summer houses. I spent time with some *Broom* editors and their families. While archaeologists usually think about conservation of things of the past in connection to the national environment, social and political events could also have a conserving effect. Neoliberal post-Soviet transformations brought many changes but preserved some Soviet materialities. Some former *Broom* editors still lived in their Soviet-era apartments with Soviet sofas and coffee tables, intermingled with new computers on old desks. Plants crowded on windowsills. Books, photo albums, cartoon catalogs, *Broom* collections, and souvenirs populated Soviet cupboards. When new furniture was purchased, the old chairs, futons, and wardrobes were not thrown out but traveled to their owners' Soviet-era summer houses. Clothing, covers, pillows, and carpets that were not needed in the city or that were replaced with new items were taken to these summer houses as well. Because of the Soviet shortage economy and neoliberal transformations, furniture and belongings had many lives until they broke, tore, or were destroyed completely. Editor in chief Juozas Bulota's apartment and summer house were like museums of the *Broom* (figure 0.3). In his Vilnius apartment a three-foot-long boar skin hung on a wall, inscribed with hexameter by *Broom* colleagues congratulating him on his birthday. His library and *Broom* issues were there, along with his photos and a portrait. In his workroom was furniture from his time.

Bulota's briefcases contained his public lecture notes. They also contained scraps of paper with questions readers forwarded to him during question-and-answer sessions. Readers asked whether it was true that the *Broom* was the most truthful and fair (Lith. *teisingiausias*) magazine. They wondered about Bulota's experience of creating humor pieces. Readers sent funny questions, such as how to overcome limited stomach capacity when you want to drink more beer.

Bulota's summer house had a shelf with a collection of souvenir dolls in national costumes that he brought from other Soviet republics and Eastern European countries. On the floor was a skin of one of the two boars he had shot and killed. Table and chairs, a sofa, a cabinet, the carpet, the lamps, even curtains, beautiful handmade pillowcases and blankets, and a carved wooden cat sculpture were from his time. He had dinner at this same table next to the wall covered with wooden planks that he procured for renovating the house. Like many others, he did not throw out old things but took them to the summer house.[50] Here also were the *Broom*'s "Best Hunter" medals, framed pictures he received as gifts, paintings of nature, and a handmade vintage farmhouse-style blanket chest (figure 0.3).

FIGURE 0.3. The summer house of Juozas Bulota, editor in chief of the *Broom*. Photo by the author, summer 2018.

The study of past materialities provided important context on the history of the *Broom*. It testified to the *Broom* as a popular media magazine, gave evidence on the editors' relationships, their statuses, the editor in chief's interests and friendships, and provided information on meetings with readers and their reception of the *Broom*.

Archives

The archival data include documents from three institutions in Lithuania: the Lithuanian Central State Archive (LCSA), the Lithuanian Archive of Literature and Art (LALA), and the Lithuanian Special Archive (LSA). Three major document collections were part of the Lithuanian Special Archive: the Lithuanian Communist Party collections, the Committee for State Security (KGB) collections, and the Ministry of Interior collections. The LSA Lithuanian Communist Party collections included *Broom* Communist Party Primary Organization meeting reports. These documents contained many detailed monthly and annual reports from 1960 to 1979 (712 pages in total) and provided information on the *Broom* editors' Communist Party work, as well as on three major *Broom* departments: the Letters Department, the Literature Department, and the Illustration Department. In the LSA's Committee for State Security collections I found several notes in the Vilnius City secret agent operations annual meeting reports; they informed me that KGB investigation materials were published in the *Broom*. I also found two anonymous letters with nationalistic content forwarded by the *Broom* to the KGB. The LSA Ministry of Interior collections contained materials of collaboration between the *Broom* and the Ministry of Interior on prevention of theft of public property, corruption, speculation, alcoholism, loafing, and youth delinquency. At the Lithuanian Central State Archive I researched Glavlit documents of 1959–1977. They provided information on the censoring of the *Broom*, as well as on Glavlit as a censoring institution. The majority of documents were in the Lithuanian language; some documents in the KGB and Glavlit archives were in Russian.

The Lithuanian Archive of Literature and Art contained information on *Broom* collaboration with other institutions, editorial work, correspondence with readers, and readers' letters to the *Broom* (representing thousands of pages of documents). I also reviewed collections of the Russian State Archive of Literature and Arts in Moscow, where I found almost no documents relating to the post-Stalinist period, which could have yielded important comparative perspectives. While *Krokodil* magazines and some editors' memoirs were available, post–World War II *Krokodil* editorial and Communist Party Primary Organization (PPO) meeting archives, as well as Russian KGB and Glavlit archives, were closed.

My comparative statements in this introduction and elsewhere in the book on the *Broom* and *Krokodil* rest on my review of the published magazine issues, secondary sources on *Krokodil*, a few primary documents, and *Krokodil* editors' articles and memoirs.

The availability in Lithuania of archives of the Communist Party Central Committee, the Communist Party Primary Organization, Glavlit, and the KGB allowed seeing the Soviet state as an incomplete, inconsistent, contradictory, and paradoxical project. The KGB did not control humor. It was not interested in ambiguities of humor or Aesopian language, but rather in explicit anti-Soviet, nationalistic, antisemitic, or anti-Russian content. It had lists of all *Broom* editors, as well as other media employees, with their addresses and phone numbers. Although I heard stories from editors about being summoned by the KGB, I did not find any record of such interviews in the KGB archives. While archives are no doubt incomplete, it is likely in the case of the *Broom* that the KGB acted as an institution that mediated and prevented actions rather than enforced control and punishment. Leading *Broom* editors addressed KGB operatives who were in charge of the *Broom* by their first names. The most exciting pieces of evidence on the *Broom* and KGB collaboration in the KGB archives were two letters sent to the *Broom* that spoke about Russification, Lithuania's occupation, and the potential death of the nation (see chapter 8). Generally, the absence of information on the *Broom* in the KGB archives told a story of editorial board loyalties to the state and the KGB's lack of interest in humor media.

I began researching Glavlit archives looking for an evil censor whose image was created in my mind from reading dissident works and memoirs. But many Lithuanian censors were regular state employees making mistakes, lacking qualifications, and having little passion for their work (chapter 4). Glavlit archives uncovered absurdities of censoring—censors carried out ideological censoring without any explicit regulations. It was fascinating to learn how censors, as well as *Broom* editors, applied ideological censoring in the absence of formalized rules and thus defined the boundaries of ideology themselves (see chapter 4). My biggest finding in the Glavlit archives were two 1968 reports specifically on the unacceptable content in the *Broom*, which provided censors' reasoning on why *Broom* literary pieces or cartoons had to be rejected (see chapter 5). Glavlit archives also helped me to position the *Broom* among other Lithuanian magazines and journals as one of the most censored official publications in Soviet times (see chapter 4).

The Communist Party Primary Organization archives provided data on the *Broom* editors' daily ideological work: discussing CP Congress materials, voting to approve the USSR's new constitution, drafting plans of ideological work, considering editors' political education, and expanding CP members' circle.

Meeting Albertas Lukša, the only then-surviving CP member of the *Broom*, as well as the long-term *Broom* PPO secretary and chair of the Letters Department, afforded me insight into what ideological work was like for *Broom* editors from their perspective. In addition to ideological agendas, the PPO reports recorded various curious events. One such record documented how the *Broom* executive secretary got drunk and tried to open a door of an apartment similar to his own, like a scene in the 1976 popular Soviet film *The Irony of Fate, or Enjoy Your Bath*. I could not tell whether the executive secretary's escapade was a joke and an example of *stiob* (Yurchak 2006) or whether it really happened (see chapter 2). In these archives, I also read about various conflicts among *Broom* editors; one such episode included accusations about an alleged underground organization in the *Broom*.

Finally, the Lithuanian Archive of Literature and Art allowed a glimpse into the editorial production of the *Broom*—selecting and rejecting satires, choosing cartoons (archives contained folders with accepted and rejected works), editing, corresponding with authors, and exchanging messages with other institutions about facts on corrupt officials, public disorders, unfinished housing projects, and various injustices. I enjoyed reading through thousands of readers' letters to the *Broom* editors documenting readers' concerns with everyday matters. Many of these letters were full of despair, and only some were funny. Readers sent photographs, drawings, satires, and small prose, which I discuss in chapters 7 and 8.

In chapter 3, I address methodological challenges in understanding archives and the political and scholarly relevance of archival data. The Communist Party and the State Security archives in Eastern European states had been used to accuse citizens of collaboration and remove them from political office (see Glaeser 2011; Tismaneanu and Stan 2018). Archives, thus, are political troves, the reading of which requires a deep analysis and juxtaposition with other data, such as interviews. Contributing to the discussion of how archives present partial and politicized truths representing the visions and values of authoritarian regimes (see Krakus 2015; Krakus and Vatulescu 2019; Vatulescu 2014; Verdery 2018), I develop analytics of *bureaucratic showcasing*. *Broom* PPO documents were records of *bureaucratic showcasing*, since the *Broom* editors' primary imperative was to address the Communist Party authorities and align their work with CP agendas discursively, to showcase hard work, loyalty, and commitment. As I discuss in chapter 3, there are no clear boundaries between bureaucratic showcasing and facts. But bureaucratic showcasing cannot be simply discounted as irrelevant. I show that late-socialist bureaucratic showcasing is a multilayered practice, integrating levels of formal, informal, and informative engagements relevant to understanding *Broom* laughter. The PPO archives, thus, are meaningful documents representing what the editors understood as important in ideological as well as *Broom* daily work, what they valued in their relations as a *Broom* collective, and how they perceived relations with authorities.

Interviews

Interviews and informal discussions with editors, artists, writers, and journalists who worked at the *Broom* for long or short periods constitute another important data set for this study. I interviewed eleven *Broom* editorial board members who worked at the magazine before 1985. Some of them had never met with former colleagues after they retired from the *Broom*. Thus, finding them involved significant detective work. Albertas Lukša and Andrius Cvirka lived in their summer houses in different parts of Lithuania. Reaching them took a day of travel over highways, gravel roads, and bumpy country roadways, making me wonder if I would find my way back. I conducted twenty-two formal interviews with the *Broom* editors (approximately forty-four hours of recording).

I also explored the creative biographies of *Broom* artists, writers, and journalists by reviewing their work for the magazine, their awards, recognition, diplomas, travel documents, and copies of their other published work to contextualize their words and art beyond the *Broom* pages. These biographies showed that the *Broom* editors were well integrated into Soviet satire and humor culture through creative and collaborative activities and participation in pan-Soviet events, including exhibitions such as *Satire in the Struggle for Peace*. Most *Broom* artists and writers were among the creative elites recognized in Russia and other Soviet republics and known in some socialist Eastern European states. Being part of the Soviet Lithuanian elite guaranteed more freedom. Some *Broom* editors traveled to Mexico, the United States, or Italy; the majority of their trips were to Eastern European socialist countries.

In addition to *Broom* artists, five family members of former *Broom* editors contributed important knowledge on the *Broom* (eight interviews, approximately nine hours of recording). I also interviewed eight artists, writers, and journalists who were regular contributors to the *Broom* (nine formal interviews, approximately eighteen hours of recording). Finally, I interviewed one editor who worked at a different media institution (one and a half hours of recording) and four former LCP CC members (six hours of recording), two of whom wrote for the *Broom* as well. Meeting some of them, like Česlovas Juršėnas, was also a transformative moment, helping me to see how limited the state was in crafting official humor as a governance mechanism (see this book's conclusion).

I also read and discussed the *Broom* with its former readers to understand their relation to Soviet Lithuanian humor. I did not conduct systematic research on readers' memories of the *Broom* but carried out some interviews and asked almost everybody born in the 1970s or earlier whom I met during my research in the 2010s what they remembered about the *Broom*. Readers' stories about older men discussing feuilletons or reading the *Broom* in their summer houses or arguing about the *Broom*'s factual material enriched ethnographic data on the *Broom*'s reception and popularity. Informal interviews with readers range from longer recorded interviews, to discussions about the *Broom* with a group of people enjoying dinner in a summer house, to spontaneous short exchanges with taxi drivers. I was unable to find people who wrote letters to the *Broom*, although some interlocutors reminisced about writing letters to other state institutions. My advertisements in newspapers and ad portals asking people to share a story about writing a complaint letter to the *Broom* went unanswered.

I organized a public roundtable, "The Vanished Laughter: The Politics of Secrecy in the magazine *Broom*," with former *Broom* editors at the Martynas Mažvydas National Library of Lithuania on April 28, 2017, an ethnographic event on its own.[51] This event provided a glimpse into the *Broom*'s legacy among its former editors, artists, journalists, and readers. It also gave *Broom* editors a forum to speak about the *Broom* in public, and to the public and to one another rather than me. This event, which I discuss in the conclusion, brought former *Broom* editors together to celebrate the *Broom* and their work for it. They were all nostalgic for the lost laughter—its intellectualism and moral appeal compared to post-Soviet joking (see conclusion). The roundtable also testified to editors' and artists' vulnerability to authoritarian stigma for their work at the Soviet humor propaganda magazine, a negative association with "collaborators" of the Soviet government.

The Unfunny Laughter

One of the questions I often get from different audiences in the United States is whether the *Broom*'s humor was funny. *Broom* humor manifested Soviet ideological principles: some of it was didactic, educational, and propagandistic. Some Soviet satire was biting. It encompassed sarcastic and humiliating laughter. Even if amusement and entertainment were parts of humor, as in comic strips (see chapter 6), they often incorporated some ideological principles, such as denunciation of the West and capitalism. However, many former *Broom* readers agreed that cartoons, comic strips, and especially foreign humor sections were very funny. Others loved small prose pieces. Some readers said it was funny because there was nothing better. But this laughter is gone. Soviet jokes are not entertaining to younger generations who grew up in post-Soviet times and who often do not even understand them.

Laughter is historical and cultural; it is related to gender, race, class, religious or political positionality (Goldstein 2003; Hall, Goldstein, and Ingram 2016). While Democratic voters note that the US president Donald Trump's 2016 electoral campaign was humorless, Kira Hall, Donna Meryl Goldstein, and Matthew Bruce Ingram (2016) remind us that it *was* amusing for Trump supporters. They claim that his success in the Republican primary in 2016 "was in part due to its value as comedic entertainment" (2016, 71). Paraphrasing George Orwell ([1945] 1968), who argued that every joke is a tiny revolution, one could say that every joke is a story, a drama, an art-politics shared by people who are recognized in such jokes and belong to a community united against the butts of laughter. To be entertained is to be in on the joke (cf. Paloff 2021) and share its moral affective universe.

While Lithuanian interlocutors often responded with pleasant smiles when I asked them about the *Broom*, they also often asked a question—why I chose this magazine for my research. Even artists and writers considered it to be an unusual research object. The *Broom* was not part of high culture, and caricature was considered a low genre. Satirists and humorists, as Soviet Jewish satirist Emil Draitser (2021, 49) argued, were "second fiddles in the literary orchestra." Moreover, humor has been perceived by cultural elites as something trivial and inconsequential. Other magazines like *Literatūra and menas* (Literature and art) or *Pergalė* (The victory) were hubs for intellectual work as well as opposition.[52] Even *Krokodil* has received only limited scholarly attention, with the exception of studies of its famous artists like Boris Efimov (Norris 2009, 2013) and its graphic satire (Etty 2019).[53] There are very few studies of other Soviet satire and humor magazines, too.[54]

The *Broom* was interesting to me because it documented the authoritarian state's attempt to govern and engage citizens at the everyday level through the intimacy of laughter. Did people laugh together with the state? I wondered. As mentioned previously, the *Broom*'s profit equaled earnings of a successful kolkhoz, while most other Communist Party magazines were subsidized by the party. While many other Soviet kolkhozes were inefficient, the "kolkhoz" of laughter brought profits to the communist state and smiles to people. The *Broom* offered an opportunity to study something genuinely popular, a magazine that was acceptable to the government and enjoyed by ordinary people.

The power of laughter was also intriguing. Throughout history, satirists and cartoonists have faced various punishments—prison for supposed treason or antigovernment conspiracy, and even executions. As I was thinking about the project on laughter, in 2015 terrorists killed twelve editors and staff at the Parisian humor magazine *Charlie Hebdo*. I also wanted to know why in post-Soviet times nostalgia for vanished laughter was so prevalent throughout Eastern Europe (see

Lampland and Nadkarni 2016). Was nostalgia indicative that there was something valuable in the authoritarian milieu? I wondered. Finally, this project allowed me to explore questions that have been at the center of my research for many years, questions about forms of political participation in authoritarian states and the nature of power and everyday opposition. It was a revelation to understand that laughter is a political weapon, but not really at the hands of the state; that the authoritarian state is not so powerful as I assumed. The wry smile on the bust that Juozas Bulota brought home on that dreary November evening in 1980 was hiding a story that this book will tell in its pages.

BANALITY OF SOVIET POWER

There was a game—you poke on a row of buttons on a sweater and say: bought, stolen, gifted. . . . The last button tells you where the sweater came from. Destiny indifferently poked on a row of . . . high school students: life, death, exile, NKVD, partisan, conformist, Siberian prisoner.

—Silvija Lomsargytė-Pukienė, 2004

On Sunday morning, June 22, 1941, Nazi bombers reached the neighborhood of Freda in Kaunas, Lithuania's interwar capital. From her house window, seven-year-old Dita followed two tails of black smoke billowing over green hills.[1] Dita's father was Jewish, her mother Catholic. That day when Dita was looking at the coiling smoke, her parents were already divorced, and her father and mother had remarried. Her father did not want to leave his second wife and a newborn son and escape to Russia, and ultimately all three of them perished in the Holocaust. Dita's half-brother died even before he started walking (Lomsargytė-Pukienė 2004, 91). Dita's mother and her new Lithuanian husband changed Dita's name to Silvija Lomsargytė to hide her Jewish identity. Mixed children were also killed by Nazis, but nobody turned them in.[2] In 1942 Dita's stepfather who gave her his name was executed by Nazis for his leftist leanings.

After the war Dita and her mother moved to Vilnius. They settled close to the former ghetto, walked on the narrow streets in the former Jewish headquarters, crossed streets with old Polish ladies dressed in black with lace gloves and beautiful hats. An old Pole used to play violin in their yard in the evenings for some money and food. This world would soon disappear under the Soviet transformation of state and society. Vilnius, a Polish territory from 1920 to 1939, was destined to become the capital of Soviet Lithuania and the city where the *Broom* was founded.

On that early Sunday morning, when Dita was looking at black smoke tails in Freda, one-year-old Andrius got into a car with his family to drive east with his parents and a maternal grandmother to escape the Nazis.[3] Their car broke down. His parents asked to join a truck filled with people retreating to Russia. Andrius's grandmother refused to let his parents take little Andrius "to that Russian hole (derogatory Lith. *į rusyną*)."[4] Andrius's parents left without him on the overflowing truck. The grandmother and Andrius returned to Freda, where they stayed during the war. Andrius did not often get to see his father, Petras Cvirka, even after his father returned from Russia a few years later, in 1944. Cvirka, a well-known Lithuanian leftist writer, joined the new Soviet elites as the LSSR Writers Union chairman in Vilnius. He died in 1947 at the age of thirty-eight, leaving seven-year-old Andrius to live in the Soviet state that Petras Cvirka helped found.

When Andrius was nineteen, in 1959, a huge monument was erected for his father in the center of Vilnius. Around that time Dita, a recent university graduate, was hired to work for the *Broom*. Andrius joined the *Broom* in 1967. In this way, Dita and Andrius both became workers at the ideological front of the Communist Party.

In Soviet studies, citizen-state relations are often explained by inquiring into agency: were they believers in communism, self-interested individuals, brainwashed by the regime, uncritical, or cynical conformists?[5] As the epigraph from Dita's memoir indicates, agency was often shaped by various circumstances. Dita spoke of herself as "a child of the war," easy to be intimidated and lacking confidence. The *Broom* provided protection during insecure times. "I was a kid of the monument," Andrius described himself when I asked why he was hired for the *Broom*.[6] He already had a family and a young son and needed money. At the *Broom*, under the "shadow" of the monument of his father, he could be more independent as an artist and challenge the ideologies of the regime that took his father away. Neither Dita nor Andrius shared an ideological commitment and determination to build communism, nor did they act to cynically pursue their self-interest or were they uncritically accepting of the status quo. Nevertheless, both became part of the Soviet regime and its propaganda apparatus.

The case of the *Broom* illustrates that the authoritarian regime can function not because of zealous believers, but rather with the help of a few indifferently chosen by destiny, as Dita claimed. I use the concept of *the banality of power* to capture the everyday commonplace process of participation in the authoritarian milieu (cf. Mbembe 2001). In this chapter I argue that joining and working for the *Broom* was a commonplace experience for those in search of security, autonomy, and self-expression.

As in Achille Mbembe's study of postcoloniality, my usage of the *banality of power* emphasizes emplacement of subjects within the system, the routinization of rules, and "systems of domination." In *On the Postcolony*, Mbembe uses the concept of the "banality of power" to refer both to the multiplication and routinization of bureaucratic and arbitrary rules and to "those elements of the obscene and the grotesque that Mikhail Bakhtin claims to have located in 'non-official' cultures but that, in fact, are intrinsic to all systems of domination and to the means by which those systems are confirmed or deconstructed" (1992, 3). Mbembe further writes that "at any given moment in the postcolonial historical trajectory, the authoritarian mode can no longer be interpreted strictly in terms of surveillance, or the politics of coercion. The practices of ordinary citizens cannot always be read in terms of 'opposition to the state,' 'deconstructing power,' and 'disengagement'" (25). Mbembe focuses primarily on the dynamics of coercion and consent among ordinary citizens and reproduction of hegemonic power relations, while my focus is on how ordinary citizens become active participants in the hegemonic regime. In this context Hannah Arendt's work on totalitarianism and, specifically, her explorations of the "banality of evil" in her study *Eichmann in Jerusalem: A Report on the Banality of Evil* ([1963] 2006) are very informative. While both Mbembe and Arendt were interested in complicity and participation in a coercive power regime, Mbembe focused on complicity among different power groups, while Arendt inquired into complicity through serving the regime.

Some examples, which help frame the analysis, are unexpected to the point that they seem to make no sense. What can be similar between an artist who drew plump, joyful characters for the *Broom* and a Nazi operative planning the Final Solution? Arendt's analysis of the 1961 trial of Adolf Eichmann, who was responsible for organizing the transportation of Jews to concentration camps, is such a displaced example. But it was Arendt's study that helped me to understand that the authoritarian Soviet regime was a commonplace experience within which editors, artists, and writers found themselves.

Arendt's concept of the "banality of evil" uncovers that participation in murderous projects sometimes can have no deep ideological roots or motives; people may drift into the Nazi Party or any other power structure in search of purpose and direction or just find themselves within it. In *Eichmann in Jerusalem*, Arendt observed that Eichmann was an ordinary bureaucrat. He performed, according to Arendt, evil deeds without evil intentions. As a result of his "thoughtlessness," a disengagement from the reality of his evil acts, he "commit[ted] crimes under circumstances that made it well-nigh impossible for him to know or to feel that he [was] doing wrong" ([1963] 2006, 276). Concerning Eichmann, Arendt argued, "Except for an extraordinary diligence in looking out for his personal advancement, he had no motives at all. He *merely . . . never realized what he was doing*" (287, emphasis in the original). Arendt emphasizes Eichmann's "inability . . . to think from the standpoint of somebody else" (49). While Arendt overstated Eichmann's thoughtlessness by suggesting he did not reflect on his actions, the fact remains that evil deeds can be performed while being disengaged from the reality of their evil nature. Evil can be banal.[7]

Although Arendt's study is quite different from mine, the uneventfulness and ordinariness of joining the *Broom* resonate with her arguments. Most editors who worked for the *Broom* did not think about reproducing authoritarian power, or contributing to its functioning and effectiveness.[8] They participated in an authoritarian governance without any deep ideological roots or motives. It was an ordinary experience that did not require a recognition of the consequences of one's actions. Still, unlike in Arendt's depiction of Eichmann, *Broom* editors were not entirely disengaged from the reality of their work. *Broom* editors' knowledge about the Soviet predicament (see chapter 3) was shaped by a history of occupations, their ethnic difference, and the political status of a new minority in the Soviet state. This knowledge became the basis for what I call *antagonistic complicity*, or relations of disagreeing consensus (chapter 6).

In her later reflections on *Eichmann in Jerusalem*, Arendt argued that the concept of the banality of evil was not necessarily the best choice (Elon 2006, xviii). The focus on individual "thoughtlessness" and glossing over questions of Eichmann's responsibility may lead us to conclude that Arendt's argument implies that evil is imminent and anything is possible. Michael Rothberg (2019) offers a different theory of political responsibility by introducing the concept of the *implicated subject*. Rothberg argues in his exploration of memory regimes and overlapping injustices that none of us are completely innocent. "Implicated subjects occupy positions aligned with power and privilege without being themselves direct agents of harm; they contribute to, inhabit, inherit, or benefit from regimes of domination but do not originate or control such regimes" (Rothberg 2019, 1). While being neither a victim nor a perpetrator, an implicated subject is a "participant in histories and social formations that generate the positions of victim and perpetrator, and yet in which most people do not occupy such clear-cut roles" (1). Implicated subjects are entangled, involved, and connected.[9]

According to Rothberg, the analytics of the *implicated subject* help to acknowledge responsibility beyond narrower legalistic categories of guilt or complicity.[10] They also allow us to recognize complexities of implication. Rothberg calls the coexistence of different relations to past and present injustices "complex implication" (2019, 8). In the case of *Broom* editors, as the introductory vignette shows, the histories of victimization and the histories of complicity with the regime were interconnected. Dita and Andrius, like many other *Broom* editors, were victims and associates of the Soviet regime. Dita's claim that she was a "war child" captures her experience of war traumas and the Holocaust. These experiences were part of her new Soviet biography (see also chapter 3). Andrius's comment about being a child of the monument reminds us of his father's accomplishments within the Soviet state. Petras Cvirka traveled with other intellectuals in

1940 to Moscow to deliver the declaration for Lithuania to be incorporated into the USSR. Their action in post-Soviet times ironically is called "bringing Stalin's sun" to Lithuania.[11] His father's fame influenced Andrius's career, while he was also affected by losing him.

Different causes shaped Dita's, Andrius's, and the founding editors' choice to join the *Broom*—a search for security and stability, autonomy and self-expression, and finding a job that corresponded with their qualifications. Andrius was studying at the Art Institute and was noticed by Stasys Krasauskas for his sense of humor. Krasauskas, an artist and a *Broom* editorial board member, met Andrius at the Neringa restaurant, where Andrius introduced himself as a "kid of the monument." Dita was a recent graduate from the Education Institute with the English-language-teacher diploma who had a job at the Science Academy. At the *Broom* she replaced her friend Elena Kurklietytė at the Letters Department. Kurklietytė left the *Broom* after she married the editor in chief of the Estonian satire and humor magazine *Pikker* and moved to Estonia.

In this book I will further explore the *Broom* artists', writers', and journalists' entanglements with Soviet history and power. This chapter focuses on the biographies of several of the founding editors of the *Broom* to understand their role in establishing the *Broom* and to contextualize this magazine as a Soviet periphery project. The next sections will take a closer look at the founding editors and their complex implications in the histories of the pre-Soviet and Soviet past as victims of the Nazi or Soviet terror and as associates of the Soviet regime.

The Founding Editors

Juozas Bulota (1918–1994) was born into a family of landowners in Putriškių village, Marijampolė district, in southern Lithuania. His father passed away when he was nine years old. He and seven of his siblings were supported by his father's brother, Andrius Bulota, a lawyer, statesman, deputy at the State Duma, and a proponent of Lithuania's autonomy in the Russian Empire. After the founding of the Lithuanian Soviet Socialist Republic (LSSR), Andrius Bulota became the chair of the juridical office of the LSSR's Supreme Council Presidium. He was shot by Nazis in 1941.

During World War II, Juozas Bulota supported Soviet partisans stationed near his village by giving them food. It is likely he did not have another choice when armed men knocked on the door.[12] After the war was over, he was granted Soviet partisan liaison status.[13] In the fall of 1944, Bulota moved to Vilnius. His uncle's fame and the need for local cadres helped him to get a job in 1944 at ELTA, a division of TASS, the Soviet News Agency.[14] It was a high-profile appointment in Soviet media. In 1949 Bulota rose to an associate editor role at the newspaper the *Truth*, a major publication of the Lithuanian Communist Party Central Committee (LCP CC), the LSSR Supreme Council, and the LSSR Council of Ministers. At the *Truth*, he started publishing his feuilletons.

According to the official version, Bulota was invited to become the editor in chief of the *Broom* because of his satirical talent (Šniukas 2018). "But the true version," journalist Domas Šniukas argued, "is this new appointment was related to the conflict with Genrikas Zimanas, the editor-in-chief of the *Truth*" (3). Šniukas writes that around 1955, Zimanas left his position as editor in chief in order to write his dissertation. Other editors at the *Truth* thought that he most likely would not return and started to criticize kolkhoz chairmen and other bureaucrats who had had Zimanas's protection. Zimanas returned to the *Truth* and retaliated against unruly editors. The *Broom*'s founding was a good opportunity to "get rid of Juozas Bulota" (3). Journalists Kurklietytė and Lukša also left the *Truth*, where they did not have good relations with Zimanas, to be hired at the *Broom* in 1957 and 1959, respectively. Elena Kurklietytė Bubnienė remembered Zimanas as "one of the most horrible ideologists in Lithuania . . . who did lots of bad things to Lithuania."[15]

Bulota's first wife had poor health and died, leaving him with a son. His second wife, Donata Vileišytė, whom he married in 1961, was a daughter of Vincas Vileišis and a member of the prominent Vileišis family. Her father had been shot by the NKVD in Sverdlovsk in 1942.[16] One of Juozas Bulota's sisters was exiled to Siberia (Šniukas 2018). Three of Bulota's relatives were shot in Siberian prison camps (see *Šluota* 1991, 3). After marrying Donata Vileišytė, Bulota never asked for permission to travel to a Western country, unwilling to draw attention to his family's biographies of repression.[17] Starting in 1969, Juozas Bulota was usually visited by his American relatives twice a year. They brought him American journals and newspapers.[18] Sometimes Bulota received the *Chicago Tribune*, *Reader's Digest*, the Lithuanian diaspora newspaper *Freedom*, and even *Playboy*. In their summer house, Bulota's family listened to the Voice of America.[19]

Jonas Sadaunykas, the *Broom*'s executive secretary, worked with Bulota from the founding of the *Broom* until his retirement. Sadaunykas suggested in his autobiographical novel that Bulota could be manipulated by the government because of his biography (Sadaunykas-Sadūnas 2002, 272).[20] While Bulota was an associate of the Soviet regime, his wife was the regime's victim, thus implicating Bulota into the history of victimization and perpetration, to use Rothberg's terms. In Soviet times he was a Communist Party member working at the ideological front, married to a Soviet enemy.

Recalling Stalinist times during perestroika in his public lecture notes, Juozas Bulota spoke about fear. His brother Andrius was in prison, his sister deported to Siberia. Bulota's brother Antanas lost jobs twice during Khrushchev's time. "I was less fearful when I was a partisan [a liaison for the Soviet Army during World War II]," claimed Bulota, than during the turbulent postwar years.[21] Bulota's son remembered that his father was always anxious that he would be fired from the *Broom*: "There were many problems and they emerged often. . . . Even if he looked cheerful and his stories amused people . . . at home [my] father was often concerned about his work. There were many complaints about him, endless problems. *Broom* staff used to get in trouble, or [when] problematic content was published in the *Broom*, he was [often] summoned to the Central Committee, [and] had to explain himself infinitely."[22] His wife Donata Bulotienė recalled how she and her husband were cautious in many situations; these were "hard times, horrible times."[23] Antanas Rimša, a regular contributor to the *Broom* in the 1970s, said that at end-of-the-year gatherings of *Broom* contributors, Juozas Bulota would ask for understanding from contributors whose works were rejected. Bulota used to say that every morning he got out of bed wondering whether he was still an editor in chief or if he had lost his job (Rimša 2007). He complained that Communist Party authorities did not understand humor and got angry at *Broom* publications (Rimša 2007). In an interview in 1991, Bulota claimed that he was often accused of vilifying Soviet reality, generalizing, giving material to enemies for their propaganda (*Šluota* 1991, 3).

Domas Šniukas (2018, 298) remembered Bulota as a "skillful diplomat who basically was the only one [among editors in chief of different magazines] who survived in his position for three decades." Dita Lomsargytė-Pukienė, introduced above, and who worked at the Letters Department in the late 1950s and early 1960s, remembered others saying that "Bulota was a coward."[24] But she thought that "he tried to ensure that the *Broom* was not closed forever. He acted carefully, but very cleverly."[25]

Following a CPSU Central Committee decision of August 10, 1956, at a meeting led by Antanas Sniečkus, the first secretary of the Lithuanian Communist Party, the LCP CC Bureau declared it would begin publishing a satirical magazine, the *Broom*, in November 1956. It is very likely that local authorities were able to reestablish the magazine because of Nikita Khrushchev's thaw, the time of relative liberalization in the media, arts, and culture (see box 1.2). The magazine had to be published in the Lithuanian language. Twice a month, fifteen thousand issues, in the size of two press sheets, would be printed and sold for two rubles per issue.[26] Bulota was appointed as editor in chief by the LCP CC. The first order he wrote was Order No. 1, accepting the position: "On October 20, 1956, I am beginning the duties of the editor in chief of the *Broom*."[27]

In Bulota's personal archive there are hiring orders from the first year after the *Broom* was founded, which show that he was in charge of forming the editorial team.[28] In addition to hiring himself, these orders included fifteen hires and five dismissals during a period of less than eight months, from October 20, 1956, to June 14, 1957. Among the fired and dismissed, one person did not pass the probation period, another was transferred to a different magazine, two others asked to leave on their own, and one quit for an unknown reason. Albertas Lukša, a *Broom* long-term journalist, was hired a year after his graduation from Vilnius University. In 2019 Lukša claimed that Sadaunykas invited him to work for the *Broom*.[29] Rytis Tilvytis was hired when he was still a student, without a diploma. Elena Kurklietytė was hired in 1957, the year she graduated from Vilnius University with a journalism diploma. She remembered that Bulota lacked staff. Bulota himself did not have a university diploma until 1960. Several other people who became longtime editors were hired without much previous experience. Eleven years after World War II, building an editorial team in a country in which many cultural elites were killed, exiled, or emigrated turned out to be a challenge for Juozas Bulota.

In 1958 in his report to the LCP CC Propaganda and Agitation Department, Bulota asked for editorial office space: at the time of his writing the editorial board had three rooms. The editor in chief had a separate room; an associate editor, an executive secretary, and an art editor shared one room; all others—a third room. Bulota wrote that many visitors came to the *Broom*, and if citizens had a complaint, they were shy to speak in front of many people, and there was no lounge for visitors.[30] Until 1984, the *Broom* moved three times: it had an office on Komunarų (currently Jakšto) Street, then Liudo Giros (currently Vilniaus) Street, and finally Pilies Alley (currently Bernardinų Street), all in the center of Vilnius.

As the *Broom* editor in chief as well as a writer, Bulota was part of the Soviet literary elite. In the 1980s he lived in the then-prestigious writers' district in brick housing, surrounded by pine forests and within walking distance from the city's center. Bulota's close friend Eduardas Mieželaitis was a recipient of the Lenin Prize for poetry in 1962. Mieželaitis was also a member of the LCP CC, later a deputy of the USSR Supreme Council, and a chairman of the Writers Union (1959–1970). Another close neighbor, whose steps Bulota heard from the apartment above, was Justinas Marcinkevičius. Marcinkevičius was a living literary legend. Both Mieželaitis and Marcinkevičius published pro-Soviet poems and poems with nationalistic undertones.[31]

Bulota had ambitions to be recognized as a satirist, in the mode of Jaroslav Hašek, a famous Czech humorist and satirist, the author of the novel *The Good Soldier Svejk*. Bulota, whose satirical works were published in many Eastern European and Soviet magazines, was awarded a distinguished journalist title in 1968 and was accepted into the Writers Union in 1971. He was, however, first of all known as the editor in chief of the *Broom*. His gravestone is marked "Writer

Juozas Bulota," but there is also a caricature of Bulota by Stasys Krasauskas on the stone, with a broom as his tie.

Bulota saved in his personal archive greeting cards from *Krokodil*'s editors in chief celebrating the New Year and other occasions. It is likely that cards and gifts traveled both ways. The 1972 minutes of the *Broom* editorial staff meeting mention a purchase of a piece of leather from the Batas shoe factory to be used to inscribe good wishes for *Krokodil*'s fiftieth anniversary.[32] Bulota's son Juozas Bulota remembered that his father did not like going to Moscow and thought the city was repulsive.[33] He was also unwilling to interact with the highest LCP CC authorities. He did not hunt with them because he was "too small a fish."[34] During perestroika, after he had retired from the *Broom* following twenty-nine years of service as editor in chief, the elder Juozas Bulota wrote in his notes for a public lecture,

> I felt I will be fired, so I left myself. I reached a certain record [of staying in office]. . . . Why? A lot depended on the authorities. . . . I used to get anonymous letters, some threatened to kill me. As you see, I stayed alive. Of course, it affected my health, but, as it is said, the devil will not take his own child [i.e., will not punish someone who has done his bidding], more so *suvalkiečio* [an ethnographic group to which Bulota belonged, mocked for its frugality].[35]

When the Reform Movement (Lith. *Sąjūdis*) of Lithuania was established on June 3, 1988, Bulota did not join its ranks.[36] He was seventy. Did his life make him doubt such political projects? In his notes for a public lecture during perestroika he wrote that "[you] cannot forgive special squad murderers [Nazis and their collaborators] who killed tens of thousands of people in Paneriai, including my relatives. You also cannot forgive those who consciously denounced, pushed people into cattle cars, [sent] their fellow countrymen [Lith. *tautiečius*] to die in Siberia."[37] In his 1991 interview in the *Broom* he said that "looking back on how far I've come, I can see everything—I had to compromise, begrudgingly follow orders that were not always the most intelligent. I'm deeply respectful of those who didn't compromise, who were imprisoned, who continued to fight, unbroken, for the freedom of all the people of Lithuania" (*Šluota* 1991, 3). Bulota's son remembered him saying that their house, situated between two hills, was well positioned to bury alive all the writers who lived there and build a monument when the government changed.[38] As it turned out, Juozas Bulota was buried close to this home, in the beautiful cemetery corner for writers. None of the former LCP CC authorities attended his funeral in 1994, with the exception of Česlovas Juršėnas, the former chair of the print media, TV, and radio division at the LCP CC Propaganda and Agitation Department.[39] In Lithuania Česlovas Juršėnas is known for his public apology in 1995 for the actions of communists against the nation and the Lithuanian state.

Jonas Sadaunykas (1925–2009) was born in Kaliekiai village, Utena district, and came of age during World War II. His grandmother was deported to Siberia and died en route. In his autobiographical novel written between 1987 and 1989, Sadaunykas wrote that mass deportations of many innocent people, primarily teachers, made many poor people turn away from the Soviets. He had to hide to avoid being mobilized for the Soviet Army.[40] He wrote about the postwar era, invoking the mutilated bodies of "forest brothers" (as anti-Soviet partisans were popularly called) in the town square and the numbers of innocent people in prison (Sadaunykas-Sadūnas 2002, 39, 80). Sadaunykas was putatively involved in the underground anti-Soviet Lithuanian Freedom Army. He agreed with charges that he betrayed the Soviet homeland and was sentenced according to Article 58 (72). In 1945 he spent almost eight months in prison.[41] When he was a student at Vilnius Art Institute, he was regularly followed by a KGB agent. "His [agent's] surveilling hawk shadow soared above him silently creating anxiety and fear" (104). This experience was so strongly imprinted in Sadaunykas's memory that he titled his memoiristic novel *The Yellow Eyes of a Hawk*.

Sadaunykas claimed that he joined the Komsomol out of fear (Sadaunykas-Sadūnas 2002, 101). He spoke of "self-preservation" as the major motive for his actions, as a way to please others, escape problems, and adjust in order to earn a living (152). "Self-preservation instinct is a powerful feeling," he argued, "and fear in such circumstances is justifiable since fear is the major expression of [the] self-preservation instinct" (152). He joined the Communist Party in 1960, which was similarly an uneventful experience, described in the third person: "The river of destiny . . . caught him and took [him] away like a small stick. He grabbed the red book [the Communist Party membership book] out of self-protection, instinctively. This book was used as a shield by many other creative intelligentsia" (281). Sadaunykas claimed that he joined the Communist Party "for Lithuania." "You had to use an opportunity, which the Lithuanian Party authorities gave us: they opened gateways to intelligentsia, while earlier they were open only for workers and *kolkhozniks*. Latvians, for example, did not do it and faced painful outcomes: the Latvian Communist Party became Russianized. . . . So does all Latvia" (281).

Unlike Bulota, Sadaunykas was not associated with leftists or pro-Soviet groups in his youth. But he was invited by Bulota to be the voice of the Communist Party at the *Broom*. Sadaunykas joined the editorial board as *Broom*'s executive secretary in 1957. For an executive secretary position, created in 1939 by the CPSU CC, a candidate had to be a member of the Communist Party, assume a leading role on the editorial board, and ensure the ideological, political position of the magazine (see Streikus 2018). Like Bulota, Sadaunykas worked for the *Truth* prior to joining the *Broom*. He was known as a "good person with a broken biography" because of his years in prison.[42] Sadaunykas's complex implication encompassed his positions in Soviet history as a victim of the Soviet regime as well as its associate.

Broom editors remembered that Sadaunykas wore a flat cap, which they called a "Stalin's cap." If I were to describe Jonas Sadaunykas based on the PPO reports, I would depict him as an ardent communist embodying the voice of the Communist Party at every PPO meeting. Artist Kęstutis Šiaulytis, who joined the *Broom* in 1978, remembered that Sadaunykas liked the fact that others were afraid of him: "He would have gotten the first prize for playing the role of a communist."[43] The editor in chief, according to Šiaulytis, "did not like to intimidate people, so this function was given to Sadaunykas: to speak in the editorial office strictly, abstain from drinking [at work], follow work hours."[44] Sadaunykas's voice quieted down in the 1970s. He was drinking more and more, while performing his loyalty to communism less and less. Reflecting in 2002 about his youth and his years at the *Broom*, he wrote that he was a servant, but it was better than being in prison. He acknowledged that his self-esteem suffered a lot; he wanted to leave his job, but "where should he go—to a factory, a *kolkhoz*, or a prison? The easiest way was to drown his conscience in vodka!" According to Sadaunykas, most of the *Broom* editors did exactly this (Sadaunykas-Sadūnas 2002, 152). Sadaunykas's Stalinist cap most likely hid insecurities and fears.[45] Enacting a communist persona was an ordinary experience. But once in a drunk state, while visiting other journalists in Ukraine, Sadaunykas reflected on his Soviet predicament by saying that Lithuania was occupied by Russians (see chapter 2).

Recalling the Sąjūdis era, Kęstutis Šiaulytis argued that Sadaunykas "was very slippery, he knew how to talk to others, so they can interpret as they wish."[46] During the time of perestroika and liberalization, in 1988, Sadaunykas published the book *Communists*. Sadaunykas's book glorified the work of an assortment of people while acknowledging them as communists. It presented seven essays—on an academic, a tractor driver, a district Communist Party Committee secretary, collective farm chairs, and a few others. When the book was published, communism was destined to die. I wondered whether Sadaunykas was forced to write this book. Most likely he wrote it voluntarily. I read his other books written in Soviet times, and they were consistent in style: glorifying some people for their work as good communists. However, the same year *Communists* was published, Sadaunykas sent a postcard to Juozas Bulota congratulating him on his seventieth birthday: "Destiny harnessed us like two horses into the *Broom* carriage for several long decades, and we pulled it as we could. During such times!"[47] In Sadaunykas's autobiographical novel written in 1987–1989 (at about the same time as *Communists*) but not published until 2002, he revealed his support for a free Lithuania. He asked whether those who returned from horrible camps in Russia and joined the work for Lithuania's freedom would forgive him and others who "conformed and kissed a fist of the occupant that was beating them?" (Sadaunykas-Sadūnas 2002, 324). Reflecting about his past, Sadaunykas noted that his life "melted like a poor-quality Soviet candy and left an unpleasant aftertaste" (323). This aftertaste would linger for years to come, until Sadaunykas would be gone, since the new state would rearticulate who counts as a victim or a collaborator. Those who were in the Communist Party ranks and in leading positions, like Bulota, Sadaunykas, and Albertas Lukša, would be deemed "collaborators."

Albertas Lukša was born in 1934 in Mančiušėnai, Širvintos district. He was still a boy when the war ended. He recalled that he used to walk five kilometers to his school on a dirt road and in snow. He sometimes rode Kaštonė (Lith., Chestnut), the family's mare. She took him to the town and then returned back home by herself. Lukša recalled that when Nazi soldiers requisitioned her, she came back on her own after three weeks by swimming over the river Širvinta.

Then Soviets returned in 1944. His father hid from the Soviet Army, and the family stayed outside their home when "*katiušos* [Lith., rocket launchers] were singing nearby."[48] Lukša recalled that at that time many waited for Americans to come; young people went to the forests to hide and fight against the Soviets.[49] Lukša remembered: "The postwar period was horrible. Fires, deadly skirmishes, (see box 1.1). dead bodies of forest brothers in a town in front of the church. . . . So many [people] went [were deported] to Siberia to never return!" (see Žeimantas 2014).

His father was a shoemaker. In the daytime, he fixed the shoes of *istrebiteli* (Rus., members of NKVD paramilitary units). At night, he cobbled for the forest brothers—the Lithuanian armed anti-Soviet resistance. Once Albertas was returning from school when a skirmish on both sides of the road erupted.[50] He was right in the middle and escaped by falling into a ditch. When he returned home, his grandmother took him on a horse-drawn carriage to a healer, since his face was swollen. The swelling disappeared, but the stuttering, which started that day, persisted. "It was a very dangerous time," remembered Lukša. There were also bandits concealed as forest brothers, "black bandits" who stole from and terrorized people, and "red bandits"—the *istrebiteli*.[51]

With a cardboard suitcase made by his aunt in 1953, Lukša traveled to Vilnius University to study journalism (Žeimantas 2014). He was fortunate to get a job at the *Truth* as a copy editor (Lith. *korektorius*). He worked night shifts. At that time Lukša published several humor pieces in regional newspapers. Like Bulota, he did not have a good relationship with Zimanas, the editor in chief of the *Truth*, who refused to publish his work. In 1958 Lukša defended his university graduation thesis on the *Broom*. The *Broom* was looking for a journalist for an agriculture position, and Sadaunykas persuaded Lukša to join the staff.[52] In 1959, at age twenty-five, Lukša started his new job. He would stay at the *Broom*, together with Bulota and Sadaunykas, for three decades.[53]

Other editors remembered that Lukša wore green riding trousers and high black boots, mimicking the style of the Soviet Army uniform. The trousers manifested his complicity to the regime and hid his dissensus. For him, working at the ideological front was an ordinary experience. At the same time he shared a complex implication as a victim of the war and postwar era and an associate of the Soviet regime. When Sąjūdis started, Lukša supported Lithuania's independence, like many other *Broom* editors.

Rytis Tilvytis was hired by Bulota in 1956 as a literary editor, and until Bulota's retirement he worked with him for many years as an associate editor. He was also a secretary of the PPO for many years. Similarly to Andrius Cvirka, Tilvytis was a child of a monumental figure—Teofilis Tilvytis, a poet, writer, and translator. From 1933 to 1940 Teofilis Tilvytis was a coeditor of *Wooden Clog*, a leftist satirical magazine in pre-Soviet Lithuania. He was imprisoned in a concentration camp during the Nazi period. When the Soviets returned, Tilvytis was appointed to leading positions in Soviet government institutions, and in 1951 he received the prestigious Stalin award. From 1947 to 1963 he was an LSSR Supreme Council member.[54] His son Rytis Tilvytis was a student of journalism at Vilnius University, graduating in 1957. Although a party member, Rytis Tilvytis often tried to distance himself from his party responsibilities (see chapter 7). He was remembered by his coworkers as someone who had the "least to do with politics."[55]

The first artist hired at the *Broom* was **Vytautas Kaušinis**, who worked at the magazine for only two weeks before transferring to another journal. On November 1, 1956, Bulota hired **Juozas Buivydas** as an art editor. Buivydas—who likely worked at the *Broom* for only a few years, since the surviving PPO reports of 1960 do not mention him—was a conservative who stood out with his orthodox Soviet political views and cartoons throughout Soviet times and after. He continued to contribute political cartoons to the *Broom* while being employed by other magazines and newspapers.

Another artist, **Algirdas Šiekštelė**, was invited to join the *Broom* in 1957, soon after Buivydas was hired, and worked at the magazine until 1972. Šiekštelė's first cartoons and drawings were realistic; however, in the early 1960s he initiated the *Broom*'s modernization. Šiekštelė and other young artist contributors, including Jonas Varnas and Fridrikas Samukas, followed by Vitalijus Suchockis,

Valentinas Ajauskas, and Zenonas Šteinys, made the *Broom* look very different from *Krokodil*, where long-established artists continued to create in the socialist realist style.

Romas Palčiauskas, famous for his comic strips (see chapter 6), worked at the *Broom* from 1961 to 1967.[56] **Andrius Cvirka** came to the *Broom* in 1967. **Kęstutis Šiaulytis**, who will be mentioned many times in this book, represented a younger generation. Šiaulytis was born after the war and did not have firsthand experience with deportations and postwar terror.[57] His implication into Soviet history was different: he never joined the Communist Party and never had any leading positions until the 1980s, when the system started to crumble. He was an associate of the Soviet regime by work affiliation, having never participated in establishing Soviet institutions like Bulota, Sadaunykas, and Lukša (see figure 1.1).

FIGURE 1.1.   The *Broom* editors. *Front row, left to right:* Česlovas Valadka, the author of the proclamation discussed in chapter 2; Juozas Bulota; Jonas Sadaunykas; unidentified man. Those identifiable in the second row include (*second from left*) Albertas Lukša, behind Bulota, and Romas Palčiauskas (*in white cap*). The man with the black sunglasses in the third row most likely is Rytis Tilvytis. The photo was taken sometime between 1970 and 1978. Lithuanian Archive of Literature and Art, LALA, f. 814, ap. 1, b. 87, l. 22. Courtesy of Juozas Bulota and LALA.

Box 1.1. A KGB agent at the *Broom*?

Leonas Kiauleikis (1927–2009) worked for the *Broom* from 1956 to 1969 and was an associate editor for eleven years (1959–1969).[58] He had no college education and was remembered as a rough person who made a lot of grammatical mistakes but wrote great feuilletons. Kiauleikis exhibited mastery of Soviet ideological language at *Broom* PPO meetings until 1969, when he had to quit because of his illegal construction and leasing schemes in the resort city of Palanga. Decades later Elena Kurklietytė vividly recalled that Kiauleikis once said that "even if a fire starts and you have to jump through the window, take your party card with you."[59] Romualdas Lankauskas, who briefly worked at the *Broom*, remembered how Kiauleikis used to spit on the floor in the office. Kiauleikis, Lankauskas said, turned him in to the KGB for "mocking Soviet reality."[60] The KGB unsuccessfully forced Lankauskas to collaborate, threatening to make him "change geographical latitude" (that is, be deported to Siberia).[61] According to Jonas Sadaunykas (2002, 278), Kiauleikis had an ambition to become the editor in chief of the *Broom*, planning to discredit Bulota and replace him. Perhaps the detailed discussions of Kiauleikis's shady schemes at the PPO meetings were Bulota's response to Kiauleikis's attempts to supplant him. According to the media, Kiauleikis was a KGB agent.[62] After Kiauleikis left, there were no other known KGB informants at the *Broom*. Laima Zurbienė, who worked at the *Broom* in the 1980s, recalled that her colleagues, when they got drunk, used to point at each other good-naturedly: "You're an informant." "No, *you* are, how else could you get a position at the *Broom* with your background?"

Zurbienė claimed that nobody knew who informed for the *Broom*. It was a very good and beautiful collective, according to Zurbienė, and the mysterious informant contributed to its spirit by not reporting on *Broom* staff.

The Soviet Periphery

Vytautas Žeimantas, a journalist at the *Truth* and LCP CC vice chair of the Propaganda and Agitation Department from 1984 to 1988, remembered in 2019,

> The farther from the war, from Stalin, the easier life was overall. . . . Little by little it got easier . . . and that ambiguity, that duality . . . was, I would say, obvious. We could sit together, look into each other's eyes and say "we are building communism" and not believe in it. . . . When the reforms started, practically all journalists, including party members who worked at the party newspapers, they all supported what? All supported Lithuania. . . . The biggest mass [of people in Soviet times] kept silent. They kept silent because of deportations, prisons, all such things.[63]

The founding editors' knowledge about historical injustices, ethnic differences, and minority status in the USSR was integral to their work for the Soviet state. This knowledge shaped antagonistic complicity, disagreeing consensus with authorities, and editors' dissensus. In the late 1980s, the leaders of the Lithuanian revolution appealed to this knowledge while promoting Lithuania's independence. Vytautas Žeimantas emphasized the editors' ethnic distinction and claimed that the *Broom* editors in the 1970s and 1980s were "all for Lithuania."[64]

As the following chapters will show, the editors' dissensus was embedded in Aesopian language (a figurative discourse with subtexts), in the hesitance to draw anti-imperialist or antireligious themes, and in a modernist style that aligned the *Broom* with Western aesthetic projects. Alexei Yurchak has argued that embracing the West among the last Soviet generations in Leningrad was—paradoxical as it may seem—a way to be "Soviet." Yurchak points out that listening to all sorts of foreign stations, enjoying American jazz, rock, and fashions was not in contradiction to being a good Soviet (2006, 181). He quotes Natan Leites, the founder of the Leningrad jazz club Kvadrat (Square) in the early 1960s and a lover of American jazz, "who thought of himself as 'quite a red person. At least, I believed in socialism'" (170). Unlike in Yurchak's case, for *Broom* editors to embrace Western modernist art was another way to distance themselves from Sovietness, to be different, to establish the Lithuanian humor tradition (see chapter 6, cf. Zhuk 2010).

The Soviet authoritarian periphery, as the upcoming chapters will reveal, was a site of contested Sovietness. The history of the *Broom* also calls into question whether Soviet satire and humor was a successful project of statecraft. After visiting the USSR, in 1978 Marian Pehowski wrote, "That sociopolitical humor succeeds in a vast nation with eleven time zones, scores of distinctive racial strains, and sixty-seven living languages is less a tribute to the universal qualities of humor than to the particular self-mocking satire that the Russians initially developed centuries ago in their federation (among the fifteen Soviet republics today) and now circulate *internationally* to Ukrainian and Lett, Tajik and Siberian" (Pehowski 1978, 726). She also argued that part of the "Russification of the remotest corners of the USSR has been the persistent internal trafficking in satire which concurrently fulfills Lenin's hopes for the press as propagandist, agitator, and organizer" (726). But it is unlikely Lenin would have considered the *Broom* as fulfillment of his hopes for the press as propagandist, agitator, and organizer for the Bolshevik cause.

One *Broom* contributor, Antanas Rimša (2007), recalled that in the mid-1970s, at the *Broom* editorial office on Liudas Gira street, there was a clay bust of Lithuanian poet Kazys Binkis (1893–1942). Binkis was a member of the modern literary leftist movement called "the Four Winds" and a leader of Lithuanian futurism, as well as author of numerous humorous and satirical poems, rhymed feuilletons, and other works. According to Kęstutis Šiaulytis, the *Broom* offices never had a bust of Lenin.[65] Rimša also remembered that editors liked to brag that Jonas Basanavičius lived in the building where the *Broom* offices were (Rimša 2007). Basanavičius was an activist and proponent of the Lithuanian National Revival who chaired the session that adopted the Act of Independence of Lithuania on February 16, 1918, the founding date of independent Lithuania's statehood after World War I. Rimša then recalled that when the editorial headquarters moved to Pilies Alley, editors bragged that they resided in the headquarters of the former count, a member of the nobility. Unlike the *Krokodil* editors, the *Broom* editors did not see the interwar *Broom* or the post–World War II *Broom* as an offspring of the Bolshevik Revolution.

The biographies of the founding editors show that the *Broom* was rooted in World War II and postwar insecurities and ethnic minority identities rather than commitment to the Communist Party ideology or the multinational Soviet state. They reveal complex implication, victimization as well as the editors' complicity with the new regime. By joining and working at the *Broom*, the founding editors secured some stability in the uncertain post-Stalinist era, and relative autonomy to serve on the editorial team and create the magazine. Juozas Bulota built the *Broom* team by inviting Lithuanian journalists, writers, and artists, who already in the 1960s looked to the West rather than Moscow for inspiration.

The dichotomy of public versus private self, often invoked in Soviet studies, does not capture the complexity of the editors' participation and implication into the Soviet history in Lithuania. The editors identified with some CP ideological imperatives, such as notions of justice (chapter 7), while dissociating from others, such as the revolutionary conceptualizations of communism. While we tend to think about complicity and opposition to the regime as antithetical positions, the *Broom*'s history shows that the editors did not occupy clear-cut roles. They were entangled, involved, opposed, and connected, as the following chapters will show by analyzing complexities of their implication. They contributed to the function and effectiveness of the authoritarian state as well as to its demise.

Box 1.2. The history of the *Broom*, 1934–1936 and 1940–1941

Konstantin S. Eremeev, the founder of *Krokodil*, was the editor in chief of *Pravda*, the revolutionary newspaper established by Lenin.[66] At the time that *Krokodil* emerged as a separate magazine—published as a supplement to *Rabochii* (Worker) and *Rabochaia gazeta* (Workers' newspaper)—there were many other satire and humor magazines. One of them was called *Metla* (Broom). It is likely that in 1934 Lithuanian artist-revolutionaries copied this name from the Soviet magazine. But the real story of how the Soviet Lithuanian *Broom* got its name is not known.

From 1921 to 1940 in Lithuania there were fifteen satire and humor magazines and newspapers, in which about fifty artists published their works (Šniukas 2004, 25). Some of these magazines or newspapers survived only a few years (25). The underground *Broom* was published for two years, from 1934 to 1936.[67] From 1926 to 1940 Lithuanian satire and humor magazines were published under the nationalist authoritarian government. After the 1935 media law, for more critical antigovernment comments editors received fines, were jailed, or their newspapers were temporarily closed (28). Editors of the newspapers were afraid to publish caricatures of President Antanas Smetona (33). Cartoons could not criticize the government, the governing right-wing Nationalist Union, or glorify communism (Šniukas 2004).

The prewar *Broom* was founded in the spring of 1934 by several Kaunas Art School students. In 1934, the magazine was published illegally by Lithuanian Communist Party artist-revolutionaries in the city of Kaunas, then the capital of Lithuania. Its first editor was Boleslovas Motuza. Around two hundred copies of the initial 1934 issue of the *Broom* were published the evening of May 1. It was sixteen pages and had a similar format to the Soviet *Broom* published after 1956. The cover of the first issue of 1934 depicted three heads, symbolizing militarism, capitalism, and clericalism, with the image of the broom above them. The first page contained a programmatic article, "Art—a Powerful Weapon," which stated that "we, a group of artists, sons of workers, and peasants, have broken free from traps of 'national art,' 'pure art,' and 'formalistic art' and other fascist art, and joined the ranks of the working class fighters" (Jonas Bulota 1984, 5). The 1934 *Broom* programmatic article announced unity with other revolutionary forces led by the then-illegal Communist Party of Lithuania against the fascist exploitative government and capitalism (6). The 1934 *Broom* contained proclamations, agitation, and communist propaganda messages (Jonas Bulota 1984). The magazine was pro-Soviet and advocated for the homeland of the proletariat—the USSR.[68] It engaged revolutionary rhetoric in the fight against fascism, the bourgeoisie, the clergy, and other "exploiters."

During the period of 1934–1936 the *Broom* published seven issues. In 1936, *Broom* publication was discontinued, most likely because of the persecution or relocation of the journal's major contributors (Jonas Bulota 1984, 6). The next and the first legal issue of the *Broom* was published on July 12, 1940, nine days before Lithuania officially became a new Soviet Socialist Republic of the USSR. The *Broom*'s artists were determined to sweep away "enemies of the people" and various "saboteurs," who dreamed about bourgeois times (7). It invited people to denounce them by writing to the *Broom*. According to journalist Jonas Bulota, brother of Juozas Bulota, in 1940–41 the *Broom* had about one hundred contributors (7). Jonas Bulota also mentions that many anonymous contributors from various regions of Lithuania regularly wrote about "shortcomings" in agriculture, administration, and cultural life in the newly founded Soviet republic (8). Starting with issue 4 of the 1940 edition, the *Broom* published translations of satires and humor pieces of

Anton Chekhov, Mikhail Zoshchenko, Il'ia Il'f, and Evgenii Petrov, Jaroslav Hašek, Valentin Kataev, and Grigorii Ryklin. It also republished feuilletons from *Krokodil* (8).

Most of the founding artists of the *Broom* of 1934–1936 joined the legal *Broom* in 1940. Stepas Žukas was not only the editor in chief of the 1940 *Broom*, but also its most visible artist, who defined the graphic tradition of the journal. In 1940–1941 the *Broom* published forty-eight issues, each sixteen pages (8). In 1941, when Žukas left Lithuania, fleeing from the Nazi occupation, publication of the *Broom* discontinued again. Bronius Žekonis, a leading editor of the illegal *Broom* in the 1930s, was executed by Nazis in 1941. Other editors escaped to Russia or joined the ranks of the new Nazi regime.

During interviews, *Broom* artists related to the pre–World War II Lithuanian graphic art tradition, most often to the popular pre-Soviet satirical newspaper *Kuntaplis* (Wooden clog) (1933–1940). The pre-Soviet *Broom* was an illegal communist pro-Soviet magazine persecuted by the Lithuanian authoritarian nationalist government. *Wooden Clog* was a legal leftist, patriotic-nationalist satire and humor magazine, which reflected the nationalistic tone in politics in general. It was antisemitic. It was also anti-Polish, since Lithuania did not have diplomatic relations with Poland because of the conflict over Vilnius. Unlike *Broom*, *Wooden Clog* celebrated religious holidays and did not publish any antireligious cartoons. In *Wooden Clog* there was no promotion of the working class or celebration of May 1. There was little on foreign policy. On the verge of the World War II, *Wooden Clog* published about Lithuania's predicament being caught between the politics of the Soviet Union and Nazi Germany. On June 15, 1940, the Soviet Army occupied Lithuania. On June 23, 1940, *Wooden Clog* announced the death of the ruling government party Nationalist Union, wrote about the lack of rights of workers under the authoritarian government, and ridiculed President Antanas Smetona, who had secretly escaped abroad. *Wooden Clog* published formerly censored articles and republished criticism against the rich and the clergy from *Krokodil*. On June 30, 1940, *Wooden Clog* celebrated the fact that the Lithuanian government and state officials had to leave for "unlimited vacation." During the Soviet occupation in 1940, *Wooden Clog* embraced the new opportunity to criticize groups and issues that were forbidden under President Smetona; but it did not emulate the revolutionary style of *Krokodil*. Fifty-one issues of *Wooden Clog* were published in 1940. On December 15, 1940, *Wooden Clog* published an obituary of itself. Its editors announced that the newspaper was not going to be published anymore since "there is no purpose" to continue publication. The board of editors who posted the announcement argued that the newspaper had fulfilled its mission, and ended in Russian (in Latin characters), "Tak budte zdorovy, živite bogato!" (Be healthy and live wealthy).[69] Its farewell note did not resonate with Communist Party ideology or revolutionary rhetoric. It must have been ironic. It is likely that *Wooden Clog* struggled financially, did not have the support of the new Communist government of Lithuania, and could not see its own future under the Bolshevik government. The *Broom*, with its revolutionary agenda, outlived *Wooden Clog* by seven months, until the Nazis invaded Lithuania on June 22, 1941.

POLITICAL INTIMACY

[There is] nothing political, only bad humor.

—KGB operative, 1972

In the spring of 1972, Česlovas Bytautas, a journalist at the *Broom*, found a proclamation in his desk drawer at work: "The *Broom* workers' pledge in honor of the October Socialist Revolution holidays."[1] The one-page handwritten text had three statements, which ironically used Primary Party Organization bureaucratic language and Communist Party ideological discourse. The proclamation declared,

1. To use press honoraria in a moderate and constructive way, the editorial staff commits to translate all foreign publications to be published in the *Broom* for free. This will facilitate saving press staff honoraria.
2. To use state funds moderately in the future, the editorial staff suggests discontinuing use of the press automobile. This will facilitate saving needed publishing house funds.
3. In light of these commitments, the *Broom* editorial staff suggests inviting the editorial collective *Švyturys* [Beacon] into socialist competition. This will facilitate a movement for saving funds in other presses.

On April 5 Bytautas brought the proclamation to Bulota's attention. He insisted that there was an underground organization at the *Broom*. It was a serious accusation that Bulota could not ignore. If Bulota dismissed Bytautas's claims, he could have been accused of covering up anti-Soviet activities at the *Broom*. According to Article 68 of the LSSR Criminal Code, "Anti-Soviet Agitation and Propaganda," agitation or propaganda used to undermine the Soviet government, was a crime punishable by law, with up to seven years in prison and potentially an additional two to five years in exile. Bulota immediately called the KGB to investigate the case.[2] A KGB operative arrived at the *Broom*'s offices. He inspected the proclamation but did not find anything dangerous there, "nothing political, only bad humor."[3] By then editors knew that the author of the proclamation was *Broom* journalist Česlovas Valadka. When the KGB operative left, the proclamation was forgotten. The *Broom* editors' attention was on Bytautas, his disintegrative role in the collective, and his "political blackmail."

As I saw the proclamation and read discussions about it in the PPO reports, many facts seemed counterintuitive: writing such a proclamation as a joke; reactions to the proclamation by the editor in chief and other editors; editors' insistence that Bytautas was sick; and the KGB operative's conclusion that it was "only bad humor." Moreover, the fact that nobody remembered this proclamation during the interviews in the 2010s was confusing. It seemed important to me, since it was one of a few cases that involved the KGB.

The proclamation is an example of *stiob*, a Russian slang term for a particular late-Soviet style of parody, what Dominic Boyer, following Alexei Yurchak, calls "the method of which was to inhabit the form of authoritative political discourse (e.g., party-state language) so perfectly that it was impossible to tell whether the imitative performance was ironic or sincere" (Boyer 2012, 212; see Yurchak 2006, 250). Boyer and Yurchak (2010) argued that *stiob* emerged in the 1970s and 1980s because of the Communist Party's emphasis on the formal orthodoxy of its discourse. Newspaper and magazine pages were filled with exceedingly formulaic, cumbersome, and sometimes absurd language. These texts were recognizable in local communist speeches, scholarly books, or Komsomol meetings (Boyer and Yurchak 2010). Boyer notes that the "pressure was always to adhere to the precise norms and forms of already existing authoritative discourse, and to minimize subjective interpretation or voice" (2012, 213). Thus, according to Boyer, political discourse was already overformalized to the point of caricature. *Stiob*'s parodic technique of overidentification sent a critical signal articulated in the language of form itself (2012, 213; see Yurchak 2006, 250). While the state identified any overt form of oppositional discourse as a threat, recognizing *stiob* was more difficult because of its formal resemblance to the state's own language (Boyer 2012, 213).[4]

The proclamation that Bytautas found in his desk drawer invoked the bureaucratic language of allocating honoraria, saving costs, and using press resources. It used formulaic language, such as "moderate and constructive way," "facilitating saving," "facilitating a movement," and "in light of these commitments," recognizable in other bureaucratic texts. It also used the Communist Party's discourse of collective commitments in the name of the October Socialist Revolution or the socialist competition among presses. The official bureaucratic and political discourse was used so well that it was impossible to tell at first glance whether it was ironic or sincere.

Most likely the proclamation listed concerns about honoraria and the cost of *Broom* production discussed at the *Broom* editorial staff meetings.[5] It is unlikely, however, that editors would have been willing to save press costs by refusing to be paid. *Broom* artists, journalists, and writers had several names that they used to sign their works, so they could get paid as different individuals and at the same time comply with the CP requirement to involve many contributors in humor production. Moreover, it is doubtful that editors were willing to engage in socialist competition. Socialist competition with other magazines had never even been discussed in *Broom* PPO reports. Bulota must have known that this was a parody. The KGB operative also identified the ironic potential of the proclamation by calling it "bad humor." Reading pages of editors' discussions of Bytautas's case, I could not stop wondering why Bulota and the KGB operative did not see it as subversive, as Bytautas suggested. If they did, perhaps they wanted to keep Bytautas under quiet surveillance, focused on his own mental health and disruptive actions. In this case, Bulota, the KGB operative, and others involved reaffirmed political intimacy among themselves.

The accusations of the *Broom* sheltering an "underground organization" were offensive to Juozas Bulota, who suggested that "comrade Bytautas's actions" were a result of his mental state. The day after the incident, a *Broom* Communist Party Primary Organization meeting was called, and Bulota recommended that the PPO secretary inquire about Bytautas's health. Bulota claimed that "such hysterical attacks [Lith. *nerviniai išpuoliai*] damage everybody's work at the press"; according to Bulota, Bytautas was to undergo medical treatment.[6] Rytis Tilvytis, the *Broom* associate editor, even suggested they consult Bytautas's doctors to get information concerning Bytautas's health. If he was healthy, "his outburst [Lith. *išsišokimas*] should be treated as a conscious attack [Lith. *išpuolis*] against the collective."[7] Tilvytis, Jonas Sadaunykas, and Albertas Lukša argued that interpersonal disagreements have to be eliminated—they could not work in such an atmosphere.[8] It was decided (1) to request that Bytautas show the proclamation to all editors, since he refused to do it after he initially showed it to Bulota and the KGB operative; (2) to learn about Bytautas's health from his doctors; and (3) to inform *Broom* communists at the next meeting [of the results], so they could evaluate Bytautas's behavior thoroughly.[9]

But at the next meeting, which took place eighteen days after the first, Bytautas argued that the editor in chief constantly nitpicked his work (box 2.1). He claimed that somebody left empty beer bottles in his desk, then the bottles disappeared the next day. He did not say why he thought this happened, but it indicated that others were rude toward him. He apologized to Bulota and Sadaunykas for his inappropriate behavior, but he still thought that it was unacceptable to leave a proclamation in his desk.[10] Like the beer bottles, the proclamation in his desk indicated disrespectful behavior toward him. From the meeting report it looked like his colleagues were making fun of him. Bytautas finally admitted that he did not really think that there was an underground organization at the *Broom*.[11] In several subsequent meetings *Broom* editors criticized Bytautas's work;[12] Bytautas felt he was a scapegoat.[13] He was even summoned to the Central Committee.

Box 2.1. The proclamation

Excerpt from the minutes of a closed *Broom* Party Primary Organization meeting, April 24, 1972. Meeting protocol No. 6.

Cde. [Comrade] Lukšienė: Why has comrade Bytautas not given this "proclamation" to the primary organization or to the Party secretary?

Cde. Bytautas refuses to give the proclamation even now, because he claims to have his own reasons. He left it at home.

Cde. Tilvytis: If similar blackmailing occurs in the future, the Party organization will have to discuss comrade Bytautas's suitability for this position. The atmosphere [created by this conflict] does not help our work in the magazine.

Cde. Sadaunykas: If the collective cannot trust Bytautas's sincerity, how can we trust him with job assignments involving work travel [Lith. *komandiruotę*]?

Cde. Bytautas changes his mind and finds the proclamation in his pocket . . .

Cde. Lukša: Comrade Bytautas just said that he left the "proclamation" at home, and now he presents it to us. How should we understand this?

Cde. Rudzinskas: How should we evaluate comrade Bytautas's behavior? If he is completely healthy . . . we have to think of it as a provocation [Lith. *iššūkis*] to the collective. Or he has to go to the hospital for inpatient treatment. The *Broom* editors, the collective, can help him in this matter.

Cde. Bytautas refuses to go to the hospital for any checkups, because he claims he is completely healthy.

Cde. Tilvytis: In this case, we have conscious "political blackmail."

[Once Tilvytis called it "conscious political blackmail," Bytautas most likely backpedals, the meeting minutes do not report about it].

Cde. Rudzinskas: Because Bytautas has understood his mistake and revokes his words [about the underground organization] we will issue only a warning.

Cde. Bytautas: I won't ever seek out trivial issues in our work.

Cde. Rudzinskas: If cde. Bytautas wished the editorial board would intervene to assure admission for treatment in the inpatient clinic.

Editors voted unanimously to issue Bytautas a warning and, upon his request, to recommend him for an inpatient treatment.

Half a year passed after the incident. At an annual assessment meeting on November 20, 1972, which was attended by two LCP CC and LCP Vilnius October District Committee representatives, Juozas Bulota again scrutinized Bytautas's behavior. He argued that Bytautas "should not cry. We have fixed his numerous mistakes. . . . At work, we accepted him and treated him like any other person; we gave him an apartment, employed his wife, but he is always against [us]. . . . He came to my office after I edited *Mascara on a Hog* and started yelling and insulting me. We cannot work in such an environment. If I am guilty of something, let me know."[14] According to the five-page typed meeting minutes, Bytautas made only a few statements. He admitted again that the proclamation was not a real proclamation; but he added that he understood that editors wanted to get rid of him.[15] Both outside representatives concluded the meeting siding with the *Broom* editors against Bytautas. Pažūsis, the LCP CC representative, mentioned the discussion with Bytautas at the LCP CC where they discussed his complaints about Bytautas's difficult material life conditions. Pažūsis disciplined Bytautas in front of everyone—"watch your own collective, do not run around [to complain to authorities]."[16] Vilkienė, the LCP Vilnius October District Committee representative, asked Bytautas whether some of his comments mean that he was still resentful toward the editor in chief.

The conflict lasted for over a year. The disintegration of relationships between Bytautas and other editors was seen as purely Bytautas's fault. At the 1973 PPO annual meeting, secretary Albertas Lukša reflected on the event for the last time:

> I have worked in the media for seventeen years, and I have never heard that a journalist would charge his editorial collective with [being an] alleged, active "anti-Soviet underground organization." Bytautas slanderously charged us with it and defamed CC employees! Certainly, competent authorities proved [to] him that his accusations were nonsense. He, however, did not settle down, told lies about us, disturbed the work atmosphere, etc. We discussed his actions, talked to him personally, but without any results. He also broke Party discipline. Twice he did not pay Party dues on time. When we discussed him at the Party meeting, and I suggested we file a report on him, he declared that we do not have a right to discuss him [i.e., his actions] and complained to the *raikom* [Rus., district committee]. . . . All communists and non-communists were against him. . . . The work atmosphere has improved significantly after Č. Bytautas left. . . . Now I think, but too late, that we were too kind to Bytautas. We had to give him a Party punishment."[17]

Over forty years after the incident, Albertas Lukša could not remember his words or the incident with Bytautas. Why couldn't Lukša remember it? Did the *Broom* CP members have to leave a paper trail in the PPO documents to suggest how seriously they addressed this case, while in fact they did not care much about it? If this is the case, the discussion of Bytautas's "blackmail" is an example of bureaucratic showcasing (see chapter 3). During interviews in the 2010s, Lukša and the artist Kęstutis Šiaulytis responded upon learning about this case that Bytautas must have been "sick" if he reported on the *Broom* to the KGB. Šiaulytis reasoned, "You see, there were no such people [like him]. Such accusations, even if they were ungrounded, would have hurt Valadka, the author of the proclamation, and the editor in chief. It was enough just to accuse somebody. And if they were not punished, it means this individual was definitely sick. . . . If there was any ground for his claims, at this level, in this environment, [they] would have been very strict. Valadka would be gone, even if he was not guilty."[18]

Šiaulytis's comment that "Valadka would be gone" indicates that authorities expected editors to prioritize the interests and integrity of the collective. Bytautas's case is more than just an unusual episode in the life of the *Broom*. It helps us understand how the magazine actually functioned on the ground, how people with different backgrounds and personalities coexisted in the Soviet milieu, in relations of political intimacy. The affair illustrates how political intimacy could be terminated by events like personal disagreements; how "Sovietness" could be mobilized for personal security and well-being by reporting about an underground organization (even if imaginary); how political intimacy could be reasserted through solidarity against a "political blackmailer"; how political intimacy between the KGB and *Broom* editors could lead to a dismissal of the case; and how what was deemed "political" was a transient quality, with a certain authority (in this case the KGB) having power to define humor as political or nonpolitical.

The proclamation case also illustrates that truth—in this case, why Valadka wrote this proclamation or why he mocked the October Revolution—was secondary to loyalty. The PPO documents do not report anything about Valadka; all attention is focused on Bytautas and his disintegrative role in the collective. Declaring him "sick" delegitimized his actions and reiterated the importance of the integrity of the collective. Bytautas's case illustrates how trust, dialogue, togetherness, and loyalty were of primary importance at the *Broom*.

More than a year after the incident, Bytautas transferred to another job.[19]

Political Intimacy at the *Broom*

Achille Mbembe (1992) argues that the banality of power creates a particular closeness between ruler and ruled, a form of "conviviality" or "intimate tyranny," a close entanglement of those who command and those who obey, as to reproduce the political episteme. While Mbembe looks at the relations between the rulers and the ruled, I use the concept of *political intimacy* to define relations of trust and coexistence among those who have different positions *within* a power hierarchy. In my case, while the *banality of power* explains the political participation of editors in an authoritarian regime (chapter 1), political intimacy is about the relational interdependence, coexistence, and trust within this regime.

Political intimacy contributed to banality of power—since power was often mediated by relationships, it was experienced as personal rather than an abstract part of the system. Relationships masked power as a tool of Soviet governance. They made it contingent, negotiable, and transient. Political intimacy usually entailed a familiar and close, affective relationship based on dialogue and reciprocity. But intimacy intensities differed, and, as in Bytautas's case, conflicts terminated intimacies.

Political intimacy mediated insecurities within the authoritarian milieu. Bulota had to defend his editors at the Central Committee when problematic content was published in the *Broom*. Usually the problematic content was published when Bulota was on vacation—which was a good opportunity for *Broom* editorial staff to push boundaries. Pushing boundaries when the editor in chief was not present also was a deliberate political strategy informed by the intimacy they shared, for they knew that this way Bulota would escape responsibility by justifying himself with his absence from work. Without his oversight, editors made a "mistake."[20]

The first cartoon for which *Broom* editors got in trouble was antisemitic, published in 1957 (see figure 2.1).[21] The cartoon "Let Me Go to the Homeland, Let Me Return to My People" was a commentary on Jewish emigration. A well-dressed Jewish man with many pieces of luggage was asking to leave for the homeland—Israel—while an impoverished man without shoes and with a hobo stick was asking to return back to the USSR, to his people. Sadaunykas, the *Broom* executive secretary at the time of the cartoon's publication, wrote in his autobiographical novel, "Khrushchev's political thaw created a massive emigration of Jews from the USSR, and many journalists and cadres from Vilnius threw their Party tickets into mailboxes and disappeared from the 'paradise' that they just recently praised" (Sadaunykas-Sadūnas 2002, 275). When the cartoon was published, Bulota was on a break because of his studies at the university (he did not have a college degree at the time). It was the only time, according to Sadaunykas, that the editor in chief yelled at him: "You killed me!" (275). Sadaunykas wrote that Vilnius's people were in a furor; the magazine traveled from hand to hand (275). Bulota had to apologize to the Central Committee authorities for this cartoon. But he did not sign the *Broom* issue with this cartoon for publication, and neither he nor others were punished (275). In this way, *Broom* editors could exert their independence and test political waters, while also not threatening the position of their editor, who in turn did not punish his fellow workers.

Bulota protected his workers from higher authorities in various ways. In cases when ideologically problematic art was published, he argued with Central Committee authorities that there was not a conscious opposition, but a mistake, one made by artists searching for different art forms. In some cases Bulota saved

FIGURE 2.1. Antisemitic cartoon by Stasys Krasauskas. Above the cartoon is an excerpt from newspapers stating that Zionists are spreading propaganda and inviting Jewish people from all around the world to relocate to Israel, where they will find real equality and brotherhood. The arrows indicate the USSR and Israel. Words on the bottom left say "Let me go to the homeland," and on the right, "Let me return to my people." *Broom*, 1957, no. 23, p. 5.

Broom editors' careers, as Dita Lomsargytė-Pukienė's case illustrates. When Lomsargytė-Pukienė was denounced in a letter anonymously sent to the *Truth*, in which she was described as a person with an unreliable biography not deserving to work in Soviet media, Bulota not only used his contacts to uncover who authored the denunciation, but also wrote a rebuttal (box 2.2). Published in the *Truth*, Bulota's response was a public performance of political intimacy for his coworker. It communicated firm trust toward her and underscored her loyalty to the regime. The act of omitting some inconvenient facts from her biography also shaped relations of political intimacy between Bulota and Lomsargytė-Pukienė. She retained her gratitude to Bulota for many years: "If not for Bulota, I don't know. If there was somebody else, more sinister [Lith. *bjauresnis*], I would be [crushed].... [The letter is] full of nonsense. My God, ... these were very serious accusations."[22]

Box 2.2. A denunciation

After graduation, Dita Lomsargytė-Pukienė worked in the publishing group at the Science Academy. When there was an opening at the *Broom*, she quit her job. Her former chair was offended by her decision and wrote an anonymous denunciation. He stated that Dita, in her work at the *Broom*, had no moral right to criticize snobbishness and other ills, since her name does not deserve to appear in a Soviet magazine or any other media pages. In the letter she was called a "lady" (Lith. *ponia*) of bourgeois manners and views. She was accused of being against Soviet media and the Soviet way of life. Her father was claimed to have been a close adjutant to Smetona (the president in interwar Lithuania). It was argued that she was proud of her family and negative toward the Soviet government. The letter writer hoped not to see her name in Soviet media or any editorial board again. It was signed, "Your reader V.M. 1959.III.15."[23]

Bulota reacted fast. He contacted a writing expert, who helped him to establish the author of the anonymous letter. Then he wrote a letter for the *Truth*, in which he defended Dita and denounced Petrauskas, the author of the denunciation and the chair of the publishing group at the Science Academy. Bulota signed with one of his own pseudonyms that he used in the *Broom*. While Petrauskas craftily presented Dita as a Soviet enemy, Bulota skillfully used other biographical facts to present her as an ideal Soviet citizen who suffered from Nazi violence and found peace in Soviet society. Bulota poetically invokes how one morning, with teary eyes, Dita's mother woke Dita and told the girl that Nazis had killed her Jewish father. Afterward Dita, along with her mother, had to hide to escape the Nazis. Bulota mentioned how Dita was saved by her stepfather, who gave her his last name to deceive the Gestapo. But soon, when Dita was nine years old, her mother had to wake her up again to tell her that her stepfather had been killed as well. The letter went on to convey how Dita struggled and sought an education. Bulota called her an orphan whose memories were fortunately fading away: "Silvija [Dita] studied, finished high school, entered the university. The Soviet government took care of an orphan: she received a stipend [to study at the university]. She successfully graduated with the university diploma and started her [independent] life." Bulota writes how she dreamed about becoming a translator, worked at a press, and loved her work. Dita's coworkers valued her for honesty and accuracy. Petrauskas's letter made her remember her life's misfortunes. He accuses Petrauskas of writing this letter in revenge because Dita left her previous job. And he even says that Petrauskas admired Dita, while she did not return any feelings.

Both letters used the facts of Dita's life freely. It was not Dita's father, as claimed in the denunciation, but her mother's brother who was the adjutant for General Povilas Plechavičius under Smetona. Bulota also fashioned an affective story that was not accurate. Dita did not know about the deaths of her father and stepfather until after the war (Lomsargytė-Pukienė 2004). But to spare her political retribution, she was portrayed as a victim of Nazi atrocities who found peace in the Soviet era.

Sadaunykas argued in his autobiographical novel that Bulota once said to him that Sadaunykas should be thankful for having had his backing for thirty years; Bulota had defended him so many times (Sadaunykas-Sadūnas 2002, 319). Sadaunykas's level of gratitude was different from Lomsargytė-Pukienė's. Sadaunykas claimed that "maybe he is right, then honor him [Lith. *tada garbė jam*]! But it was very hard to interact with a person who did not need friends, only superiors and money! But thanks to him for not informing against me!" (319). While these words do not describe every aspect of the two men's thirty-year relationship, which must have encompassed all kinds of interactions while working together, they reveal that political intimacy weathered various disagreements but was not necessarily built on deep friendships, but rather on mutual understanding shaped by belonging to the same political milieu.

The editors reaffirmed their political intimacy with Bulota on various occasions, including his birthdays. On his sixtieth birthday, Bulota received hexameter verses eulogizing him on a boar's skin. In a humorous way they recognized Bulota's work as the editor in chief of the *Broom* and his patronage of the *Broom* collective:

A Letter of Honor

To the strong Holder of the *Broom* handle,
The Defeater of rabbits and hare,
The Owner of joke books and bits,
The Scrubber of evildoers' and liars' skin,
The Scolder of us, the miserables, in some cases (but also a fierce
     defender when necessary!)
JUOZAPAS
BULOTA-
DOVAINIS[24]

. . . .

We wish you many years

. . . .

And most importantly, as is the custom,
We wish to our lovely p a t r o n,
To lead us holding the handle of the *Broom* firmly
     Many more years through this unsettling world!

Political intimacy among *Broom* editors was reinforced by Soviet ideologies of collective responsibility at the workplace. Trust at the workplace, accepting coworkers' opinions, self-criticism, support of the collective, work discipline, and good relations with the editor in chief were integral to political intimacy at the

Broom. At PPO meetings *Broom* CP members expressed support for one another, complimented one another on work done or initiatives undertaken, chided one another for incomplete work, and expressed mutual responsibility and commitment to the affairs of the magazine. There was almost always consensus about issues considered.

Being an exemplary collective was related to the good reputation of the *Broom.* In 1963, Albertas Lukša reminded editorial staff, "We all have to fight for the honor of the press!"[25] In 1972, Juozas Bulota argued that "if there are any disagreements in the collective, we should not take trash out [Lith. *nebūtina nešti šiukšles iš namų*]. We can take care of shortcomings ourselves, in the collective."[26] He concluded, extending the metaphor to the whole of Lithuania, "All our country is one house, and we do not take anything from this house out. We want it to be clean and beautiful."[27]

Broom editorial staff tried to avoid conflict. In one of the PPO reports, Keblytė, one of the *Broom*'s staff, was described as someone who goes "wild" (Lith. *išsišoka*) and does not work hard. Lukša mentioned that "we have to find means to make the 'climate' in the press better."[28] Rytis Tilvytis, the PPO secretary, wrote in the annual PPO report that Keblytė had abused her position and discredited the editorial board.[29] Bulota argued that "we need to show humanity toward Keblytė, but in some cases we need an 'ax.'"[30] He also cautioned that "we should not pit one colleague against another"[31] and admitted his guilt in whatever had happened. Acceptance of guilt (or at least accountability), usually by Bulota himself, was a form of relational responsibility, connecting editors to a morally interdependent collective.[32]

Political intimacy implies impermanence: it was a process shaped every day and interrupted by conflicts leading to disintegrations of intimacy. When conflicts occurred over inappropriate behavior and the breaking of work discipline, in many cases the majority of the editors discussed these cases. In recurrent cases of not showing up at work without justification, excessive drinking, unacceptable behavior in the family, not paying CP dues, or not performing work well, editors could receive a verbal reprimand. Informal conversations, as well as warnings, reprimands, fines, and job transfers, worked to check loyalties and to reaffirm the power relations. Although political intimacies were sometimes terminated by different parties, in most cases the intimacies persisted.

Political Intimacy and Sociality

Political intimacy was constituted and reaffirmed in particular forms of sociality, including hunting sprees and rituals of drinking. One iconic Soviet example of reproduction of political intimacies among Communist Party elites was hunting, an institution integrated into the Soviet political elite culture (Grybkauskas 2016).

According to Grybkauskas, in some cases, during hunting trips Politburo members solved political, economic, and even international issues (Važgauskaitė 2020). Hunting events allowed for personal exchanges about work, career, and personal matters (see Važgauskaitė 2020). Saulius Grybkauskas claims that hunting provided an opportunity to see whether an individual might be fit for a specific position, while higher-ups got familiar with his communicative skills and knowledge, or how he behaved in a drunken state (see Važgauskaitė 2020). Hunting was an important part of a political career path, and, Grybkauskas argues, it was hard to avoid it even if one did not like to hunt. An invitation to join a hunting trip expressed authorities' recognition. Hunting also reaffirmed loyalties of members to one another; outsiders were not invited to hunting (see Važgauskaitė 2020). According to Grybkauskas, the forest provided space for secret (since some offices were bugged) and unconstrained conversations among the hunting partners (see Važgauskaitė 2020). It was a space where political intimacy was constituted and reaffirmed in a personal and homoerotic matter. As Martha Lampland claimed, "such events also were characterized by homoerotic bonding, emphasizing a masculinist ethos or community, while tangentially underscoring the second-class status of women in socialism."[33] In Lithuania, hunting was a male affair, illustrating that political intimacy was gendered.

Juozas Bulota, the editor in chief, participated in hunting rituals with editors in chief of other magazines and journals (figure 2.2). Traditional hunting trips for journalists were organized annually by editors of the magazine *Mūsų gamta* (Our nature). The hunting event was sometimes joined by an instructor or a chair of the Communist Party Central Committee. (The Central Committee had its own hunting events.) The editors and journalists lined up and blew a traditional hunting horn. They ate traditional *biguzas* (Lith., sautéed cabbage with sausages). They also rarely shot anything, and everybody bragged how they missed shooting a rabbit or a boar—or they missed on purpose to get the *Broom*'s funniest hunter medal, awarded to the goofiest marksman by Juozas Bulota.[34] Cartoons and stories about hunting were part of *Broom* joke lore. Like fishing jokes, hunting jokes spoke primarily to male readers.

Rituals of drinking were another form of sociality that united *Broom* editors and contributors. Editors' recollections about their work at the *Broom* were punctuated by phrases such as "We didn't show up in the mornings"; "We went out for 'coffee'"; "We gathered in bars and restaurants to discuss everything"; "We had a good time"; "It was a wonderful time, full of celebrations"; "We worked little and then went out for drinks"; and "Artists from Tallinn took a taxi to come to Vilnius to drink with us."[35] In the *Broom* press headquarters on Pilies Alley in the 1980s, the third floor was a "café" where the editors gathered.[36] Andrius Cvirka remembered,

FIGURE 2.2.   After hunting, 1975: Juozas Bulota is at right center by a tree stump. Photo by K. Verbickas, Lithuanian Archive of Literature and Art, LALA, f. 814, ap. 1, b. 86, l. 13. Courtesy of editor in chief's son Juozas Bulota and LALA.

Luckily, I was not involved. First, my head was not so strong [he had low alcohol tolerance]. Second, I had children early. . . . They [other editors] used to assemble in the afternoon, collect money, then I quietly escaped. Sometimes I took a shot. It was like this in those times. I had a strategy: if I have to, I take one shot, and then others forget [about me]. Well, if you start refusing, it's the end. . . . I managed not to become a drunk, but many of ours, they ended their lives [early] because of schnapps [vodka].[37]

The *Broom*'s editorial Communist Party organization meeting reports routinely discussed absenteeism, drinking, and lack of discipline among the *Broom*'s artists, writers, and journalists.[38] Nevertheless they continued drinking. Bottles of cognac, vodka, or wine were used as bonuses to encourage other colleagues involved in the *Broom*'s publication to do their jobs well. Artist Romas Palčiauskas recalled how he used to pack his big briefcase with bottles of wine, go to the printing house, and give them to workers, so they could adjust colors better: "They made it a bit better, but how much wine can you give them?"[39] In many other cases, alcohol was a token of recognition and appreciation; it created relations of reciprocity and mutuality.

Drinking created obligations to one another, interdependence as well as trust, which were at the core of relations of political intimacy.[40] Drinking mitigated political risks, uncertainties, and inequalities through the bond of intimacy and solidarity. Juozas Bulota, did not usually drink with his coworkers. According to his son, this was because of an ulcer in his youth. He was also older than many of the artists and fellow journalists. Since drinking was about equality, mutuality, and reciprocity, abstaining reaffirmed his status as the editor in chief. Bulota reasserted his political intimacy with the collective in another way—while *Broom* artists celebrated various occasions on the third floor of the *Broom* "café," he used to sit in his office on the second floor to protect his collective from unexpected guests. Moreover, Bulota was forgiving. Lomsargytė-Pukienė remembered that in the early 1960s "men used to get drunk, did not show up at work, and he disapproved, but his disapproval was, I would say, fatherly."[41] On Bulota's birthday in 1977, *Broom* editors wrote him a humorous note to take home to his wife to avoid a conflict for returning in a drunken state. They called him their "fake leader, because he noticed us drunk many times, but pretended he did not see."[42]

On September 14, 1978, the PPO met to discuss *Broom* executive secretary Sadaunykas's case. On August 10, Sadaunykas had spent a night in the Vilnius drunk tank (Lith. *blaivykla*), a sobering-up facility for intoxicated people, and was reported to the LCP Vilnius Lenin District Committee. Sadaunykas wrote in his statement to the *Broom* PPO secretary Albertas Lukša, "On August 10 of this year, around 10 p.m. I was returning home drunk from guests, and I got into the wrong house, No. 45 on Antakalnis Street instead of No. 49 [his home]. The yard and corridors were very similar, and I opened a similar apartment with my apartment key. [There was] the same nonstandard bell like mine. The landlady of that apartment (citz. Volkova) called the police, and I was taken to the drunk tank."[43] At the PPO meeting Sadaunykas conveyed that he was very worried about what happened. He promised the other editors he would not only work harder in the future, but also stop drinking.[44] Bulota reminded him that they had already discussed his drinking and emphasized that "if he [Bulota] notices him drunk or drinking at work, as a communist and the leader of the press, he will have to take the strictest administrative measures."[45] Sadaunykas received a verbal reprimand, and in a few days the *Broom* PPO met to discuss questions of work discipline in the collective. As his autobiographical novel testifies, Sadaunykas did not stop drinking until much later (Sadaunykas-Sadūnas 2002).

The houses that Sadaunykas had mixed up were very similar, just a block apart. It was Thursday, a regular workday. A day before the incident Sadaunykas was at a PPO meeting where he discussed with other editors the notes from the CPSU and LCP Central Committee plenary meetings. Sadaunykas's case curiously resembles the extraordinarily popular film *The Irony of Fate, or Enjoy Your Bath*, a 1976 classic Soviet romantic comedy directed by Eldar Ryazanov. The uniformity of public architecture is an object of irony in the film. The main character, after celebrating New Year's Eve and getting drunk with his friends in a *banya* (Rus., sauna), finds himself in Leningrad rather than Moscow. He takes a taxi "home" and enters a building that looks exactly like his own, with the same number and on a street with the very same name. His keys open the door of the apartment, and even the furniture is nearly identical. The comedy develops when the tenant of the apartment finds the main character in her bed. Did Sadaunykas use the film to justify what happened? It may have been so. Like the proclamation introduced at the beginning of the chapter, his written explanation might have been an example of *stiob* (Yurchak 2006), which uses official discourse so well that it is impossible to tell whether it is ironic or sincere. *Stiob* also was multidirectional—authorities could perceive it as legitimate and sincere, while others could laugh at its oppositional message. Antanas Rimša, who was a regular literary contributor to the *Broom* from 1972 to 1978, recalled that when Antanas Pakalnis was forced to leave the *Broom* for drinking, he wrote on his request to leave his job something like "I am leaving because the editors are fools." Bulota had no other choice but to countersign in the corner, stating "I approve" (Rimša 2007). Humorous exchanges between editors and their inner circles were common at the *Broom. Stiob* might have been one of the humor genres they used in these exchanges.

Rimša recalled that at annual end-of-the-year gatherings of *Broom* contributors in the 1970s, conversation and speeches ended with prize awards in the amount of seventy rubles for the best publications. Afterward, Gediminas Astrauskas, the literary editor of the *Broom*, announced that "these days you will not find a fool who would not drink away his prize" (Rimša 2007). They all went to celebrate at a restaurant, and drinking lasted for hours. Somebody's hat would be passed to collect money; the four awardees were expected to contribute thirty rubles, while everybody else five rubles. They collected between 250 and 300 rubles in the first round (Rimša 2007). The second, third, and even more rounds followed, until they left one by one or in groups. The last person was so drunk he most likely was not able to say to others "see you next year" (Rimša 2007).

The *Broom* magazine is full of stories about drinking, some of which were probably taken from the *Broom* editors' experiences. A tipsy father, worker, or lover were frequent subjects of this humor:

> From an explanation given to the factory's Comrades' Court [volunteer tribunals to try petty offenses]:

Comrades, these facts are slanderous. I did not swear. I was drunk, and I was going back home to my wife. I stopped at the fence and tried to talk to myself in order to understand how well I would be able to explain myself at home.[46]

Sadaunykas's drunk tank stay after he mixed up houses, described as a "single" event in the PPO documents, was not an exception. Andrius Cvirka recalled how he and Sadaunykas spent another night in the drunk tank. They took an editor from Poland to the Gintaras (Amber) restaurant. One of the *Broom* artists started loudly explaining sensitive facts about Lithuania's history:

Sadaunykas told me to quell him. Of course, it was not possible to quell him. Instead, I started something myself. . . . When Sadaunykas and I got out to the street, they put us in a car. We thought that we would be taken home. They took us [to the drunk tank], undressed us. It's good they did not give us a shower. I was quiet, subservient, did not kick or bite, nothing [*smiles*]. They laid us down on clean beds [in the drunk tank] on Kosciusko Street. Importantly, at night, I think, they did not turn the light off. They probably wanted to see who is doing what. We were not together, and suddenly, I do not know at what time, a local [staff member] came. He told me, if I wanted, [I could] get dressed and go. I was very sleepy, where would I go now? I turned on the other side and slept until the morning. Sadaunykas and I were released in the morning. Drowsy, we went to the Literatų café. We stayed there awhile, then left. Nothing, no word [about it at the *Broom* office], not even at the meeting.[47]

Bulota and the collective protected Cvirka and others. But since the other Sadaunykas instance was reported to the LCP Vilnius Lenin District Committee, Bulota had to take action.[48] The subsequent meetings on work discipline and drinking were ultimately performative, held to demonstrate to authorities that action had been taken, but also performances that shored up political intimacy. Bulota most likely was angry not so much that his coworkers got drunk, but that they got in trouble and were reported. After Sadaunykas's incident with mixing up houses, Bulota seems to have lost patience. He emphasized as never before that there should be no drinking, neither with the regular contributors of the *Broom*, nor separately at the press. "Not even celebrations of anniversaries. . . . I will personally check during and after work hours. Otherwise, if a bad habit repeats, we will have an argument, and you may have to quit the job."[49] Whether Sadaunykas's story mimicking the Soviet film was true or a parody of Soviet life remains a mystery.

Hierarchies of Political Intimacy

Political intimacy was unequally distributed along hierarchical lines: editors shared political intimacy among themselves and with the leadership of the *Broom*, but not with the LCP CC authorities, some of whom shared political intimacy with Juozas Bulota or a few other *Broom* editors. *Broom* journalist Albertas Lukša remembered one case when Central Committee ideologists came to check on the *Broom* after Lionginas Šepetys, the LCP CC secretary, stated publicly that *Broom* had an unclear direction.[50] The Central Committee ideologists were checking the documents in the Letters and other departments. But then Bulota called an editor from Trakai, and he and the Central Committee ideologists left for that city (located seventeen miles from Vilnius) to eat *kibinai* (traditional ethnic Karaite pastries). This was the end of inspections. Vytautas Žeimantas, a *Truth* journalist and *Broom* contributor, remembered that "Bulota was quite strong. He had a good backing, that is, good relations with authorities. I think by executing that common policy he had opportunities to say more."[51] Česlovas Juršėnas, an LCP CC instructor in 1973–1975 and the chair of the print media, TV, and radio division of the LCP CC Propaganda and Agitation Department from 1983 to 1988, did not recall any conflicts with the *Broom* or any directions he had to give the editor in chief. According to Juršėnas, "the editor in chief was cautious [Lith. *apsidraudėlis*]."[52]

Broom journalist Albertas Lukša had personal connections to some people in ministries who provided him with information for publication in the *Broom*.[53] Lukša recalled that Juršėnas used to come to chat and spend time with him. As students at Vilnius University, they had both worked at an internship in Ignalina, where they shared a room and even a bed, since "there was nowhere to live. We lived at the old lady's [house].... At that time no one said that a man cannot share a bed with another man."[54] Lukša's personal connections with Juršėnas guaranteed some protection to the *Broom* and gave a sense of control and security to *Broom* editors.

Besides the episode of Bytautas and the proclamation described at the beginning of this chapter, *Broom* editors had a few other encounters with the KGB. Another incident involved Sadaunykas. Once while visiting Ukrainian colleagues and after several shots of alcohol, Sadaunykas announced that Lithuanians and Ukrainians were occupied by Russians. Sigitas, a KGB operative, showed up at the *Broom* before Sadaunykas even returned home from Ukraine.[55] The editorial board meeting followed, and Sadaunykas was questioned about his statements. But there were no other repercussions. Calling a KGB operative by his first name, Sigitas, meant that some *Broom* editors knew him well. Most likely the collective reassured him that Sadaunykas was loyal, that it must have been a bad humor from a drunken state, that they would take responsibility to make sure it would not happen again. The *Broom* editors' protection must have been the shield from the "yellow eyes of the hawk" that Sadaunykas talked about in his autobiographical novel (chapter 1). This protection was binding, with obligations of reciprocity and commitment to the collective.

This chapter illustrates that power as experienced within the *Broom* collective was not only banal; it was an intimate experience, integrating individuals into a political milieu through deep relationships, which mediated power relations and insecurities inherent in an authoritarian system. These relations entailed bonds of togetherness, trust, and loyalty, shared sociality and solidarity, feelings of security and recognition, and senses of belonging. Political intimacy secured limited autonomy and self-expression. As Valadka did in the opening vignette with Bytautas, editors could privately joke, as long as they shared camaraderie with the collective, recognized hierarchies, and remained loyal to the authorities. As argued above, political intimacy contributed to the banality of power—since power was always mediated by relationships, it was experienced as personal rather than an abstract part of the system. Relationships also masked power as a tool of Soviet governance. Dita Lomsargytė-Pukienė and Andrius Cvirka (introduced in chapter 1), joined the *Broom* as a workplace with good colleagues, not as a place of dissemination of Soviet propaganda.

Multidirectional laughter that became the hallmark of the *Broom* emerged and was secured by relations of political intimacy. Algirdas Radvilavičius, who worked at the Kaunas Military Commissariat and was, in his words, "part of the system," recalled his experience of multidirectional laughter at the *Broom*: "They [the *Broom* editors] rejected [his cartoons]. A lot was rejected. I take a good cartoon [to the *Broom*], you know, which is already a bit critical of authorities [Lith. *ant valdžios*]. Well, you know, they laugh, but say 'we won't publish it. . . . Oh hell [Lith. *čia velnias*], we can get in trouble.'"[56] Restaurant visits and hunting trips solidified political intimacy among journalists, editors, and Communist Party authorities. Since political intimacy mediated relations between censors and *Broom* editors, it aids in understanding why *Broom* editors and artists claimed they were relatively free to create satires and cartoons (chapter 4). Political intimacy also helps us explain how the Soviet predicament discussed in the next chapter could be lived through and laughed at.

3

THE SOVIET PREDICAMENT

> We are a small [Communist] Party faction entrusted with a very powerful weapon—the media. We have to use the flame of satire more effectively in the battle for a common cause—communism.
>
> —Jonas Sadaunykas, journalist and executive secretary of the *Broom*, 1972

An old, clattering bus wound through a rural landscape of barley and wheat fields and blooming green meadows. The now-crumbling walls of former Soviet collective farms poked out through the otherwise lush, green landscape, testifying to the collapse of the Soviet Union. On the bus, passengers clutched their few belongings as the ruins and meadows, barley and wheat, passed by. I got up to ask the driver to stop at a crossroad on a gravel road. "There will be a man with a big dog waiting for me," I said, and moved to a front seat so as not to miss them. After a few hills up and down, there was an old man and a tiny, mixed-breed dog. As I mumbled about a big dog again, the driver and passengers burst into laughter. They knew Albertas Lukša and his Mika; there was no doubt I was in the right place.

Lukša and I greeted each other as the bus disappeared down the hill. Ten-year-old Mika took the lead on our long way to their home. Lukša showed me an archaeological site with ancient stone pillars, a tall cross, and an old tree with a stork's nest (figure 3.1). We walked down to the dark river Širvinta, then back up to his house. Stasė Lukšienė, Lukša's wife, waited for us in their garden. The garden was a theater of nature and art: fruit trees and bushes, flowers and herb gardens populated by puppets, masks, and decorations from the time when Stasė Lukšienė led a theater association. In a shadow of apple trees was a table with country cheese, ham, honey, and vegetables, all decorated with flowers.[1]

Albertas Lukša was born in a nearby village in the summer of 1934.[1] He was six when the borders in Europe were redrawn again and Lithuania became part

FIGURE 3.1. Former *Broom* journalist Albertas Lukša and his dog Mika at the archaeological site by an eleven-meter cross and an old tree with a stork's nest in Liukonys village, July 29, 2015. Photo by the author.

of the Soviet Union. In 1958 he graduated from Vilnius University, and in 1959 he joined the *Broom*. In 1962 Lukša joined the Communist Party. He was the *Broom* Communist Party Primary Organization (PPO) secretary for many years, and many reports held his signature. I made this journey to ask a simple yet profound question: What was it like to work for the authoritarian state at its ideological front?

Forty years ago Lukša, the PPO secretary and the editor at the Letters Department, was in his forties. At that time most *Broom* PPO meetings took place behind closed doors. The *Broom* artist Kęstutis Šiaulytis recalled that the magazine's CP members went into a meeting through the office door with serious faces and came back even more serious. "They did not talk to us about what happened at the meetings."[2] I imagined Lukša would take me into this secret world.

I wanted to know what happened behind these closed doors. How important was the ideological work? I wondered what it meant to Albertas Lukša to serve the Communist Party.

My knowledge of the relevance of ideology in late socialism was informed by insights such as Václav Havel's (1978) on living a lie, being submissive to the government, and hiding true beliefs, and Gale Stokes's (1993) on disillusionment in communism in Eastern Europe after the Prague Spring in 1968. Communism, I thought, was the ideology of an authoritarian state to justify and legitimate its power, but that it did not appeal to ordinary people as well as journalists like Lukša. During my interviews, some former *Broom* editors and contributors dismissed the PPO meetings as pro forma activities, a "tribute to those times." Kęstutis Šiaulytis, the long-term *Broom* artist who was not in the CP ranks, called various imitations of *Krokodil* artistic style a "mere show" (Lith. *butaforija*). He remembered, "[Nobody was interested in Communist Party platforms] unless somebody wanted to make a career. There was no psychological mimicry. Moscow was so far away that it was beyond our perception."[3] Vytautas Žeimantas, a CP member and correspondent for the *Truth*, as well as a regular contributor to the *Broom*, compared the Communist Party's ideological discourse with that of Aesopian language:

> Everybody said what they had to say for the protocol. . . . They all knew each other. . . . If a time came to meet and write a protocol, they could produce anything. . . . I am confident that they [the *Broom* editors] most likely drank and wrote protocols down [without any discussion]. I think so because when I visited them, there was always a shot glass, always coffee, always all rooms smelled good; all . . . that duality . . . was obvious. We could sit together, look into each other's eyes and say, "We are building communism" and not believe it.[4]

According to Žeimantas, there was no point in looking at the PPO documents at all.[5] But the PPO documents were my major data on the *Broom* as the CP ideological institution.

On that beautiful sunny day at Lukša's home I asked if the *Broom* CP members fabricated reports in any way. Albertas Lukša responded without any hesitation, "No, we did not." I was taken aback, as Lukša continued to speak of his work at the PPO as the serious, committed, and commonplace work of a professional. Lukša unexpectedly shifted my attention from thinking about ideological work as a "mere show" to wondering about its meaning and significance.

Building on this encounter, in this chapter I inquire into the meaning and significance of ideological work at the *Broom*. I argue that the concepts "living in the lie," "disillusionment," "camouflage," or "Aesopian language" fail to capture the prevalent relation of the *Broom*'s CP members to their ideological work. Instead, I claim that *Broom* CP members experienced ideological work as a heavy burden of the *Soviet predicament*. This concept documents editors' relation to power emergent in their experience of communist responsibility: hard work for the Communist Party; burdensome compliance with the Central Committee, GLAV-LIT, and the District Committee PPO initiatives; a demanding ideological self-education and self-discipline; and a wearisome role as a communist vanguard in charge of educating others. The *Soviet predicament* was also interconnected with disciplining oversight by the Lithuanian Communist Party Central Committee or District Committee and, in a few cases, the KGB.

In *The Unbearable Lightness of Being* (1984), Milan Kundera's characters oscillate between lightness, which is freedom from any burden, and heaviness, which weighs on their lives whether through love or other commitments. Kundera writes that "the absolute absence of a burden causes man to be lighter than air, to soar into the heights, take leave of the earth and his earthly being, and become only half-real, his movements as free as they are insignificant" (Kundera [1984] 2005, 5). Kundera's characters find meaning and significance in heaviness, to which they return because lightness becomes unbearable. "The heaviest of burdens is therefore simultaneously an image of life's most intense fulfillment. The heavier the burden, the closer our lives come to the earth, the more real and truthful they become" (5). While there was distancing from and disregard of Communist Party ideological imperatives, a pro forma enactment of expected behavior, and some examples of *stiob*, most of the time *Broom* CP members, including Lukša, undertook their PPO tasks with seriousness and found meaning and significance in ideological work. While it may sound paradoxical, the heaviness of the Soviet predicament contributed to their lives' intense fulfillment.

To say that it was meaningful and significant to work at the Communist Party ideological front is not to argue that *Broom* CP members believed in communism. On the contrary, the concept of the Soviet predicament implies lack of commitment to Communist Party ideological work. I imagine, if I had a chance to go back in time to 1970s Vilnius and ask editors if they were building communism, my question most likely would have been met with a knowing smile or puzzled look at the silliness of the inquiry. But even back then, Lukša believed in some Communist Party ideological imperatives, such as helping ordinary people. Serving the working class was a celebrated Communist Party ideal.[6] There were real issues *Broom* editors had to address: youth delinquency, mismanagement of kolkhozes and enterprises, or factory administration unfairness toward workers. Targeting these issues in investigative journalism, satires, and cartoons, as well as administering editorial office work, gave meaning and significance to editors' lives.

Ideology was not limited to Khrushchev's or Brezhnev's speeches or the resolutions of CPSU congresses. The *Broom*'s satire and humor contributed to the Sovietization of everyday life through ideological socialization—it projected Soviet notions of labor, consumption, and leisure; leadership and authority; public and private spheres; city and village life; sociality; morality; materiality; and social and historical justice. The ideological work of the *Broom*'s editors targeted various "shortcomings" in society, from inefficient governance in factories, corrupt officials, and lazy bureaucrats to violations of public order, and bad customer service. Various immoral types were also chastised in its pages—speculators, liars, womanizers, alcoholics, pilferers, and procrastinators—making the *Broom* a moral arbiter. The humor media, as a disciplining and punishing force, contributed in its own way to governing Soviet citizens.

The Soviet ideological project reshaped everyday life. Riding on a bus almost three decades after the Soviet Union collapsed, I could still see traces of everyday Soviet life through disappearing kolkhoz farm ruins. People came to work, maybe drove a kolkhoz bus or a truck, went back home to newly built Soviet housing districts, and shopped at local stores, which sold bottled milk and bread without any packaging. There was candy, which was available in many other places in the USSR, and sausages, most likely under the counter, since they were in shortage (see Klumbytė 2014). People sent their children to schools where they learned the Lithuanian and Russian languages, studied the rich Lithuanian cultural heritage, and learned to idolize Soviet cosmonauts conquering the cosmos. They were taught to love Lenin, the great *vozhd* (Rus., leader) of the Bolshevik Revolution. Maybe in the evenings these kolkhoz workers read the *Broom*, which portrayed everyday life, satirized various social problems, and taught them about Soviet virtues.

The Soviet Predicament

The publishing office never had more than eight CP members from 1960 to 1979, the period for which PPO archival data exists. They made up about half of the editorial staff of the *Broom*. Juozas Bulota (1918–1994), the editor in chief; Jonas Sadaunykas (1925–2009), the executive secretary; Rytis Tilvytis (1933–2005), the associate editor; and Albertas Lukša (1934–2021), a journalist and chair of the Letters Department, were the core members of the *Broom*'s PPO for many years (see also chapter 1).[7] When Leonas Kiauleikis left in 1969, Lukša and Tilvytis divided among themselves the PPO secretary work. Almost every year at the annual assessment meeting, both of them asked others not to reelect them for this position.[8] I thought these requests were evidence of dissociation from their party work, but Lukša argued that he made the request in order not to draw LCP CC instructors' attention to himself.[9] Humility and the implicit critical position toward one's PPO secretary work were embedded in this request, as well as an indirect appeal to be recognized for carrying a heavy burden of PPO secretary responsibilities.

At the *Broom*, the ideological work had to be overseen by the editor in chief, an associate editor, the executive secretary, and the Communist Party members of the *Broom*. A PPO was the lowest level of the Communist Party government at various institutions, including the editorial offices. PPOs were central to the fulfillment of the CPSU objectives. The *Broom* PPO executed the party agendas, planned ideological work, admitted new party members, and ensured that party discipline was maintained. The PPO of the *Broom* was headed by the elected secretary and a deputy secretary, who were in charge of organizing meetings and writing annual assessment reports. All party members, which numbered from five to eight employees, were expected to attend PPO meetings.[10] An LCP District Committee representative or an LCP CC instructor attended annual assessment meetings at the *Broom*. The LCP District Committee was an oversight institution subordinate to the LCP CC.

At the PPO meetings, *Broom* CP members discussed *Broom* party members' work, and its shortcomings. The PPO reports sometimes invoked the achievements of the *Broom* and its very popularity as evidence of successful communist work.[11] Some meetings took place on the occasion of various important Soviet events: the October Revolution anniversary, Lenin's birthday, Victory Day, or the acceptance of the USSR Constitution. CP members had to approve editors' biographical profiles (Lith. *charakteristikas*), which served as letters of reference, required to gain permission to travel to foreign countries. In fall or winter, *Broom* CP members had annual assessment meetings, in which they read and discussed the annual report recapturing that year's accomplishments and reiterating communist work problems (see box 3.1). At the end of these meetings those assembled elected a new PPO secretary and an associate secretary.

Box 3.1. Excerpt from the 1976 annual PPO assessment report

Vilnius, November 3, 1976.

The annual assessment meeting of the *Broom* editorial office.

The chair of the meeting is J. Sadaunykas, secretary R. Lukšienė. All five Broom Communist Party members were present. The meeting was also attended by

P. Jankauskas, a representative from the Lithuanian Communist Party Lenin District Committee.[12]

The meeting agenda:

1)   The Primary Party Organization secretary R. Tilvytis's report;
2)   Elections of a Party Organization secretary and an associate secretary.

[The official assessment follows:] This assessment period coincided with historic events in our country's life. The CPSU's Twenty-Fifth Congress and the beginning of the tenth five-year period [directed at] increasing the quality and work efficacy fostered a great political upheaval and creative activity at work [Lith. *kūrybinį darbinį aktyvumą*] by the Soviet people, which resonated around the world. These two events set the direction for our country's further development and raised specific tasks for building communism in all spheres of political life and industry. Soviet people joined the work to make our country thrive[,] and [they] joined the struggle to fulfill the tenth five-year period plans. The Soviet country, devoted to its major principle [of promoting peace] in foreign politics, further struggles to reduce international tensions by achieving important positive changes. Preserving peace is a very important condition for future creative work [Lith. *kūrybingam darbui*] in the country.

The Party raised important new goals to be achieved in all spheres of life. Ideological workers, the print media, as well as our magazine editors play a great role in this work.

How have the communist editors contributed toward the fulfillment of the goals raised by the Party?

Ours is the satire magazine, therefore our means to achieve these goals are different from other print media. The core of our work is to reveal and unmask [Lith. *iškelti ir demaskuoti*] the obstacles, shortcomings, and phenomena, which prevent [society] from achieving Party goals in building industry and culture. Our task is also to uncover bourgeois ideology, in its various manifestations, because, even if international tensions are subsiding, there is not and could not be any convergence in the ideological sphere. On the contrary, the ideological struggle is becoming stronger.

The Party Organization [of the *Broom*], the [editorial] administration, has devoted and will devote considerable attention to reflecting on the pertinent problems of our times.

In the Party meeting devoted to the analysis of the CPSU CC project for the Party's Twenty-Fifth Congress, "The USSR people's economy development major directions in 1976–1980," the communists of the editorial board approved [the project] unanimously. In this meeting it was emphasized that all workers of the editorial office have to effectively contribute to fulfillment of the [CPSU's Twenty-Fifth Congress] goals. While welcoming the Twenty-Fifth Congress, we must make fact-based critical material more relevant [Lith. *suaktualinti faktinę-kritinę medžiagą*]. We have to present it in more depth and skillfully seek its greater effectiveness. [End of the excerpt of the official assessment.]

The report further offers examples of how the *Broom* contributes to CPSU's Twenty-Fifth Congress agendas by publishing art, satires, and feuilletons. It discusses the CPSU Twenty-Fifth Congress's goals and tasks that are important to the *Broom* collective and addresses collaboration with readers and Broom's active role in fighting against social problems, the importance of the Letters Department's work, as well as that of the Literature and Illustration Departments. It proceeds to discuss shortcomings of the magazine and emphasizes its popularity in Lithuania and beyond. Next, editors praise Broom CP members for their character and work, address questions of further communist education, discuss publishing delays, and finish by mentioning that the following year the *Broom* will celebrate the sixtieth anniversary of the Great October Socialist Revolution. Tilvytis asks not to be reelected as a secretary of the PPO.

Communist Party membership was associated with higher positions at the editorial office, and therefore it provided editors with recognition and prestige. In the 1970s and 1980s, as Kęstutis Šiaulytis recollected, professionalism was very important, but LCP membership added another layer of power.[13] Bulota became the editor in chief without a university diploma. It was mandatory that he was a CP member. Kiauleikis, an associate editor from 1959 to 1969, had no college education either. Kiauleikis was also a CP member. In the 1970s, the *Broom*'s PPO did not have an artist among its members. Artist Andrius Cvirka remembered that he was lucky to escape this Soviet predicament; he did not join the Communist Party. Arvydas Pakalnis joined the CP ranks and replaced Cvirka as the chair of the Illustration Department (see chapter 6). According to Kęstutis Šiaulytis, "Pakalnis was more obedient, Cvirka was very independent. It was hard to control him."[14] Šiaulytis remembered how party membership transformed Pakalnis:

> When he went to a Party [PPO] meeting, he became focused, suddenly looked like a different person, you know, but otherwise, he liked to drink, play table games [such as] finger soccer with coins, and he liked to go out downtown, drink a shot at a café. He was from Kaunas [the second-largest city and former capital of Lithuania]. He felt like a free artist. But when he went to the [PPO] meetings, only at that very moment, a minute before the meeting, he became serious. After the

meeting, he moved papers for half an hour or so, and then came back to himself and became human again. I think he felt recognized when he was accepted to the party.[15]

The heavy weight of ideological work is recorded in the *Broom* CP members' ongoing struggle to meet the party requirements, to achieve efficacy and efficiency in their ideological work, and to participate in political self-education. From year to year, the *Broom*'s Primary Party Organization failed to accomplish many PPO obligations, from regular scheduling of the Communist Party PPO meetings to improving publication of anti-imperialist and antireligious cartoons, to succeeding in communist self-education. In the 1960s, the PPO meetings did not comply with the Communist Party requirements of a regular schedule. At the end of the 1960s and the beginning of the 1970s, the number of party meetings increased. In 1973, the *Broom* CP members took pride in achieving a regular schedule of meetings: the PPO met once a month, in compliance with CPSU regulations.[16] However, it was a short-lived achievement. Already in 1974, the PPO met only six times to discuss PPO communist work and twice to address personnel issues.[17]

Among the most rigorously criticized topics every year was the lack of political education. The *Broom*'s CP members criticized each other for the lack of a serious attitude toward effective political education.[18] Most of the time the magazine's party members engaged in "independent" political education: they committed to reading political education books and attending lectures and seminars organized by the Union of Journalists, the Union of Writers, or other institutions. They accepted decisions to engage in political education regularly, control political education more rigorously, and listen to each other's reports on self-education.[19] Comrade Rabačiauskaitė, from the Lenin District Committee, noted at the *Broom* PPO annual assessment meeting in 1975 that "it is very hard to engage in self-education, you have to be very determined."[20] In most cases, indeed, as the *Broom* CP members acknowledged themselves in the reports, "political education was neglected."[21] Editors most likely chose individual political education because it provided them with some leeway: nobody looked over their shoulders at how many pages of Communist Party literature they read or how attentive they were at a seminar. In 1978 it was decided that the editor in chief Bulota and the associate editor Tilvytis would go to lectures organized by the LCP CC. Albertas Lukša would attend the LCP Marxism-Leninism night school. Other editors had to attend a theoretical seminar on ideological work and political economy.[22] In 1979 Lukša reported that he had missed many lectures at the LCP Marxism-Leninism night school. Bulota and Tilvytis claimed to have attended lectures organized by the LCP CC. However, other editors missed some seminars without any serious justification.[23]

Editors reflected on the heaviness of ideological work in their individual commentaries about PPO responsibilities. Tilvytis seemed to often feel guilty for his poor performance in his role as a PPO secretary and overburdened by his Communist Party service. In the 1975 annual report, Tilvytis finished his ten-page statement with the following words: "It is hard to say much about myself. My comrades and I know that I am not doing a good job as an organizer [of PPO work]. . . . I would like to openly thank communist Juozas Bulota for [his] friendly help and support organizing the party work at the editorial office."[24] Tilvytis had reiterated his unfitness and unwillingness to serve as a PPO secretary several times before; as he acknowledged, it was his "character."[25] One of the *Broom* artists recalled that Tilvytis's drawers were full of papers, and he used to push them closed with his foot. Better organized and more detailed annual reports testify to Lukša's superior organizational skills. These skills, however, did not illustrate Lukša's deeper devotion to communism (see chapter 1), even if they were more exemplary forms of engagement with party ideological agendas. Out of a limited number of party members beyond Bulota and Sadaunykas, there were just a few people who could be assigned a role of a PPO secretary.

The ideological work was always incomplete. Many times *Broom* CP members invited a more cutting critique of social, political, and economic developments to be published in the *Broom*.[26] They criticized the quality and narrowness of investigative journalism.[27] They argued that publicizing their journalistic investigations did not have any strong impact (see chapter 7).[28] They noted the importance of going out "to the people," including collaborating with residents in rural areas to get information about problems in the region.[29] They often mentioned a lack of political caricature or cartoons devoted to antireligious and antinationalist themes. Editors spoke of the importance of building a big circle of activists, regular contributors, who would provide material to the *Broom*. They also referred to a lack of effective collaboration with other institutions, such as the police, the prosecutors' office, or people's control (Lith. *liaudies kontrolė*).

This self-criticism was a form of bureaucratic showcasing (discussed in the next section) meant to demonstrate the editors' hard work and concern about shortcomings. But it also illustrated their serious engagement with agendas that provided practical guidelines for their work. In 2014 Lukša recalled some of the lectures organized by the LCP CC as useful. The editors' pragmatic engagement with ideological work was integral to the banality of power. Beyond thinking about building communism, editors had daily tasks related to publishing the magazine and addressing pertinent issues of their time.

Bureaucratic Showcasing

PPO archives implicate individuals into the political history of their time, and, in the case of the *Broom*, into Communist Party work, state ideology, and propaganda. In Eastern European states, archives have been used to remove citizens from political office and denounce them for their collaboration with the authoritarian regime (see Glaeser 2011; Tismaneanu and Stan 2018). In 1991 the Communist Party was banned in Lithuania. Since the ascendancy of Sąjūdis, membership in the Communist Party was stigmatized. Attribution of what I call "authoritarian stigma," a negative association with "collaborators" of the Soviet government, was especially prevalent after the collapse of the USSR in 1991 (see conclusion).

The *Broom* staff members' and contributors' opinion of these PPO archives are indirect commentaries about their sense of belonging to post-Soviet history and their loyalties. Vytautas Žeimantas (see above) dissociated himself from Soviet history even though he was a representative of the *Truth*, the leading Communist Party newspaper, and in 1988–1989 worked at the LCP CC. Lukša most likely took his own work for Lithuania for granted. His journalism and PPO secretary work were the major anchors of his identity. By affirming that the PPO documents are truthful representations of ideological work at the *Broom*, Lukša emphasized his professionalism and commitment to the *Broom*. In 2014, at the celebration of his eightieth birthday at the Lithuanian Journalist Union, Lukša reflected on the meaning and importance of his work:

> Nowadays young talented satirists do not need Aesopian language; they can be extreme [in their writing], and the boomerang from those above will not come back. And then, at the time of "mature social-ism" . . . I often contemplate in my cozy home by the quiet river Širvinta. Did I do anything useful to an ordinary person with my work? At least I tried. I did not accumulate any wealth, even if I could get bribes. The former Broomers [Lith. *šluotiečiai*] subscribed to an unwritten code of honor. And the happiness of my life was my work—I went to it as to a party. I longed to be at work.

Although Lukša does not speak about his ideological work specifically, rather his work at the Letters Department, his work with letters was closely interconnected with ideology (see chapters 7 and 8). Helping ordinary workers was a cornerstone of Communist Party ideas of justice. It was also a humanistic ideal. In both cases, Žeimantas's and Lukša's memories were interconnected with inscribing oneself into the new narratives of post-Soviet history. Both journalists were also reclaiming their own dignity by locating themselves in the past as moral subjects.

Reconstruction of *Broom* CP members' ideological work requires consideration of how PPO documents were produced (see box 3.2). PPO meeting reports were assembled, edited, changed, and even crafted with a particular audience in mind—the Communist Party District Committee and the LCP CC to which the *Broom* was accountable. PPO reports cited and referenced CPSU and Lithuanian Soviet Socialist Republic (LSSR) Communist Party resolutions and other Soviet Communist Party texts, which reaffirmed Communist Party agendas by repeating that *Broom* CP members are "in support of" CPSU CC resolutions. Those PPO reports documented *Broom* editors' unanimous support of the party agendas, their commitment to CP member work and ideology, and their continuous political education and seeking to involve non-CP members of the *Broom* in their activities. In some cases, *Broom* CP members also delivered reports on various communist themes, which they explored individually, recirculating ideological discourse from a variety of sources, such as books about Lenin or seminar materials about achievements in Soviet industry.

According to Vytautas Žeimantas, a journalist and member of the LCP CC, PPO reports had to be written in case somebody checked your work. But some PPO reports provide evidence of seemingly genuine commitment to the ideological discourse: personal invitations to be sincere in editorial and communist work; invoking Brezhnev's speeches in personal statements; and some initiative and creativity in engaging with communist agendas.[30] As in the case of Lukša's claim that his work as the PPO secretary was truthful, such discourse most likely displayed pragmatic engagements with power, illustrating its banality. Editors related to ideology not in terms of belief or disbelief but primarily engaging its utility when it was significant in their everyday work at the magazine.

In her analysis of Romanian secret police files, Cristina Vatulescu (2014, 13) contends that although they were "sometimes wildly skewed records of historical fact, the files are at the same time priceless representations of the values, apprehensions, and fantasies entertained by the secret police. While a personal file can mislead about the particulars of a victim's fate, its close reading can be abundantly revealing about what the secret police understood by evidence, record, writing, a human nature, and criminality."[31] *Broom* PPO files also provide such information: about the unquestionable authority of the Soviet Union Communist Party; the importance of communist ideals, such as collectivism and anti-intellectualism; projected advancement to the communist future; struggle with "enduring shortcomings"; commitment to anti-imperialism and atheism. These files also document Soviet notions of collective responsibility, accountability, and the relevance of criticism and self-criticism. They illustrate that economic issues were of primary importance; thus, agriculture and industry, technology and machinery, work and production, and workers' daily life informed PPO meeting discussions. In the pages of the *Broom*, these issues were covered in satirical critique of inefficiency, procrastination, disorder, lack of safety, mismanagement, or cheating at workplaces.

The PPO documents testify to *Broom* CP members' mastery of the party's bureaucratic language. But PPO documents also tell us about certain truths: editors embraced values of the collective. They were interconnected by relations of political intimacy and were committed to helping ordinary people. PPO documents also provide important historical data, such as a failure to live up to the certain standards of the Communist Party, as evidenced in the irregular schedule of the *Broom*'s PPO meetings and lack of engagement in political education. In the 1960s the *Broom* PPO failed to contain modernist trends and significantly increase its number of political cartoons.

Contributing to the discussions about archives in authoritarian states, I introduce the analytics of *bureaucratic showcasing* to conceptualize *Broom* editors' strategies of documenting their ideological work. Bureaucratic showcasing emphasizes editors' performative engagement directed at manifesting their commitment to the CP ideological work. At a PPO meeting in 1962, at which CP members of another magazine, *Soviet Woman*, were present, Povilavičiūtė from the *Soviet Woman* suggested magazine editors ask the LCP District Committee for an example of how to write their own PPO reports.[32] This request was scratched out by somebody who reread the typed report and hoped to conceal the editors' awareness that the reports had to be *written* in a specific way. There is some evidence that in some cases, *Broom* CP members exaggerated their accomplishments, copied parts of the annual reports instead of writing them, and even lied. It is likely that was what happened when the PPO secretary and an associate editor of the *Broom* was Leonas Kiauleikis, who later lost his job at the *Broom* for his illegal machinations. In 1960, there were only three PPO meeting reports. But Leonas Kiauleikis, an associate editor, claimed at the annual assessment meeting that there were eleven, the number of PPO meetings required by the Communist Party.[33] An inspection report for that year in Russian mentions only three meetings as well.[34]

In the case of the PPO archives generally there are no clear boundaries between bureaucratic showcasing and facts. At the same time, bureaucratic showcasing provides important facts about the relevance of the Communist Party ideology and editors' struggle to incorporate it in their work. Some criteria that I developed to read these documents helped me to understand different layers of the formal as well as the consequential (see box 3.2). Thus, late-socialist bureaucratic showcasing is a multilayered practice, integrating levels of formal, informal, and informative engagements relevant to understanding *Broom* laughter.

Box 3.2. Making sense of the PPO documents and bureaucratic showcasing

I dragged two big folders with 712 printed-out pages of photocopied material of the PPO meeting minutes and reports back and forth over the Atlantic several times, since during the initial stage of research these copies were my major source of data. There were too many highlights, Post-it notes, and comments on almost every page to leave them behind. Some of my colleagues in Lithuania, who think these documents are of little value, would be disappointed by my close reading. But they were all I had in the beginning, in addition to some interviews. Doing historical ethnography entailed seeking additional data and exploring multiple contexts. As I found new archival sources, I compared the new data with the *Broom* PPO data. The interviews helped me to interpret the archival data; however, the interviews were also partial, biased in different ways, mediated by interlocutors' relations to the past and the present. I compared different answers of interlocutors to the same questions, building my own picture of the *Broom*. With the exception of Albertas Lukša, a longtime secretary of the PPO, none of the editors knew firsthand about the PPO meetings and documents. But even Lukša could not remember many things. I asked questions about fifty-year-old events, in some cases.

There was no doubt that the *Broom* PPO documents were meaningful productions, as well as documents of bureaucratic showcasing. Some criteria that I used helped me to understand different layers of bureaucratic showcasing in editors' ideological work:

1) *Abstract vs. specific engagement with ideological work.* For example, editors emphasized the importance of reading Lenin's or other ideological works and sometimes gave titles or argued that they discussed these works at the meeting. However, in most of these cases there were no details provided on what was read, how it was relevant, or what was discussed at the meetings. Engaging with issues in an abstract way signaled to me that editors engaged in bureaucratic showcasing.

2) *Casual vs. original and creative input in ideological work.* For example, celebrating the anniversary of the October Revolution in 1977, editors decided to republish cartoons from other countries rather than coming up with original artwork for such an important CP holiday. Lack of initiative, originality, and creativity suggested relative disengagement from ideological work.

3) *Nonfulfillment vs. carrying out plans and decisions.* For many years, *Broom* editors complained about the lack of antireligious cartoons, and although they took some steps to remedy the situation, antireligious cartoons continued to be underrepresented (see chapter 6). Nonfulfillment illustrated that discussion of the necessity of antireligious cartoons was a

case of bureaucratic showcasing. Interviews show that editors published even antireligious cartoons of questionable artistic quality when they received them, to comply with CP ideological requirements (chapter 6). Thus, while discourse on the lack of antireligious cartoons was a case of bureaucratic showcasing, it also informed editors' actions in some cases.

4) *Routine vs. atypical events and actions covered in the documents.* Aligning *Broom* agendas with CP ideological discourse, discussion of ideological work, and self-criticism was routine, offering redundant examples of bureaucratic showcasing, while some events, such as the episode with the proclamation discussed in chapter 2, were rare and provided additional information on the *Broom* editors' relations with one another as well as with other institutions.

Some other aspects were also relevant in understanding bureaucratic showcasing:

5) *Silence.* Editors rarely spoke about *Krokodil*, which could have been an inspiration for the artists and writers of the *Broom*. Most likely that reticence illustrated the *Broom*'s relative disengagement with the pan-Soviet *Krokodil*, which was confirmed by interviews. Moreover, since documents were in the Lithuanian language, these documents did not address Russian-speaking audiences and CP authorities in Moscow. There was no need to showcase affinity to *Krokodil* in the PPO reports.

6) *Inconsistencies.* As discussed in chapter 2, Bulota argued several times that he was not going to tolerate drinking at the *Broom* headquarters, yet never-ending issues with editors' drinking had been consistently reported in the PPO documents and were confirmed by interviews. Having a record on paper of the policy of "non-tolerance" at the *Broom* might have indicated assertion of Bulota's authority and protection of the editor in chief in case others' exuberant drinking drew authorities' attention. His "non-tolerance" policy illustrates bureaucratic showcasing, even if it might have informed some of Bulota's actions. Interviews confirm that in most cases Bulota disregarded others' drinking.

7) *Differences in opinion.* While there was a general agreement on most issues, when opinions differed it indicated important events or conflicts, as in the case of the proclamation discussed in chapter 2. Unanimous opinions and conflicts provided important data on political intimacy in the *Broom* collective. Unanimous opinions were also cases of bureaucratic showcasing illustrating integrity, agreement, and a good work culture at the *Broom* collective.

I also looked at whether discussions changed in any ways when the LCP District Committee representatives or the Central Committee instructors were present at the PPO meetings, and did not find any important differences in discourse. I compared PPO thematic plans with the published materials in the *Broom* and found that thematic plans were not consistently followed; however, some themes discussed in the plans, such as criticizing bad service at cafeterias or bad organization of work at enterprises, were represented in the *Broom*.

The abstract style of some PPO reports also raises the question of whether some discussions at the meetings happened at all. The 1976 report states in vague terms that "the speaker J. Bulota analyzed historically significant resolutions in detail, raised important goals related to the improvement of quality and work effectiveness, which the magazine workers will have to solve in their everyday work."[35] In most cases, such reports mentioned "carefully" or "in detail," instead of providing the substance. One report described how "A. Lukša takes time to discuss a number of articles in the project of the [new USSR] Constitution. He concurs with the project and points out that the discussion of the project shows the rights of Soviet citizens to all the world."[36] Such abstract summations contrast with detailed discussions logged in reports of some other regular PPO meetings.

In his study "Soviet Hegemony of Form: Everything Was Forever until It Was No More," Alexei Yurchak (2003) emphasized the importance of the performative aspect of Communist Party ideological discourse. Yurchak asserts that a unanimous raising of hands in an affirmative gesture at a Soviet Komsomol meeting in late-socialist Leningrad was, to its participants, usually an act of recognition of how one must behave in a given ritualistic context in order to reproduce one's status as a social actor, rather than an act conveying a "literal" meaning. In this sense, Yurchak interprets, the raised hand was a positive response to the question "Are you the kind of social actor who understands and acts according to the rules of the current ritual, with its connection to the larger system of power relations and previous contexts of this type?" (2003, 485–86). The *Broom* editors' invocations of the CPSU holidays, CPSU leaders, and CPSU CC resolutions were performative, as captured in the concept of bureaucratic showcasing. However, the editors did find meaning and significance in parts of their ideological work beyond performative engagement with the Communist Party agendas and rituals. Investigative journalism, as argued by Lukša, had real effects by restoring justice to some people (see chapter 7).

Soviet Ideology of Everyday Life

The *Broom* editors were aware of the role of laughter as a political tool of the state. Like Soviet satirists and *Krokodil* editors (see Gérin 2018; Norris 2013; Oushakine 2011), they admitted that "laughter is a weapon" at the ideological front, necessary to fight against the imperialist West as well as transform everyday life. The editors were aware that, like other literary genres, satire plays an important role in creating a communist society using the means of artistic persuasion. At their PPO meetings, the *Broom* editors argued that "every word of satire has to serve the cause of the Communist Party and implementation of its ideas."[37] According to the 1964 CPSU CC Plenum materials, a satirist had to drag everybody who would hinder the creation of communism into the daylight, without leaving out anybody or anything that gives rise to negative consequences. Satirists must also choose an artistic form of expression, an angle and a perspective of observation, that would allow them to, as artistically and persuasively as possible, reveal defects and shortcomings in life (see Kulpinskas 1966, 6). In 1973 Juozas Bulota argued that "laughter is also politics. If people laugh [when they read the *Broom*], it means they are happy with our life and the system."[38]

Responding to Soviet party congresses, local Lithuanian Communist Party directives, or communist leaders' speeches, the *Broom* addressed, in feuilletons, satires, and cartoons, a variety of topics, from environment pollution, work discipline, work of public patrols, effectiveness of agriculture vehicles, corruption and theft, collective farm events, and public entertainment. The magazine also targeted various issues related to readers' everyday life, such as dry cleaning, shoe repair, hygiene, or moral themes of alcoholism, unemployment, and hooliganism (see box 3.3). It routinely addressed themes related to collective farms and village life. One of the important concerns for the *Broom*, also directed by Communist Party imperatives, was not to become a city magazine. In a 1971 PPO meeting, the editors addressed the question of the lack of culturedness among the workers at a collective farm: "not every house has separate towels for hands and a face."[39] At a 1973 PPO meeting, *Broom* CP members claimed that they needed to better understand village teachers' everyday life. "We have to inquire why many of them quit their jobs, also how students are transported to a more distant school, how farm directors help in this matter."[40] They were interested in cultural life, issues of clubs, libraries, culture house activities, but also good manners and other everyday issues.[41]

The intensity of ideological work depended on important events in the USSR, from the anniversaries of the October Revolution to the beginning of harvests.

Kęstutis Šiaulytis remembered that the ideological work came in the form of campaigns (Lith. *vajus*):

> During the [editorial board] meetings in this building they used to tell us, sowing had started, so we had to write about sowing. If it's harvesting—about harvesting. In some cases, a campaign was started in Moscow, [for example] about a loss of construction materials. Over there, they counted how much it is produced and how much it is used, and they saw that the difference is huge. These differences were, indeed, related to various causes. I was told that when they built the Ignalina nuclear plant, drivers were paid for the number of trips they made. There were some who used to dump concrete in a nearby forest, then went back to get another load. Instead of two, he made three trips. There were lots of cases like this. I remember in the Russian media they published on digging unnecessary quarries only to make more money, completely useless. . . . So the idea [on what to address in the *Broom*] used to come from the Soyuz [Lith. *Sąjungos*, i.e., Soviet Union]. It was in all Soyuz that you had to [respond to this matter], but it was again just a couple months, and everybody forgot about it. Harvesting or sowing started, and the discussion turned to different things.[42]

The *Broom* addressed household issues primarily in the annual March issue devoted to the International Women's Day. The March issues satirized men's contributions to cleaning, cooking, and rearing children (see Lukošienė 2016). In one cartoon by J. Juozapavičius, men celebrate at the table on the March 8 Women's Day and raise a toast to "our dear women," while women are serving them.[43] Another cartoon by A. Kazakauskas shows a women's march against men. They carry hanging laundry as a banner.[44] Artists and satirists also engaged the themes that Women's Day was the only day when men remembered women's hard work, and that men were ignorant about household chores, or incapable of doing them well.

Since the *Broom*'s primary task was to address public rather than individual issues (see chapters 7 and 8), it often focused on life outside the family and home. One of the major concerns was productive labor, central to Communist Party ideology. The *Broom* was to fight against procrastination, absenteeism, abuse of work discipline, pilfering, drinking, immoral leaders, and favoritism.[45] Workers who called in sick just to stay home, take a vacation, or go hunting or fishing during work hours were ridiculed in the *Broom*. In Rimantas Baldišius's cartoon of 1985, a man with a suitcase walking through a corridor says, "I can feel the smell of coffee. It means everyone is at work already."[46] Readers got the joke, since in Soviet work culture, coffee signified taking a break and socializing.

Consumption was also an important ideological sphere connected with readers' everyday life experiences.[47] The *Broom* criticized retailers absent from their workplace. Shoppers frequently found signs hanging on shop doors with messages such as, "The salesclerk has gone to make a call."[48] Another announcement—"We don't work *today*. It's cleaning *hour*" (Lith. *sanitarinė valanda*; emphasis added)—referred to popular cleaning days (or hours) during which institutions were closed to address hygiene concerns and orderliness.[49] For many workers this was a day off from their regular work responsibilities (Klumbytė 2012). Another common reason for closing was "technical difficulties," which could entail any variety of excuses to close. Cartoons and jokes also ridiculed the tradition of *blat* (favors, connections).

People's behavior was also a focus of concern for the *Broom*. Various negative personal traits, such as subservience, hypocrisy, bragging, interest in the material realm as opposed to the spiritual (but not the religious), arrogance, careerism, lying, laziness, and civic irresponsibility were criticized (see Klumbytė 2012). The magazine poked fun at speculators, people who resell goods for profit, as well as their customers. Greed was despised, while modesty and simplicity were admired, as was "spirituality"—defined as a quality that entails disinterest in material things, respect for others, conscientiousness, honesty, sincerity, open-mindedness, simplicity, and responsibility to the public (see Klumbytė 2012).[50]

In 1976, the *Broom* provided a long-term plan on themes to be addressed in its pages following the CPSU Twenty-Fifth Congress Resolutions. This plan was the most comprehensive projection of thematic work documented in the *Broom* PPO archival documents between 1960 and 1980. It incorporated topics on economic themes, including work control and efficiency; production; transportation and supply; construction and organization of construction site environment; issues of technology; machinery and repair; work ethics, discipline, and culture; and the daily needs of workers (see box 3.3).

The *Broom* promoted social and public order, officials' responsibility to ordinary people, employers' fairness toward their employees, good service, and respect toward each other.[51] As chapters 7 and 8 will show, *Broom* readers embraced social and moral values about work relations, public order, and consumption. Nevertheless, readers and *Broom* artists and journalists reinterpreted official ideology. *Broom* editors also addressed ideological discourse in a way that sometimes paralleled unofficial jokes or hid unacceptable messages (see chapter 6).

Box 3.3. The 1976 long-term plan of the *Broom* press

Responding to Soviet party congresses, local Lithuanian Communist Party directives, and communist leaders' speeches, *Broom* editors drew plans of what to address in their pages. The below list is the most comprehensive record of topics
in the PPO documents of 1960–1979 illustrating editors' plans for the magazine's
content based on the CPSU Twenty-Fifth Congress Resolutions. The entire document is translated to show the variety of areas of interest, from environmental pollution to effectiveness of agricultural vehicles to people's daily needs and morals.

1. Questions of farm leaders' behavior—their snobbishness [Lith.
   suponėjimas]; mistreating the retired; disagreeable relations with
   specialists; neglect of kolkhoz people's daily needs [Lith. *nesirūpinimas
   kolūkiečių buitimi*].[52]
2. Technical provision [Lith. *techninis aprūpinimas*], work conditions, work
   culture in animal husbandry [Lith. *gyvulininkystės*] farms as well as in
   mechanical workshops [Lith. *mechaninių dirbtuvių*]; mechanization,
   supply of work clothing, footwear, recreation rooms, showers, order and
   cleanliness inside.
3. Use of agriculture machinery (efficiency), conditions of its repair.
4. Negative aspects of rural everyday life. When X gets richer, disorder
   prevails. Neglect is related to habits of [life in] the past.
5. The activities of *druzhiny* [people's voluntary patrols].
6. Shortcomings of work discipline: alcoholism, unexcused absence from
   work [Lith. *pravaikštos*].
7. Misuse of funds due to weak control, deliberate appropriation of funds.
   Falsification of documents for a higher pay [Lith. *prirašinėtojai*].
8. Protection of water, nature. Fights with poachers.
9. Moral themes. Material about parasites [humans] [Lith. *veltėdžius*],
   alcoholics, asocial elements, street people [Lith. *valkataujantys*], loafers,
   unemployed alimony payers [Lith. *alimentininkus*]. Hooliganism of the
   "golden youth." From a courtroom [journalistic stories from a courtroom].
10. [A regular column] Aunt Agnieška's corner:
    a. A raid on city stores (regarding cleanliness, culture).
    b. Regarding child daycare choice, quality and appearance.
    c. A piece on poor people [Lith. *kampininkai*]—people who walk several
       kilometers in N. Vilnia to get water from wells.
    d. Dyeing and laundering of clothes, repair of shoes.
    e. Problems of toys in day care centers.
    f. . . .

11. Reserves for increasing labor productivity [Lith. *darbo našumo didinimo rezervai*]—advancement of technology [Lith. *technikos pažanga*], discipline.
12. Quality issues in light industry, etc. (permanent headline).
13. Problems of introducing new technology into production.
14. Complex mechanization [Lith. *kompleksinis mechanizavimas*], especially in auxiliary works [Lith. *pagalbiniuose darbuose*].
15. Falsification of workload: work carried out by machines assigned as a manual work norm.
16. Full utilization of machines and equipment.
17. Economizing of raw and other materials, their ineffective use.
18. Reserves of surplus and unnecessary materials, machines, and equipment.
19. Faster expansion of a new stock of goods [Lith. *spartesnis plėtimas naujo prekių asortimento*].
20. Problems of spare parts and repair of machinery in certain enterprises of the republic.
21. Local roads. Disorderly temporary access roads and related [financial] losses [Lith. *laikinų privažiavimo kelių nesutvarkymas*].
22. Safety at work and problems of its improvement.
23. Problems of supply [Lith. *tiekimo nesklandumai*].
24. Problems of storage of goods in district cooperative union [Lith. *rajkoopsąjungos*] depots (influence on quality).
25. Problems of nutrition in workers' and school canteens.
26. Order in enterprise shops as well as in their territory.
27. To construct fast, well, and cheap.
28. Influence of construction material storage on the quality of future buildings.
29. Work quality depending on speeding up plans [Lith. *plano šturmavimo pasėkmės darbo kokybei*] ([based on] a raid on recently finished objects).
30. Uninstalled and unused construction machinery [Lith. *technika*].
31. Regular withholding of transport [Lith. *prastovėjimai*]—a reason for losses.
32. Projects doomed to be scrap paper at the stage of their planning (design of equipment, lines of technology when equipment is not produced anymore).
33. "Increase" of work productivity at the price of unanticipated costs.
34. Automobile incidents [Lith. *automobilizmas*] (with State Auto Inspectorate).
35. Signing off unfinished construction objects.
36. Driving empty transport and withholding transport.
37. Literary materials (verses, humor pieces) written in relevant production, economic life questions.

38. Atheistic themes. Political satires [Lith. *pamfletai*] against capitalist plots and unmasking bourgeois lifestyle.

39. Problems of cultural life: construction of culture houses, their renovation, supply of inventory, daily life conditions [Lith. *buitinės sąlygos*], conditions of culture workers, circulation of cadres [Lith. *kadrų tekamumas*], recreational evenings and their programs.

40. Attendance of libraries, work conditions, cadres of librarians.

41. Culturedness and behavior in public space.

42. Visual agitation, advertising, cleaning parks and squares, etc.

Material for cartoons and illustrations

43. Production of items that are old-fashioned and have no demand.

44. Complex machinery.

45. Topics of morality.

46. Problems of raising labor productivity.

47. Violations of work discipline and its criticism.

48. Problems of spare parts in agriculture.

49. Problems of irregular provision.

50. Violating plans and signing off on construction objects [that were still unfinished].

51. Themes of culture.

52. Circulation of [any workplace] cadres [Lith. *kadrų tekamumas*].

53. Problems of the use of young specialists.

54. Matters of user safety in agriculture and industry.

55. Making work conditions better on the farms.

56. Questions of quality: speeding up [Lith. *šturmavimas*]—a trap to quality and positive motivation at work.

57. Criticism of transportation work.

58. Political cartoons on pertinent international life issues.

59. Atheistic themes.

The heaviness of the Soviet predicament was a generational experience.[53] The founding editors of the *Broom* lived through World War II, lost families in the Gulag and the Holocaust, experienced the violent postwar era and the end of Stalinism (chapter 1). Engaging in ideological socialization of their readers, they supported new regime projections about emerging social order. However, none of my interlocutors said anything close to "socialism and communism were good and right" or that they "had a deep feeling that we lived in the best country in the world," as did Yurchak's (2006, 97) interlocutors, representatives of the last Soviet generation from Leningrad. Ideological work was a heavy Soviet predicament, even if it gave meaning and significance to their lives, and even if they accepted some of it as important for creating *Broom*'s laughter.

Decades after World War II, *Broom* journalist Dita Lomsargytė-Pukienė's mother could still not eat watermelons. They always evoked freight cars from the Soviet Union arriving in Kaunas full of watermelons for "starving Lithuania." In the Kaunas train station, banners for "starving Lithuania" swiftly disappeared, so people would not make fun of them—or rather, would not become angry about them, writes Lomsargytė-Pukienė (2004, 67). In Sri Lanka, Carolyn Nordstrom described how in the midst of the chaos of the 1983 anti-Tamil riots, in which thousands were killed over seven days, one local woman left all her things by the road as they became too hard to carry on her way home. She abandoned her handbag with bank cards, money, glasses, and licenses; then her medicines; then presents and blessed religious relics for her family; then her suitcase. But she did not let go of the heavy watermelon. She carried it all night long, through all the pandemonium and horror (Nordstrom 2004, 6–7). In Sri Lanka, carrying this watermelon most likely represented holding on to the everyday life that the watermelon was associated with. In Lithuania, refusing the watermelon was negating the everyday life associated with Soviet occupation. The Sovietizing of Lithuania and reorganizing of everyday life and sensible orders took many decades and millions of watermelons. Watermelons played an important role in integrating Lithuania into the Soviet empire of taste, which included mass-produced products circulating throughout the USSR. These products reconfigured sensory experiences and tastes (see Klumbytė 2010). Communist ideology reached into intimate experiences of everyday life, including people's laughter. While trains brought watermelons, *Broom* curried laughter.

CENSORIAL INDISTINCTION

We were more free than others.

—Romualdas Lankauskas, 2016

With little green plastic buckets in hand we headed to pick raspberries in the garden. The bushes are taller than I am, dotted with big red berries, and I can hardly keep pace with Adomas Subačius, who is eighty-eight years old. Subačius was an associate editor for several decades at a publishing house in Kaunas. He vividly remembered censors from Glavlit (the Main Directorate for Literary and Publishing Affairs), the major censorship agency.[1] "The censor was Jewish," says Subačius, smiling. "He used to come to announce new requirements. We would celebrate his visits, having a couple of drinks whenever he came around. Sometimes, we called him on the phone to ask if there were any new requirements and invited him to a restaurant." Before Subačius was promoted to associate editor, censors used to return their proofread books and tell the editorial board, "There are errors." The editors searched for errors, could not find them, then invited the censors to a restaurant. Everything took place secretly, Subačius assured me. Editors worked in a partially mysterious space, navigating state secrets. Drinking together at a restaurant helped editors to understand censors' expectations and how to produce ideologically correct books.

One day, Subačius took a Kaunas city photo album for approval to Glavlit. In one photo, there was a view with nature and a chimney. Censors told him to conceal the chimney, so "the enemy couldn't find out about the factory." On another occasion, there was a house in a photo of Kaunas that had to be cropped out for security reasons. This way factories and houses disappeared from photographs. Once, laughed Subačius, he was on a road with the director of a political press—the LSSR national press for political and scientific literature. A tourist map published by this press was in Subačius's hands, but instead of reaching a destination, they arrived at a clover field. According to the map there should have been a road. They both stared into the clover field for a while and decided to ride through it. "How come," Subačius asked his colleague as they bumped through the field, "this is the map you published?" The director assured him that everything must be correct, everything was reviewed and approved. "But it was because of censorship," smiled Subačius; they [censors, authorities] made roads disappear, so "the enemy could not find us. . . . This enemy had much better maps."[2]

My conversation with Subačius in a raspberry garden captured many important developments in the late-Soviet political culture of censorship: the arbitrariness of censorship regulations and control, the importance of relations and political intimacy among censors and editors, and the displaced reality that censorship created. My initial expectation that I would learn what was specifically censored in Soviet times was futile. As we headed back, our buckets were full of raspberries, but I lacked solid data on censorship.

Glavlit's censoring mission centered on state military, strategic, or other secrets, as well as ideological content.[3] Ideological censorship, a branch of Soviet censorship that focused on politically and ideologically unacceptable content, was particularly relevant to studying the *Broom*. Brian Kassof (2015, 72) notes that "ideological censorship was a symbol *par excellence* of the oppressive nature of Soviet power." In the Soviet and East European contexts, the stories of Aleksandr Solzhenitsyn, Czesław Miłosz, Milan Kundera, and Václav Havel reflect primarily upon censors' ideological work. They describe censorship as a repressive institution, which suppressed works and lives, killed creative thought, destroyed literature, and condemned writers to silence.

Lithuanian intellectuals who created in the Soviet era have also portrayed censorship as an institution of the state's repressive control. Writer Tomas Venclova (1985) wrote about a "faceless" censor, whom the author in Soviet times did not meet, whose name he did not know, and with whom he struggled in an unequal fight all his life. Writer Marcelijus Martinaitis (2003) recollected in 1994 that "the essence of the Soviet system was generally *total censorship*, which interpenetrated almost everything" (emphasis added). During the international Sakharov hearing in Munich on August 1, 1975, Jonas Jurašas, a Lithuanian theater director, testified about censorship in terms of "the persecution of an entire nation [of Lithuanians]" that contributed to "decades of continuous destruction, occupation and genocide of a nation of three million" (Jurašas 1977).

These stories are remarkable and memorable because they capture the conflict between an author and the regime, a drama of freedom and repression and the dilemmas of creativity and ideological compliance. They are intrinsic to our understanding of Soviet authoritarianism. However, I argue, they do not describe all relationships between authors and censors. *Broom* editors, artists, and journalists invoked the presence of censorship and self-censorship, yet, they recalled that they were relatively free, as claimed by Romualdas Lankauskas in this chapter's epigraph (see also box 4.1).[4] Artist and regular *Broom* contributor Jonas Varnas maintained that there were generally no restrictions. When I objected that erotic themes were not permitted, he argued, "We made women climb into a bed in clothing. And it was even funnier [than drawing a naked body]."[5]

This chapter illustrates that *Broom* editors' and artists' positionality toward censorship in terms of relative freedom encapsulates relations of political intimacy with censors, as well as banal opposition. Claiming to be relatively free entailed two seemingly opposite stances: agreeability with censors and authorities on the official expectations for publishing, along with shared trust and understanding—but also transgressions of ideological censoring requirements when publishing jokes or cartoons with hidden messages.

If I had learned what was censored from *Broom* editors, maybe I never would have opened the door to the Lithuanian Central State Archive to read Glavlit documents and find out about the *Broom* and the Glavlit censors' work. But even reading through the hundreds of pages of Glavlit censors' reports, which included notes on the *Broom* as well as other magazines and print media, I was not able to compile a consistent and comprehensive list of censored ideological content. With the exception of some major unlisted taboos, such as critique of the socialist system, the Communist Party, or the highest authorities, there were no explicit regulations on what ideological content had to be censored.[6] Subačius's story in the introductory vignette about going to a restaurant with censors to find out and agree about ideological correctness started to make sense to me, as well as *Broom* editors' claims about relative freedom. Eventually I realized that I had chosen to study an object—ideological censorship—that officially did not even exist. While secret factories were listed in *Perechen'* ("The List"), the manual on forbidden information in open media, there was no secret or any other list on ideological censorship.[7] The 1936 and 1977 USSR Constitutions stated that Soviet citizens were guaranteed by law freedoms of speech and the press.[8] Glavlit was not mentioned in the Soviet media, phone books, information manuals, or encyclopedias (Truska 1997). Since 1967, Glavlit censors had not been called "censors" anymore; they were "editors" (see also Streikus 2018, 92).

Box 4.1. What was censored in the *Broom*?

An excerpt of an interview with contributing Broom artist Vladimiras Beresniovas (Vlaber).

VLABER: There was censorship . . . it was everywhere. Not only in the *Broom*. . . . It was everywhere . . . in the newspapers. At that time I published [cartoons] in Kaunas *Truth*. . . . If it was a political cartoon and if there was something not right, they did not accept it. You had to celebrate the CPSU [Communist Party of the Soviet Union]. . . . "Long live [the Communist Party] . . ." then all is all right.[9]

NERINGA: I ask everybody, what were you not allowed to draw? Radvilavičius said that you could not draw a desert island.

VLABER: No, you could. It was allowed. . . . Something is not right here. . . . There were a lot of drawings . . . with a desert island. . . . A lot. . . . Plenty in the *Broom*. . . .

NERINGA: Others said, "Everything, we could draw everything." Andrius Deltuva told me that "everything had to be very abstract." Did editors allow naked bodies?

VLABER: Well . . . it was allowed, why not? . . . it was possible . . . yes.

NERINGA: Radvilavičius said if you draw a bull, there should be no sexual organs [*laughs*]. Now you are saying differently. I'm trying to understand.

VLABER: Well, maybe he thinks this way. I think differently. Maybe he did not draw because he was afraid that he would not get published. I don't think this way. If you draw well, so what? . . . What's the big deal if you show a leg [uncovered]? Nothing. You do not show everything [*laughs*]. You could not draw Brezhnev—you couldn't, and that's it. Any political leader . . . well, you could not show them . . . in a negative light. Only from a good side. For example, now you can do everything. . . . Putin, Obama, Bush, you can draw the way you want; well . . . nobody prohibits [anything]. But there is also an internal thing. . . . I, for example, do not want to draw anything negative. I don't want this. Others, they do.

NERINGA: I think about this freedom, how much you—

VLABER: This freedom also . . . it also has [limits]. . . . You are never free. Freedom does not exist. . . . You are always dependent.

This chapter, then, is about an unusual research object—*censorial indistinction*, the invisibility and opacity of ideological censorship, recorded in the recollections of *Broom* editors and artists. *Censorial indistinction*, I will argue, was shaped by inconsistent and arbitrary censoring practices, resulting from censors' lack of knowledge, incompetence, errors, or ignorance; censors' inability to control ambiguity and multiplicity of meanings; and, importantly, relationality—that is, co-constitution of censoring practices among authors, editors, censors, and Communist Party authorities. *Relationality* refers to the embeddedness of censorship in interactions mediated by relations of political intimacy, that is, trust and coexistence within the same political episteme (see chapter 2). Political intimacy among editors, censors, and Central Committee authorities was the major pillar on which ideological censorship of the *Broom* rested. In the case of "total censorship," however, political intimacy among authors, censors, and authorities was disrupted, disintegrated, or absent. Memories of censorship as "total control" thus recorded this disruption or disintegration of political intimacy and indexed a conflict among authors, on the one side, and authorities and censors on the other.

This chapter focuses on censorial indistinction and the *Broom* as an object of ideological censorship. It first briefly describes the changing censorship policies in Lithuania after the establishment of Glavlit in 1940. Next, it explores Glavlit's censoring practices by focusing on errors that censors made. It further analyzes Glavlit censors' ideological censoring strategies and the censoring of the *Broom*. The section "Control of Contexts" shows how potential ambiguity of meanings and contextualization posed challenges to ideological censorship. The last section discusses censorship as mediated by relations of political intimacy. Since censorship in late socialism was relegated to the presses themselves, the next chapter will discuss how the *Broom* editors censored *Broom* contributors' and readers' works and shaped the political aesthetics of *Broom* texts.

Vilnius Glavlit Censorship

Lithuania was incorporated into the Soviet Union in the summer of 1940.[10] In the fall of 1940, Glavlit was founded in the city of Kaunas, and it ceased functioning in 1941 when the Nazis occupied Lithuania.[11] In August 1944, after the Red Army had advanced on the western front, Glavlit was reestablished, this time in Vilnius (Streikus 2018; Truska 1997). Many prewar history books, encyclopedias, religious books, and literary works were immediately forbidden as ideologically unacceptable (see Gudaitis 2010). The works of authors who emigrated, joined the anti-Soviet resistance, or were deported to the Gulag had to be eliminated (see Gudaitis 2010). Various genres were targeted by censors, from "the Lithuanian fairy tales," which were prepared for publication by a "nationalist" author, to dictionaries, which did not include the new Soviet vocabulary and thus "did not serve the masses and failed to contribute to the communist education of society" (Gudaitis 2010). According to Gudaitis, more than 10 percent of Lithuanian printed books "experienced repressions of [Soviet] censorship." Epp Lauk (1999) writes that in the case of another Baltic state, Estonia, nobody knows how many books were destroyed under Soviet rule, but estimated numbers range from ten to twenty million (Veskimägi 1996, 307, cited in Lauk 1999, 30). New books, magazines, and other print media had to speak about the new communist society and meet Communist Party ideological requirements.

In post-Stalinist Lithuania, censorship existed at various levels: presses, Glavlit, the Central Committee, and the KGB (Sabonis and Sabonis 1992; Streikus 2018). The post-Stalinist era also was defined by the growing importance of editorial boards vis-à-vis Glavlit. Presses, Glavlit, or the Central Committee not only censored, but in some cases saved works from censors' cuts and changes; editors and censors helped authors to write in ideologically acceptable ways or defended them when conflicts emerged (see Sabonis and Sabonis 1992). Every piece of art or literary work had a history of censoring; some works also had a history of post-publication censoring, sometimes including the organizing of public campaigns, as the discussion below shows, against the author.

The *Broom* was established in November 1956 when ideological censorship came to a temporary halt owing to the CPSU's Twentieth Congress, during which Khrushchev delivered his Secret Speech.[12] But the liberalization of censorship was short-lived. The secret CPSU CC letter of December 19, 1956, "Regarding strengthening of the work of political mass party organizations and the prevention of anti-Soviet hostile element attacks," requested giving a decisive response to various attempts to rethink the party line toward literature and art (Zezina 1999, 198, cited in Streikus 2004, 45). On January 16, 1957, Antanas Sniečkus, the first secretary of the Lithuanian Communist Party, met with Lithuanian communist writers to discuss the limits of post-Stalinist freedom (see Streikus 2018, 82). Sniečkus emphasized that a strong ideological war was taking place, which affected literature. The party did not recognize any intermediate ideology between communist and bourgeois ideologies (82). Another important event was the Manege Affair. On December 16, 1962, and March 7–8, 1963, Khrushchev and other members of the party leadership visited an anniversary art exhibition, "Thirty Years of the Moscow Artists' Union," and met with writers and other cultural figures in Moscow's Central Exhibition Hall, or Manege. He expressed his disapproval of abstractionists and imitators of Western art (Ermolaev 1997, 13), ranting against some works in terms of "filth and fecal messing, decadence and sexual deviance, concluding, 'gentlemen, we are waging war on you'" (Reid 2005, 673). As Susan Reid notes, after the Manege Affair the Central Committee Ideological Commission reasserted party control over the arts along with the central principles of Socialist Realism, *partiinost'* (Rus., commitment to the

Communist Party and identification with the proletarian cause) and *narodnost'* (Rus., accessibility to the people) (673). The Manege Affair is known in history as the beginning of the end of the cultural thaw in the USSR (Reid 2005). In 1963 an ideological campaign against formalism and abstractionism in art and literature began (Streikus 2004, 49).

Until 1968 almost every year (with the exceptions of 1958, 1962, 1964, and 1965) Glavlit recorded ideologically unacceptable *Broom* content (see table 4.1). From 1968 to 1978 there is only one entry about the *Broom* recorded in Glavlit. The lack of Glavlit interventions after 1968 was likely related to a new wave of tightening of ideological control. On January 7, 1969, the CPSU CC passed a resolution "regarding press, radio, television, cinematography, culture, and art institution leadership responsibilities for increasing the ideological-political level of published materials and repertoires," which more explicitly than ever specified to editorial board leadership that they have to produce ideologically impeccable publications (Streikus 2018, 93). According to Arūnas Streikus (93), this resolution, along with the suppression of the Prague Spring, the expulsion of Aleksandr Solzhenitsyn from the Writers Union in November 1969, and the firing of Aleksandr Tvardovsky from *Novyi Mir* magazine in February 1970, signaled the end of the thaw.[13] In Lithuania, a notorious moment that marked the end of the thaw was the 1969 Congress of LSSR culture workers, during which Antanas Sniečkus, the first secretary of the Communist Party of Lithuania, expressed concern "about petty themes [Lith. *dėl tematikos susmulkėjimo*] in contemporary literature, about manifestation of bourgeois philosophical ideas and formalist experiments." Sniečkus declared that "at the Board Plenum of Writers Union, writer Jonas Avyžius aptly noted that nowadays it is fashionable to raise a flag of shared humanism forgetting who is holding it, that is, forgetting that the flag of shared humanism can only be in the hands of supporters of the socialist regime" (*Pirmasis Lietuvos TSR kultūros darbuotojų suvažiavimas* 1971).

The control of censorship fluctuates in both democratic and authoritarian regimes, along with the understanding of threats and insecurities to society, the ruling elites, and the state. A more restrictive censorship control was implemented after the revolutions of 1956 in Hungary, 1968 in Czechoslovakia, and youth riots of 1972 in Lithuania (see Ermolaev 1997; Streikus 2018). According to Streikus (2004, 45), "for Lithuanians 1972 has the same meaning as 1956 for Hungarians and Poles, and 1968 for Czechs and Slovaks." The year 1972 is remembered for Romas Kalanta's self-immolation. The nineteen-year-old high school student set himself on fire in the center of Kaunas, leaving a note that read, "Only the system is responsible for my death" (see Swain 2015). This event led to massive riots of youth in Kaunas. The year 1972 is important for other reasons as well, namely, the first underground publication of the *Chronicle of the*

Lithuanian Catholic Church, which was the major, longest-running, and best-known dissident periodical in Lithuania (see Tamkevičius 2021). In 1972 the Central Committee replaced three editors in chief of major magazines (Streikus 2018). Secret LCP CC documents and some decisions, such as the replacements of the LCP CC Propaganda and Agitation Department chair and the editors of more liberal presses, confirm that after the events of 1972, the Central Committee was determined to strengthen ideological control (Streikus 2018, 103). Insufficient control of some print media was believed to have contributed to the 1972 youth riots (Streikus 2018).

The *Broom* participated in the 1972 ideological campaign by planning to fight against youth delinquency and nationalism. On May 31, 1972, two weeks after the self-immolation of Kalanta, the *Broom* organized a PPO meeting to discuss "questions of the struggle against surviving bourgeois ideals in people's consciousness: against occurrences of nationalism, drinking, etc."[14] Referring to the May 1972 events at the meeting, Juozas Bulota argued that the *Broom* had to "emphasize struggle against hooligans, long-haired men, who drink and disturb the peace, engage in obstructive behavior, and even commit crimes."[15] This meeting shows that in the case of important events like youth riots, the *Broom* participated in joint initiatives of the regime. However, in the following summer issues of the *Broom*, there were no cartoons or articles that would illustrate the editors' agenda in practice. The Kaunas events were not immediately addressed. Cartoons against hooliganism and long-haired men, or against bourgeois nationalism, appeared in some *Broom* issues, but not in relation to the Kaunas events.

Ideological censorship was officially terminated on January 1, 1990, when the law on print media and other means of information was passed (Streikus 2004, 63). Glavlit formally operated until Lithuania established independence on March 11, 1990 (63).

Censors' Errors

Vilnius Glavlit, headed by director Mykolas Slizevičius (in office 1955–1988) and associate director Borisas Gurvičius (in office 1945–1986), encountered not only various institutional constraints, such as censorship policy changes, lack of censors, and high employee turnover, but also inefficient work by censors.[16] Censors' errors, usually instances of overlooking ideologically unacceptable content or state military, strategic, or other secrets, are one of the major concerns in Vilnius Glavlit's reports. If censors deleted or corrected too much, they were blamed for making ungrounded corrections (Lith. *nepagrįsti išbraukimai*). Both overlooking state secrets and ideological errors, and over-censoring, were not acceptable.

What do censors' errors tell us? Discussions of censors' errors in Glavlit reports illustrate how at the institutional level various factors contributed to censorial indistinction. Some censors lacked necessary knowledge, or struggled with the obscurity of regulations or difficult work conditions. Censors made errors not only because of institutional constraints, but also because of lack of vigilance and commitment to their work.

The censors of Glavlit often attributed errors they made to institutional constraints. From the mid-1950s to the mid-1970s in the Glavlit PPO documents, censors complained about the lack of staff and resulting "unbearable work conditions."[17] They pointed out that they read too many pages and worked day and night shifts.[18] The Glavlit PPO reports document that censorship work was not very attractive. It was poorly paid, with a heavy workload, and offered neither prestige nor special benefits.[19] But in 1957 the USSR Glavlit claimed that if you look at the errors made by Vilnius Glavlit censors, it is clear that high workloads and changing of cadres cannot explain censors' errors. Many errors were made by experienced censors. According to this report, it happened because of "inattentive reading."[20]

The Glavlit director Slizevičius and associate director Gurvičius often drew attention to the lack of vigilance, self-discipline, and responsibility. From their perspective, inattentive reading was the major reason why censors made errors. Censors were blamed for reading too fast, and in some cases not even being familiar with censorship manuals. The loyalty of censors was assumed—that is, the error was never a political mistake, but a procedural mistake. Some censors received reprimands or fines. If censors' poor work persisted, they could be transferred to another workplace. Interestingly, some censors used the phrase "burning down" if they were caught making important errors, which had repercussions such as job losses. The phrase "burning down" was used by *Broom* editors as well. "Burning down" referred to game-like relations in which there were winners and losers. Both censors and editors thus were willfully or unwillfully playing with "fire."

Censors rarely admitted having read materials inattentively. In addition to complaining about the workload, in some cases they argued about a lack of knowledge of how to censor materials.[21] They justified their errors by referring to the obscurity of regulations of ideological censorship and difficulties in censoring ambiguous content. Censors also talked about the impossibility of avoiding subjectivity.[22] In 1961 one censor commented on his colleague's error, "I also missed ideological errors [in materials]. I did not notice them. Sometimes it is hard to understand what is allowed, what is not."[23] The same year, at the meeting on political vigilance, another censor requested a meeting with representatives from the Central Committee, so they "could tell us how to evaluate the past" by "giving a good lecture," so that censors could be good helpers to the Central Committee.[24] At the August 31, 1967, meeting, a censor noted that "it is hard to evaluate creative writing. You have to be very educated, a good critic, and be above [more knowledgeable than] a writer."[25] At the same meeting Glavlit associate director Gurvičius regretted that they did not have any editor who would "be higher than a writer." He also thought that it was impossible to avoid subjectivity, since "*The List* does not state what literature we have to veto."[26]

Analysis of the "political-ideological errors," however, also tells a different story, not reducible to institutional constraints, lack of attentiveness, or obscurity of regulations. Reading Glavlit PPO documents, I discovered that some censors disregarded violations in censored works.[27] On February 23, 1965, the Lithuanian Glavlit PPO report mentioned that some censors were accused of not reading some materials.[28] Reports, memoirs, and interviews on censorship suggest that generally censors did not act as "witch hunters" aiming to capture minor ideologically disapproved messages. Their censoring work in some cases was mediated by political intimacy shared with censors and authors, dialogue and negotiation, understanding and openness, as well as flexibility when the boundaries of what was to be censored were obscure. An important inspection report of LSSR Glavlit work that took place in September 1967 documents that censors reported many errors to editors verbally, not in writing, as was required (see Streikus 2018, 92). *Broom* contributor and artist Jonas Varnas remembered that at public exhibitions of cartoons there were many cartoons very critical of Soviet realities. These exhibitions had been regularly organized since 1968 by cartoonists, who also published in the *Broom*. Artists were able to sneak ambiguous cartoons in, people flooded the exhibitions, and high Central Committee and government officials also came. "They valued [art], [they] were not evil, [but] very tolerant, did not put any obstacles for us . . . just a bare minimum. They were afraid for themselves. What if they got caught? The signature sanctioning the exhibition will be theirs."[29] Varnas (2017) also emphasized that censors looked primarily at words, not images, and that people from Glavlit as well as the Central Committee suggested what was not to be publicized (see introduction). Glavlit PPO reports also referred to political intimacy among censors and cultural elites, and condemned censors for trying to make deals with writers—that is, letting them publish some ideologically problematic or ambiguous content.[30]

Like *Broom* PPO documents, Glavlit annual reports and reports to the LCP CC and Moscow Glavlit were documents of bureaucratic showcasing driven by imperatives to illustrate hard work, loyalty, and commitment. Openness about errors in censoring was also fostered by the communist ideological requirement of critical introspection and reflection on work. Like *Broom* editors, Glavlit censors were expected to criticize themselves and analyze shortcomings in their work.

Nevertheless, censors' errors tell us that ideological censoring was limited in its reach because of institutional constraints, censors' limited knowledge of what to censor, and lack of vigilance and commitment to their work, as well as political intimacy between censors, editors, and authors. One is left to wonder whether Glavlit was not plagued by procrastination and a drinking culture, which defined other workplaces and was laughed at in the *Broom*. Procrastination and drinking are even documented in several Glavlit reports. The report of August 21, 1964, tells us that many censors were late two, fifteen, or even fifty minutes on the day when officials from Moscow Glavlit paid what was most likely a surprise visit. In Kaunas, one Glavlit censor was found asleep on chairs, drunk.[31] Jonas Varnas (2017), remembering Glavlit censors, remarked with a smile on his face that they liked to drink.[32]

Glavlit Ideological Control Strategies

In the context of changing and ambiguous regulations and lack of knowledge of how to censor ideological content, what was the rationale that guided censors' decisions? Glavlit censors' ideological censorship of print media was justified by the following overlapping categories: (1) *generalizations* about negative developments of socialism had to be avoided; (2) *misrepresentations of reality* (Lith. *neatitinka tikrovės*) had to be corrected; and (3) published content had to be *ideologically correct*. The three categories used by Glavlit censors—generalizations, misrepresentations of reality, and ideological incorrectness—overlapped. All of them could be called, in censors' terms, "political-ideological errors."

"Generalizations" violated the principle of "enduring shortcomings," an important ideological imperative for interpreting negative events and processes in society. "Enduring shortcomings" implied that various negative issues are temporary, "survivals" from the earlier periods, which would disappear in a communist society. These negative issues could be attributed to specific individuals but could not describe communist society in general. "Generalizations" could even be politically subversive; as Glavlit PPO reports indicated, they could incite opposition via religious or nationalistic stances. For example, Glavlit reported about the memoir by E. Bilevičius, a former LSSR fishing industry minister, in which he introduced problematic facts about administration in Moscow. He claimed, according to the Glavlit report, that ministers were invited to "Moscow to account for an unfulfilled plan and were yelled at; they [ministers] could not even say what was their opinion."[33] In the report it was argued that in reading Bilevičius's memoir, "one could conclude that the fishing industry was established in Lithuania under Moscow's dictate and an administration that disregarded others."[34] Glavlit director Slizevičius reported that the "negative facts [in the memoir] are presented in a too general way. It [generalization] could be understood in a wrong way and used by a bourgeois nationalist for anti-Soviet propaganda." He also expressed reservations about publication of Bilevičius's memoir: "Most likely publishing it would not be appropriate."[35]

If facts or interpretations did not comply with the Communist Party line and Marxist-Leninist ideology, censors deleted them, justifying that they did not correspond to reality or were politically or ideologically incorrect. Authors could not undermine the image of the communist regime as the best social, political, and economic system, and therefore the achievements of Western capitalist societies or pre-Soviet Lithuania could not be presented in a better light. One could not mention that grain and potato harvests in Soviet Lithuania were much lower compared to those in pre-Soviet Lithuania.[36] The friendship of Soviet nationalities or proletariat internationalism was beyond criticism. There could be no oppression in the USSR, and thus (as in one prayer book), Saint Mary could not be asked to save the nation drowning in troubles and dying from oppression.[37] Affects were also tailored according to ideological imperatives; one could not laugh at public demonstrations, such as at May 1 International Workers' Day parades. Censors could not accept irony directed at Lenin's monument, as when "Druzhinniki [Lith. *tvarkdariai*, voluntary people's patrols] with red armbands closed entrances to [Lenin's] monument and left Lenin [to stand] alone."[38] People could not watch foreign movies with "great interest" or dislike Soviet "historical-revolutionary movies" that received little attention.[39]

Descriptions of the past had to celebrate the friendship of Soviet peoples and the leading role of the great Russian nation. Soviet World War II heroism was unquestionable. One author argued that people in a kolkhoz rarely smile, unlike in newspaper reports. "According to the author," censors argued, "it looks like our newspapers represent life in kolkhozes in a wrong way, that people live worse than they [newspapers] describe them."[40] Censors requested deleting the statement from *Broom* journalist Leonas Kiauleikis's collection of feuilletons that mentioned the annual consumption of 470,000 liters of vodka in Vilnius.[41] The newspaper *Moriak Litvy* (Lithuanian sailor) could not publish a World War II veteran story about how the veteran killed his friend and how they showed mercy to enemies and gave them an opportunity to retreat.[42] The Soviet Army had to be portrayed as a heroic fighter against fascism. A story about Soviet Army soldiers in the winter of 1944–45 burning galleries and columns of a wooden church—the burial site of famed Lithuanian figure Kristijonas Donelaitis—could not be disclosed.[43] Lithuania's incorporation into the USSR had to be presented as an expression of a unanimous will of the people of Lithuania. Thus, it could not be published that among all teachers in Soviet Lithuania in 1945 there were only five communists and ten Communist Youth members.[44]

Unacceptable were scholarly and research findings that did not portray socialist society in the best light, such as a conclusion to a 1959 biology article noting that in Lithuania, workers' nutrition was substandard, that many did not eat breakfast, only 50 percent consumed meat, and 34.5 percent did not eat eggs.[45] The 1960 economics study could not publicize facts showing inefficiency of Soviet kolkhozes by stating that kolkhoz workers produced 80 percent of potatoes, 70 percent of milk, and 55 percent of meat in their personal plots. The importance of personal plots in the economy of collective agriculture, as well as the suggestion that private farming could be strengthened, was ideologically unacceptable.[46]

The acceptable reality was a displaced reality; it was a "reality" that corresponded to Communist Party ideology, reaffirmed the party's authority, and was constructed through censors. Ideological correctness projected the view that the communist regime was the best, that citizens lived good and fulfilling lives, and there were no social, political, or economic problems. Negative developments were the result of the incompetence of single individuals or survivals of the "bourgeois" past. They were singular, not generalizable to the regime or society.

The *Broom*, as the next chapter will show, was also expected to shape this reality in its satires and humor. Subject to Glavlit, the Central Committee, and KGB monitoring, the *Broom* had a mandate to provide a forum for criticism under the ideologeme of "enduring shortcomings." The *Broom* criticized real events or circumstances—alcoholism, bureaucracy, poor service, irresponsible workers and bosses, and environmental pollution—more openly than any other public media. Therefore, readers remembered the *Broom* as a "gulp of fresh air," while they smirked at and criticized mainstream Soviet media. This state mandate to criticize "enduring shortcomings" also contributed to *Broom* editors' perception that they had relative freedom to create their own works.

Censoring of the *Broom*

Even if the *Broom* had a state mandate to criticize Soviet life, it had to criticize "enduring shortcomings" in an ideologically acceptable way (see chapter 5). *Broom* editors and artists sometimes intentionally, sometimes accidentally failed and were regular targets in censors' reports.[47] The *Broom* was among the most often mentioned magazines from among forty magazines, journals, and newsletters controlled by Glavlit. Glavlit censoring of the *Broom* illustrates that the majority of censored materials related to ideologically unacceptable laughter in the magazine: laughing at authorities, mocking party and government resolutions

FIGURE 4.1. "Expulsion from Eden," by J. Augustinas. The small letters at top read, "Recently the prosecutor's office of the republic uncovered several embezzlement cases." The cart says "Food Commerce," and the lawn sign reads "Paradise." Juozas Bulota, the editor in chief, received a party reprimand for publishing this cover cartoon. *Broom*, 1959, no. 15, front cover.

or political slogans, portraying everyday life in ideologically unacceptable ways, or misrepresenting history. Nevertheless, while some magazines or publishing houses had their editors in chief replaced, the *Broom*'s editor in chief received only one reprimand, in 1959, for a vulgar *Broom* cover (figure 4.1).[48] Česlovas Juršėnas, an LCP CC instructor in 1973–1975 and the chair of print media, TV, and radio division at the Central Committee of the LCP Propaganda and Agitation Department from 1983 to 1988, remembered the *Broom* as "quite disciplined" compared to other magazines.[49]

The year 1968 stands out in the history of censoring of the *Broom*, since Glavlit produced two reports to the LCP CC reflecting on unacceptable *Broom* content.[50] These reports provide unique information: in contrast to other reports, which include only short entries on censored content, the 1968 reports discuss material in detail (see table 4.1). The first report, on print media of May 17, 1968, singled out the *Broom* for having published a satirical message, a feuilleton, and a poem, all considered ideologically unacceptable. The editors were blamed for not being demanding enough.[51] The second report, of October 31, 1968, was a four-page, typed document exclusively on ideologically problematic content in the *Broom*. The October report mentions four unacceptable poems and one satirical advertisement, which were removed from the *Broom*, plus several unacceptable erotic cartoons and a cover, which were published (see table 4.1). It also discussed some works in the *Broom* that had an "unwelcome ambiguous political undertone."[52] Since such a number of unacceptable pieces had never been reported before 1968, it was a signal to the *Broom* to tighten editorial censorship and be more vigilant.

The May report mentions that *Broom* no. 21, 1967, planned to publish a satirical "Open Letter" in which kolkhoz workers expressed dissatisfaction with a new retirement law. According to this law, they would be required to retire even if they wished to continue or were able to work.[53] In this same issue, the *Broom* also planned to place J. Dalgis's feuilleton "Mummies," in which, according to the Glavlit report, loafers are rightly laughed at and condemned, but the author presents a problematic conversation at a nightclub:

> "Hold on, boys. Most likely we will hear something about his fiftieth birthday; I already heard this, dude," warned Alfonsas.
>
> "You are right," spoke Ignas, slowly. "You cannot hide from propaganda even at the nightclub. . . . But does it matter?"
>
> "Where can you find purpose? It's an empty category. A fiction. We all will be turning fifty this year . . ."[54]

This conversation invoked the Bolshevik Revolution, which also turned fifty in 1967.[55] The general negative tone might have also been unacceptable, since literary pieces had to be positive and future-looking (see chapter 5).

The last example of the May report is A. Pabijūnas's satirical poem "Vyriausioji sąžinė" (Highest conscience). In the poem millions of consciences gather and elect the highest. The highest conscience is above everything; nobody has to discuss or disagree about anything anymore or worry about or repent anything. Everything is done by the highest conscience. Yet if you do not comply, you are thrown out of the conscience.[56] The censors most likely disapproved of the implicit critique of the government and censored the poem before publication.

The October report indicates that it was not the first time the *Broom* had published unacceptable materials. In this report, Glavlit director Slizevičius argued that "recently, remarks [to the *Broom*] did not decrease but increase."[57] He claimed that "the magazine often publishes erotic drawings in the Foreign Humor" section.[58] He also wrote that when Glavlit informed the editorial staff about the cartoons, the number of such materials in the *Broom* decreased.[59] In the October report, Glavlit argued that the *Broom* planned to publish a satirical advertisement page devoted to food industry workers. Glavlit expressed its concern about the idea to place a "mocking satirical page devoted to the Day of food industry workers":[60]

> "DEAR CUSTOMERS!"
> Our meat packing plant products, such as—
> C a n n e d f o o d
> "Nevėžis," "Tourist breakfast," "Liverwurst for children," "Liverwurst
>   with milk," "Minced pork," "Brain liverwurst," "Arctic" also
> S a u s a g e s
> "Dawn," "Dew" and similar and so on.
> Y o u c a n b u y
> in the stores of Austria, France, Spain, Holland, Cuba, Yugoslavia,
>   Czechoslovakia, Poland and other foreign countries.[61]

In the published version *Broom* editors replaced "In the stores of Austria, France, Spain, Holland, Cuba, Yugoslavia, Czechoslovakia, Poland and other foreign countries" with "only under the counter."[62] This change conformed to the rule that you cannot praise foreign countries and show any inadequacies of your own. It also illustrated that shortcomings have to be attributed to individuals— salesclerks selling goods under the counter—rather than to systemic failures.

The October report also lists four poems, which had "an unwelcome political undertone."[63] Glavlit director Slizevičius expressed concern that A. Pabijūnas, the author of one poem, had already tried to publish his poem, with a different title, in another magazine:

We are tied like dogs	Nuo visų moderniškų standartų,
To all modern standards,	Kuriais lyg šunes esam pririšti—
(In poetry, thinking, and everyday life),	(Poezijoj, mąstysenoj, buity),
You sometimes wish to escape to a barn,	Taip kartais norisi pabėgt į tvartą,
Tell your name to the rams,	Ir avinams pasakius savo vardą,
And read them something from the	
newspapers.	Ką nors iš laikraščių jiems paskaityt.

In the October report, Glavlit censors also mentioned they had asked the *Broom* to remove a satirical poem, "Everyday Lyrics," by L. Valaitis, which addressed a gap between socialist ideals and reality, and criticized state farm directors:[64]

Our life	Mūsų gyvenimas
is full of poetry	pilnas poezijos
Cities turn beautiful	Puošiasi miestai
As new houses rise.	naujais namais.

And only in passing
    We organize sessions
On issues of trash disposal.

. . . .

Our life
    is full of poetry.
Projects appear
    For saunas in state farms.
State farm directors, of course,
    Will not go there,—
They will have them in villas,—
    who can
        take it away?
So, the life is
    full of poetry.
And with a song
    It's easier to live.

But
we need
    apparently
      more
self-cleaning sessions.

Ir tik, tarp kitko,
    rengiame sesijas
Šiukšlių valymo klausimais.

. . . .

Mūsų gyvenimas
    pilnas poezijos.
Dygsta projektai
    ūkių pirtims.
Ūkių vadovai, aišku,
    kad neis į jas,—
Vilose maudysis,—
    negi
      atims?
Taigi, gyvenimas
    pilnas poezijos.
O su daina
    ir gyventi smagiau.

Tačiau
    apsišvarinimo sesijų
Reikėtų
    matyt,
      daugiau.

TABLE 4.1 Glavlit censored content of the *Broom*

YEAR OF (PLANNED) PUBLICATION/ RECORD IN GLAVLIT REPORTS	CENSORED BEFORE OR AFTER PUBLICATION IN THE *BROOM*	CENSORS' EXPLANATIONS
1957/1958	A cartoon about Jewish people leaving the USSR for Israel (discussed in chapter 2). Published in the *Broom*, 1957, no. 23, p. 5. **Censored after publication.**	Politically unacceptable.[65]
1959/1959	Cartoon on the cover with a man and a woman covered only with fig leaves, leaving their paradise of material wealth escorted by a policeman-angel (discussed	Vulgar cover.[66]

YEAR OF (PLANNED) PUBLICATION/ RECORD IN GLAVLIT REPORTS	CENSORED BEFORE OR AFTER PUBLICATION IN THE *BROOM*	CENSORS' EXPLANATIONS
	in chapter 6). The top of the cover mentions several recently uncovered embezzlement cases (figure 4.1). *Broom*, 1959, no. 15. **Censored after publication.**	
1960/1961	A cartoon with young people running from a village to a city and leaving only old people in a kolkhoz. *Broom*, 1960, no. 18. **Censored before publication.**	Generalized unacceptable message.[67]
	Vulgar cartoons (no other details provided). *Broom*, 1960, no. 15. **Censored after publication.**	Vulgarity.[68]
1961/1962	Feuilleton "A New Fairy Tale." *Broom*, 1961, issue number is not provided. **Censored before publication.**	In the feuilleton an ungrounded general conclusion is reached that kolkhozes in the republic engage in cheating (Rus. *ochkovtiratel'stvom*). Generalization does not correspond to reality.[69]
	Poem "The Misérables."[70] **Censored before publication.**	[no explanation provided].
1963/1964	A satirical poem. **Censored before publication.**	Generalized critique of leading workers of the republic.[71]
1966/1967	A postcard. **Censored before publication.**	An improper (Rus. *neprilichnyi*) drawing on a postcard prepared for publication by the *Broom*.[72]
	A feuilleton "A Duke in the Press." *Broom*, 1966, December issue. **Censored before publication.**	It presented Lithuanian grand duke Vytautas from a wrong [historical] perspective.[73]
1967/1968 May 17 report	Satirical "Open letter." *Broom*, 1967, no. 21. **Censored before publication.**	This letter expresses "collective farm workers' dissatisfaction with the new pension law, which presumably forces them to retire when they could and are willing to work."[74]
	J. Dalgis's feuilleton "Mummies." *Broom*, 1967, no. 21. **Censored before publication.**	The author rightly condemns loafers; however, "without any grounds presents their talk in the nightclub."[75]
	A. Pabijūnas's poem.[76] *Broom*, 1967, no. 23. **Censored before publication.**	[no explanation provided]

(Continued)

TABLE 4.1 (Continued)

YEAR OF (PLANNED) PUBLICATION/ RECORD IN GLAVLIT REPORTS	CENSORED BEFORE OR AFTER PUBLICATION IN THE *BROOM*	CENSORS' EXPLANATIONS
1968/1968 October 31 report	A satirical advertisement suggesting that Lithuania's meatpacking plant products can be bought abroad, indicating their unavailability in Lithuania. *Broom*, 1968, no. 20. **Censored before publication.**	An unacceptable satirical advertising on the page devoted to the Day of Food Industry Workers[77]
	Several foreign humor cartoons with erotic content (discussed in chapter 6). *Broom*, 1968, nos. 14 and 15. **Censored after publication.**	Erotic content[78]
	Three poems by A. Pabijūnas. *Broom*, 1968, no. 19. **Censored before publication.**	Poems have unacceptable political undertones.[79]
	A satirical poem on everyday life by L. Valaitis. *Broom*, 1968, no. 9. **Censored before publication.**	[After reading this poem] "our society can create a wrong view about our life and [that] is not welcome ideologically."[80]
	A photo of a smiling young woman in a bikini. A woman is portrayed in a net like a "fish." A disheveled kolkhoz brigade leader holds the net and claims that such a fish is neither good as a snack, nor could [she] weed [kolkhoz] turnips. *Broom*, 1968, no. 13, cover. **Censored after publication.**	"Such covers made no sense and had no idea."[81]
1970/1971	The cover and a vignette devoted to what would have been Lenin's one hundredth birthday (discussed in chapter 6). **The published issues were destroyed before circulation.**	The LCP CC publishing house violated Section 6 of the "Unanimous Rules" and published the *Broom* without the editor in chief's signatures on some illustrations.[82] (Vilnius Glavlit annual report for 1970, signed January 12, 1971) All published issues of the *Broom* no. 7 were destroyed because of an unacceptable vignette devoted to what would have been Lenin's one hundredth birthday.[83] (Vilnius Glavlit report to LCP CC, May 5, 1970)

YEAR OF (PLANNED) PUBLICATION/ RECORD IN GLAVLIT REPORTS	CENSORED BEFORE OR AFTER PUBLICATION IN THE *BROOM*	CENSORS' EXPLANATIONS
1979/1980	An epigram, which describes that we are drowning in a sea of resolutions, which are rarely implemented.[84] *Broom*, 1979, no. 20. **Censored before publication.**	[no explanation provided]
1983/1984	J. Sadūnas's humor piece "A Meeting in a Sauna," in which he ridicules party and government resolutions on strengthening work discipline.[85] **Censored before publication.**	[no explanation provided]
	Visockis's satirical poem in which he ridicules political slogans.[86] **Censored before publication.**	[no explanation provided]

Note: The table is based on Glavlit annual reports and Glavlit reports to the LCP CC. Shaded rows mark the two special reports by Glavit censors written in 1968. These reports provide the most extensive reviews of unacceptable content in the *Broom* in the magazine's history.

The 1970 Glavlit annual report, signed by director M. Slizevičius, argued that the LCP CC publishing house violated Section 6 of "Unanimous rules" and published the *Broom* without the editor in chief's signature on some illustrations.[87] On May 5, 1970, shortly after the incident, the LCP CC received a more comprehensive description of what happened—all published issues of the *Broom* no. 7 were destroyed because of an unacceptable vignette devoted to what would have been Lenin's one hundredth birthday (see chapter 6).[88] After the 1970 incident, censors did not mention the *Broom* for many years, until 1979. In 1979 Glavlit ordered the *Broom* to remove an epigram, which described people drowning in a sea of resolutions that were rarely implemented.[89] In 1983 the *Broom* had to take out J. Sadūnas's (J. Sadaunykas) humorous piece "A Meeting in a Sauna," in which he ridiculed party and government resolutions fighting for stronger work discipline.[90]

Censorship was also executed by the LCP CC Department of Propaganda and Agitation. Much of the LCP CC critique was verbal, and it was not recorded anywhere. It was also usually post-publication censorship, enacted after the magazine was already published and distributed, and nothing could be changed. In such cases, both *Broom* editors and Glavlit censors were held responsible for unacceptable *Broom* content. In the 1975 *Broom* PPO documents, editors mention that they had received critical commentaries from the LCP CC's Department of Propaganda and Agitation regarding J. Kunčinas's "Kaunas Resident X in Vilnius, Vilnius Resident X in Kaunas."[91] The humorous story presents a Kaunas resident as a judgmental snob excited about material things during his visit to Vilnius. During the discussion at the *Broom* PPO meeting, Pranas Raščius, the chair of the Literature Department, argued that he suggested adding "X" to avoid generalizations about Kaunas or Vilnius residents. Nevertheless, the Central Committee representatives still thought that generalizations were not avoided. Raščius also argued against the Central Committee critique on hidden meanings (unspecified in the report) since he did not imply any subtexts that were attributed to this piece by the Central Committee. In 1975 Bulota had also received critical remarks from the LCP CC's Department of Propaganda and Agitation about a published poem by L. Valaitis that had allusions to the beards of Marx and Engels and was written in a "screaming tone."[92] In 1979 the LCP CC Propaganda and Agitation Department warned the *Broom* about A. Deltuva's cartoon "Matryoshki" (Russian nesting dolls), since, it was reasoned, the cartoon implies that "Russians drink a lot" (figure 4.2).[93] "As a result," argued R. Tilvytis, a *Broom* associate editor, "the drawing is shocking and distasteful, we should be more careful in the future when selecting drawings for publication."[94]

In some instances the LCP CC invited artists to explain their unacceptable cartoons.[95] In addition to disciplining, such invitations to the CC must have raised artists' and editors' vigilance. It is possible that in some instances the LCP CC reacted to dissatisfaction voiced by readers. At least one case is known of a ship captain writing a letter to authorities at the Moscow Central Committee, denouncing the *Broom* for publishing erotic cartoons. *Broom* contributing artist Radvilavičius recalled this case (see also chapter 6):

> Some sailor cut almost naked ladies—but they were not completely naked—from the *Broom* [cartoons], from the "Foreign Humor" section. . . . [The ladies] were beautiful, decent. . . . In Moscow at some kind of CC meeting they showed these cartoons and said, "Look what's going

FIGURE 4.2. Andrius Deltuva's cartoon "Matryoshki" (Russian nesting dolls) was criticized by the LCP CC Propaganda and Agitation Department for implying that Russians drink a lot. *Broom*, 1979, no. 14, p. 5. Courtesy of Andrius Deltuva.

FIGURE 4.3. "Gentlemen, Don't Tell Me We're Going to Die without Fulfilling Our Dream: World War III?!" The figure to the right of the speaker was identified as Brezhnev by a vigilant reader. By Kęstutis Šiaulytis, the *Broom*, 1982, no. 2, back cover. Courtesy of Kęstutis Šiaulytis.

on in the Soviet Union. . . . It's a new bourgeois-type magazine published in Lithuania" [Smotrite, chto tvoritsia v Sovetskom Souize, . . .
eto novyi burzhuaznyi kakoi-to zhurnal'chik, kotoryi vypuskaet Litva].
There was a huge scandal. Bulota [the editor in chief] stuffed sausage,
etc., into his suitcase [Lith. *čemodanas*] and settled everything. . . . [The
one who reported it] was a captain. The captain of a ship. There was a
name, everything. He reported to the [Moscow] CC. . . . You could not
even show the sex. If it was a bull, it couldn't have a sex. Sexless, soulless
[*laughs*]. . . . It was indecent [to show sex].[96]

In another case, an unknown vigilant citizen from Klaipėda sent a cartoon by
Kęstutis Šiaulytis, published as a back cover of the 1982 issue, to the KGB. The citizen cut the cartoon from the *Broom* and wrote "Brezhnev" on it. Šiaulytis's cartoon portrayed American gentlemen discussing their "dream: World War III." The
reader from Klaipėda identified the corpulent, sluggish bodies of the bureaucrats
as Brezhnev and his cronies rather than Western capitalists (figure 4.3). Kęstutis
Šiaulytis argued that he did not draw Brezhnev. According to him, Western capitalists
were usually not portrayed as sluggish, therefore the cartoon characters must instead
have reminded this reader of Brezhnev and his cronies.[97] *Krokodil* artist Boris Efimov and other artists' cartoons actually portrayed capitalists as corpulent figures, an
aesthetic commonly used for drawing capitalist characters. Yet since *Broom* laughter
was often multidirectional, many cartoons could have been suspected of having a
subversive message (see chapter 6). It is possible that the person who denounced the
Broom was not a Lithuanian, since the port city of Klaipėda was a multinational city.

Control of Contexts

Humor, as Tanja Petrović (2018, 203) reminds us, is full of ambiguities, elusive-
ness, and resistance to clear-cut interpretations.[98] Moreover, meaning is "always a
function of context, and every image-object has its social and historical contexts"
(Mazzarella 2013, 196; see also Jevsejevas 2014). William Mazzarella argues in his
study of censoring of films in the 1910s and 1920s, and after the 1990s in India,
that "'contextualizing' an image-object does not tell us everything we might want
to know about its potential. Establishing its meaning does not quite account for
its social force" (2013, 196). Editors and censors developed strategies to contextualize texts and images. At the *Broom*, editors followed *Krokodil*'s contextualization
practices. To avoid ambiguities in anti-imperialist cartoons, soldiers, tanks, and
missiles had to be marked with "US" or the dollar sign to guide readers' interpretation, as in Šiaulytis's cartoon with the American gentlemen (figure 4.3; also
see cartoons in chapter 6). Nevertheless, as the case of Šiaulytis's cartoon shows,
readers came up with their own interpretations.

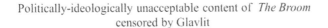

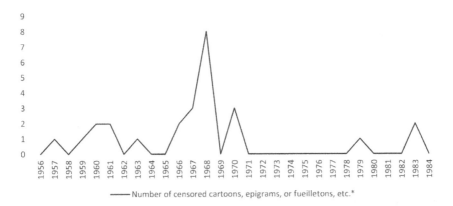

————— Number of censored cartoons, epigrams, or fueilletons, etc.*

FIGURE 4.4.   Glavlit censoring of the *Broom* by year: a distribution of ideological errors in the *Broom* from 1956 to 1984. The table is based on Glavlit annual reports and Glavlit reports to the LCP CC. The year indicates when censored content had been set for publication.

* When the number is not mentioned in the reports, the number is listed as "1." If reports mention several censored items but do not specify how many, the number is "2."

Among the strategies of contextualization used by editors was adding ideological statements to cartoons produced without an ideological message in mind. *Broom* artists rarely drew cartoons on specific political topics.[99] Since the *Broom* had to publish on political themes, and political cartoons were always lacking, editors used to select a cartoon and add an ideological statement to illustrate the "required" ideological content. A cartoon by Arvydas Pakalnis published as a cover of the *Broom* in 1981 could have been one such cartoon. It depicts a salesclerk telling a family of snowmen with two small snow children, "I'm sorry, but currently we do not have any nice clothing for kids, you should come in the spring . . ."[100] Above the cartoon is a quote from the CPSU CC project for the Twenty-Sixth Party Congress: "Special attention has to be paid to the production and quality of children's items." Looking at the cartoon, I wondered how it was published. The laughter embedded in this cartoon to me was not a "positive satire" (one providing a constructive alternative), but laughter at the state, explicating inability to provide for citizens and absurdities they have to bear trying to get clothing. But the cartoon *was* acceptable, since it was contextualized. The authorities could see it as an illustration of the CPSU CC project for the Twenty-Sixth Party Congress. Similar cartoons with snowmen were published in *Krokodil*. If artists were scrutinized about the cartoon, they could point to *Krokodil* as a source of inspiration. However, similar cartoons in *Krokodil* and the

Broom did not have the same meanings. In the *Broom* they could imply criticism of authorities and even anti-Sovietness, because of different historical and political contexts, while in *Krokodil* they were less likely to be perceived as anti-Soviet.

The cartoon "Expulsion from Eden" (1959) by J. Augustinas (figure 4.1) was contextualized in a similar way to the cartoon with snowmen. In the right corner of "Expulsion from Eden," in small letters, was written, "Recently the prosecutor's office of the republic uncovered several embezzlement cases." However, portraying a policeman as an angel might have elicited laughter at the Soviet police as well. Naked figures, religious symbolism of "Eden," "Paradise," "fig leaves," and the policeman-angel created a sharp satire overwriting contextualization. Bulota received a strict reprimand for publishing this cartoon. Nevertheless, it looks like the cartoon itself should not have been received so negatively by authorities. Perhaps the editor in chief had previously failed to comply with the ideological line of the regime, and this cartoon was a last straw, or there were real-life events that contributed to negative interpretation of the cartoon. In the Communist Party documents this is the only recorded reprimand in Bulota's entire career.

Although the state, censors, and *Broom* editors aimed to control ambiguities and guide readers in their interpretations through contextualization, they could never foreclose all possible interpretations or anticipate the contexts in which meanings could be produced. In an authoritarian state, many readers were accustomed to reading between the lines. When free expression is controlled, the search for details and meanings is intrinsic to reading a text or understanding an image (cf. Jevsejevas 2014; Satkauskytė 2018). Thus, censorship control shaped Aesopian language.[101] It pushed authors to create in an allusive and ambiguous way to escape censoring and readers to search for various hints and meanings. In this sense, Aesopian language and censorship were codependent. As Kęstutis Šiaulytis's cartoon with the American gentlemen shows, interpretations surpassed the *Broom*'s editorial control or Glavlit censorship. Readers could have looked for hidden meanings, and vigilant Soviet citizens could inform the Communist Party authorities or the KGB concerning hidden meanings even if they were not intentional, as in Šiaulytis's cartoon. But such cases of denouncement were rare. It is more likely that readers laughed when they recognized Brezhnev rather than reported it to the KGB (see chapter 6).

Glavlit reports and *Broom* PPO documents, as well as censors' memoirs, devoted a lot of time to questions of ambiguity. The *Broom* editors' comments, such as "we passed," "we did not burn down," or "censors did not look for faults," reflected their awareness of multiple potentialities of content. In their memoirs, censors reported that in the case of any creative work they were very much afraid of potential generalizations, abstractions, and ambiguities, which could always imply a criticism of the regime (cf. Sabonis 1992). Lithuanian writer Marcelijus

Martinaitis writes about censors' search for secret contextualizations: he heard that censors read the first letters or words of poem lines to see whether unacceptable words or phrases emerged from them, or they held pages with Lenin's or Stalin's images against the light to see if on the other side of the page there was any inappropriate word written that might be visible on the images (Martinaitis 2003). Sadaunykas recalled that several editors read the *Broom* one more time carefully when the first issue was published, to make sure there was no ambiguous or negative information, such as "Away with the oppressors of the people!" on the other side of the page with the "great leader" (Lenin) (Sadaunykas-Sadūnas 2002, 167).

Algirdas Radvilavičius did not speak in terms of relative freedom to create, but like many other artists he could think only of a few categories that were censored. He claimed that during the Soviet era he was afraid that a cartoon of his might be placed in an inappropriate context: "What if it was published abroad and included [as an illustration] for an [anti-Soviet] article? It would be terrible."[102] One of Radvilavičius's cartoons portrayed a child carrying a birdhouse and a black cat following him. The child was celebrating the spring, argued Radvilavičius. The child would "mount a birdhouse on a tree, little birds would come." Radvilavičius then pondered what would happen if this cartoon was placed next to an article discussing political events in the United States: "It could lead to a tragedy." The cat could be interpreted as the US going to rip apart the new spring birds of the Soviet Union.[103] A similar cartoon with cats greeting spring birds with a welcome sign was drawn by *Broom* contributing artist Jonas Varnas. The cats stand up on their hind legs on birdhouses, holding a poster saying "Welcome" while the birds circle around. This cartoon is another site of multidirectional laughter, with cats being just cats or potentially representing the state, the USSR, or any authorities in power. In one case, Bulota pretended to be naïve and allowed the publication of a poem, "Lady," which spoke about a lady who pokes her nose everywhere, wants to establish her own order, and everybody hates her (*Šluota* 1991, 3). Censors did not even call him; they took the ready-for-publication issue of the *Broom* straight to the Central Committee. The poem was deleted, and Bulota was summoned to the Central Committee for a serious conversation (*Šluota* 1991, 3). The problem was the context; the poem was placed in the *Broom* at the time when Soviet tanks entered Prague in 1968. "Lady" became a reference to the Soviet invasion of Czechoslovakia.

Like Radvilavičius's cartoon with the cat, any theme or image could become politicized because of an image-object potential "social force," as argued by Mazzarella. A desert island could become a political image because its recurrence in cartoons could indicate lack of talent and originality, thus undermining socialism with poor art. A leaning wooden wayside shrine could pass as a cartoon of religious criticism, but it could also express nostalgia for religiosity in a pre-Soviet era. That these multiple potentialities emerge in diverse contexts contributes to our understanding of why censoring power could never be total, why there was an awareness that anything could become a potential problem, or, from another perspective, as many of *Broom* artists and contributors claimed, that there was relative freedom to create.

Relative Freedom

Censorship was relational. It was mediated by relations of political intimacy. Political intimacy among editors and censors made searches for hidden meanings and subversive content unnecessary. Writer and *Broom* regular contributor Vytautė Žilinskaitė recalled that editors declined, without any particular reason, to publish some of her pieces. But Glavlit was different: "You could make a deal with them."[104] She had received the *Krokodil* humor prize numerous times and had a *Krokodil* journalist identity card. She also had connections in Moscow. She knew Glavlit director Slizevičius. She bitterly recalled rejections of her work by Lithuanian editors and questioned their decisions: "In Moscow they did not read Lithuanian. . . . It's only if somebody complained about it." She recalled one of her feuilletons about a big fish swallowing a small fish that censors immediately rejected. The bigger fish was telling the little one, "You will be safe in my belly, you will live well, and eat well. You will feel well." It was about the Soviet Union, Žilinskaitė admitted, and it was too obvious about the paradise in the larger fish's belly.[105]

Magazine editors and censors often had similar objectives—to prevent publication of ideologically problematic content (see also chapter 5). Glavlit censors trusted many editors in chief to deliver "clean" materials; editors in chief trusted their staff and contributors to bring them acceptable work. At *Broom* PPO meetings, literature editors made efforts to prevent ambiguity and apolitical messages, to "make sure everywhere you can feel a political platform."[106] Artists and journalists remembered having followed, as artist and *Broom* contributor Šarūnas Jakštas noted, unwritten rules.[107] Jonas Varnas agreed that "there was an internal censor. It did not make any sense to draw [unacceptable cartoons]. We knew they would not be published. You can try to sneak your thought out, [only if you] mask it diligently. Sometimes we were lucky to mask it well. All [readers] understood [the content], but the editor in chief is not a dumb guy. If he publishes and later deciphers [the hidden meaning], then it's not all right. Then he is not going to publish you for several months, if you make him angry that you deceived [him]. Who wants to be deceptive?"[108]

There is very little data on the *Broom* editors' interactions with Glavlit censors. Kęstutis Šiaulytis, a *Broom* artist and the art editor in the 1970s and 1980s, claimed to have never met a Glavlit censor who approved the *Broom* for publication. He could not meet anybody at Glavlit, could not talk to anybody there; he handed in a *Broom* issue to a receptionist, then came to pick up the approved issue from a designated place.[109] Since the *Broom* was generally trustworthy, in the 1970s and early 1980s Glavlit approval was most likely an automatic process. As the recollections of *Broom* contributing satirist Žilinskaitė or contributing artist Varnas illustrate, artists and satirists knew the censors because they encountered them when they organized cartoon exhibitions, prepared their work for international exhibitions, or published books. Juozas Bulota, who was in his position of editor in chief for three decades, must have known Slizevičius and Gurvičius, who were the appointed director and associate director of Glavlit the entire time Bulota was in office. There must have been relationships that connected the *Broom* editor in chief and Glavlit leadership. It is very likely that various censoring issues were not formally recorded at Glavlit or in other archives. Censoring was discussed by phone or in person, which contributed to its indistinction.

The conflicts that did take place over censored works could lead to the disintegration of political intimacy among authors, editors, censors, and authorities. Romualdas Lankauskas, who worked briefly for the *Broom* in the late 1950s or early 1960s, painfully remembered Communist Party elites' criticism of his work at the National Creative Workers Meeting attended by LCP first secretary A. Sniečkus at the Russian Drama Theater in 1963. The form of his novel *Vidury didelio lauko* (In the middle of a big field) was ironically called "a white guard form" (Rus. *belogvardeiskaia*, i.e., antibolshevik, anticommunist), playing with the associations of the Russian word "form," which could mean "a form" and "a uniform." During Eduardas Mieželaitis's public address as chairman of the LSSR Writers Union at the board plenum in 1963, Mieželaitis (*Literatūra ir menas* 1963, 3) argued that Lankauskas's novel "insulted people who just recently endured all difficulties of the war against fascism." "After this," Lankauskas recalled, "I thought, I am finished. Because after such a speech—[you can go to] prison."[110] Unlike in Soviet novels, which portray the heroism of Soviet troops during World War II, in Lankauskas's novel there are no heroes or war patriotism, no evil-versus-good plot. Two Lithuanian soldiers, one on the Nazi side, another on the Soviet side, do not know why they must die. The book portrayed World War II as a human tragedy. In the case of Lankauskas's work, formalism, pessimism, "bourgeois pacifism," unheroic presentation of World War II and a Soviet soldier, abandoning the socialist realist style, and following Western literary trends were unacceptable. For Lankauskas, the public denigration campaign at the Russian Drama Theater left a deep imprint for many years. In his autobiographical contribution to the book *Rašytojas ir cenzūra* (Writer and censorship), Lankauskas called Glavlit "almighty" (Lankauskas 1992). While Lankauskas's texts were not anti-Soviet, politicization of his work in light of the Manege Affair contextualized it as contradicting Soviet ideological values.

The *Broom* participated in this ideological campaign by publishing a skill-fully crafted parody of Lankauskas's other novel, *Tiltas į jūrą* (A bridge to the sea, 1963), which told the story of a young person in search of life's purpose, lost and unable to find direction. The *Broom*'s parody mocked Lankauskas's style and writing. Lankauskas recalled Rytis Tilvytis's parody as a sort of death sentence, his "execution."[111] Most likely around the same time, an epigram about Lankauskas circulated among some members of the Vilnius creative intelligentsia, ridiculing him personally: "The young are too young, the old are too old [for Lankauskas]. He strolls down the street taller than himself."[112]

The images of "total" and "almighty" censorship describe the process of disrup-tion, disintegration, or absence of political intimacy among authors, editors, cen-sors, and authorities. As mentioned previously, Lithuanian dissidents, some writ-ers, poets, and theater directors, invoked "total censorship" relating to the Soviet history of censorship. Jonas Jurašas, a Lithuanian theater director, claimed in the 1980s that "I simply could no longer stand the conditions I was living under—the censorship, the total control" (1987, 23). He wrote a letter to his censors and "the scoundrels from the Ministry of Culture," which captures the rupture of political intimacy that Jurašas viscerally experienced: "I will never forget that day on the banks of the Sventoji [*sic*] [river] where I was writing it. As I got the last words down, I was shaking and felt ill. I threw up, perhaps symbolically, separating from a sickening part of myself which I had always hated but which I had been forced to live with, as if I'd been serving a life sentence with a boring cellmate" (Jurašas 1987, 26). Jurašas emigrated to Australia in 1974, then lived in Germany, and eventually settled in the United States.[113] Jurašas's experience of censorship as "total control" stands in sharp contrast to the *Broom* editors' views of their relative freedom.

It is hard to say whether censorial indistinction describes other editorial boards, cultural or other spheres. Bulota was known to have "his back covered" (see chapter 1). The fact that he stayed in his position for almost three decades illus-trates that he was able to navigate censorship and assure authorities of his own loyalty. Another layer of protection was his Communist Party membership. As mentioned, other editors lost their positions, and rotation was regular (see Ivana-uskas 2010; Streikus 2018). Nevertheless, some important facts suggest that cen-sorial indistinction might have defined other cultural sites, not only the *Broom*. Vilius Ivanauskas (2014, 656) notes that "the personal relationship between the management of the UW [Union of Writers] and Glavlit influenced decisions in doubtful situations about whether to publish or not to publish a book." Ivanaus-kas (2010, 59–60) also claims that belonging to the official cultural elite guaran-teed various privileges and milder censorship, as these people could access special library collections and have greater influence while communicating their ideas to the public. He argues that writers' and artists' opposition was sanctioned by the system—the case exemplified by banal opposition in the *Broom* as well. In some cases when critical works were published by highly respected cultural elites, the government representatives had to "grind their teeth" (Ivanauskas 2017, 108); in others, critical works were published because censors were not sophisticated enough to capture hidden meanings (2017, 113). Ivanauskas quotes Marcelijus Martinaitis, who tells us that "there was a certain form of protest to do something that was not allowed" (Ivanauskas 2017, 111), which echoes *Broom* artist Šiaulytis's statement "it was in fashion to be against [the official platform]" (see chapter 6). Martinaitis's and Šiaulytis's quotes indicate that certain forms of opposition were integrated into everyday official life. According to Arvydas Anušauskas, the KGB labeled the cultural elites as a "constructive opposition" (cited in Ivanauskas, 2017, 130). Ivanauskas (2010) notes that in the 1960 and 1970s, official cultural elites increasingly supported national ideology, expressed support for ethnic and local interests, and shared indifference toward the regime. He concludes that official cultural elites contributed to the erosion of the Soviet system and strengthening of nationalist processes in the 1980s (2010, 53). According to Ivanauskas, cultural elites who were unorthodox communists (he uses the term "conservatives") had a dominant role in official culture.

Lankauskas's reflection cited in the epigraph about his work at the *Broom*, that "we were more free than others," captures the *Broom* editors' and artists' experiences of censorship in the authoritarian context. Power, including the power of the censoring institutions like Glavlit or the LCP Central Committee, was commonplace and mediated by relations of political intimacy. The *Broom* editors' experience of censorial indistinction, that is, the opacity of ideological control in an authoritarian state, illustrates their codependence with censors and authorities, which helped to maintain the regime itself as well as to advance multidirectional laughter. The artists' and editors' relations to the regime, reflected in their engagements with censorship, were rooted in banal opposition, not dissidence.

POLITICAL AESTHETICS

Life is beautiful, life is beautiful.

—Juozas Aputis, 2007

At the 2007 Turin International Book Fair, the Lithuanian writer Juozas Aputis recalled censorship in Soviet times: "I had written a short story. . . . One editor who had to read this short story tells me, you know, if your hero cries twice 'Life is terrible, life is terrible,' [a reader] will say that socialist life is terrible. You have to change it, [the editor said,] and I changed it. Instead of 'Life is terrible,' I wrote twice: 'Life is beautiful, life is beautiful'" (Aputis 2007). Since the context of the story did not change, "life is beautiful" even more strongly suggested how terrible life was. Aputis's encounter with censors illustrates how authors and editors had to embed interpretations of experiences and shape sensory and emotional perspectives for their readers in an ideologically acceptable way. Nevertheless, their works also expressed their dissensus and were sites of multidirectional laughter.

Although we tend to associate authoritarianism with violence and art with creation of beauty, authoritarianism is an aesthetic project. Authoritarian regimes use art for propaganda purposes, to promote certain perspectives and legitimize state power. Crispin Sartwell (2010, 1) argues that "ideology *is* an aesthetic system" (emphasis in the original). Nazism, Sartwell contends, was an art-political system, as the example of its emphasis on "purity" of the nation and the conception of order illustrates. In Sartwell's perspective, "Whether a political ideology is true or false, admirable or repugnant: answering these questions is not exclusively a matter of understanding its texts or speeches or assertions, but also requires seeing these as part of a multisensory aesthetic surround or context. The aesthetic embodiments of political positions are material transformations and interventions, with concrete effects" (18). Soviet laughter was a venue of materialization of art-politics. The *Broom* editors had to communicate that "life is beautiful," or that it was going to be beautiful in the future no matter what "enduring shortcomings" the *Broom* had to fight against. Censorship implemented political aesthetics by portraying everyday life in a positive way, in accordance with Communist Party ideology. Censorship was thus an integral part of the state's art-politics.

Already in the 1920s, Soviet cultural elites formulated some aesthetic principles for Soviet laughter, including avoiding hidden allusions and metaphors, rejecting "laughter for laughter's sake" (perceived as a landmark of the bourgeoisie's "spiritual idleness") and producing a positive, future-looking satire (Oushakine 2012, 201). Remembering the founding years of the pan-Soviet satire and humor magazine *Krokodil*, Manuil Semenov, its editor in chief in post-Stalinist times, wrote that the self-contented laughter of a snob, a vulgar smile, or a plain and stupid joke was not *Krokodil*'s laughter, which was "permeated with the highest civic consciousness, combatting with the spirit of the Party, with militant truth and justice" (Semenov 1982, 25). The *Broom* editors shaped political aesthetics by promoting reality-based writing that addressed pertinent issues of their time, positive future-looking views, and a focus on real, everyday concerns. They rejected abstract philosophizing, intellectualism, mysticism, and ambiguity. They argued that there could be no literature for literature's sake, humor for humor's sake, but only critical and publicly engaged writing. Commitment to professional writing and high-quality work was part of this political aesthetic, since misspelling a word could shed a negative light on a communist state and be seen as subversive. Literary scholar Algis Kalėda, in his book *Lietuvių tarybinė satyra* (Soviet Lithuanian satire), wrote that satire would be more persuasive and effective if problems are presented at a high aesthetic (Lith. *meninis*) level (Kalėda 1984, 18). Moreover, beyond writing style, political aesthetics were shaped by promoting a certain vision of the world through censoring some ideologically unacceptable representations. *Broom* editors suggested Marxist interpretations of Lithuanian history, rejected positive depictions of capitalism and Western countries, and crossed out vulgar portrayals of Soviet society. As this chapter shows, editors often justified their interventions in terms of professionalism and literary quality of the magazine, which concealed politics behind aesthetics and censorship behind editing, in this way contributing to censorial indistinction, as analyzed in the last chapter.

In the last decades of the Soviet Union, there were almost no traces of censors' work (Martinaitis 2003).[1] Lithuanian writer Marcelijus Martinaitis (2003) ironically notes, reflecting on the interconnection between politics and aesthetics, that most changes were made by authors themselves in collaboration with editors, which means the authors learned about censors' attitudes on "how to improve the artistic level of work." In this chapter I discuss how the *Broom*'s censorship was located in editors' attitudes toward texts, editing, and comments to authors. First, I focus on how editors selected works for publication and how they communicated with readers about their works. Second, I analyze editing of accepted texts. I pay specific attention to editorial changes made to ensure ideological correctness of works. The last part of the chapter discusses the limits of the *Broom* editors' censoring, and their failures to enforce political aesthetics. Since the practice of censoring is very much connected to the suppression of certain content, various editing interventions, as well as the editors' rejection of certain works, can be called censoring. The *Broom* editors, however, did not think of their editing as censoring. From their perspective, they sought to prevent rather than control and suppress, to protect themselves and their authors rather than denounce them. In this chapter I use both terms, "editing" and "censoring," interchangeably.

This chapter discusses *Broom*'s ideological editing of fictional and fact-based pieces—feuilletons, satires, epigrams, and poems, submitted to the magazine by its regular contributors (journalists, writers) and amateur writers. The *Broom* editors' letters of rejection to authors did not mention misrepresentations of reality or ideological incorrectness (the justifications used by censors in Glavlit PPO reports); rather they criticized authors' lack of literary skills, humor, or the overall literary-aesthetic quality of their work. In this respect, the Glavlit censors' conceptualization of editing was very different from that of the *Broom* editors. Unlike *Broom* editors, censors usually were explicit about the politics behind aesthetics.

Selecting Literary Works for the Broom

Since the archives are not complete, the actual numbers of *Broom* submissions that were declined and that were accepted are not known. In the 1970s the *Broom* editors claimed to have fifty-eight contributors, among poets, prose writers, and small-genre contributors.[2] Smaller prose was more likely to be published than longer satires or feuilletons. The acceptance rate of literary submissions from amateur writers was not high, even if the *Broom* officially welcomed submissions from everyone. The *Broom* had high professional creative-writing standards, which many authors could not meet; it is likely that most pieces were written by professional journalists and writers, either *Broom* staff or regular contributors from other presses. To show a diversity of authors, the editors used different names for their own contributions; all *Broom* regular writers and artists had several pseudonyms.[3]

People sent their contributions from cities and villages all over Lithuania, and in rare instances from other Soviet republics.[4] Some authors introduced themselves: a high school student, a kindergarten teacher, a designer, an agricultural worker, an engineer, a driver, a worker. Authors often asked *Broom* editors to write back; they gave their addresses and work and home phone numbers. They requested that editors return their manuscripts if they were not accepted. In many cases they wrote on notebook paper. Some sent contributions on white letter paper, and only rarely were the texts typed, indicating that a submission most likely came from a member of the creative intelligentsia.

The *Broom* editors had ultimate authority to decide about the circle of contributors, the quality of submissions, and the publication of submitted work. If the *Broom* received a promising submission, the editors could ask the author to stop by, so that they could help him or her to improve it. Editing involved hefty rewriting and changing the content to ensure literary quality and to enforce *Broom*'s topical, stylistic, and other standards. For the *Broom* editors it was sometimes easier to borrow an idea from works submitted, to completely rework authors' submissions rather than closely work with authors to prepare their works for publication. As some authors' complaints to the *Broom* show, in such cases editors tended not to acknowledge contributors' authorship. Many contributors, however, did not expect their works to be published unchanged. They sometimes wrote directly that editors could make changes, perhaps hoping to have a better chance of being accepted. Authors also might ask for advice on how to write and what themes to choose. Some authors even apologized for writing and taking editors' time, submissively recognizing their authority.

One man in 1971 wrote that being published in the *Broom* was like winning a car in the lottery. His humor piece, "A Miniature Cake," was about a man who decided not to celebrate his birthday because, the character reasoned, drinking at birthdays is unethical and unhealthy. He started considering this plan with his wife, but soon they realized that it would be impossible. They must invite one family since they were invited by them; some people would come under any circumstances, and if they came, the uninvited would learn about it and would gossip disappointedly. This piece was not very funny; it dealt with trivial issues, but it also connected with the *Broom*'s tradition of satirizing people's small-mindedness. I wondered, as I read it, if perhaps it could have been rewritten and made more humorous.

The author of "A Miniature Cake," a department chair at the Research Institute of Textile Industry, complained in his letter to the *Broom* that he had sent ten or twelve humor pieces previously, and none of them had been published. He wrote that *Broom* editors suggested he learn how to write and look for new forms. All his rejected pieces, he argued, had subsequently been published by other newspapers and magazines. In his letter he presented himself as a knowledgeable scholar and a writer: he had published about four hundred articles, essays, and humor pieces, including some that were republished abroad, and he was a coauthor of two books. He mentioned that he had read the *Broom* starting with its first issue, and he could not see how his humor pieces were worse than others written by authors who were part of the "publishing monopoly."[5] The man wondered, "I often ask: why does the *Broom* not let in any new authors? Why these same names? Is the honorarium more important than expanding the network of active contributors [Lith. *aktyvas*]?" Gediminas Astrauskas, the editor of the *Broom* Literature Department in 1971, responded that the magazine published works by many authors, and his humor piece was not going to be published because it was not original. He suggested the author offer it to "those different newspapers" that had previously published his work, in this way reaffirming the *Broom*'s unquestionable authority.[6]

Jeronimas Laucius, an electrical engineer, had much better luck with his submission: without any publication record, he became a *Broom* author. "The *Broom* was my destiny," he remembered in 2019.[7] Laucius was an associate director of a Vilnius factory. He vividly recalled February 22, 1977: the director of the factory had reproached him at work, and he was driving home, talking to himself in the car. It was as if he heard somebody telling him, "You will be a writer."[8]

"I was born on February 22 for the second time," he recalled. "I stopped the car at Lake Baltis, sat on a stump, and started writing. First time in my life. Started writing. In winter. Alone, alone, in a notebook."[9] Back in Vilnius, he called the *Broom* from a phone booth on Kalvarijų Street to ask if they would accept a handwritten submission. He was afraid to open the door to the *Broom* press; he wondered how he, an engineer, could approach literary people. He received nine rubles for his first text, and ten the next month for another. Laucius said that the *Broom* was "my sanctuary, my road."[10] He used to wait for each issue, stop at the newsstand to ask if they received the *Broom*. Writing earned him a second salary. He started to publish in other media, and later wrote books. Laucius joined the Central Committee in 1980. They did not know, according to Laucius, that he was a writer. He recalled that his coworkers at the Central Committee later teased him for being a poet, and colleagues at different presses disliked that he was from the Central Committee. In 1988 Laucius became the editor in chief of the children's magazine *Žvaigždutė* (Little star). Reflecting on his writer's career, he was happy that he had received an education in electrical engineering. The work at a factory, he argued, gave him important knowledge and an understanding of ordinary people's lives. He not only read the *Broom* itself but also books on logical thinking in order to become a more original and better writer. He became part of *Broom*'s "nice collective," as he remembered it, and enjoyed coffee and drinks with its editors when he stopped by to pick up his honorarium. The *Broom* published about one-tenth of his aphorisms. They were published with his last name or without any name. One of his favorite aphorisms was "It cannot be worse. But it is!" which he had been using to describe life in the post-Soviet era as well.[11] Laucius, who was in his seventies during our interview, still stops by the spot where the phone booth was in Soviet times, the booth from which he called the *Broom* in 1977, to bring that important moment back to life.[12]

The *Broom* inspired people like Laucius to write humor pieces. Some *Broom* authors admitted in their letters to editors that they decided to write because they had been inspired by the *Broom*. While seeing occasional work from amateur writers in the *Broom* might have encouraged them to write, they also felt that they had something worthwhile to say, since the *Broom* published material about the everyday lives of ordinary people.

Archival data suggests that the *Broom* received many submissions, and editors could afford to be selective. In 1971, at least 279 submissions were rejected.[13] In the rejected works, people wrote about speculators, alcoholism, cheating, and generational and interpersonal relations. Emulating *Broom* publications, submissions often included satires with animals. In one response to an author, the *Broom* editor wrote that they were not going to publish the author's quite good work because "at the *Broom* we started a fight against 'the zoo' recently. These animals have been spreading everywhere!"[14] In another response, editors wrote, "Frankly, we are tired of these bus trolley-bus themes. That topic has been done to death."[15] Explaining why another work would not be published, one editor wrote, "We write so much about alcoholism and anti-alcoholism that I really feel like going somewhere and getting drunk."[16]

A lot of creative work by authors was denied publication in the *Broom* because, as editors argued, it did not meet quality literary standards. The *Broom* editors advised potential contributors to better develop the form of their poems; find more interesting, newer, more serious, and more meaningful themes; present original insights; send only their best pieces; and let work sit in a drawer for a while. Sometimes editors got impatient and blunt and told authors that they needed to study literary theory, read, and learn for many more years before submitting their work again for publication.[17] During a public meeting with *Broom* readers, Bulota was asked by a dissatisfied reader how many submissions end in "the drawers of the *Broom*. We also want to write."[18] When authors asked what the *Broom* would suggest writing about, editors in some cases directed them to read and learn from the *Broom* itself. Pranas Raščius, the chair of the Literature Department in 1965, responded to one such inquiry, "What concerns requirements for satirical poetry, please read other works by poet-satirists, analyze poems published in the *Broom*, and you will get an idea of what our magazine requirements are."[19]

Rejection letters indirectly demonstrated the *Broom*'s commitment to shaping political aesthetics in ideologically acceptable ways. Abstract philosophizing was not liked, and *Broom* editors suggested that potential authors write "reality-based" pieces. Authors had to "focus on real, mundane [*žemiškas*] themes."[20] "Intellectualism" was not acceptable; editors invited many to write in a simpler way.[21] Narrow and trivial themes were also not accepted, such as themes concerning quarrels between husband and wife. Works were rejected because they "sound dull" or were "banal," "too long," or "naïve," showed "little humor," or did "not [demonstrate a] sufficient literary level." Recurring facts and developments, rather than idiosyncratic cases, were expected objects of the *Broom*'s humor. Thus, when *Broom* editors asked authors to be original, "original" implied a specific pool of themes usually covered by the *Broom*. At the same time, excessive writing on the same topics was also not acceptable. The chair of the Literature Department wrote to the author of several humor pieces on drinking, "Comrade Stankevičius, we read your humor pieces. . . . [You write] as we say, about 'vodka' themes, which are on the rise. Most likely there is a reason for it. But we cannot publish all, otherwise it will look like people do not do anything else, only gulp down [vodka]. The literary level of the humor pieces is not high either. Good luck!"[22] Different editors in different years added their own reasons for rejection. Unlike other editors at the Letters Department whom Laima Skrebutėnaitė succeeded, in 1980 she emphasized that the *Broom* needed more publicly engaged themes (*visuomeniškesnių*).

Some submissions were rejected because of lack of "sharpness." Cutting satire and "sharpness" were socialist humor tools used to fight against "enduring shortcomings." Khrushchev famously claimed that "satire is like a sharp razor; it shows human tumors and quickly, like a good surgeon, takes them out."[23] Many editors did not consider "sharpness" a socialist or political quality of their criticism, but rather a tool of justice and important critique that benefited people and defended them against the authorities. At the *Broom*'s PPO meetings editors criticized their own work published in the *Broom* for lack of sharpness. Nevertheless, Albertas Lukša, who worked with Juozas Bulota for almost three decades, remembered him as very careful and having stayed in power just because of lack of "sharpness."[24]

Censoring Pedagogy

In 1964 a reader submitted a piece called "The Power of Pedagogy" for publication in the *Broom*.[25] The feuilleton negatively portrayed teachers and students. It depicted how students at one school humiliated the teacher by arranging a trap by the door. When the teacher opened the door, a garbage can fell right on his head. The author of the piece described contemptuously how the teacher tried to free himself from the garbage can. The amused students were looking at the pieces of eggshells stuck on the teacher's nose while the teacher was staring back at them with "little swine eyes." After this incident, one of the students, the originator of the trap idea, was taken to the teachers' break room; other students followed and listened by the door. The yelling voices of teachers and the principal meant that "reeducation" was in progress. After about half an hour, the teachers had to call an ambulance for the student. Although the author of the feuilleton did not go into the details of what happened, there is little doubt that the student was physically abused. The chair of the *Broom* Literature Department wrote to the author of this piece: "Where did you come up with such a school, sadistic students, and bloodsucking teachers? From what country, what epoch? . . . It's not funny here, but my hair stands on end."[26] The editor's reaction was mediated by the *Broom*'s political aesthetic standards—such brutality was not possible in the Soviet Union. It communicated that "life is terrible." The piece could not be published in the *Broom* because it "misrepresented reality," as the editors' questions indicated, even if the events could have really happened. According to Akvilė Naudžiūnienė's study (2021), unsanctioned physical punishment in schools coexisted with other official disciplinary measures against students.[27]

The editor's response to the author of "The Power of Pedagogy" illustrates that the *Broom*'s censoring was pedagogical. The *Broom*'s editors educated its authors, instructing them how to aesthetically imagine socialist reality. Various other submissions that portrayed everyday life in dark colors were not accepted: "Nobody behaves like this on a bus," claimed a *Broom* editor in her response to one author (1968); or "It is hard to believe that a television editor takes bribes."[28] In some cases, submissions were rejected because they were about "unusual problems in rural areas," such as kolkhoz workers using kolkhoz machinery to harvest individual plots.[29] All these submissions most likely were based on real events, but it was only a particular type of reality that the *Broom* could criticize.

Broom political aesthetics advanced certain moral and emotional sentiments encoded in humor. You could not laugh at just anything; editors anticipated specific moral reasoning in satirical laughter. Open moralizing was not acceptable; neither were "altercations" or "declarative statements."[30] In one response letter, the editor suggested not to criticize people for simply picking mushrooms. Maybe, suggested the editor (teaching the author ideologically acceptable moral reasoning), you should have looked at it from another angle: "They are picking mushrooms instead of working, skipping a workday for a boletus or two."[31] Similarly, a fisherman could be mocked for not working, but his statement—"If somebody would pay me a salary, I wouldn't do anything else, I would sit and sit in a boat"—had to be deleted.[32] Editors deleted words about salaries in a short humor piece with a fictional character named Kindziulis. A sociologist is inquiring into a worker who is behind a production schedule:

> "What do you lack most in your job?"
> Here came Kindziulis and stated:
> "A salary . . . "
> The sociologist:
> "What season of the year is the most delightful to you?"
> Kindziulis intervened again:
> "Vacation . . ."[33]

Only the second part, about vacation, was approved for publishing. Mentioning salary was a sensitive topic, since citizens could not question the fairness of the socialist state and its payment policies. Moreover, a socialist citizen could not work just for a salary; one would enjoy the work for its own sake, since it allowed one to participate in building socialism. In such instances aesthetics intertwined with politics—some fictional characters, behaviors, and contexts were not possible because of ideological incorrectness.

Since the *Broom* was at the center of humor culture in Lithuania, it participated in educating other humor producers about political aesthetics. Juozas Bulota, in his 1965 article about wall newspapers, argued that creators of wall newspapers have to avoid vulgar and distasteful images (Bulota 1965, 6). He mentioned that in a transportation bureau wall newspaper, the drunks are portrayed so naturalistically that it is difficult to look at them. He asked, can they be less disgusting and vulgar? (6). At one meeting with satirists, Bulota discussed many problematic examples; some pieces were unacceptable because they compared people with animals or used swear words. One feuilleton was criticized for depicting a drunk person with snot on his face walking on all fours to the outhouse, where he could hardly find his belt. Bulota lectured that "angry laughter" was not acceptable. A writer could not enjoy laughing at shortcomings, as if they would not concern him. A feuilletonist had to "feel responsible for shortcomings occurring, he has to worry about them."[34]

Editors' selection of literary works for publication illustrates that ideological correctness was more important than factual reporting. Public engagement, as well as satirical criticism, was imperative. Sentimentalism, philosophizing, and other "bourgeois aesthetics" were disapproved of. There could be no humor for humor's sake. Laughter, not anger, had to frame characters' emotions. Optimism rather than pessimism was required. The *Broom* promoted a particular humorous or satirical writing style, created certain aesthetic tastes where vulgarity, obscenity, anger, and swear words were rejected in favor of conscientious and responsible humor at the service of society.

Ideological Editing

At the *Broom*, editor in chief Juozas Bulota held the primary responsibility for enforcing ideological correctness. Journalist Albertas Lukša argued that Bulota "had to make sure nothing [unacceptable] would surface. . . . He had to save his own skin."[35] Every literary submission, before it reached the editor in chief, underwent review by journalists or writers at the Letters or Literary Department. Submissions that were accepted for review were typed on letterhead paper and given a final review by the editor in chief, an associate editor, and an executive secretary. Most of these pieces were read by all of them and edited with different-color pens.

The *Broom* editors followed several general content editing imperatives that shaped the political aesthetics of the magazine. A satirist could not generalize about negative aspects of everyday life (they had to be singular or temporary) and had to write in a positive, reaffirming language. Cartoons and satires had to have a positive corrective stance. The critique was to be directed at overcoming temporary shortcomings, survivals of the past. Moreover, as table 5.1 illustrates, certain editing strategies were routinely used by *Broom* editors. Based on my analysis of the editing of submissions to the *Broom*, these strategies can be grouped into the following categories:

1. The government and the Communist Party, and also the highest state institutions and authorities above the city level, were beyond criticism.
2. Socialism was the best political regime, and thus capitalism could not be portrayed in a positive light; foreign goods or relations with foreigners were not to be mentioned.
3. Social and political developments that would present Soviet life in a negative way, such as prostitution, crime, homelessness, unemployment, or lack of rights and freedoms, could not be discussed.
4. Interwar Lithuania had to be presented as an exploitative, capitalist, and nationalist country. Lithuania's history had to be articulated from the perspective of Marxist class struggle; any mention of Lithuania's occupation was censored.
5. In the USSR, nationalities coexisted on friendly terms, and any negative depictions of ethnic groups and nationalities were censored.
6. Vulgar or obscene themes were not acceptable.
7. Religion could not be mentioned except in a negative light and in the context of promoting atheism.

Using these editing strategies, the *Broom* followed the long tradition established in Soviet satire more generally, including in *Krokodil*.

TABLE 5.1 Censoring by the *Broom* editors

CATEGORIES	CENSORED WORDS AND EXPRESSIONS IN SUBMISSIONS RECEIVED BY THE *BROOM*	SUBSTITUTIONS (BY *BROOM* EDITORS)	NOTES AND INTERPRETATION OF *BROOM* EDITORS' EDITING
The government and the Communist Party	**Moscow** (in a sentence threatening to complain to Moscow: "I will show you! I will get [a complaint] to Moscow!")[36]	**The very top** (Lith. *Iki pačio viršaus nueisiu!*)	Unlike other edits in this issue, "Moscow" is struck through with red ink by the editor in chief. It may suggest the importance of it. Moscow, like Brezhnev or Lenin, could not be used casually in a text, especially if it was humorous.
	A minister[37]	**A chair of the food industry department**	The government could not be criticized.
	The government (Lith. *valdžia*)[38]	**Those in charge** (Lith. *vadovaujantys*)	Diffusing meaning, the criticue of the government was not allowed.
Capitalism and Western countries, goods, people	**Do I have relatives abroad?**[39]	**To whom will I write a letter?**	Removing the specificity of the statement by replacing it with a vague phrase; references especially to foreign countries, goods, and relatives were often deleted from texts.
	"Fiat" (a foreign car brand)	**"Žigulių"** (a local car brand produced in the USSR)	Foreign goods should not be desirable, local brands have to be celebrated. The author in the original text mentions "Fiat" in describing a man waiting in line to get a car.[40]
	West Germany[41]	**Germany**	Capitalist countries were only mentioned in critical and negative texts. The author mentions "West Germany," describing a need for new equipment to be delivered from West Germany.
	Foreign-brand jeans[42]	**Jeans**	References to foreign goods were often deleted. According to the original text, "A truck of foreign-brand jeans" was delivered to the store and a customer requested a pair the next day, but a salesclerk pretended not to know anything about it.

Category	Censored word/expression	Replacement/result	Explanation
Social and political developments (which present Soviet life in a negative way)	**Prostitutes**[43]	**Ladies of the night** (Lith. *"laisvo elgesio moterys"*) in a sentence about Geneva	"Prostitutes" might have sounded too obscene.
	Bad teachers, corrupt editors, etc.[44]	Not published	The ideological position was that in the USSR there were no bad teachers or journalists.
	"What do you lack most in your job? . . . **A salary.**"	Deleted	Issues like unemployment or low salaries could not be mentioned.
	Women's rights year[45]	**Women's year** (in a sentence "If the year 1975 is women's rights year, why do we need March 8 this year?")	Most likely "rights" had to be deleted since women were considered to have rights in the USSR, so speaking in terms of rights was unnecessary.
Interwar Lithuania (had to be portrayed in a negative way)	**"Ponia"** [Lith. Miss, Mrs., lady][46]	**"Comrade"**	Using the pre-Soviet "bourgeois" tradition to address a woman by her status was unacceptable.
	"All is ours / Only we are Russians' / Lithuania is not ours"[47]	Not published	Nationalistic poem referencing the history of occupation.
Soviet nationalities or ethnic groups	**Ivanas** (a common Russian name)[48]	**Antanas** (a common Lithuanian name)	Avoiding ethnic references and nationalistic critique.
Vulgar or obscene themes	**"The counter edge deeply creased her doughy thighs"**[49]	Deleted	Too vulgar.
Religion	**"Honor your father and mother, but remember your boss's birthday."**[50]	Deleted	References to the Bible had to be avoided or used only in specific contexts, such as antireligious texts.

Note: A list of censored words and expressions in texts accepted for publication in the *Broom*.

As the table illustrates, editing of the *Broom*'s literary humor pieces involved changing general references to particular (e.g., the "government" to a "local official"), foreign to local (e.g., a foreign car brand, "Fiat," to a car produced in the USSR, i.e., "Žiguliai"), "bourgeois" language and realities to Soviet language and realities (e.g., "miss" to "comrade"). One could not indiscriminately mention relatives abroad, traveling to West Germany, or buying foreign brands of cars or jeans. Writers could not criticize Soviet policies, the highest authorities, or Soviet life in a general way.

To enforce political aesthetics the *Broom* editors *deleted* certain perspectives on everyday realities and history, especially if they were associated with the so-called bourgeois Lithuania or Western countries; or *substituted*, that is, changing unacceptable words or descriptions into those deemed acceptable, shifting emphasis, or reinterpreting (e.g., changing "God" with "god" and anti-Russian sentiments into anti-tsar sentiments). Deleting was the most intrusive type of editing: everyday realities, people, and historical events disappeared, creating a displaced reality. Substitution involved changing an otherwise acceptable original to avoid potential ambiguities, generalizations, or unacceptable political connotations.

A review of published *Broom* issues, along with interviews and archival data, suggests that editors were aware of the need to portray reality in brighter colors. In cartoons, drunks were presented as cute, comic figures with red noses rather than lying on a bench with wetted pants or dirty and reeking of alcohol, as some interlocutors remembered. Rejecting vulgar jokes, one editor argued that they better fit a party table than magazine pages.[51] Depictions of intimacy and sexuality also followed Soviet moral values of modesty and propriety in social and personal life (see Klumbytė 2012). The *Broom*'s editors deleted a wife's advice to her husband about wearing a certain kind of underwear and washing his armpits.[52] One submission described an impolite saleswoman turning her back on a customer; the comment "The counter edge deeply creased her doughy thighs" was crossed out.[53] There were no lice, bedbugs, urination, and swear words in *Broom* texts. Socialist everyday life could not be portrayed in an obscene or cynical manner or with a strong sense of indignation. By editing texts, editors directed readers on how to experience the material world: "R. Diktas [who was just promoted] was in a brilliant mood. He looked with disdain at how people climbed into a bus as if they were flies sticking to honey on bread. He walked on the Antakalnis street without rush, grumbling under his breath: 'Communism is still far away from us. . . . People do not understand basic things—it's healthy to breathe fresh air in the morning.'" Comparing people to flies and creating such a negative image of early rush hours was not acceptable. Editors had to censor a critical reference to communism. All of the above, with the exception of the first sentence, was crossed out. The story started with R. Diktas already at work, taking care of his own affairs.[54]

The general imperative to depict Soviet life positively is implicit in the *Broom*'s silence about deep problems in Soviet society. The *Broom* did not publish about prostitutes or criminals, psychiatric hospitals, or disabled people. Topics of unemployment, homelessness, crime, and militarism emerged only in the Foreign Humor section or cartoons criticizing capitalist countries (see chapter 6). Most readers did not even submit work about prostitutes or criminals; most authors intuitively felt these limits and self-censored. Although authors sometimes failed to articulate Soviet everyday life in an ideologically correct way (as in "The Power of Pedagogy"), the content of the majority of submissions was acceptable.

Broom editing strategies contributed to shaping readers' perspectives of other countries, the USSR, history, society, and everyday life and providing frameworks for how readers should interpret their own experience. Following Communist Party ideological imperatives, the *Broom* had to create a particular aesthetic of good society, happy people, and a just regime in which shortcomings were singular and temporal. While the West was defined by crime, homelessness, unemployment, racism, poverty, violence, and militarism, life in the Soviet Union was overall "beautiful." Nevertheless, as the introductory vignette suggests, editing did not always eliminate subtexts, sometimes purposefully.

The Threats of Satire

Broom editing, guided by Communist Party ideological imperatives, was not necessarily effective. The always present distance between readers and butts of laughter in a satire created space for multidirectional laughter. Writers and editors could hide under narrow-minded, negatively portrayed characters, apparently satirizing them and their ideas and at the same time relating important facts or opinions. Mikhail Zoshchenko, a Soviet author and satirist, especially popular in the 1920s and 1930s, presented unacceptable opinions as perspectives of the "bourgeoisie" (McLean 1963), thus allowing the reader to know that different points of view exist. Since speculators, loafers, hippies, and decadent youth populated the pages of the *Broom*, they could speak about the West, religion, youth culture, consumption, deficits, "bourgeois" Lithuania, and many other topics otherwise forbidden in the public space. Under the guise of criticizing these views, the *Broom* editors shared them with the public. Authors could use negative characters to cast political messages otherwise unacceptable in the *Broom*.

In one unpublished humor piece, a fictional character speaks about Lithuania's occupation. The author describes him in a negative way: he gets on a bus, takes two seats and puts his hat on a third, and proceeds to sing and irritate other passengers with his impolite and provocative questions about imperialism and free Lithuania. He speaks about the tricolor flag of prewar independent Lithuania and about Soviet occupation:

> —All is ours
> But we are Russians'
> Dear Lithuania is not ours.[55]

The *Broom* editors did not say explicitly why the submission was rejected. The official reason was a "lack of humor," this way presumably misrecognizing nationalist "bourgeois" content. While the author of this piece hid his own political message in satirical laughter, *Broom* editors concealed their actual reasons for rejecting it, invoking a lack of humor. Another voicing of Lithuania's occupation in a reader's letter to the *Broom* was reported to the KGB (see chapter 8).

Yet another humorous piece about the Soviet past was heftily edited to express some facts in an ideologically acceptable way by satirizing them, thus distancing, discrediting, and morally rejecting them as the thoughts of an immoral character. This fictional humor piece tells how a woman writes a denunciation letter of her coworker Užbaltienė, who dares to criticize her new dress in front of all their coworkers. The letter writer ponders how to hurt her coworker as much as possible. In the original submission, her letter mentions the following facts about Užbaltienė (parts in bold were deleted or otherwise edited by the *Broom* editor):

> Užbaltienė's grandfather was **a large landowner. Her father killed peaceful Soviet citizens when he served in the German police.** Her brother during the first postwar years hid in the woods and **did the same** [served in the German police during World War II]. As a matter of fact, Užbaltienė herself did not drop far from the tree—**she did not hide that she was against the current regime. Her beliefs, most likely, were inherited in her early youth as well as her habit of taking others' things.** For her type it doesn't mean anything to embezzle from the public![56]

The edited version (changed parts in bold):

> Užbaltienė's grandfather was **a relative of a large landowner's cousin. Her father pleased Germans: when a pig was in their yard, he used to**

take his hat and say, "gut morgen" [*sic*].[57] Her brother during the first postwar years hid in the woods and **worked as a ranger**. As a matter of fact, Užbaltienė herself did not drop far from the tree—**when she was two years old, she turned against the current regime. Already then, she started seizing others' things—she took her friend's doll.** For her type it doesn't mean anything to embezzle from the public![58]

For some readers this piece could still invoke postwar resistance (hiding in the woods), collaboration with Germans, and the prewar landowner class. It also mentioned theft of property and satirized theft as an anti-regime action by claiming that taking a doll from a friend at two years old leads to embezzlement of public property in adulthood. In this way *Broom* political aesthetics integrated potentialities for multidirectional laughter that served and undermined the regime all at once.

Even if *Broom* editors tried to catch potential "political undertones," censoring objectives could rarely be fully achieved because of potentialities of the text (chapter 4). Like Glavlit censors, in some cases *Broom* editors perceived political undertones where they did not exist; in other cases they omitted the embedded undertones. Kęstutis Šiaulytis recalled that if hidden meanings or unacceptable content were not too obvious, the editor in chief would let it get published.[59]

The *Broom* was a primary forum for shaping political aesthetics of humor in Lithuania. Its commitment to professional literary standards meant that it was not open to many amateur writers. Nevertheless, it advanced the image of writing about people's everyday concerns, publishing the offerings of some workers and technical elites among those of journalists and intellectuals, and giving hope to would-be authors that their works might one day be published. The final authority to create political aesthetics, which advanced certain themes and emotional and moral positions, and promoted forms of laughter and satirical writing standards, belonged to the *Broom* editors. Political aesthetics directed readers on how to experience the material world, and framed their sensory and emotional perspectives. While authors' submissions suggest that they engaged this aesthetics while writing satires, feuilletons, or small humor pieces for the *Broom*, readers' letters of complaint portrayed Soviet life in negative ways, telling an often dystopian story (see chapter 8).

The *Broom*'s editors strove for professionalism in their editing and writing to deliver literary quality, humorous content, and relevance to the public, rather than politics and ideology. It is likely they misrecognized some aesthetic strategies, such as censoring obscene descriptions, as connected to ideological imperatives of the state. This chapter showed that both professionalism and literary quality were mediated by Communist Party ideological imperatives. By concealing politics behind aesthetics, the *Broom* editors' censoring strategies contributed to the indistinction of censorship and opacity of ideological control in an authoritarian state (see chapter 4). Nevertheless, editors were not always able to bear their censoring mission easily, nor did they intend to uncritically implement Communist Party political aesthetics. The *Broom* was a site of multidirectional laughter, which most explicitly defined its graphic satire, discussed next.

MULTIDIRECTIONAL LAUGHTER

The opposition was not to the regime, but to its foolishness.

—Kęstutis Šiaulytis, *Broom* artist, 2013

April 22, 1970, was approaching. All newspapers, journals, and other media were preparing to celebrate what would have been Lenin's one hundredth birthday. *Krokodil* would publish a cover with Lenin, world revolutionaries, and communist leaders, emulating Vladimir Serov's painting *Peasants Visit Lenin* (*Khodoki u V. I. Lenina*, 1950), depicting a friendly meeting around a table between Lenin and three peasant men. Andrius Cvirka was entrusted with the graphic design for *Broom*'s contribution. He chose a 1918 drawing by Mikhail Cheremnykh, with a behatted Lenin atop the globe and, with a large broom, sweeping away his enemies: the tsars, a priest, and a capitalist (figure 6.1).[1] Cvirka framed most of the pages with a vignette of hammers and sickles, laurel leaves, red stars, and the number *100* (figure 6.2). The Leninist issue was taken to a printing house. When somebody realized that there appeared to be a hidden message against the regime, 114,082 copies were already in print.[2] Thousands of printed copies had to be destroyed. Andrius Cvirka remembered,

> I took an old cartoon by one Russian, with a globe and Vladimir Il'ych with such a cap [Lith. *su tokia kėpka*] . . . with the broom cleaning imperialists or scum. . . . But I did a kind of nonsense. . . . They started printing. Can you imagine . . . 120,000 [copies]. And you cannot stop it. . . . They printed about half of the issue. They saw terrible sedition, well, anti- . . . anti-Soviet, antistate. I created an ornament, maybe even Birutė [Cvirka's wife] created it, since she helped me a little. From laurel leaves, a hammer and a sickle . . . [and the number] *100* . . . This [was]

kind of an ornament, and I made a frame from it for half of the issue devoted to the anniversary of [Lenin's] birth. But I did not think that on one side *100* looks good, and on the other side it [turns into] *001*.... When they turn a transparent film [Lith. *plėvę*] and attach it, you get a mirror effect. They printed half of the issue, and they had to throw it out in the garbage. There was a huge scandal. Can you imagine, so much paper ... [tossed] into the garbage.[3]

Cvirka had to redo the Leninist issue. He recalled it with irony: "The cafeteria-style diluted color of *kisielius* [Lith., a tart fruit drink made with starch, similar in color to the faded red on the cover], I had to replace with the color of revolutionary blood. [I] defended [the too menial image of] Lenin fervently sweeping [Lith. *besišvaistantį šluota*] by bringing up [similar] images of Lenin [casually dressed,

FIGURE 6.1. The original cover of the issue celebrating the one hundredth anniversary of Lenin's birth, created by Andrius Cvirka (*Broom* 1972, no. 7). Thousands of copies of the printed issue had to be destroyed.

FIGURE 6.2. The original interior border design of the Lenin hundredth anniversary issue, created by Andrius Cvirka (*Broom* 1972, no. 7).

with a cap] in school history textbooks where he was portrayed ... dragging a log assisted by a squad [Lith. *šutvė*]."[4] The major issue was the border on the top of the page. One could read it as *001* instead of *100*, which could elicit laughter that would undermine Lenin and the regime. Moreover, as Juozas Bulota claimed, for some *001* brought to mind the "WC" (water closet, i.e., toilet) sign (*Šluota* 1991, 3).

Cvirka replaced the border of hammers and sickles, laurel leaves, red stars, and the number *100* with a straight red line.

Bulota was summoned to the Central Committee. It was decided to destroy the printed issues, and he had to take responsibility. Bulota reasoned that he was not fired because the CC leaders were afraid to send a negative message about Lithuanian affairs to Moscow (*Šluota* 1991, 3).

It was a big failure for Andrius Cvirka. Cvirka remembered that similar incidents, whether his fault or someone else's, occurred regularly, and Bulota would have to pay a visit to the Central Committee. The Illustration Department had been a source of problems for the *Broom* since the mid-1960s. Many new, young artists who contributed to the magazine in the late 1960s and 1970s were graduates of the Vilnius Art Academy, which encouraged experimentation and independence.[5] They distanced themselves from the socialist realist tradition and introduced new aesthetics (often defined as "modernist" by the artists themselves), which became central to the *Broom*'s identity as a modern Lithuanian humor magazine. The *Broom*'s leading editors continued to condemn modernism and formalism in *Broom* PPO meetings until the 1980s. Cvirka's failure was symptomatic of his and other artists' departure from the principles of Soviet art-politics: *partiinost'* (Rus., commitment to the CP), *ideinost'* (Rus., correct ideological stance and socialist content), and *narodnost'* (Rus., art for the people). During Cvirka's time as the chief editor of the Illustration Department, from 1973 to 1979, Bulota had to oversee the department personally, even soliciting themes in some cases, to boost its ideological profile. In 1975 Jonas Sadaunykas, then executive secretary of the *Broom*, noted that "we have to pay special attention to artists, because they can come up with the devil knows what."[6] In 2014, Cvirka agreed: "From us who were younger, they [the leading editors] could expect anything. Sometimes we did it on purpose, sometimes accidentally."[7] In 1976 Bulota and Sadaunykas recommended the artist Antanas Pakalnis as a potential candidate for the Communist Party, and therefore a candidate to lead the Illustration Department as well.[8] At the same time, it was still expected that Cvirka could improve and organize the artists' work ideologically.[9] In 1978 Bulota complained that Cvirka showed too little initiative, that the Illustration Department did not publish enough cartoons on political and economic themes.[10] He claimed that "Cvirka lives like [he's] in a vacuum. You can make such a conclusion looking at the works he submits."[11] Justifying Cvirka's demotion in 1979, Bulota summed up, "Cvirka is not able to organize work, paid little attention to political caricature, does not put enough effort into balancing with [the] ideological side." Bulota also complained about Cvirka's difficult character and his "dismissing [political] anniversaries in some cases."[12] In 1979, at one of the *Broom*'s Party Organization meetings, Bulota impatiently claimed, "We must revive counterpropaganda. We have to revive political cartoons in the *Broom*. We have to increase the honorarium for political cartoons and decrease the honorarium for simplistic jokes. Let the authors feel it in their pockets."[13] This same year the chairmanship of the Illustration Department was given to Pakalnis, who soon joined the Communist Party.[14]

Cvirka himself recollected that he had purposefully tried to transgress the boundaries of political aesthetics endorsed by Communist Party ideology and to irritate the editor in chief: "You can plant a bomb.... I tried to make as much harm to poor Bulota as I could."[15] Cvirka's *Broom* cartoons illustrate his search for an individual style; his minimalist drawings and experiments with unfinished lines and even blurry images express his dissociation from the socialist realist aesthetic. Cvirka never joined the Communist Party. He was, however, a "kid of the monument"—in 1959 a huge monument was erected in Vilnius to his father, a well-known Lithuanian writer who had worked for the Soviets until his untimely death in 1947 (see chapter 1).[16] Artist Vladimiras Beresniovas remembered Cvirka as "freer than others ... he was not afraid of anything. He did not care."[17] He was "very independent," recalled Šiaulytis.[18] Cvirka's father's monumental shadow protected him. The Leninist issue, however, was an accident, not a "bomb." Even his celebrated father's name could hardly have protected Cvirka if this accidental "bomb" had exploded, causing a scandal.

Most of the *Broom*'s artists and contributors did not try to submit any cartoons with openly transgressive messages. *Broom* artist Kęstutis Šiaulytis recalled that the editor in chief pretended that he did not see hidden texts if they were well concealed. Once in the 1970s Šiaulytis showed his new drawing to Bulota: in the summer a saleswoman sells ice cream, in winter from the same cart she sells flu medicine. Agitated, Bulota crossed out the drawing with a pen, something he did not usually do. "The health sector was a sensitive topic; there was a shortage of medicine. I did not have anything [subversive] in mind," recalled Šiaulytis.[19]

In the 1970s the PPO documents repeatedly note that artists had too little contact with the magazine activists, who were regular contributors to the *Broom*. The artists did not care enough about current events. They scarcely cooperated with other editorial board members. They did not address political, economic, or agriculture themes. The *Broom* was constantly lacking antiimperialist and antireligious cartoons.[20] Unlike *Krokodil*, it rarely published positive cartoons, the poster-like cartoons that promoted communist ideals or celebrated Soviet achievements. Richard Stites (2010, 353) writes that in the time of the Cold War, the overall picture of Soviet life was "a cross between an idyll and an epic." Pastoral descriptions, images of growing prosperity, peaceful and optimistic scenes constituted the idyll, which folded into the epic of "high energy achievements in technology along the road to progress" (353). These themes were portrayed in *Krokodil*, as in the cartoon by Ivan Semenov, "At the Table All Are Welcome . . ." which displayed people of different Soviet nationalities raising their glasses to toast the USSR's fiftieth anniversary at a huge table with an image of the USSR map. At the center of the map were the Kremlin towers, while from the Baltics to Kamchatka various symbols represented Soviet achievements—BAM (the Baikal-Amur Railway), electric power plants, oil drilling rigs, factories, and farms. Andrius Cvirka's award-winning cartoon celebrating the USSR's fiftieth anniversary is one of the *Broom*'s rare positive cartoons (figure 6.3), depicting a full-rigged ship, its sails in the designs of the flags of different Soviet republics. Nevertheless, it sharply contrasts with a *Krokodil* cartoon published on this same occasion. Cvirka's cartoon may leave the reader to wonder where the boat is sailing, who the captain is, and why it

FIGURE 6.3. The award-winning *Broom* cover by Andrius Cvirka was devoted to the USSR's fiftieth anniversary. On the left, upper corner: "Happy New Year!" *Broom*, December issue, 1972, no. 24. Courtesy of Andrius Cvirka.

is an old-fashioned wooden ship rather than the famed Soviet military cruiser *Aurora*. Compared to *Krokodil*'s cover, the Broom illustration's celebratory tone is not forthcoming.

In the 1960s and 1970s various *Broom* editors' discussions at the PPO meetings reasserted the central principles of Soviet art-politics embedded in socialist realism, such *partiinost'*, *ideinost'*, and *narodnost'*. *Broom* editors related socialist realism with correct stances, invitation to struggle (abstract art does not invite one to struggle), accessibility to broad audiences, and artists' responsibility to the masses.[21] They argued that it was imperative to create an artistic language understandable to the masses, which they juxtaposed to the bourgeois style defined by intellectualism and individualism.

Although after Khrushchev was ousted from power in 1964 an anti-formalism campaign paused in the USSR (Streikus 2018, 340), the *Broom*'s editors, as well as some other more conservative culture workers, censors, and Communist Party Central Committee authorities, continued to argue against formalism. In the late 1960s, for the *Broom*'s leading editors, modernist art was still a sign of poor art, lack of professionalism, and artistic immaturity. Executive secretary Jonas Sadaunykas encouraged artists to follow the traditional direction of the *Broom*: "realistic, simple, and understandable to every reader." He reminded contributors about the *Broom*'s tradition from 1940–41, when artists created realistic and simple cartoons. Sadaunykas condemned other styles as technically inept: "All our art has developed in a realistic direction until now. . . . We cannot draw open snouts [Lith. *išsižiojusių snukių*], people-squares [Lith. *žmonių kvadratų*], scarecrows [Lith. *baidyklių*]. Drawing this way shows that you are trying to hide your inability to draw well."[22] *Krokodil* could have been mentioned as an example of socialist realism, but it never was.

At the PPO meetings the editors developed plans to teach and guide artists who were "not free from the influence of Western bourgeois ideology."[23] Artists were expected to go to rural areas together with journalists, so they could get a better sense of the real life to be covered in their work.[24] They were also obliged to attend various seminars for political education (low participation was common among both Communist Party members and nonmembers).[25] Editors' language invoking Communist Party ideological imperatives for *Broom* aesthetics and political education was an example of bureaucratic showcasing (see chapter 3). The leading editors did not reject modernist cartoons, which populated every issue of the magazine. But it is likely that Bulota, Sadaunykas, and perhaps some other editors personally preferred realistic drawings. As late as 1979, Bulota at the PPO meetings was still speaking against modernism or ultra-modernism, even if the artists had been drawing modernist cartoons for over a decade. At a meeting in 1979 Bulota claimed that "ultramodernity and attempts to outcompete the

West will take us in the wrong direction. We have to denounce the bourgeois lifestyle."[26] In the 1970s and 1980s the next generation of Central Committee members took on new leadership roles, including Lionginas Šepetys, the LCP CC's secretary for ideology (in office 1976–1988), and Česlovas Juršėnas, the associate chair of the LSSR Council of Ministers Culture Section (1975–1978) and chair of the LCP CC's Propaganda and Agitation Department of Press, TV, and Radio (1983–1988). Šepetys and Juršėnas, along with other new Central Committee members, were more flexible and pragmatic than their predecessors, such as Vladas Niunka, Antanas Barkauskas, and Genrikas Zimanas, regarding ideological principles (see Streikus 2018, 99). It was during this time that modern trends started to be recognized, to be fully accepted in the 1980s (Streikus 2018, 99–100). Although officially disapproved of during different periods of time, modernist style, unless it created ideologically inappropriate content (e.g., Lenin drawn in an abstract way), was also disregarded by Glavlit censors (see chapter 4).[27]

Artists' achievements continued to inspire them to further distance their art from the socialist realist tradition. In the 1970s, the *Broom*'s cartoons were republished in different Soviet and Eastern European satire and humor magazines, including Bulgaria's *Strshel*, Hungary's *Ludas Matyi*, East Germany's *Eulenspiegel*, Poland's *Szpilki*, Ukraine's *Perec*, Belarus's *Vozhyk*, Latvia's *Dadzis*, Estonia's *Pikker*, and the Soviet *Krokodil*.[28] The *Broom*'s artists participated in Soviet and socialist Eastern European art exhibitions and won prizes.[29] In 1974, the *Broom* won second place in the USSR for graphic design of the magazine.[30] Unlike any other Soviet satire and humor magazine, already in the 1960s the *Broom* published comic strips. While in the 1970s and 1980s *Krokodil* also published more diverse cartoons, unlike the *Broom* it continued to be defined by the socialist realism of many of its artists.

In this chapter I argue that partial rejection of Communist Party ideological prerogatives, an emulation of Western style, and the creation of a distinct graphic art tradition are examples of artists' *banal opposition* to Soviet social, economic, and political developments and the regime's structures of authority. I introduce this term to conceptualize editors' relation to power and their dissensus. While in the Lithuanian language "banal" has a negative connotation, I do not use it that way.[31] In my conceptualization, the banality of opposition is a routinized, commonplace disagreement, which is still acceptable within structures of power, but at the same time threatens to subvert them. It is the opposition within the system itself, institutionalized, and accepted by authorities. This opposition affirmed the boundaries of state authority, while exposing their porousness. Such opposition was expressed in action, such as publishing cartoons in Aesopian language, and in inaction, as in refusal to publish antireligious cartoons.

Opposition is historically contingent and dependent on a particular under-standing of agency. Anthropologists and historians who conducted research outside Western contexts critique notions of agency based on Western concep-tions of rationality, freedom, and autonomy as requisites for political action (see Mahmood 2011 on Egypt; Krylova 2000 on the USSR). The concept of *banal opposition* stems from a particular form of agency, *antagonistic complicity*, rooted in authoritarian structures and relations. My concept of *antagonistic complicity* captures subjects' situatedness within authoritarian structures of work and rela-tionships of authority, at the same time it implicates consensus as well as opposi-tion embedded in action. "Complicity" in popular usage may imply association, collaboration, collusion, commitment to joint actions, sharing of ideas, or con-sent to wrongdoing. It tends to preclude a tension among those who consent and the authorities in authoritarian states. In authoritarian settings, consensus could exist without unity, solidarity, and shared beliefs. Moreover, it can entail conflict, disagreement, and dissensus. By introducing the concept *antagonistic complicity*, I recognize alternative forms of opposition, different from the opposition of dis-sidents or ordinary people to the state, as well as alternative forms of agency dif-ferent from that of a collaborator, a self-interested subject, or a resisting subject.

While artists were creating the Lithuanian graphic art tradition as different from Moscow's, they were not an antistate underground organization. Kęstutis Šiaulytis's statements that "it was in fashion to be against [the official platform]" or "the opposition was not to the regime, but to its foolishness" succinctly cap-ture the banality of opposition.[32] Jonas Varnas similarly argued that "I do not want to brag, but we tried to undermine the Soviet government, but legally, so the wolf is well and the sheep are not hungry."[33] The repercussions that artists faced were reprimands, administrative fines, demotions, or transfers to other jobs, not prison. As Šiaulytis aptly argued, artists "felt that like in other Soviet offices you can do something in opposition when authorities do not see it, but . . . would not get very angry when they found out about these tricks."[34]

Multidirectional Laughter

The *Broom* had to have an ideological direction and implement the Soviet art-politics. *Broom*'s laughter, however, was multidirectional—serving and under-mining the regime all at once. Officially the *Broom* was the LCP CC propaganda magazine, and its editors, artists, and journalists worked on the ideological front. But there was always some humor that made you wonder—how could this be published in Soviet times? Many examples of graphic art and many sat-ires or feuilletons embedded critical messages that were generalized by readers as critiques of the regime.[35] Thus, the magazine could be read as a propaganda magazine or an oppositional magazine or both.[36]

In the *Broom* there were four major categories of graphic art: (1) current-issues cartoons (Lith. *gamybinė karikatūra*); (2) political cartoons (propaganda cartoons); (3) foreign (Western, capitalist) humor cartoons; and (4) comic strips. *Current-issues cartoons* discussed current events, focusing on developments in Soviet economic and social life, such as inefficient work at collective farms, discipline issues in factory workplaces, quality of production, bureaucratization (Lith. *biurokratizmas*), or morality questions. *Political cartoons* reflected political agendas of the Soviet Union, commenting on foreign politics and expressing Soviet anti-imperialist struggles. *Foreign humor cartoons* included graphic art republished from Western magazines. They integrated themes, from bank robberies to sexuality, not covered in the main pages of the *Broom*. *Comic strips* were published from 1966 to 1978 and represented an innovative graphic art tradition in the USSR. Since the mid-1960s, *Broom* graphic art had become a site of rearticulation of socialist realist tradition.[37]

All four groups contained multidirectional humor. Some anti-imperialist cartoons might be straightforwardly propagandistic, but if recontextualized by editors or readers could still be read as a critique of Soviet rather than US or Western European militarism. Some contributing artists, like conservative Juozas Buivydas or modernist Fridrikas Samukas, did not use subtexts or Aesopian language to communicate opposition; others, like Andrius Cvirka, used oppositional messages on purpose or by accident. Cvirka recalled that Heinz Valk, the art editor at the Soviet Estonian satire and humor magazine *Pikker*, made a bet with his acquaintances that in every issue of *Pikker* "he would publish something for which he could be shot and that he would hide it so well that nobody will notice.... The rumors were spreading about it among us. They [the Estonian artists] used to visit Lithuania [and the *Broom*] often."[38] None of the *Broom* artists had a similar agenda. Most of them were careful, but also willing to take some minor risks.

Current-Issues Cartoons

The editor in chief and the executive editor reminded colleagues at PPO meetings that the Communist Party had entrusted the *Broom* with a powerful weapon—the media—in order to fight against "survivals of the past" and various current ills.[39] The Communist Party expected the *Broom* to engage in economic issues, such as industrialization, agriculture, and production, which were central to Communist Party ideology. Related questions of embezzlement and financial violations, bureaucratism, work efficiency, productive labor, work discipline, workplace relations, workers' everyday life, and their morality were targeted by *Broom*'s graphic satire.

Some current-issues cartoons were devoted to fighting with bureaucrats and dishonest managers. Various cartoons poked fun at bad managers for not taking care of public property, failing to serve the collective, laziness, and lack of commitment to the public cause. Officials and managers were also taken to task for their chronic absenteeism and procrastination. On the 1970 cover of the *Broom*, Arvydas Pakalnis's cartoon featured a circle of tables and bureaucrats; every second table was empty, with a note on it: "I'm at a meeting."[40] Bureaucrats were a common object of criticism, since Soviet humor magazines could not criticize anybody above local Communist Party leadership.

Many current-issues cartoons discussed consumer experiences, shortages, and favoritism. Salesclerks were portrayed with their hands in the till or providing poor service; consumers were standing in lines to buy low-quality goods. Some wary consumers brought calculators to stores and tallied their purchases along with salesclerks. A cartoon by Valdimaras Kalninis shows two tables with scales; the bigger table has huge scales that obscure the smaller table, so the customer cannot see the second scale. This cartoon invoked the widespread practice of salesclerks giving short change or overcharging for purchases. Readers recognized the culture of double standards where salesclerks adjusted their scales to show more weight than there actually was, while other consumers, usually acquaintances and friends of store staff, were surreptitiously provided with better cuts of meat, cheese, or vegetables at lower rates and actual weights.

Alcoholism was a serious social problem, regularly emphasized in PPO meetings in the 1960s and 1970s as an important target for the magazine. The *Broom* artists portrayed men as incurable drunks, while women were devoted fighters on behalf of the family.[41] Some women gossiped and craved material goods, but these vices seemed to be minor when compared to the moral degradation of men. A cartoon by Andrius Deltuva depicted two drivers whose trucks had smashed into each other. The men had a bottle in front of them and appeared drunk. Both of them told the traffic police officer writing up the report that they had just had a few shots to celebrate the fact that they had survived the accident.[42] Similar themes occurred not only in cartoons but also in satires, feuilletons, and small prose.

On the surface, current-issues cartoons seemingly served the Communist Party agenda to fight "enduring shortcomings" with tools of graphic satire and humor. Many of the cartoons responded to themes outlined at party congresses, in remarks of General Secretary Brezhnev, or in speeches of the Lithuanian Communist Party first secretary Petras Griškevičius. Cartoons that skillfully dealt with pertinent issues received annual awards. In 1975 Vytautas Veblauskas received an award for drawings on industrial themes, and Arvydas Pakalnis won an award for his cover drawings on kolkhoz themes.[43]

Laughter in the current-issues cartoons was multidirectional: while some cartoons reproduced Soviet ideological agendas, others embedded Aesopian meanings; many cartoons embedded both ideological and Aesopian messages. In 1983 Kęstutis Šiaulytis drew a cartoon with kolkhoz workers waiting for a bus in the hollow of a tree, sheltering from winter cold (figure 6.4). Šiaulytis recalled that he expected it to be published as a *Broom* cover and called "Our bus stop, the best in the district."[44] In the published version, one of the men smiles and comments, "Imagine how jealous the passengers waiting in other bus stops must be . . ." The cartoon was a critique of poor infrastructure at the imaginary kolkhoz called

FIGURE 6.4. "Imagine how jealous the passengers waiting in other bus stops must be . . ." (words in the speech balloon in the published version). The original cartoon by Kęstutis Šiaulytis was published in the *Broom*, 1983, no. 3, p. 7. Courtesy of Kęstutis Šiaulytis.

"Rye." The message of the cartoon was consistent with the Communist Party ideology. This cartoon, however, could be read as a critique of the state's inadequate attention to public spaces, of authorities' inability to serve the working people, or of the regime itself.

The leading *Broom* editors were consistently concerned with low attention to kolkhoz realities. In 1976 at the end of a meeting, Juozas Bulota argued that "we do not spend enough time in kolkhozes, enterprises, we do not know life well enough from primary sources. We have to recognize critically that we have become inert and have taken the easiest way. Therefore, it is important to become deeply concerned about the current situation in enterprises and kolkhozes. We have to talk more to kolkhoz workers, leaders, and other specialists."[45] Since the *Broom* constantly lacked cartoons on rural life, Šiaulytis, a *Broom* artist hired around 1972, made visits to kolkhozes his own personal agenda. He started a "village diary," where he recorded various events, painted, and drew illustrations and caricatures, many of which were published in the *Broom*. Šiaulytis loved these trips, and he continued his diary for many years after.[46] He did not think of his Soviet-time "village diary" as a means of implementing Soviet ideological agendas. Moreover, these cartoons were a site of experimentation with the modern style—Šiaulytis was known for the long noses of his cartoon characters, which also appear in the winter bus stop cartoon.

Šiaulytis's cartoons were an example of banal opposition. The graphic modernism of his cartoons conflicted with Communist Party priorities to produce socialist art accessible to the masses. But it was a concealed form of opposition still acceptable to the *Broom*'s editor in chief, the LCP CC instructors, and Glavlit. He knew how long noses had to be (but not too long!) to avoid irritating authorities. Such opposition affirmed the boundaries of state authority, as well as exposed their porousness.

Political Cartoons

Anti-imperialist Cartoons

Political cartoons engaged politics at the state level. Most often editors and artists called them "anti-imperialist cartoons." The majority of them were directed at the United States, its foreign politics, militarism, and capitalism. From the 1970s on these cartoons were usually published on the back cover of the magazine. As in other socialist and Soviet satire and humor magazines, the West was portrayed as struggling with unemployment, crime, corruption, and the exploitation of the poor by warmongering industrialists and generals. In socialist countries these issues were minor compared to in Western capitalist countries. As Randall Byt-werk argued in East Germany's *Eulenspiegel*, "the major problems are rudeness, defective merchandise, laziness, ugly cars left rusting by the side of the road—and dealing with the threat of war from the West" (Bytwerk 1988).

Cartoons on American imperialism and militarism portrayed the US Army's brutality. American soldiers, although often themselves victims of US militarism, were also negatively presented as violent and criminal "yankees." In one cartoon, a veteran has a sign, "I am looking for a job." A cartoon of a veteran with a thief's mask and a gun suggests he uses his Vietnam experience in civilian life, as a criminal.[47] In another cartoon a happy crowd with flowers and a photographer meet "Johnny" coming from Vietnam. They ask, "What is new, Johnny?" Johnny opens his shirt wide to show the scars on his body.[48] Another cartoon portrays an officer extending his hand to a soldier in a wheelchair who has no hands or legs and saying, "Let me press your manly hand."[49] One cartoon shows two soldiers drinking and pondering going to Vietnam for two months: "Those who come back, they always get acquitted."[50]

The *Broom* had to follow *Krokodil* in its coverage of political events. Discourse on foreign policy was generally framed by Moscow (see Grybkauskas 2016). Kęstutis Šiaulytis recalled,

> We had to draw cartoons that were analogous to cartoons in *Krokodil*. You could not present your own discussion of these events or decide what to draw. . . . You had to draw on the theme that was clearly for-mulated and already drawn [by artists] in *Krokodil*, the *Truth*, or else-where. . . . The Republic of South Africa, the USA, the Free Radio . . . practically there were about ten themes that were known. Racism, oth-ers, you take them and re-create, that is, find a new humorous perspec-tive. . . . These themes were known for twenty to thirty years.[51]

However, the graphic language of enemies in the *Broom* was different from that in *Krokodil*. Boris Efimov, a well-known Soviet political cartoonist whose career spanned the entire Soviet period, considered the role of a Soviet cartoonist to "create laughter" by mocking the enemy (Norris 2013). This kind of laugh-ter demonstrated political consciousness (52). Stephen Norris notes that in the Soviet Union, Efimov's caricatures were held up as examples of a "'healthy form of humor,' one that could produce 'moral laughter,'" where viewers could derive satisfaction and pleasure from, in Vladimir Propp's (2009, 145) terms, "seeing that evil is exposed, disgraced, and punished" (Norris 2013, 52). In *Krokodil*, various generals were portrayed as warmongers planning the destruction of the world. Privates were the robot-like army marching to die, or disfigured men going back home. Some unemployed and homeless former soldiers turned into disgruntled robbers. In *the* Broom, there were almost no monstrous enemies, no grotesque exaggerations of imperialist and capitalist characters.

A cartoon by *Broom* contributing artist Algirdas Radvilavičius portrayed two US soldiers: one is telling the other that he once dreamed of being a general, and now he dreams of becoming a deserter (figure 6.5).[52] His criticism of Western militarism contrasts with the plump and amicable figures of the soldiers. Radvilavičius's propaganda cartoon is a site of multidirectional laughter: the enemy that is portrayed as a relatable human figure becomes a symbol of any military. In Soviet times Radvilavičius worked in the Kaunas Military Commissariat, as a military associate to the chief physician. He was not in the LCP or the KGB. During our interviews in the 2010s, he spoke of saving some people from being drafted into the Soviet Army or sent to military hot spots. It is possible that his negative sensibilities about the Soviet Army were embedded in the cartoon with the US soldiers, making it a propaganda cartoon as well as an opposition statement.

— Žinai, Džoni, kažkada aš svajojau būti generolu...
— Na, o dabar!
— Dezertyru!..

Algirdas RADVILAVIČIUS

FIGURE 6.5. "You know, Johnny, I once dreamed of being a general . . ." "What about now?" "A deserter! . . ." Algirdas Radvilavičius's cartoon portrays the US soldiers as plump and unthreatening figures. *Broom*, 1971, no. 12, back cover. Courtesy of Algirdas Radvilavičius and Donatas Bartusevičius.

The grotesque can also be multidirectional. As argued in chapter 5, writers and editors could hide under negatively portrayed characters, apparently satirizing them and their ideas while at the same time relating important facts or opinions. Serguei Oushakine (2012) has argued in the case of the 1920s–1950s theories of Russian comedy that with their grotesque masks on, Soviet jesters "could tell the truth" (209). Since the grotesque supposedly prevented readers from identifying with negative characters and estranged the satirized message, authorities and censors ignored its potential to deliver oppositional messages.

In the 1960s and early 1970s artists criticized US military actions in Vietnam, Laos, and Cambodia.[53] In one of the cartoons a shadow of the Statue of Liberty is falling on Vietnam, Cambodia, and Laos.[54] In a cartoon by G. Kunickis, one soldier is telling another, "Look, Johnny, now all the world knows our language" as they are walking on a globe with "Go Home" signs posted everywhere.[55] Just a year later, similar graphic ideas were used to express the springtime of communist nations in a cartoon called "Every Spring." In this cartoon the globe is populated by red flags in the same graphic style as "Go Home" signs in Kunickis's cartoon. The globe is also encircled by music notes, suggesting the global spring of the communist nations. An alien in a spaceship overlooking the globe wonders what kind of "interesting phenomena take place on this planet."[56] In the context of the "Go Home" cartoon, one could wonder whether "Every Spring" was not seen by some readers as a commentary on Soviet imperialism. The cartoonist Algirdas Šiekštelės's commentary—"Every spring interesting phenomena take place on this planet"—is ambiguous, making this political cartoon an example of multidirectional laughter.[57]

To avoid ambiguities, all anti-imperialist cartoons had to be marked with a sign, such as stars and stripes indicating the American flag, or symbols such as "US," "$," or "NATO" (see also chapter 4). The same language of signs was used in *Krokodil* and other Soviet humor magazines. In the 1960s some cartoons were also marked with a Nazi swastika. Kęstutis Šiaulytis in 1988 revealed that "US" actually could have referred to the "Union Soviet," not the "United States," by publishing his cartoon in the *Broom* in which two men had a conversation about the "US" symbol while producing moonshine. One asked whether it meant "United States," and another responded, "No, Union Soviet."[58] It was an inside joke of *Broom* artists expressing their banal opposition. *Broom* readers could have laughed at some anti-imperialist cartoons as commentaries on Soviet imperialism, as in the work of Radvilavičius, Kunickis, or Šiekštelė, while accepting anti-Western propaganda in other cases.

Some cartoons addressed social problems in the United States such as unemployment, poverty, and racism, to illustrate that American democracy is unfair to its people. These issues were also portrayed in class terms: the working class was poor, lacking opportunities to seek education, while capitalists were exploiting working-class people to become even richer. This critique of American freedom and democracy also addressed high military spending, taxes, crises, and inflation, which impoverished people. In one such cartoon the Ku Klux Klan is shooting and making a Statue of Liberty silhouette out of bullet holes in the wall.[59] Another image portrays a KKK member holding a detached hand of the Statue of Liberty.[60]

In the *Broom* and *Krokodil*, racism was another topic that artists addressed to expose American democracy.[61] Antiracist cartoons emphasized discrimination against people of color. In one cartoon by Arvydas Pakalnis, an African American boy is looking at an apple marked "college education." The boy, who is standing on three one-dollar coins, gazes up at the apple, which symbolizes forbidden fruit. The cartoon is titled "Fruits of Education in the World of Capital."[62] However, some cartoons portrayed people of color in racist imagery with abundant hair, long hands, sometimes half-naked, and with various accessories. In this way, racist imagery in the *Broom* coexisted with critiques of racism.

For the twenty years for which the PPO archives exist (1960–1979), Communist Party members at the *Broom*'s Party Organization meetings complained about the absence of strong political cartoons and the lack of anti-imperialist and antireligious themes in the *Broom*'s art.[63] Artists rarely volunteered them; the editor in chief had to solicit them. Andrius Deltuva remembered how Juozas Bulota encouraged him to send political cartoons by complaining when Deltuva sent him various other drawings.[64] Bulota accepted even lower-quality political cartoons to fill the gap. At the PPO meetings the editors even considered raising a honorarium for political cartoons to encourage people to draw them.[65]

The *Broom*'s artists often published political cartoons under their pseudonyms, not their real names, since they wanted to dissociate themselves from propaganda art.[66] Such a strategy expressed their antagonistic complicity, the disagreeing consensus, as they enacted banal opposition to the Communist Party agendas. Moreover, many anti-imperialist cartoons were so routinized and formulaic that they were not funny anymore; they were predictable. Readers admitted during interviews that they skipped them, as they skipped the *Truth* editorials or first pages of a book quoting Lenin. The *Broom*'s anti-imperialist cartoons never reached the anti-imperialist zealotry of *Krokodil*, partly because artists had to be very careful while drawing anti-imperialist themes, and partly because it was not the fight they were engaged in. The *Broom* never had an artist like Boris Efimov, whose political cartoons served as a powerful weapon in the state's arsenal against imperialist enemies (see Norris 2013).

Antireligious Cartoons

Algirdas Radvilavičius, who regularly contributed his artwork to the *Broom* beginning in 1962, was among very few artists who drew antireligious cartoons. "Don't think of me as godless [Lith. *bedievis*] or *bezbozhnik* [an atheist]," Radvilavičius said, looking at me with a friendly expression as we drank tea in his apartment in Kaunas. There was a big cross on the wall, right in front of us (figure 6.6). "When the Russians came in 1939, my father served in Panemunė [a suburb of Kaunas city] for Raštikis [the commander of the Lithuanian army]. In his office there was this cross. [Soviets] told him to throw it away. They destroyed everything that was sacred. . . . My father brought the cross from Panemunė on his shoulders and hid it. If [the Soviets] saw that he was carrying it, they would have shot him."[67]

FIGURE 6.6. Artist Algirdas Radvilavičius with his wife, Anelė Radvilavičienė, in their Kaunas apartment, July 12, 2014. The cross behind them decorated their room in Soviet times when Radvilavičius drew antireligious cartoons. Photo by the author.

After the war, around 1948, a police officer used to come to check documents. One asked, bewildered by the cross on the wall, "Where is the portrait of Stalin?" After this visit, Radvilavičius drew a portrait of Stalin and hung it next to the cross. When Christmas came, the priest paid a visit but did not say anything about the artwork. But the police officer was happy to see the new addition.[68]

At the PPO meeting in 1963 Bulota argued that the *Broom* has to "criticize the servants of the cult [Lith. *kulto tarnus*], their greediness, hypocrisy."[69] Bulota said that "atheistic propaganda cannot be only anticlerical. Discrediting servants of the cult should lead to rooting out religion."[70] Atheistic propaganda, when it was published, however, was primarily anticlerical. At the November 23, 1973, PPO annual meeting, in one of his longest statements on the *Broom*'s antireligious agenda, Bulota expressed the magazine's contradictory stance on antireligious propaganda, suggesting the publication should engage in anticlerical propaganda, laugh at illogical religious dogmas, but not hurt believers' feelings:

> [We] do not have to laugh at feelings of the believers. The old people will not turn away from religion. We have to think about our [Lithuania's] youth, so it doesn't get caught into church traps. We understand that religious propaganda from abroad often entangles with anti-Soviet propaganda. . . . Priests blessed nationalist bandits [Lithuanian anti-Soviet resistance forces] and helped Germans. Now they try to reach children through their mothers.
>
> What can our editorial office do? We can show reactionary activities of priests in the past. We have to use our poets; we can laugh at priests through cartoons. We can show that they live very well from offerings from believers. . . . We have to laugh from real facts. Artists could solve this question knowledgeably by laughing at illogical religious dogmas. Atheistic propaganda is a part of our general ideological work.[71]

Nevertheless, like other political cartoons, antireligious propaganda had always been in short supply at the *Broom*. When asked why the *Broom* artists were unwilling to draw antireligious cartoons, contributing artist Jonas Varnas joked that "editors were getting older and did not want to be on bad terms with God."[72] Radvilavičius responded to the *Broom*'s need for antireligious propaganda, but his cartoons were "not against God . . . [but] against the greediness of people. Look, an old lady is giving him money, she is giving to god [Lith. *dievuliui*], but he puts it into his pocket,"[73] he said of his old cartoons. Radvilavičius remembered,

> You take a bunch of [political] drawings to the editor in chief. He takes one, looks at it: "You know, it's a weak drawing . . ." I felt myself that it was very weak. They [still] published it [because they lacked political

cartoons]. OK. Later, they paid a higher [honorarium]. . . . Others do not draw [political cartoons], so the editor in chief does not have them. The editor in chief gets invited to the CC [to explain why this is the case]. Then he tells me, "Draw some [political cartoons]." I say, "OK," and drew more. He supported me, paid a [higher] honorarium.[74]

Many of Radvilavičius's cartoons were anticlerical. Some of them were based on real stories: "This is our Vilijampolė church [in Kaunas]," he says, describing one drawing. "This person [priest] robbed it . . . this butterball. . . . He built his house higher than the church. But this is the truth. It's neither against God, nor against the devil."[75] Yet despite the *Broom*'s Party Organization requests and material incentives to promote antireligious critique, such critique remained scarce in the *Broom* in the 1970s and 1980s.

Banal opposition in the case of the *Broom*'s political cartoons primarily emerged in the artists' reluctance to draw them. At the August 28, 1973, meeting on drawing on political-economic themes, Andrius Cvirka, who was the chair of the Illustration Department at the time, was asked by PPO secretary Tilvytis, "Why do artists participate in exhibitions with great enthusiasm but are not so willing to draw [political cartoons] for regular *Broom* issues?"[76] Cvirka responded by affirming that artists lack enthusiasm to draw routinely for the magazine. The executive secretary Sadaunykas asked him again, more directly, why young artists draw little on political and economic issues. Cvirka answered that they are not prepared for that.[77] Cvirka's evasive answers signaled the *Broom* artists' relative disengagement from Communist Party political agendas.

Foreign Humor

Many readers made a habit of opening the *Broom* from the back, to look at its most interesting section—the Foreign Humor page. Foreign humor was republished from newspapers like the British *Daily Mirror* and *Sunday Times* and magazines like the American *New Yorker*, the British *Punch*, the French *Paris Match*, and the Italian *L'Europeo*.[78] In some cases, the source of foreign cartoons was not known, and so they were published without any reference to their origin, or the magazine guessed their source.[79] In the 1960s, 1970s, and 1980s, foreign humor was published on the last pages (fourteen or fifteen) of the *Broom*.

Some foreign humor resonated with political cartoons; it depicted negative scenes about unemployment, poverty, violence, or lack of humanity among people in Western capitalist countries. One cartoon from the *Sunday Times* portrayed two men dressed as new recruits: "I decided to go to the Army, since I cannot stand violence in civic life . . ."[80] A *New Yorker* cartoon depicted a man angrily asking a passerby for handouts: "Parasites [Lith. *veltėdis*] also have to eat, dear sir!"[81] In one *Punch* cartoon a family is driving a convertible car and complaining about the ugly advertising billboards all around. But when they reach a place without billboards, the view instead is of garbage, broken cars, and falling-apart houses.[82]

Foreign humor was often entertaining without the satirical underpinning of current-issues humor or the reproachful propaganda of political cartoons. While some of these foreign cartoons could have been perceived as a critique of Western life, many readers disregarded the propagandistic messages the same way they neglected the anti-imperialist cartoons on the back cover. They seemed to have enjoyed a different humor genre, jokes that were not otherwise allowed in the Soviet public space, and topics that were censored if used to describe Soviet society. Foreign cartoons, like Western movies, provided a glimpse into another world: cowboys, bullfighting, psychiatrists, suicides, robberies, homelessness, swearing, and sexual encounters. They could also, as Thomas C. Wolfe (2005, 70) argues be "alluring glimpses into lives of ease and abundance, as the inverted image of the relative deprivation of Soviet citizens." Sergei I. Zhuk (2010), writing about the city of Dniepropetrovsk in the 1970s, argued that middle and high school students found Western adventure, detective, and science fiction stories more exciting and interesting than traditionally didactic and boring stories in the Soviet books. Moreover, these Western books were part of the school curricula for "extracurricular reading" (107). In Lithuania, too, Western adventure books coexisted with movies and music from the West. Books by Thomas Mayne Reid, Alexander Dumas, James Fenimore Cooper, Jules Verne, Edgar Allan Poe, and Arthur Conan Doyle were available in Lithuanian bookstores. Zhuk (305) argues that by the end of the 1960s, Western cultural products like jazz and rock music, although traditionally considered to be anti-Soviet, were accepted as legitimate elements of Soviet entertainment. Some music groups were discouraged or forbidden, however, if their repertoires contained harmful ideas: "punk, violence, vandalism, eroticism, religious obscurantism, religious mysticism, racism, neofascism, cult of strong personality, sex, homosexuality, nationalism, anticommunism, anti-Soviet propaganda, and the myth about the Soviet military threat" (Yurchak 2006, 216). Alexei Yurchak claims that "Imaginary West," an idealized version of the West, was an "indivisible and constitutive element of Soviet reality" (2006, 161). As mentioned in chapter 1, according to Yurchak (170), in the case of late-Soviet Leningrad, ultimately the position emerged that "there was nothing intrinsically wrong with being a fan of Western jazz, a follower of Western fashion, or a person interested in the foreign press if one was also a Soviet patriot." *Broom* editors and readers invoked a different symbolic geography by aligning Lithuania with the West and against things Soviet.[83] Thus, cartoons were interpreted in the context of different imaginaries of the West.

These cartoons very likely were also perceived in the context of unofficial humor that portrayed the West in a positive light. Kateryna Yeremieieva (2014), based on her analysis of the Ukrainian satire and humor magazine *Perets*, and unofficial jokes, argues that while official humor presented "Western" enemies, they were absent from unofficial discourse. The West, in unofficial discourse, claims Yeremieieva (28), often was associated with freedom and material prosperity.

Dark humor, which can expose matters that are generally taboo, or issues that are considered painful or serious in a society, was included in the foreign cartoons section: a surgeon showing his patient that he actually attached a foot in place of a hand; a nurse excitedly asking during surgery whether she could take a piece of a patient's body that is not needed for her cat; a child wrapped in bandages in a stroller being pushed by a mother with whips and a flail on her belt; a child following a funeral procession and rolling a funeral wreath like a plaything.[84] Such humor could not be represented by the *Broom* current-issues cartoons, which discussed "enduring shortcomings" and bourgeois survivals, not painful and deep realities. When *Broom* artist Kęstutis Šiaulytis drew a highway with a cemetery as the median strip between the lanes, Bulota told him to place it in the foreign cartoon section.[85]

Censoring of foreign humor was different from censoring of current-issues cartoons, since it described Western societies, not socialist countries. For example, *Broom* artists rarely drew prisoners, and when they did, there was no discussion of prison systems. A prisoner in current-issues cartoons was an abstract figure; artists could play with images of stripes and cell bars to produce a comic effect. In one of the foreign humor cartoons a prison guard is shown feeding an upset prisoner in a cell with a spoon while the prisoner rejects the meal. A guard kindly says, "Take another spoon. . . . Don't be upset, I guarantee—Huggins will be back!" Two other guards are looking through the cell window and broken bars through which prisoner Huggins has escaped.[86] Escaping from prisons could not be discussed in the *Broom*. Moreover, depicting prison guards feeding and trying to comfort a prisoner would be problematic, since it questioned the guards' authority and mocked the state's security system. The cartoon with an upset prisoner represented unreliable prison systems in Western countries. In one letter written in 1970, a would-be contributor wrote that he loved cartoons with prisoners. His own cartoon, which the *Broom* had rejected, depicts a hockey player in a prison-striped uniform aiming at a puck attached with a chain to his skate.[87] As the art editor noted in his response to the author, the leading editors were rejecting themes with prisoners at the moment, even if the cartoons were of high quality.[88]

Kęstutis Šiaulytis remembered that artists occasionally tried to include naked figures in a foreign humor page.[89] Images of a nude body in Soviet print media were rare. Thus, various partially dressed bodies contributed to *Broom*'s popularity. Juozas Bulota was once told by Antanas Sniečkus, the first secretary of the Communist Party of Lithuania, not to publish "naked ladies!"[90] In his notes for a meeting with readers during perestroika, Bulota mentions that the *Broom* was criticized as the only magazine that published pornography.[91] Several inappropriate foreign media cartoons with erotic images were reported by Glavlit to the LCP Central Committee in 1968 (figure 6.7).[92]

— Žiūrėk, kad į kadrą nepatektų rėmai!

FIGURE 6.7. For many readers, *Broom*'s Foreign Humor section was the magazine's most interesting. The caption for this cartoon was "Make sure that the frame is not in the photo!" Glavlit reported the *Broom* to the LCP Central Committee for this and several other erotic cartoons in 1968. *Broom*, 1968, no. 14, p. 15.

The son of the editor in chief (also named Juozas) remembered that his father received a reprimand for publishing an image from banned *Playboy* magazine with the words "Here it is, this capitalist, capitalist world . . ." (in other versions "Here it is, the decadent West!" or "Here it is, America!").[93] Although I was not able to find the image from *Playboy* with these words, it is likely that some images from *Playboy* or similar foreign magazines were published. According to Bulota's son, *Broom* issues with the image from *Playboy* were sold out immediately from newsstands:

> One year father returned from vacation or from a work trip and discovered that the *Broom* had published a photo of a partially undressed woman from the American magazine *Playboy*. It was on the inside of the *Broom* cover with the words "Here it is, this capitalist, capitalist world . . ." Everybody got the message, what this is all about, and all copies were sold out on the same day. When people from the Central Committee found out that such a thing was published, they told [editors] to collect the magazine [issues] from newsstands, bookstores, and so on, from everywhere where the magazine was sold. However, the copies were sold out on the same day, or the next day, so there wasn't anything to collect. . . . Of course, a big scandal erupted, and my father was called to the Central Committee. . . . First of all, it was published from the capitalist world, as they called it then, a "partially pornographic photo." Father received a strict party reprimand "for spreading pornography among the Soviet people."[94]

Portrayals of nude bodies, crimes, and foreign life, justified by editorial boards as "unmasking capitalism," were common in other Soviet magazines (see Streikus 2018, 222–23). Antanas Drilinga, the editor in chief of the magazine *Nemunas*, recalled how he was invited to the Central Committee for publishing the script of *West Side Story*, a musical romantic drama about New York City street gangs. When he defended his publication in terms of "unmasking capitalism" and "contra-propaganda," the Central Committee official told him not to play the fool. "Such contra-propaganda is more effective than propaganda itself! You show forbidden fruit, who would not fall for it! You have to unmask wisely, purposefully, from the Party position" (Drilinga 2005, 173, cited in Streikus 2018, 222). While the *Broom*'s Communist Party members criticized their artists in the PPO documents, in other instances they also justified their art as an unsuccessful search for new forms, stressing that there was nothing political. These presumably unsuccessful searches for new forms were routine manifestations of banal opposition in multidirectional laughter.

Foreign humor could have provided a retrospection on Soviet society and everyday life for readers as well. A cartoon of a woman composing a letter while sitting next to a stroller with her three crying babies, writing "Dear Mother, I live with three other girlfriends in my room," could reference Soviet life.[95] One could wonder if the 1972 foreign humor cartoon about hijacking a plane was not associated by readers with the 1970 hijacking of a plane by two Lithuanians (father and son, Pranas and Algirdas Brazinskas), who killed a flight attendant and made the plane land in Turkey. In the foreign cartoon, a flight attendant is telling the plane captain, "It's a terrible chaos, Captain. All passengers are plane hijackers, and all of them want to fly to different destinations."[96]

Andrius Cvirka remembered how *Broom* artists once created a macabre dark-humor cover around 1968. They followed foreign cartoons and depicted creatures biting each other's heads off.[97] Not long afterward, Cvirka and Rytis Tilvytis went to Moscow to attend the All-Union Congress of Soviet Artists. During the Congress, a speaker asked from the podium if there was anybody from Lithuania. The two men stood up. The speaker noted he would like to talk to them after the event. Cvirka recalled that it was clear that the discussion was not going to be pleasant. Cvirka and Tilvytis decided not to go. Tilvytis later thanked his companion for suggesting he skip the after-talk meeting. Some Latvian attendees later told them that it was about the macabre cover. "Litovtsi" (Rus., Lithuanians) had a poor reputation already then, recalled Cvirka.[98]

Comic Strips

José Alaniz has argued that the Soviet government and most ordinary Russians by the last decade of Soviet power shared ideas about Western comics that could be captured by the words of N. S. Mansurov (1986, 153, cited in Alaniz 2010, 70): "They mainly show adventures using violence and weapons and do not pursue the objective of moral edification. The badly executed drawings foster bad taste[,] and with its elements of adventure and militarism the primitive content produces a defective system of values, ideals and conceptions. The Western comic strip entertains but does not educate the younger generation. Recent Soviet children's publications show attempts to use comic strips devoid of the negative features inherent in the Western comic strips."[99]

In the Soviet Union, comic strips were disapproved of as simplistic, an impediment to "real" reading, even dangerous mass-culture products of the capitalist world (Alaniz 2010). Alaniz (33) argued that initial disapproval of comic strips was also related to attempts to eliminate illiteracy in the first decades of Soviet power and the creation of educated citizens. Artists were expected to contribute positive attitudes, be informative, and provide moral guidance. In the postwar era, comic strips were regarded as light entertainment for children (65), as in the case of the Russian *Veselye Kartinki* (Merry pictures, 1956). Post–World War II Eastern European satire and humor magazines featured comics, including *Szpilki* (Poland), *Dikobraz* (Czechoslovakia), and *Ludas Matyi* (Hungary) (68). The French Communist Party journal *Pif Gadget* and the books by Danish communist cartoonist Herluf Bidstrup were also accessible in the Soviet Union (68).

The idea to create comic strips for the *Broom* first came to Česlavas Valadka, a journalist and satirist for the magazine who created ideas and words for comic strips in the beginning, then intermittently helped Romas Palčiauskas (see figure 6.8).[100] Like foreign humor cartoons, the comic strips spoke about Western realities, and in some years were even signed by Palčiauskas and other contributors with English-version names: Roy Paltchauskas (Romas Palčiauskas) and Charly Walladka (Česlavas Valadka) and Company; or Romas Paltch (Romas Palčiauskas) and Jonas Bool (Juozas Bulota). In 1966 when the first comic strips were published, many households still did not own personal TVs. Children would gather at some neighbor's home to watch short evening programs. Even in the 1970s, exciting visual images, journal picture clippings, or candy wrappers were collected and exchanged by children. In this context, having, exploring, and discussing colorful and action-packed comic strips offered novel entertainment for children and youth. Some readers created their own books from *Broom* comic strips. Children and adults could enjoy thrilling stories of gangsters, Vietnam war scenes, episodes including street shootings, crimes and drugs, strikes and protest actions, pilfering and bank robberies, and sexualized images of women with partly covered big busts and tight dresses.

Comic strips first appeared in the *Broom* in 1966, in issue 24, and continued to be published with some breaks until 1981 (see table 6.1).[101] The first comic strip, *Heart, Knife, and Colt* (Lith. *Širdis, peilis ir koltas*) was renamed *Fred—the Wooden Leg* (Lith. *Fredas—medinė koja*). When the strip about Fred with a wooden leg was discontinued, *Blinda—Leveler of the World* (Lith. *Blinda—svieto lygintojas*) took over. *Blinda* focused on a legendary heroic Lithuanian outlaw who robbed from the rich and gave to the poor. Most likely the artists aimed to invent adventure themes focused on local history rather than the West. *Blinda* was soon replaced by *Jack and Bobby*. *Jack and Bobby* was reminiscent of *Fred—the Wooden Leg* in its focus on Western themes. *The Adventures of Smoky and Pewit* (Lith. *Suodžio ir Pempės nuotykiai*) was published briefly in 1973 (table 6.1).

The most popular comic strip, *Jack and Bobby*, was first published in issue 13 of 1968. Palčiauskas, who drew *Jack and Bobby*, conceded that *Jack and Bobby* most likely was Česlavas Valadka's idea as well. For Palčiauskas, the most difficult

FIGURE 6.8.   Česlavas Valadka, *left*, and Romas Palčiauskas, the founders and creators of the *Broom* comic strips, walk by the editorial office of the *Broom* on Liudas Gira (currently Vilniaus) Street in Vilnius. Photo was taken in the 1960s. Courtesy of Romas Palčiauskas.

part was creating a plot for the strips. He borrowed character types with cowboy boots and hats from American western films. The figures of tall and slim Jack and short and stout Bobby reminded readers of Palčiauskas, who was very tall and slender, and Valadka, who was shorter and heavyset. But the figures, according to Palčiauskas, mimicked famous Danish comic actors Karl Schenstrøm and Harald Madsen, also known in pre–World War II Europe as Pat and Patachon, or as Ole and Axel in the USA.[102] The Kennedy brothers—President John F. Kennedy and his younger brother (and attorney general) Robert F. Kennedy, also called Jack and Bobby—were not Palčiauskas's prototypes.[103] When we met in the summer of 2021, Palčiauskas was excited to hear that the Kennedy brothers were also Jack and Bobby: "Such coincidence!"[104]

TABLE 6.1 A distribution of publication of comic strips in the *Broom*

	1	2	3	4	5	6	7	8	9	10	11	12	13	14	15	16	17	18	19	20	21	22	23	24
1966																								H
1967	H	H	H	H	H	H	H	F	F	F	F	F	F	F	F	F	F	F	F	F	F	F	F	
1968	L	L	L	L	L	L	L	L	L			L	JB	JB	JB	JB	JB	JB	JB	JB	JB	JB	JB	JB
1969	JB	JB	JB	JB	JB	JB	JB	JB	JB	JB	JB	JB	JB	JB	JB	JB	JB	JB	JB	JB	JB	JB	JB	JB
1970	JB	JB	JB	JB	JB			JB	JB	JB														
1971																								
1972																								
1973	A	A	A	A	A	A	JB	JB	JB	JB	JB	JB	JB	JB										
1974														JB										
1975																								
1976																								
1977																								
1978	JB	JB	JB		JB	JB	JB	JB	JB	JB	JB	JB	JB	JB	JB	JB	JB	JB	JB	JB	JB	JB	JB	JB
1979	JB	JB	JB	JB	JB	JB	JB	JB	JB	JB	JB	JB	JB	JB	JB	JB	JB	JB	JB	JB	JB	JB	JB	JB
1980	JB	JB	JB	JB	JB	JB	JB	JB	JB	JB	JB	JB	JB	JB	JB	JB	JB	JB	JB	JB	JB	JB	JB	JB
1981	JB																							

Note: Abbreviations for the most popular comic strip series: *Jack and Bobby* (**JB**); *Heart, Knife, and Colt* (H); *Fred—the Wooden Leg* (F); *Blinda—Leveler of the World* (L); *The Adventures of Smoky and Pewit* (A).

In the mid-1970s, the publication of *Jack and Bobby* was temporarily discontinued. Palčiauskas was interested in animation, so he took another job at an industrial factory to create advertising. While at the factory, he created dolls to produce animated advertising. These dolls were later used for *The Adventures of Smoky and Pewit*, which focused on everyday issues such as shopping or skewed moral behavior, and appeared briefly in the *Broom* in 1973. This new series had to address socialist everyday issues and provide a critique of "enduring shortcomings." There were no thrilling stories, very little action, and no sexualized female characters, since socialist citizens had to be portrayed differently from people in Western countries. Most likely *The Adventures of Smoky and Pewit* was not very popular, and Palčiauskas returned to his Western-style *Jack and Bobby* in half a year. From 1974 to 1977 some comic strips series were still published, but not *Jack and Bobby*. Publishing of *Jack and Bobby* resumed in 1978 and continued through most issues until 1981 (see table 6.1).

Comic strips were published on the last page of the *Broom*, taking the place of the political anti-imperialist cartoons. While *Fred—the Wooden Leg* and *Jack and Bobby* had to expose the evils of capitalist life, many readers enjoyed them for their action, unconventional themes, and entertaining humor. Announcing the publication of the comic strip *Heart, Knife, and Colt*, the *Broom* introduced the leading characters Fred as a superman and Jenny as a sex bomb.[105] There was also Mister Hopkins, a greedy millionaire involved in various financial machinations, such as sending bombs in boxes marked "Flowers for the children of Vietnam." In *Broom* issue 14 in 1968, an announcement about *Jack and Bobby* stated, "Attention! Attention! From this issue of the *Broom*, you will get excited, thrilled, and entertained by *Jack and Bobby* adventures in the country of the freest initiative. You will learn how these unemployed men hope to become millionaires and what happens afterward."[106] Naïve and adventurous, Jack and Bobby get into all kinds of trouble by trying to find jobs and become millionaires. They encounter rich people, bank robbers, and racist militant activists. Palčiauskas remembered that for the editor in chief it was important that they speak about the unemployed.[107] In one episode Jack and Bobby are hungry, so they steal sausage and successfully escape from the police. In another cartoon they realize that people pay a lot of money for dogs, so they decide to create their own business by stealing dogs and then reselling them. In other episodes they try to get benefits for joining the army, fool military personnel by signing up as radiomen, and blow up a minefield. In one comic strip, Jack and Bobby come up with a plan to desert the army by hiding in coffins. When the coffins arrive home, Jack and Bobby climb out, scaring protesters and military officers (figure 6.9).

Comic strips were generally considered a decadent capitalist genre. In 1972, at *Krokodil*'s fiftieth anniversary celebration in Moscow, Juozas Bulota in his speech

FIGURE 6.9. The original of a *Jack and Bobby* comic strip. Jack and Bobby desert the army by hiding in coffins that are flown back from Vietnam. Upon the coffins' return, an army officer orders the funeral director to escape protesters by driving directly to a crematorium. The coffins are covered with Coca-Cola blankets, and the musicians are told to play a tango. But Jack and Bobby and other soldiers emerge from the coffins, scaring the army officer, the funeral director, and the musicians. Courtesy of Romas Palčiauskas.

devoted a good deal of attention to the *Broom*'s comic strips. He argued that the comics were tremendously popular among the young. He admitted that the *Broom* editors had doubts "whether such a serious magazine can use such an unserious form," and that they wondered whether comic strips could become a genre of Soviet political satire.[108] At PPO meetings, editors' discussions of comic strips were shaped by two conflicting positions—condemning them as an art form built on Western influences, and trying to justify them for exposing negative lifestyles in Western countries. On October 23, 1974, at a PPO annual meeting, Sadaunykas, the executive secretary, regretted that the magazine's popularity had dropped after they stopped publishing Palčiauskas's comic strips. He suggested that they should publish the strips again, maybe with another artist.[109] According to Sadaunykas, the "form of comic strips was, it seems to me, quite acceptable, the content even more so—it unmasked the capitalist way of life."[110] Bulota remarked that the *Broom* was the only magazine in the Soviet Union that published comic strips.[111] At one 1975 meeting, Bulota urged artists to think of new forms—for example comic strips, but keeping in mind a realistic presentation.[112] At the same time Bulota himself enjoyed comic strips and signed them as "Jonas Bool" when he contributed ideas, or even when he did not.[113]

Palčiauskas remembered how children used to buy the *Broom* at newsstands and immediately look at his comic strips first. During our interview in 2014, he recalled how others used to say "we grew up with your comic strips." Palčiauskas could not explain why his comic strips were so popular—"maybe because of the action," he said.[114] According to Kęstutis Šiaulytis, Palčiauskas's "American ladies were also running half-naked" in his comic strips; "no question it was one of the important factors of the comic strips' popularity."[115] Šiaulytis argued that "Bulota most likely observed a shortage of this theme in print media, and thus it was useful [to include half-naked bodies] in humorous form, and it yielded popularity for the magazine."[116] Palčiauskas recalled Bulota noting that the circulation went up by eighty thousand. "I remembered it [the number], since I thought that's how many fans I had."[117] According to official publication records, the magazine's circulation did go up in 1969, from just over 70,000 to 114,000. The number never went below 100,000 in the 1970s, and it is likely that comic strips contributed to the popularity of the *Broom*.

Palčiauskas did not intentionally oppose Communist Party ideology in his comic strips. When I asked him in 2014 why he did not join the Communist Party, he said, "It was not for me; all the meetings, bureaucratic things, were absolutely foreign to me."[118] A talented artist, he visualized ideas in his comic strips, shunning the structured bureaucratic life and conflicts at the editorial office and beyond. He introduced a new aesthetic language that was entertaining and exciting, despite the propagandistic content. Comic strips told stories from Lithuanian editors' and artists' imagination—even if under cover of "being critical of the West"—with action, thrilling encounters, entertainment, and adventure, all of which conflicted with the political aesthetics supported by the regime. Readers excitedly embraced this kind of humor. One such reader, who was a child when the comic strips were published, remembered dreaming of visiting the "West" while reading *Jack and Bobby*.[119] *Jack and Bobby* strips, thus, were sites of multidirectional laughter. Unlike Andrius Cvirka, Palčiauskas drifted into the experimentation and opposition that were becoming popular, without intentionally transgressing ideological imperatives.

Banal Opposition

The antagonistic complicity of editors and artists was an open secret. Česlovas Juršėnas, an LCP CC instructor in 1973–1975 and chair of the Press, TV, and

Radio Division at the LCP CC's Propaganda and Agitation Department from 1983 to 1988, recollected that even establishment writers were privately very critical of the regime, but rarely expressed it in public.[120] Generally, artists and journalists did not even try to publish openly subversive messages. In this sense, the story of the *Broom*'s authoritarian laughter tells us more about the official political culture in Lithuania and the ability of a communist state to integrate and absorb certain critiques and opposition than about anti-regime dissidence. Moreover, the banal opposition that emerged in the *Broom* was to some extent an outcome of its editors' privilege and prestige, granted to them by the state. They were considered loyal, and their transgressions were seen as accidental. It may seem paradoxical that Andrius Cvirka, the son of an iconic Soviet Lithuanian statesman and a leftist writer, was the *Broom*'s most independent artist. Artists experimented with style and form, embraced modernist graphic art, and looked for inspiration to Eastern European and capitalist countries rather than Moscow. Their cartoons undermined the political aesthetics of socialist realism. Moreover, some artists used Aesopian language to communicate hidden meanings. None of this was supported by the *Broom* PPO officially. But unless there was an identifiable, ideologically problematic message, the editor in chief, the associate editor, and the executive secretary did not censor cartoons.

Cartoons and stories about pollution, becoming more frequent in the 1970s, and especially in the 1980s, coded a negative commentary about Soviet industrialism. In the USSR, economic growth through industrialization was a primary goal; the government and the military contributed highly to ecocide, the degradation of environment and health, according to Murray Feshbach and Alfred Friendly Jr. (1992). According to Jūratė Kavaliauskaitė (2011), eco-nationalist movements of the late 1980s in Lithuania were also movements to preserve ethnic identity and "Lithuanian Green Organization"–supported sovereignty from the USSR. In the summer of 1988, an ecological protest march through Lithuania advanced the idea to "clean consciousness and rivers" by cleaning pollution and trash from the environment and "getting rid of lies, accepting historical truth, spiritual renewal, freedom" (Kavaliauskaitė 2011, 244). In Vytautas Veblauskas's cartoon, men stand in front of a factory with chimneys emitting dark smoke. They are dressed in Western-style clothing, one smoking a cigar and holding a cane. One says to another, "I bought a shipment of gas masks. They are cheaper than cleaning devices."[121] On the surface the cartoon communicates the author's critique of immoral Western capitalists. However, a reader could see other, hidden texts behind the obvious: it is the Soviet "bourgeoisie" rather than the Western one that behaves this way. The pollution is *Soviet*, and it pollutes *our* homeland, Lithuania. Such messages intensified after the greatest environmental disaster in the USSR, the nuclear power plant accident at Chernobyl in Ukraine in 1986, which released ten times the radioactivity of the Hiroshima atomic bomb. The perestroika movement in Lithuania started as an ecological movement and soon acquired explicit nationalist undertones (see Kavaliauskaitė 2011).

Broom cartoons interconnected with unofficial humor. The *Broom* provided themes and characters for private jokes and language for readers' discontent with everyday life and the regime (see chapter 8). The Voice of America sometimes read Kindziulis's jokes from the *Broom* with the intention to disclose critical discourse in Soviet Lithuania.[122]

Some of the *Broom*'s cartoons resonated with jokes circulating in the private sphere. In one such joke a Russian wanted to buy a car:

> The man goes to the official agency, puts down his money and is told that he can take delivery of his automobile in exactly ten years.
>
> "Morning or afternoon?" the purchaser asks.
>
> "Ten years from now, what difference does it make?" replies the clerk.
>
> "Well," says the car-buyer, "the plumber's coming in the morning."[123]

This joke could not be published in the *Broom*. However, references to unfinished construction projects and the unavailability of plumbers to fix leaky pipes and faucets regularly appeared in the *Broom*'s pages. For those who knew unofficial jokes, the *Broom* cartoon on plumbers could be read in the context of general critique of the Soviet public service economy. It could also be interpreted as a critique of the system itself. Moreover, themes and characters of the *Broom*'s humor were used to create unofficial jokes:

> A good handyman is hard to find, complains a woman.
> Here came Kindziulis and said: "You have to search with a bottle!" (cited in Venckūnas 2010)

> A woman laments anxiously to her friend: "My husband is not returning home from work after so long . . . Maybe he is having an affair?"
> Here came Kindziulis and said: "Don't think of the worst, maybe he just got into an accident . . ." (cited in Venckūnas 2010)

Both examples would be too vulgar and thus unacceptable to be published in the *Broom*. Private jokes ridiculed communism, the Communist Party, Soviet heroes, and Russians, none of which could be published in the *Broom* either:

> A teacher is telling students that soon inspectors will come from Moscow, that they have to tell them something nice. One girl stands up: "My cat just had three kittens. They all want to join the Party." The teacher decides that this is good news to share, so the next day the girl is asked

to share that with the inspectors. The girl announces: "My cat had three kittens. One wants to be a communist." Everybody starts wondering why just one. She adds that the other two opened their eyes already. (cited in Važgauskaitė 2019)

People were complaining to Khrushchev that there was no food. Khrushchev responded: "We are going to communism. Nobody eats on the road. We will eat when we reach the goal." (cited in Važgauskaitė 2019)

The *Broom* artists' graphic art in many cases violated the principles of political aesthetics endorsed by the Communist Party. *Broom* artists and contributors did not comply with the socialist realist imperative to be explicit about content and avoid intellectualism and ambiguity, favored the humor of capitalist countries, and indirectly criticized the Soviet regime. They created disruptions in ideological visions of the state and, as argued in chapter 8, shaped imaginings of socialist dystopia. While modernism became accepted by LCP authorities by the 1980s, the principles of *partiinost'*, *ideinost'*, and *narodnost'* continued to define Soviet art-politics until perestroika. In the end, banal opposition was transformative: when consensus no longer was enforced and supported by Soviet power structures, it disintegrated with glasnost and perestroika. Thus, the Orwellian note ([1945] 1968) that "every joke is a tiny revolution" could apply to the *Broom* as well. After January 13, 1991, when Soviet troops tried to reclaim power in Lithuania, the *Broom* published a special edition in support of Lithuania's independence.

SATIRICAL JUSTICE

It is possible that the power of laughter will be stronger than some articles of the criminal code, and satire and humor will gradually take over and successfully fulfill many court and administrative functions.

—Albertas Lukša, *Broom* journalist, 1958

"Will there be KGB in communism?"
"No, by then people will learn to self-arrest themselves."

—The *Broom*, 1991

On April 1, 1975, at 12:00 p.m., Julijona Siudikaitė, a worker at the Kova (Fight) factory, accidentally ran into a huge tobacco sheet stack near the exit. Four heavy tobacco piles, weighing twenty kilograms each, crashed onto her from two meters above. The manager of her work brigade advised Siudikaitė to return to her workplace. Siudikaitė worked in pain. The next day her pain became unbearable, and she had to go home. The managers persuaded her to keep everything secret. They promised to pay for her sick leave. At a polyclinic, Siudikaitė was diagnosed with "right thigh and body contusion" (Valadka 1977a, 2).

Siudikaitė never returned to work. On that fateful April day, she had broken her spine. At the time that she wrote to the *Broom* in search of justice, she was confined to bed, unable to take care of herself and her teenage son, surviving on a small pension from the factory. Somebody advised her to write to the *Broom*. In 1977 the magazine received her letter about the unfairness of the factory administration. She wrote that if the factory authorities recognized her disability as a work injury, she would have received higher disability benefits.[1]

After receiving Siudikaitė's letter, *Broom* journalists visited the factory. The director of the factory described Siudikaitė as a dishonest person whose injuries were not from tobacco piles, but from a metal carriage she accidentally knocked over. The administration claimed she had been sick with spine problems before. The *Broom* journalists requested Siudikaitė's sick leave reports. Reviewing these reports, they could not find any record of spine problems. Then they visited Siudikaitė at the hospital. She couldn't sit; she could hardly stand with a cane. She told the *Broom* journalists that "I cannot say when I [last] worked. . . . The factory allocated me a two-room apartment. But when I got injured [they tried to hide the case]. At the Polyclinic No. 1, they told me that it's too late. [If] they had acted right away, they could have helped, but as time passed, my spine became permanently crooked. I will have to go through a third surgery, otherwise my legs may get paralyzed" (Valadka 1977a, 3). The *Broom* journalists asked if her coworkers and representatives from the trade union visited her at the hospital. But "instead of a response, a tear of bitterness ran down the cheek of a communist shock worker" (Lith. *komunistinio darbo spartuolės skruostu*) (3).[2] She wished she could take care of her fourteen-year-old son (3).

The fact that the spine injury was not recognized and diagnosed in the beginning was used by the factory administration to argue that her spine problems were unrelated to the accident at work. In June 1977, *Broom* journalist Česlovas Valadka published an article, "Be Careful—a Human Being!" on Siudikaitė's case. Valadka argued that satirists have to be objective and that all the facts made him think that the factory administration was wrong (Valadka 1977a, 2–3). He mentioned that Siudikaitė's case was concealed because a serious work injury would have compromised the reputation of the department where she worked, as well as affect factory socialist competition ratings (2–3). The administration continued to neglect safety requirements, since tobacco stacks were not taken away from the exit (3).

Valadka's article was sent to several state institutions. On August 10, 1977, the *Broom* received a response from the Republic Prosecutor's Office, assuring them there was no doubt regarding the conclusions made by the competent medical commissions. Lithuania's Trade Union Council, the LSSR Ministry for Social Services, and the LSSR Health Care Ministry, however, recognized that the injury was work related. At the PPO meeting, the *Broom* editors concluded that "the employees of the Republic Prosecutor's Office most likely did not examine the matter well enough."[3] In October the *Broom* published a note to readers on this case, saying that J. Antanaitis, the Lithuanian Republic Trade Union Council secretary, confirmed that the council and Kaunas city health care experts had reviewed Siudikaitė's case again and established that the initial decision about the disability was incorrect (Valadka 1977b, 15). The factory administration was ordered to pay Siudikaitė injury benefits every month.

Two years passed. On November 1, 1979, another letter from Siudikaitė, this one seven pages long, reached the *Broom*. This time Siudikaitė asked for the *Broom*'s help receiving compensation for her injuries from the insurance agency. Siudikaitė wrote with a deep sense of injustice: "They did not respond to my complaints ... then they responded that the Polyclinic had not given them accurate documents. ... All year round I went there [to the Kaunas City State Insurance Office], stood on stairs in pain by the door of the Commission. Just to hear that I was sick only ten days because of this injury . . . and that they will pay me for a minor injury. . . . I received fifty rubles."[4] She also cited the Lithuanian SSR Chief State Insurance Board decision of March 14, 1979, which overruled the previous decision to pay her insurance benefits for a minor injury; it stated that she should not have received any insurance for her minor contusions.

There are few details mentioned about Siudikaitė's life outside the workplace and unrelated to her injury in her letters, *Broom* publications, or *Broom* journalist correspondence with other institutions. She introduces herself by stating that she has worked at the factory for nineteen years and claims to be a good worker: "I always put an effort to fulfill socialist obligations as much as I could (Lith. *įsipareigojimai*). I did not get any fines, did not commit any misdemeanors." She had received recognition as a Communist Work Achiever (Lith. *darbo spartuolis*) in 1968. The *Broom* journalist calls Siudikaitė a Stakhanovite—hardworking and productive—most likely to introduce her as a good person and gain sympathy from *Broom* readers and representatives of institutions in charge of Siudikaitė's case. According to the published article in the *Broom*, she often suffered from ulcers before the accident. It is likely she was not married, since in Soviet times most Lithuanian married women changed their surnames to their husbands', adding the ending "-ienė." Her letter of 1979 has many grammatical mistakes. Her 1977 letter, in contrast, is written with a typewriter and has few grammatical mistakes. Most likely she wrote it with somebody's help, since typewriters were not owned by ordinary people. Nevertheless, her letters give an impression of Siudikaitė as a competent complaint writer. She effectively presents herself as a vulnerable person suffering from injustices inflicted by unfair state institutions. She also includes important, detailed evidence on her case: a thorough description of the accident, doctors' decisions, the dates of sick leaves and hospitalizations, and verbatim citations from correspondence with the insurance office.

Siudikaitė's predicament illustrates how the *Broom* acted as an institution of satirical justice through journalistic investigation, public exposure, and satirical critique. I use the concept of *satirical justice* to refer to fairness restored or propagated using media exposure, public social critique, derision, ridicule, caricature, or shaming into improvement. The *Broom*'s satirical justice in some instances fulfilled legal and administrative functions when other state institutions failed. Although *Broom* journalists celebrated their work as bringing justice to "ordinary people" such as Siudikaitė, I show that satirical justice was intrinsic to authoritarian state governance and reaffirmed its structural injustices. In its own way, as discussed below, satirical justice reproduced the harm people experienced as a result of centralized power and Communist Party authority and the structural processes that minimized opportunities for some people to achieve the quality of life that otherwise might have been possible (cf. Young 2003).

Satirical justice was integral to authoritarian governance: first, it reaffirmed the authority of the state; second, it was justice by fear and negative publicity; and third, it served state preventive and propaganda aims. These three aspects of satirical justice contributed to reproducing structural injustices. Through censorship, the *Broom* foreclosed the possibility of potential disputes on systemic redistribution of resources, rights, and freedoms, and on a good life as imagined by *Broom* readers rather than Communist Party ideologues. Moreover, *satirical justice* was a journalism of public exposure and shaming, disciplining, and fear. It was selective and partial; it punished some "ordinary people" like shop salesclerks, while ignoring injustices perpetrated by state officials. Emil Draitser (2021, 117), a Soviet-time freelance contributor to *Krokodil*, wrote that "a Soviet satirist is hardly the same as an investigative journalist in the West. His job is not to dig out some unseemly truths about, say, corruption or abuse of power. Mostly, he ridicules things the state apparatus has proved wrong and worthy of criticism." According to Draitser (176), it was common to blame "some little man for any of the system's faults." Factory administration, as in Siudikaitė's case, were the highest-level officials the *Broom* could criticize. Some interlocutors remembered that their teachers or coworkers were afraid of becoming objects of the *Broom*'s negative media publicity. Nevertheless, they remembered satirical justice positively in the absence of a functioning legal and administrative system. Some bureaucrats, collective farm managers, or factory leaders did get punished, even if these punishments were not systematic, as argued below. After *Broom* journalists' investigations they received reprimands, fines, were transferred, or even fired from jobs.

Letters to the media like Siudikaitė's usually were a measure of last resort. In his speech of September 12, 1984, celebrating the fiftieth anniversary of the *Broom*, Juozas Bulota noted that people called for help when they "could not find it anywhere else."[5] For many people seeking justice could have been an ordeal that lasted several years. The indifference and lack of accountability of multiple institutions recorded in readers' complaints ranged from factory administration to doctors to the Republic Prosecutor's Office. Editors claimed in the PPO reports that in some cases the *Broom* restored justice for an "ordinary worker" when official and legal institutions failed. Yet even if the *Broom* occasionally restored justice, it functioned like any other state institution in many respects: it could not launch journalistic investigation in every case; the most important cases had to be approved by the Central Committee before publication; it re-sent letters to often unresponsive institutions in other cases; and it used the letters as a measure of prophylactic disciplining and propaganda. Following the Communist Party principle of "enduring shortcomings," which declared that shortcomings are singular and temporal, *Broom* journalists often attributed blame and responsibility to single individuals without addressing structural injustices.

The *Broom* was part of the USSR's system of journalism, which was an instrument of consolidation of Soviet power and a "weapon" in class struggle. Critical participation of citizens in state governance was the Marxist ideal integrated into Communist Party ideology and policy on communication with the "masses."[6] During the entire Soviet period, people sent letters to Soviet political leaders, party and government agencies, public figures, journals and newspapers. Those letters consisted of complaints, denunciations, petitions, requests for assistance, confessional declarations, airing of opinion, and threats (Fitzpatrick 1996a). Sheila Fitzpatrick (1996b, 837) defines a denunciation as "a written communication to the authorities, voluntarily offered, that provides damaging information about another person." In Stalinist Russia, as studies show, whistleblowing could be on behalf of others, seeking to restore justice and accountability (cf. Fitzpatrick 1996b). The letters to the *Broom* most often were personal grievances. The major intent of the complaint writer was to express injustices suffered and restore justice, not to accuse others of wrongdoings, even if wrongdoings were mentioned. In some instances, these grievances did not even mention the names of the accused. Letters to the *Broom* also lack the revolutionary rhetoric of letters written in the Stalinist period in Soviet Russia. There is little talk about loyalties to the regime or duties to report, a type of the language that Stephen Kotkin (1995) referred to as "speaking Bolshevik."

In this chapter I focus primarily on letters and complaints that report personal grievances. In the first place, many of these letters ask to pay attention to certain issues and restore justice. Second, the writer is a humble or an angry applicant or an active citizen, announcing various injustices to the *Broom*. Third, a complaint is based on facts, often including places where events took place and people's names. Fourth, the complaint is a letter of (potential) satirical content laughing at "shortcomings." If readers could not see satirical content, they often asked the *Broom* to laugh at wrongdoers for them.

In this chapter, I look at the circulation of people's complaints from the moment they were received to their publication in the *Broom* to illustrate how satirical justice functioned as an institution of an authoritarian state while at the same time helping some ordinary people. Chapter 8 will focus on Soviet materialities and explore complaints about services, living conditions, and disorderly public spaces.

The Institution of Complaints

The right to complain to the media and state institutions was guaranteed by the USSR's constitution and laws. In Soviet Lithuania, right after World War II, the state encouraged citizens to write letters (Marcinkevičienė 2007).[7] Recourse to complaint was further encouraged by Khrushchev's de-Stalinization and decentralization of the institution of complaints by making the "executive committees of local soviets the primary arbiters for a host of everyday problems, and thus staunch the flow of letters to Moscow" (Bittner 2003, 282). In the late 1950s, two Central Committee decrees were passed: "On improving the activities of the soviets of the workers' deputies and strengthening their ties with the masses" (January 22, 1957) and "On the serious shortcomings in the examinations of the letters, complaints, and declarations of working people" (August 2, 1958). In 1968 the Presidium of the Supreme Soviet of the USSR announced that citizen proposals, applications, and complaints are "important in implementing and protecting individual rights, strengthening the state apparatus and citizen contacts, an essential source of information, which is important in solving current and future issues in state, economic, social, and cultural development. It is one of the forms through which workers participate in governance. Citizen's appeals reinforce people's control in state and social institution work, and fight against formal correspondence, bureaucratism, and other shortcomings in their work."[8] The 1968 resolution laid the groundwork for normative communication with citizens. It established how questions have to be answered, in what time, and declared the right to appeal to a higher institution if necessary (White 1983, 45). The 1977 Article 58 of the Constitution of the USSR reinstated a citizen's right to complain to state and public bodies and receive responses within the time limit established by law.[9] These provisions were part of legislative directives earlier, but none of them were part of the constitution until 1977 (White 1983, 46).[10] Their inclusion into the constitution revealed the growing importance of citizens' letters.

The number of letters sent by citizens of the USSR to state institutions greatly increased from the 1950s to the 1980s (White 1983). Between the Twenty-Fourth and Twenty-Fifth Party Congresses (1971–1975), the CPSU CC received more than two million letters and seventy-eight thousand verbal addresses (47). Republic, territorial, regional, city, and district party committees between the Twenty-Fifth and Twenty-Sixth Party Congresses (1976–1980) received nine million letters and six million verbal addresses (47). The Letters Department of the Central Communist Party newspaper *Pravda*, with a daily circulation of over ten million copies, received about five hundred thousand letters from its readers every year (White, Gardner, and Schöpflin 1987, 190). B. A. Grushin estimates that in 1966 and 1967 the newspaper *Komsomol'skaia pravda* received between nine hundred and one thousand letters daily, or three hundred thousand annually (Grushin 2003, 178). The Soviet national daily press altogether received between sixty to seventy million letters per year (White Gardner, and Schöpflin 1987, 190).

The *Broom* received from one to three thousand letters annually in the 1960s and 1970s.[11] In the 1964 publication celebrating the thirtieth anniversary of the magazine (since its founding in 1934), journalist Jonas Bulota, a brother of the editor in chief, emphasized that "the *Broom* had been receiving thousands of letters from workers, collective farm workers, and intellectuals—from ordinary, decent Soviet citizens, who help to expose and eliminate many various shortcomings and disorders."[12] In the 1977 Primary Party Organization meeting, Albertas Lukša claimed that in every issue of the *Broom*, ten letters on average were used by the magazine.[13] In the 1970s, one-third of received letters were used in some fashion by the *Broom*, while two-thirds were forwarded to other institutions.[14] In 1980 Juozas Bulota in his note to the LCP CC Propaganda and Agitation Department wrote that in 1979 the *Broom* had published about eighty important investigative pieces.[15]

Scholarly interpretations as to why complaint writing was encouraged in the USSR range from arguing that the practice curbed citizens' discontent to suggesting that it fostered socialist democracy. Martin Dimitrov argues that in the Brezhnev period, the leadership valued complaints because they provided information that "could be used to identify issues of concern to citizens and to address them before they had been transformed into sources of mass discontent" (Dimitrov 2014a, 342). He even speculates that "responsiveness to complaints was important for preventing the escalation of individual dissatisfaction into mass disturbances" (352). In Dimitrov's approach, letter writing emerges as a quasi-practice of socialist democracy, which included communication of popular opinion about governance and policy implementation, expression and monitoring of trust, and information on corruption or distrust in the elites, an input "from below" (Dimitrov 2014a; see also Dimitrov 2014b). In the Khrushchev years, Stephen Bittner relatedly suggests, the Central Committee decrees of January 22, 1957, and August 2, 1958, "were part of a broader attempt to rationalize the hyper-centralized state and improve popular satisfaction with the workings of government. They reflected Khrushchev's sense that Stalinism had produced 'an extreme stifling of local initiative' that had distorted the interaction between citizens and state" (Bittner 2003, 283).[16] In a similar vein, Gleb Tsipursky (2010, 55), in his study of complaints against bureaucrats, argues that the Communist Party sought to limit corruption and minimize any alienation between people and the state, reduce economic inefficiency, and maintain its role as a moral and ideological vanguard (see also Kozlov 1997). Analysis in this and the next chapter of the processing and circulation of letters to the *Broom*, as well as their content, shows that, in general, letters did not help to build government accountability (among higher-ranking authorities), strengthen the legitimacy of the state, or build citizens' trust toward the state. Some complaint writers expressed trust toward the *Broom*, but this trust most likely coexisted with general distrust of the state (see also chapter 8).

Satirical justice was an institution of an authoritarian state embedded in its power structures and authority relations. Like Soviet elections, writing letters of complaint was a form of political participation that reaffirmed the ultimate authority of the state.[17] Moreover, as discussed below, satirical justice fulfilled a prophylactic and propagandistic function, governed by fear of media exposure and public humiliation. The next chapter illustrates that in the case of the *Broom*, complaint writing did not foster unity between citizens and the state in most instances, nor did it strengthen the regime's legitimacy. Citizens' letters often expressed their dissensus. None of the Primary Party Organization documents or interviews with *Broom* staff provide evidence that the *Broom* intended to counteract or curb existing opposition to the regime, as claimed by Dimitrov in the case of letters to the CPSU CC. The *Broom* initiated themes and solicited letters from readers or fellow journalists following Communist Party agendas. Thus, what appear to be grassroots opinions were also state-initiated or solicited attitudes. *Broom* Communist Party members *did* speak about the importance of the links to the people as well as the *Broom*'s role in serving them and gaining their trust. Analysis of *Broom* journalists' correspondence with other institutions, readers' letters, and interviews reveal, however, that this role was circumscribed by the power structures and unresponsiveness of different institutions. Even if the *Broom*'s journalists helped some people like Siudikaitė, the major role of their publication was preventive and propagandistic. Publications served as a warning to ordinary people and lower-ranking officials about potential outcomes if they committed illegal or immoral acts. They propagated the idea that the Communist Party media could achieve justice.

Natalia Roudakova, in her study of Soviet investigative journalism and letters of complaint, writes that the party-state needed journalists because at least "once in a while the Soviet state needed to *be seen* as accountable to its citizens" (Roudakova 2017, 51, emphasis in the original). The party preferred to "keep the amount of negative publicity by the press to a minimum, opting to sweep as many issues as possible under the rug. This was thus the major tension journalists balanced between the party's encouragement of criticism and the simultaneous fear of it. In that space, Soviet journalists were able to push the limits of the 'sayable' as long as they did one of two things: abstained from criticizing the party itself and remained committed to the socialist project as a whole" (51). The *Broom*'s journalists and editors inhabited tensions between encouragement of criticism and fear of it; openness to reader's complaints and the necessity of soliciting letters on particular themes and reflecting Communist Party political, economic, social, and cultural priorities; willingness to help ordinary people and the struggle with irresponsiveness of state institutions; and the imperative to write about officials while self-censoring.

At the Letters Department

At the *Broom* Letters Department, work with letters took place in several stages. First, each letter received by the *Broom* was registered. Then, a *Broom* journalist reviewed the letter and either queued it for an investigation or resent it to other institutions (the LCP District Committee, ministries, etc.). Other institutions had to check letters and respond to the *Broom* on measures taken. The *Broom* did not have enough staff to follow up on all letters; often journalists in other cities and regions would be asked to check letters for the *Broom*, for which they received an honorarium.[18] If *Broom* journalists carried out an investigation themselves, the magazine might publish its findings and then send the published article to certain institutions, as in case of Julijona Siudikaitė. *Broom* journalists might respond to a complaint writer after receiving information on the issue from other institutions, other journalists, or after resolving the issue themselves. The work at the Letters Department also included recruiting journalist-activists from other city or regional journals who could check facts of complaints from their areas, as well as recruit complaint writers and solicit complaints on certain themes.

In the 1960s, editors introduced new permanent sections that publicly shamed wrongdoers: "Scoundrels Corner" and "The Carousel of People Who Create Defects." In the 1980s, the *Broom* published sections documenting readers' involvement in satirical justice: "Based on Readers' Letters," "We Received a Letter," "Defend the Disadvantaged," and "Real, Not Made Up."[19] As early as 1941, readers' letters, as well as facts gathered by staff journalists on various social problems, were presented in the *Broom*, when sections included "Riding the Broom," "We Answer Readers' Inquiries," "A Reporter Is Looking for Garbage," and "I Want to Sweep You!"[20] Compared to 1941, after 1956 fact-based material lost its revolutionary seriousness and refocused on new issues. The bourgeoisie, landlords, nationalists, and religious activists had already been "swept away," so journalists turned to the working class and "enduring shortcomings." One of the well-known sections, "After the *Broom* Wrote" (*Brūkštelėjus*, or *Šluotai brūkštelėjus*), appeared beginning in 1956. In this section, the *Broom* published short reports about resolved cases. It reported about officials who were fired, transferred to other jobs, or demoted, about reprimands and fines, or the termination of bonuses. In the section "In the Bureaucrats' Lounge" the *Broom* named institutions that did not respond to the magazine's inquiries or that responded formally but avoided resolving the issues at hand.[21]

Work with letters was among the most important undertakings at the *Broom*. In 1964, at the annual PPO meeting, editors claimed that work with activists, regular contributors to the *Broom*, and letters from working-class people was the most important task for communist and noncommunist members of the editorial board.[22] In the 1960s through the 1980s, the *Broom*'s Communist Party members consistently discussed their work with fact-based material at Primary Party Organization meetings. Editors spoke about a lack of staff to deal with letters, an insufficient group of activists, unresponsive institutions, lack of visits to investigate letters, scarce letters from some regions of Lithuania, dull topics, and inadequate coverage of specific themes, such as agriculture. They criticized themselves for not following their prospective plans and reminded everybody that socialist commitments had to be actual, not empty blabber.[23]

Published, fact-based material had to reflect Communist Party political, economic, social, and cultural priorities.[24] In some years, editors argued that it was important to avoid household issues and minor topics (Lith. *buitiškumo*). In 1964 Rytis Tilvytis argued that the *Broom* would receive more letters if it published about minor issues, such as broken fences, dug-up streets, or garbage.[25] Responding to a decreased number of letters, in 1966 Tilvytis, the Primary Party Organization secretary, pressed again: "We should understand the questions of the industry in broader terms—we should write not only about defects, but also about the households of industry workers, their everyday life, not only production concerns. This is very important. The reader should feel that the editorial office has not forgotten about him, [and] is interested in his problems. Then he [or she] will write to us for help or some advice."[26]

Although there was no shortage of letters, there were not enough letters reflecting the ideological agendas of the LCP. In 1963 at the PPO meeting, the *Broom*'s party members discussed the idea that writing on certain issues in the magazine would encourage readers to address these themes in their letters.[27] In 1965, during an open meeting with the staff of the editorial office, editors discussed whether letters had to be "organized" by sending journalists to the regions, going on business trips, and recruiting letter writers. The *Broom* subsequently recruited activists to report and write for the magazine by visiting enterprises and kolkhozes.[28]

Fact-based material and feuilletons thus were based not only on readers' letters but also on information from activists, as well as from other institutions. In 1977 there were seventy activists in Lithuania who sent information or material to the *Broom*.[29] The *Broom* published material upon request from ministries, participated in various inter-institutional campaigns such as youth delinquency prevention, and published satirical pieces based on the Internal Affairs Ministry, People's Courts, or, in very rare cases, KGB information.[30]

The *Broom* editors claimed to have achieved effectiveness of published critical material by 1977 (see box 7.1).[31] Effectiveness meant that the *Broom* received more responses from different institutions to its critical material; these responses were more comprehensive and less formal; and it published more follow-up material.[32] In 1977 there were 248 responses to forwarded materials from various ministries, party and executive committees, and other institutions and organizations about measures undertaken. Thirty-seven of the 248 responses were used for "After the *Broom* Wrote," to inform readers on what measures had been taken to address the issues raised in their complaints.[33] Fact-based material in that section of the magazine appeared in eighteen out of twenty issues in 1977.[34] "After the *Broom* Wrote" was, according to Lukša, a "barometer" of the effectiveness of published fact-based material in the *Broom*. He also recalled that most institutions had to be persuaded to respond to criticism published in the magazine.[35] As the chair of the Letters Department, Lukša was especially proud of critical material that targeted higher authorities (see box 7.1).

Box 7.1. Effective critical material published in the *Broom* in 1977

In 1977 Albertas Lukša summarized the work of the *Broom*: criticism published in the magazine helped to restore justice for people, address economic problems, expose wasted state funds, and fight defects and negligence in construction work and manufacturing.[36] In the 1977 Primary Party Organization annual report, Lukša introduced some of the major feuilletons published in 1977:

- Issue no. 3, "Depreciated Bubbles," criticized director N. Baršauskienė for economic and financial violations and forging documents in the Rasa factory in Klaipėda. Many others benefited from the fraud, including the chief engineer and the director's personal driver. For financial mismanagement, chief accountant K. Vangalienė received a reprimand. A senior personnel officer received a reprimand for illegally hiring part-time workers and for poor documentation. The director of the factory was fired. Workers who were hired illegally were fired.[37]
- Issue no. 4 included a follow-up piece on "Reporting with a Sauna Whisk" (originally published in 1976, *Broom* no. 21), which criticized different enterprise leaders for using public funds for parties in a kolkhoz sauna. They returned the money that was spent. The kolkhoz director, V. Radavičius, received a strict party punishment for organizing and hosting sauna parties and was fired.[38]
- Issue no. 4 included "A Man of Good Deeds from Nemakščiai," which criticized director Juozas Kuncius of the Raseinių region Nemakščių state farm for building houses from farm funds and selling them to workers for less

than the cost of construction. The *Broom* journalists satirized Kuncius's "kindness." He also had been allotted five cars, which he resold to others. He was criticized for mismanagement of the farm and shortcomings in his work and leadership. He was fired.[39]

- Issue no. 12. "Magicians" criticized the director and the chief accountant of the Varėna secondary vocational school for misusing student food coupons. The lawsuit was closed because no criminal activity was found. The LSSR prosecutor's office subsequently informed the editors that the facts published in the *Broom* were checked again, and the lawsuit was reopened.[40]
- Issue no. 13 included Č. Valadka's "Be Careful—a Human Being!"[41] (discussed in this chapter's introductory vignette).
- Issue no. 14. "New Timurovtsy" criticized Vilnius region collective farm "March 8" leaders for a disorganized machinery base.[42]
- Issue no. 15. "Strolling around Yards" criticized several farm authorities for mismanagement of agricultural machinery and disorganization of farm areas.[43]
- Issue no. 16. "Factory Is Me" criticized the director of a reinforced-concrete construction factory in Telšiai for disrespectful behavior with employees and mismanagement of the factory. The director was fired.[44]
- Issue no. 16. "Boorish Initiative" described mismanagement of a Širvintos region pig farm. The head of the farm, S. Pinkevičienė, was critically evaluated at the kolkhoz Primary Party Organization meeting and given a warning. Her case had to be reviewed at the joint meeting of all collective farm workers. Veterinarian N. Piktelienė was issued a reprimand.[45]
- Issue no. 19. "Stupid History Repeats Itself" ridicules experimental medical herbs farm director V. Ošakaitė's deals with "gypsies". There can be no business with private dealers.[46]

The range of readers' complaints included everything from "moral" issues, such as impolite behavior of salesclerks at stores, to minor offenses, such as illegal building of garages, to, in rare cases, crimes, such as embezzlement, which could lead to many years in prison. The *Broom* criticized kolkhoz and factory leaders, depot and shop managers, repair shop or construction workers, salesclerks, and cafeteria staff. There were far fewer letters on neighbors or community members. Some families disagreed about their shared communal apartment kitchen, and one family reported on another by denouncing the wife for stealing from a store where she worked. In a letter from the city of Kapsukas, it was reported that neighbors' yards were not clean and that one resident built an illegal garage, which was rented to motorcyclists who disturbed the peace for thirty neighbors.

Another neighbor was reported for building an illegal swine shelter at the end of the house.[47] Some letters accused groups of individuals, such as ensemble artists or teachers. These letters constituted a minority of complaints. The director of the ensemble "Vilnius Aidai" (Vilnius echoes) responded to the *Broom* in regard to a letter of complaint, assuring readers that during the visit of his ensemble to a village there were no drunk artists, that their program was not of a lower quality, and that the costumes, criticized for "diversity of colors" (Lith. *margumynai*), were in fact designed by Vilnius Model House artists.[48]

Readers sometimes manipulated facts or dramatized the situation in order to draw the editors' attention. Some letter writers exaggerated problems with construction work, arguing that their house was going to fall down soon.[49] Others claimed that they had to eat potatoes and other vegetables soaked in sewage water.[50] When the facts could not be confirmed, the *Broom* editors responded to the letter writer suggesting that probably not everything was as bad as had been outlined, and sent the letter writer the results of their investigation. In some cases, the editors even argued that the letter writers were to some extent responsible for the situation themselves.

Letter writers often presented themselves as powerless, disappointed, or angry, submissively asking the *Broom* to "please help" solve the issue for them. In some cases, they wrote that the *Broom* was their only hope. Others wrote that they had already contacted various institutions: "They all make promises, comfort us, but we, poor people, just wait and wait forever."[51] Many readers also expressed trust in the *Broom*.[52] They addressed it in kind words, like "respected *Broomy*," mentioned that they always read the *Broom*, that the *Broom*'s pursuit of justice made them happy. The readers also called the *Broom* "powerful." "It's a weapon," wrote a man from Vilnius, asking the *Broom* to investigate a brewery in the center of the city that was producing such a terrible smell that he had already seen two women getting sick near it.[53] Belief in their right to justice was expressed by many letter writers, especially those of a higher social status. Such letters came from journalists, legal consultants, or even policemen. Sometimes the letter writers mentioned that they were good citizens, hardworking, and devoted to the public interest, in this way expecting to draw the editors' attention.[54] In rare cases readers asked, "How can a communist behave like this?"[55] or emphasized that "we have to fight against remaining shortcomings," this way invoking the official discourse.[56]

The *Broom*'s editors might transform the cases described in some letters into satirical accounts. Sometimes the letters were completely re-created by the addition of fictional material. For example, a comic account based on a letter about the flooding of an apartment building described how strong men wearing fishermen's boots were sent to rescue the inhabitants' jam and mushroom jars, a tricycle, a basket of potatoes, skis, and other goods stored in the basement.[57] One of the rescuers put on a gas mask, and another put a wooden peg on his nose before descending into the basement with candles. The *Broom* laughed at the local municipal workers who had not maintained this building over the course of many years. They wrote that they were preparing a project based on which "residents would be advised to keep potatoes under their sofa with built-in storage, and jam and mushrooms in washing machines or accordion cases" (Pelėgrinda and Saulius 1979, 7). In such accounts, *Broom* journalists enacted satirical justice by using the means of negative media publicity, public social critique, and ridicule, aiming to bring justice to ordinary people.

Satirical Justice

Satirical justice as a Soviet institution had its beginnings in the Bolshevik Revolution and related to a specific revolutionary mission to fight with the foreign and internal enemies of the new communist state. For Anatoly Lunacharsky, the people's commissar of enlightenment from 1917 to 1929, satirical laughter was never kind (Gérin 2018, 34). It had to expose, disarm, humiliate, defeat, and conquer (34). It must often be cruel (34). According to Lunacharsky, "To say that you are laughable actually means that I see you as degraded. It means I won't even honor you with serious criticism. . . . In this sense, laughter cannot be absolutely just. Nor should it be kind-hearted either. Its function is to intimidate by humiliating. Now, it would not succeed in doing this, had not nature implanted for that very purpose, even in the best of men, a spark of spitefulness or, at all events, of mischief" (cited in Gérin 2018, 34). Annie Gérin notes that satirical campaigns in postrevolutionary Russia were "rooted in a kind of institutionalized hatred. . . . Hatred is an emotion that pushes those who hate to desire the disappearance or the outright devastation of the object of their scorn. . . . In this sense, satirical campaigns served a very specific rhetorical purpose, that of symbolic destruction" (171).

K. S. Eremeev, the creator of *Krokodil*, and his followers saw satirical justice as a tool in defense of achieved revolutionary justice (Semenov 1982, 22). *Krokodil* was a "reliable guardian from those whose greed or stupidity jeopardized conquered revolutionary justice" (22). I. P. Abramsky, who worked with Eremeev at *Krokodil* after its founding, recalled that Eremeev created a first- and second-degree "*Krokodil* order" award to be given to the most malicious bureaucrats who obstructed the work of the state apparatus (Semenov 1982, 22). *Krokodil* wrote about these awardees and invited people to send them greetings. Manuil Semenov (1982), editor in chief of *Krokodil* in the post-Stalinist years, boasted that the awardees were terrified when a postman paid a visit with numerous greetings from the readers of *Krokodil*. Readers sent these awardees poems, drawings, and even collective letters from plants and factories. They shamed and humiliated "*Krokodil* order" recipients. As this case illustrates, *Krokodil* condemnations were a public event. Its laughter was formidable and denunciatory (Semenov 1982, 23).

According to Communist Party ideology, the state would eventually die out and crime gradually disappear (see Berman and Spindler 1963; Kareniauskaitė 2017). Official law as an instrument of coercion was to become obsolete. In 1958, Albertas Lukša, then a twenty-four-year-old student at Vilnius University, wrote in his university degree thesis,

> It is possible that the power of laughter will be stronger than some articles of the criminal code, and satire and humor will gradually take over and successfully fulfill many court and administrative functions. Thus, satirists should not be afraid of unemployment. I am confident that they will find work not only in communist society but will also have a secured place in the future [of] spaceships [and] interplanetary expeditions. Laughter will always be a warrior, a friend, and a pedagogue; it will follow a person all [one's] life.[58]

Such perspectives most likely prevailed in the official discourse until the 1980s. In 1966 another graduating student, Steponas-Vytautas Kulpinskas (1966, 55), ended his fifty-five-page university graduation thesis analyzing satire and humor by restating Lukša's words verbatim without citing him. Lukša's captivating arguments were tempting to copy, but most likely they were not original either. They expressed pan-Soviet ideas about satire and humor and their future. Lukša joined the *Broom* as a journalist after graduation from the university, and later became the chair of the Letters Department, the position he stayed in for many years (see chapter 1). While the utopian future for laughter he envisioned as a student had not been realized, humor did serve an important role as an arbiter of justice.[59]

As argued at the beginning of this chapter, satirical justice was integral to authoritarian governance. Satirical justice did not eliminate social injustices. It contributed to reproducing structural injustices by never questioning state authority and delegating responsibility to particular individuals as well as arguing that injustice occurred only in single cases. Justice and injustice, according to Iris Marion Young, "concern primarily an evaluation of how the institutions of a society work together to produce outcomes that support or minimize the threat of domination, and support or minimize everyone's opportunities to develop and exercise capacities for living a good life as they define it" (Young 2003, 7). In Soviet Lithuania, structural injustices included harm people experienced as a result of centralized power and structural processes that minimized opportunities for some people to achieve a greater quality of life than otherwise would have been possible (cf. Young 2003). In the case of the *Broom*, satirical justice directed at lower-ranking officials or ordinary people, negative media publicity, and public humiliation were means of reaffirming structural injustices. Criticizing salespeople stealing some candy, bus drivers charging for a ride and pocketing the money, or old women reselling alcoholic drinks subjected them to public shaming and humiliation, while higher authorities could not be touched. Moreover, the *Broom*'s journalists or readers seldom raised questions about the impunity of authorities, social stratification, redistribution of resources, unequal opportunities, and individual rights and freedoms, topics common in informal jokes rather than *Broom* humor.

The Authority of the State

Satirical justice had to be ideologically correct. Information about problems like sexual violence in the Vilnius psychiatric hospital, for example, could not be published in the *Broom*. After receiving a letter on the "amoral behavior of the hospital staff with patients" in 1958, the *Broom* editors forwarded it to the LSSR Health Care minister and noted, "This is not the first signal regarding amoral behavior of the hospital staff with patients"[60] (cited in Vaiseta 2018, 161). Tomas Vaiseta writes about the LSSR Council of Ministers Soviet Control Commission report that established that one doctor sexually abused patients for two years (Vaiseta 2018, 160). A seventeen-year-old girl died two days after being sexually abused (160). In another case a therapeutic program assistant stole hospital inventory—six towels, four flat sheets, and three top sheets—from a psychiatric hospital in Švėkšna. She was sentenced to ten days in jail and demoted to cleaning staff, while the doctor who was accused of sexual violence was not sentenced, stayed in his job, and the chief doctor who protected him later became the director of another psychiatric hospital (161).[61] How could such behavior be punished? one could bitterly ask, since officially neither psychiatric hospitals nor sexual violence existed in the USSR. Juxtaposing these two cases uncovers paradoxes of Soviet justice—sexual violence was covered up, while stealing some sheets and towels was punished by a jail sentence. The *Broom*'s participation in the Soviet justice regime was delimited by what it could criticize. By not publishing the letters complaining about psychiatric hospitals, the *Broom* reaffirmed state authority to define what kind of justice would be pursued and in this way contributed to the prevalence of structural injustices.

Soviet Lithuanian media almost never touched anybody above the authorities of a regional executive committee. If misdeeds of higher authorities were covered in the media, in many cases it was with the Central Committee's approval. The *Broom* could not question the authority of the government, and thus none of the existing inequalities, such as the different rights of government officials and ordinary people, could be questioned either. As Natalia Roudakova writes about Soviet journalism generally, "Questioning the leading role of the party in society, the lives of Soviet leaders, the desirability of communism, and so on . . . raising any of those topics was considered anti-Soviet propaganda" (2017, 60). If a reader sent a complaint about the lack of freedoms, *Broom* journalists could forward it to the KGB. Complaining had to be ideologically correct.

Although the regime officially encouraged strong criticism, *Broom* journalists feared publishing material on ideologically sensitive issues that criticized higher authorities. In 1975 Juozas Bulota reflected on this tension: "Nobody prevents us from providing highly critical material. But sometimes it is hard to criticize even the director of a kolkhoz who has protection in Vilnius. . . . Although we are always supported [by the Central Committee], it's not good that a satirist has an internal censor: 'What will happen to me for this?'"[62] In a 1980 note to the LCP CC Propaganda and Agitation Department, Bulota remarked that G. Siminenka, the LSSR regional industry minister, called the *Broom* and asked him not to publish information about bad work conditions in Kaunas's Pirmūnas (Leader) factory. Siminenka said that he would complain to the LCP CC authorities if the information got published. Bulota noted that such a position of the minister did not help fight shortcomings.[63] In this same note, Bulota complained that the *Broom* rarely received letters from the Kupiškis and Raseiniai regions, since authorities there did not like criticism.[64]

Vitas Tomkus, a journalist who was hired by the *Broom* around 1981, recalled that the editor in chief asked him to write on garbage piles in the Vilnius region or polluted rivers in other regions, to prevent him from publishing critical material on officials (Tomkus 1988, 60). Tomkus said that he had been disciplined by Bulota when he worked at the magazine; he was told not to think of himself as better than others (62). Tomkus wrote that Bulota said that if he, Tomkus, was a party employee (Lith. *partinis darbuotojas*), he would have done the same as the party employees he was ready to criticize, that the same things happened everywhere, and it was impossible to change anything. Tomkus reflected that the editor in chief was partly right: "The biggest problem is that you cannot live honestly" (62).[65] Tomkus once published a story about some enterprises that protected their employees who spent nights at a drunk tank and did not show up at work. They were instead granted sick leaves for missed days (19–26). An LCP CC Vilnius Committee Propaganda and Agitation Department instructor criticized the *Broom* for this article. Recalling the event in his memoir, Tomkus wondered, "After such incidents how can I listen without any irony to calls from high tribunes for stronger and more open publicizing of our shortcomings?" (23). Tomkus recalled the words by B. Motuza, who was one of the *Broom*'s founders when it was published illegally in 1934–1936: "I read [the] contemporary *Broom* and cannot understand. What are you afraid of? I recall when we published the underground *Broom*. We risked our own freedom and sometimes even life. What can happen now for criticism? A written reprimand? Losing a job? Is it more threatening nowadays than [losing one's] freedom and [facing] death?" (26).

Certain issues of injustices, such as selective allocation of apartments, were rarely covered in the *Broom*. Albertas Lukša remembered how he was able to "achieve" (Lith. *iškovojo*) three apartments for different families. In one case, a family with three children lived in poor conditions and could not get an apartment. The workplace where the father of this family was employed allocated apartments to other workers, helping them skip the line. No other government institutions were able to help. Lukša did not remember other details. Such cases were not published in the *Broom*, and they were very rare and memorable.[66] Analyzing cases similar to Lukša's, historian Dalia Marcinkevičienė has argued that the media itself served as a *blat* channel, illustrating that its justice was personally motivated and random. She writes about a disabled woman named Liuba who earned the trust and support of the *Truth* journalist J. Baužytė by writing complaint letters. Baužytė helped her to get an apartment and a job. Later Liuba also asked her for help getting a Volga, a prestigious Soviet car (Marcinkevičienė 2007). Vytautė Žilinskaitė, a leading Lithuanian humor writer and a *Broom* contributor, remembered that she used her status as a *Krokodil* special journalist to get several apartments for people in need.[67]

Although the *Broom* journalists were generally protected by the Central Committee and had the Communist Party mandate to publish criticism, they were also persecuted for such criticism when it targeted higher-ranking officials. In 1977 the *Broom*'s newly hired editor V. Katilius, on a raid with the traffic police, collected information on traffic violations and noted the name of one violator. The violator, N. Polemčikas, saw Katilius write down his name and realized that negative information about him might appear in the media. Polemčikas was a captain and a senior assistant to the director of the Republic Military Commissariat. He asked Katilius for his name and workplace, intending to prevent publication of information about his violation. The next day, Captain Polemčikas called the *Broom* and requested that editors give him Katilius's home address on behalf of the commissariat. It was a signal not to proceed with the publication, otherwise Katilius would have to deal with the military commissariat. *Broom* staff told Polemčikas to make this request officially in writing. Polemčikas refused and promised to find Katilius anyway. Tilvytis, at the time the secretary of the Primary Party Organization, mentioned that they had to report this incident to the LCP Central Committee.[68]

While some lawbreaking officials were punished, in many cases their punishment included reprimands, warnings, or transfers to other jobs.[69] Tomkus recalled Bulota saying in the early 1980s, "You most likely still do not understand the task presented for satire. It's not Khrushchev times when you can write about ministers. You cannot blindly discredit these employees. Do not forget that they will have to work afterward. . . . Do not be too harsh, be considerate and well-meaning, so they can be successful leaders after they take into account your criticism" (Tomkus 1988, 26). *Broom* artist Leonidas Vorobjovas's cartoon, published in the *Broom* in 1985, reflected on the limits of justice. In it, a man holding a glass of beer jumps, gracefully and smiling, over three hurdles marked "Warning," "Disciplinary note," and "Reprimand."[70]

Justice by Fear

Criticism was often directed at lower-ranking workers—salesclerks, waiters, cafeteria, or shop staff. In these cases negative media publicity reproduced structural injustices by disciplining and threatening some ordinary people while claiming to defend others. Such media publicity did not eliminate the root causes and reasons for injustice. In most cases it did not address the responsibilities of leadership. Instead it enacted governance by fear of media exposure, public humiliation, and shaming.

Elena was born in a small village in western Lithuania in 1935. Her homestead became a front line during World War II. Her family was deported to Germany by the Nazis. When the war neared its end, they were sent back to Lithuania by the advancing Soviet Army. Her family of rich farmers became poor *kolkhozniks*. She had to work in a village shop, and later moved to Klaipėda, which was still in ruins, where she found a job at a food store.[71] Elena remembered,

> [The store administration] had to provide for "state authorities." Everybody from the Executive [Committee] used to come, take goods under the table, the director [of the store] had everything ready for the most important [people] [Lith. *aprūpindavo glavniausius*], such as . . . priests, doctors, and state authorities. They used to take everything. And then these NKVD, all these war veterans . . . [received so much, even canned] peas. They used to get everything. . . . I used to take [some] for myself . . . first of all for myself . . . but not actually for neighbors or others. . . . Well, somebody could have noticed if you take too much.

Elena also remembered the *Broom*:

> Yes, yes. God forbid, [if] they publish about you [*laughs*]. They wrote once about me. I put thicker paper [on a scale]. I weighed candy. They were expensive, chocolate. I think it was "Bear" candy. Only the bosses used to buy them. Kosolapaia ["Clumsy Bear," a Soviet chocolate brand],

I think it was [*laughs*]. You know I put [paper] on the other side of the weight, you know these [weights] were with an arrow. . . . They used to check. You have to weigh [candy] in the same kind of paper as you put on [the other side of] the scale. . . . I think somebody was from the press [of the *Broom*]. . . . They did not write my name, only the name of the store. . . . My daughter was born. I needed money. So I put a piece of thicker paper. . . . I learned about it [the publication] from our director. She said, "Our store ended up in the *Broom*. It's interesting who [cheated customers]. There is no name or last name, but it is written that it was the bread department." There were only two shifts. She could have found out, but most likely since she was the wife of the police chief, she made sure nobody inquired [into this case]. Nothing happened. I did not get a reprimand, nothing.[72]

In the context where the highest authorities acted with impunity, the *Broom*'s satirical justice may have appeared arbitrary to the butts of its laughter. Elena, who lost her family's wealth, land, and her own future opportunities because of World War II and Soviet occupation, had to see how the Soviet police, new settlers from the USSR, and new Lithuanian Soviet elites received the best products, did not have to stay in line, and lived better lives and had opportunities and rights inaccessible to people like her. In this context the *Broom* editors' discourse about "taking pants down"—that is, shaming cheaters like Elena—may have appeared hypocritical and unfair.[73] The store director did not punish Elena. Not punishing her was also a way to keep her silent, since the director herself was engaged in sales through the back door for the privileged. Elena was overcome by fear: fear of exposure, public humiliation, and punishment.

Satirical justice of the *Broom* suggested moral perspectives on how various minor offenders have to be approached: through derision, ridicule, and humiliation. Some followers took *Broom* lessons to the extreme. Juozas Bulota in a 1965 article about wall newspapers wrote that people in factories and enterprises should avoid creating vulgar and distasteful images. He mentioned that he once saw a depiction of a worker with a pig's head, since she did not clean her workplace after her work hours. Bulota thought that the dignity of the worker would be hurt. He also criticized a photo showcase in one of Vilnius's cafeterias. "Who are these criminals, who are featured in the showcase—maybe murderers or hooligans? No, here we see photos of some children and serious, elderly people. It so happens they all committed a big crime: [they] did not buy a [bus] ticket for four kopeks. . . . People with high education and serious elderly workers, who maybe forgot to buy the ticket because of their absentmindedness" (Bulota 1965, 6). Tomas Vaiseta writes about how one worker saw a report about himself in the

Vingis factory wall newspaper, the *Mirror of Shame*, and broke the glass display case (Vaiseta 2014, 167). Another time, a worker from the Eidukevičius association tore down the wall newspaper the *Flashlight of Komsomol*, in which she was derided, after which she was reported to the police (167). Satirical justice in these cases brought anger rather than resolution and reconciliation. Even if Bulota criticized some wall newspapers and photo showcases, the *Broom* itself set an example for these satirical justice engagements at workplaces.

Many *Broom* editors, collaborators, and readers mentioned that the name of the *Broom* was used to scare others, invoking the potential of becoming an object of satirical laughter. Juozas Bulota, the son of the editor in chief, even claimed that some people were more afraid of journalists showing them *Broom* ID than they were of the KGB. He remembered his father saying "humor is a terrible weapon. In some cases, people would rather go to prison than get derided and laughed at in the *Broom*. . . . You had to be very careful with such things, because somebody may have a heart attack or die."[74] Manuil Semenov, the editor in chief of *Krokodil*, recalled in 1982 that *Krokodil* was used as a tool of threat, which he described as "sweet music": "I hear words accidentally overheard in a store or on the street, [they sound] like a sweet music: '[Report] them to *Krokodil*, rascals! It's for *Krokodil*! I will take it to *Krokodil* and find justice!'" (Semenov 1982, 54). *Krokodil*, according to Semenov, was "the highest satirical institution" for its readers, an institution comparable to the court (54). He cites a foreign journalist from a capitalist country who, after a visit to *Krokodil*, reported in his own newspaper that a threat to write about some infraction in *Krokodil* had more impact than a threat to report it to the court (55). Joyfully, Semenov declares that "*Krokodil* is above [the] court and prosecutor's office!" (55). Instead of relying on judicial institutions to bring justice and hiding individuals' identities to protect them from discrimination and threats, Semenov, as well as the *Broom* editors, celebrated opportunities to expose people to public shaming and condemnation.

Readers' positive perspectives of the *Broom*'s satirical justice coexisted with negativity toward complainers. Tomas Vaiseta (2014) writes that the notion of a "complainer" in workplaces in Soviet Lithuania had a negative connotation. In the *Broom*'s Primary Party Organization annual report of October 24, 1977, Rytis Tilvytis, the PPO secretary, said that in some cases people who wrote letters to the *Broom* were harassed.[75] Albertas Lukša, in his 1977 report, mentions that some journalists were unwilling to check readers' complaint letters requested by the *Broom* because, they hint, in their regions there is no support for "the objective critical genre and its authors."[76] Complaints disrupted routinized relations at work collectives or communities, as well as relations of interdependence and political intimacy. They could serve as a form of revenge, with true or doubtful facts. Alexei Yurchak (1997) considers similar reporting and complaint writing as a form of action available to "activists"—regime supporters who were disliked by "normal" people. The complaint writer could have been associated with the betrayal of the collective or individuals, with mean or selfish motives. The *Broom* also criticized letter writers who wrote simply to accuse somebody rather than seek justice.

The journalists as well as representatives from different institutions were careful not to publish letters with slanderous intentions. They always gathered information about a letter writer, not just an accused person. If it was somebody with a criminal background, not a respected member of the work collective, his or her complaint was scrutinized. Among themselves, journalist-activists who checked the *Broom* letters ironically called some letter writers "truth hunters" (Lith. *tiesos ieškotojai*), reminding the editors that some letter writers were not beyond reproach, too. In one reply to the *Broom* by an editor from the *Komunistinis rytojus* (Communist tomorrow) who checked a prospective case, he said that the complaint was revealed to be groundless.[77] The accused brigade chairman was reported to be an "industrious and honest person. A communist since 1948. When he was on vacation, there was no order in the brigade. But when he came back, everything is in place again." Higher authorities were said to be satisfied with the brigade chairman. The "truth hunter," on the other hand, often skipped a workday and currently had not shown up at work for a week.[78]

In some instances, journalists from other presses who were asked to check facts wrote on behalf of the accused and suggested the *Broom* editors refrain from disciplinary actions. If the accused person had not been the subject of complaint before and was on good terms with others, reputedly a "good person," journalists could suggest waiting before proceeding with the case. Once a journalist wrote against a complainer herself, a woman who sued a factory that she said violated the rules. The factory administration did not at first make any attempt to reconcile the dispute, and now that the woman "feels that she can win the case . . . we cannot expect any concessions or good will from her."[79] In another case a journalist mentioned that there was already an article in the *Raudonoji vėliava* (Red flag) titled "You Have to Answer to Yourself, Lašiau," where the complaint writer was criticized as a snitch (Lith. *skundikas*) and graphomaniac (Lith. *rašinėtojas*), who kept searching, without grounds, for justice.[80] Another letter, from the Syrius factory, argued that one "comrade" liked to write complaints to local and national newspapers and journals for financial reasons (honoraria from the publisher). He would complain about various shortcomings at the factory, such as disorder, but he had never stopped by the director's office or talked to the chief engineer or even the department chair.[81] Justice, as these cases showed, was relational and personal, the truth depending not only on facts, but also on personalities and power relations. Political intimacy with the members of the collective could have served as a protective shield from potential media exposure.

Prevention and Propaganda

Satirical justice had a preventive function—publication of negative cases was a warning to other people that they would be punished for similar behavior. It also was a form of propaganda showing that the media could achieve justice. By writing about cases like Siudikaitė's, the *Broom* advocated for fairness, respect for ordinary workers, and accountability of lower-ranking officials. Although the *Broom* was sometimes effective in restoring justice, as the Siudikaitė case in the introductory vignette illustrates, in many other instances it primarily aimed to raise the issue, rather than to solve it. In 1977, Albertas Lukša claimed that "a lot of fact-based material in the magazine is published out of purely preventive considerations. We do not get any response [from institutions] on this material. They [the published pieces] include various articles and feuilletons based on control institution [data], investigation, inspection, and court material. The impact of this material . . . is not direct, because its 'characters' had already received their share [punishment], according to their merits, without the help of feuilleton writers. However, when we announce a negative fact, it has a preventive influence on a reader."[82]

Some so-called preventive material was prepared in collaboration with Internal Affairs Ministry departments. According to Rytis Tilvytis's report to the LSSR Internal Affairs Ministry Political-Educational Work Department, in 1973 the *Broom* published a number of fact-based feuilletons and other critical material "fighting with enduring shortcomings, specifically against speculators, all [kinds of] embezzlers and public property thieves, hooligans—public order violators, drunk drivers, dishonest sales people."[83] In 1974 almost every issue of the *Broom* published material, according to the editor in chief, about "thieves of public goods, speculators, briberies, parasites, alcoholism, irresponsible waste of state funds, bad management, all kind of cheaters, preventive material on fire safety questions, [and] teen education themes. We criticized drunk drivers, etc."[84] These pieces, in Bulota's words, "contributed to the prevention of legally punishable and publicly denounced crimes."[85]

In 1977 the *Broom* published a true story by Liudmila Paškevičienė, a policewoman from a facility for drunks. According to Paškevičienė, she and her colleagues worked as educators, nurses, and moralists. They lectured the drunks and showed anti-alcoholism films. Drunks arrived at the facility from everywhere: the streets, public squares, transportation hubs, restaurants, and even workplaces.

They were grouped into three categories: first, a boozer (Lith. *latras*) whom you have to wake up and take to the facility for drunks because he cannot get up himself. Boozers usually are found on the pavement, in a park, or on a bench. The two other categories are drunks who can walk and drunks who are aggressive. The story provides names and employment of people who stayed at the facility for drunks. Paškevičienė discusses how badly alcoholism affects family relations:

> Jonas Gečas has good hands. His work was valued at the Vilnius furniture factory. However, his taste for alcohol is also special. It's already been a couple of years that he drinks without stopping. . . . The facility for drunks is like a home for him. And his family doesn't have time to relax. Drunk and rowdy Gečas fights. His swearing hurts his young son who cries because of such "happiness." [Because of his father's drinking,] his performance at school is also affected. (Gelvaitis 1977, 5)[86]

"There is no cock without a crest, and no larger collective without its boozer," moralizes Paškevičienė (Gelvaitis 1977, 5). She claims that although the drunks are taken by the scruff of the neck at work and taught manners, they still keep drinking. The collectives take responsibility for such workers, because they are their collective problem and collective shame, according to Paškevičienė (5).

In another story on drinking, in a feuilleton titled "Attorney's Speech," A. Brička (a pseudonym for journalist R. Tilvytis) ironically presented an attorney defending Angelė Ginkūnienė for diluting vodka and cognac in a cafeteria. According to the attorney, her actions were beneficial because none of her customers got drunk, so they showed up at work on time the next morning. She also saved working people's health and energy and contributed to the state's wealth. Moreover, she contributed to family well-being, since husbands did not return home completely drunk. It is so nice when "a loving mother kisses a husband, happy kids run around, and dishes, pillows, and cactuses are not destroyed. Such ideal harmony strengthens the most important cell of the state—a family."[87] After giving several other justifications, the attorney concluded that Ginkūnienė was doing a job beneficial to the state. Therefore, the court was asked not only to recognize her innocence, but also to acknowledge that she positively contributed to workers' health, productivity, and happiness.[88]

In a 1980 *Broom* article, a journalist recounted accompanying a traffic policeman on a raid in the city of Šiauliai. They met two men, serving as people's patrols, who were taking an intoxicated man to a drunk tank. The *Broom* published a photo showing how the people's patrols were carrying an intoxicated man, who was not able to walk by himself, up the stairs.[89] They also visited an older woman, a speculator who was reselling vodka and cheap wine. Then they went to the store in which this old lady used to purchase vodka behind the counter, and several apartments where drunks used to gather (Lith. *lindynės*). In one apartment, eighteen-year-old E. Trinkūnaitė drank with her mother in the company of men. The article mentioned that Trinkūnaitė gave her newborn child to a state orphanage. Her photo, with her words "What can you do to me?" was placed in the *Broom*.[90]

Another article described how *Broom* journalists spent a night with policemen disciplining drunk hooligans, uncovering pilfering and stealing cases, and dealing with drunks. One of the photos that ran in the *Broom* portrayed two men in beds in a drunk tank; one of them is sleeping, the other is smiling, undressed and partially covered with a blanket.[91]

Broom journalists sometimes published court material on men who did not pay alimony for their children. The *Broom* listed names, how long the men were unemployed, and how much they owed their children. They also placed images of speculators, often with things they were selling, such as fur coats, fur hats, cloth material, blouses, gloves, or food items. One woman was caught reselling a golden ring at a Vilnius store. She asked for twenty-five rubles more than its original cost, the *Broom* reported. The *Broom* received images and information on speculators and drunks from the police and the courts.

Individuals and various institutions participated in the *Broom*'s satirical justice undertakings by sending in unsolicited examples of funny conversations or sayings. In 1972 the *Broom* published messages from Klaipėda's People's Court exposing ridiculous explanations by several men:

> MYKOLAS K.: "My neighbor started running. She was scared. I chased her. I wanted to apologize since I grabbed a chair from her, but she thought I wanted to beat her."
>
> EUGENIJUS N.: "I asked for a cigarette from a man in front of me. He said that he doesn't smoke. I did not believe it, and I asked him again. He got angry and wanted to take me to the police."
>
> VASILIJUS K.: "I dated Danguolė. I wanted to talk to her, but her father, who has bad nerves, grabbed me by my shirt. Then I insisted that I want to speak to Danguolė. Then the police came, and I left with them."[92]

In rare cases, the *Broom* facilitated the reopening of lawsuits, acting on information it received from other state institutions, journalists, or readers. In 1977 the *Broom* published an article about the financial misappropriation of secondary vocational school funds in Varėna in the amount of twenty-one thousand rubles. Student coupons were used for various "receptions," this way appropriating large quantities of food products and money. The lawsuit was discontinued, since there were no facts or circumstances constituting a breach of a law. The director of the school and the chief accountant received severe reprimands. The *Broom* editors could not credit the fact that nobody was really found guilty for the disappearance of twenty-one thousand rubles. The *Broom* published a feuilleton, "Magicians," in which editors laughed at the magic used to transform student food coupons into various food items and alcohol. The feuilleton ended with a sentence indirectly accusing the legal institutions of complicity in a crime: "One more piece of magic happened: twenty-one thousand [rubles in] state funds disappeared, but nobody was guilty. From a big cloud only a small gentle spring drizzle of reprimands." After publication of this feuilleton, the LSSR Prosecutor's Office informed the editors that facts published in the *Broom* were reviewed, and the lawsuit was reopened.[93]

When in 1971 a bicycle valued at twenty rubles was stolen from a student, the Alytus Region Internal Affairs Department refused to press charges since the issue was minor. A student complained to the *Broom*, and the editors forwarded his letter to the Ministry of Internal Affairs, which instructed the department to open the case and take measures to find the bicycle.[94] In 1970 the *Broom* mediated in another case when a bag of flour and jars with jam and apples were stolen in the town of Miroslavas. While two men were found guilty of stealing the flour, jam, and apples and were given a public reprimand and fines of fifteen and twenty rubles by the Comrades' Court, they did not pay the fines for the stolen items.[95] The *Broom* intervened after receiving a letter about the unpaid fines. A letter from a prosecutor, copied to the *Broom*, asked the city Executive Committee, which oversaw Comrades' Court decisions, to intervene in this case, so that the fines were paid.[96] While the thefts took place in March 1970, the letter from the Prosecutor's Office wasn't sent until January 1972, making the two women, who lost flour and preserves, wait almost two years for justice to be carried out. Another letter by a kolkhoz worker from the Anykščiai region complained that the Comrades' Court and other institutions did not punish a man who beat him up because the family of this "hooligan" had connections. He bitterly concluded that only god will punish hooligans (box 7.2).

Box 7.2. Reader's letter: There is no justice in the world

I sometimes read in the magazine *Broom* about very funny accidents, and we also had a funny accident, which should be reported in the magazine.[97]

I will write how hooligans are punished. Hooligans will be punished by god.

In Anykščiai region, on the "May 1" collective farm lives Jonaitis Pranas and his son Jonas. Jonas returned from the Army just two years ago, but he is already known for his bravery. He beat up Grinius Bronius. Next Šiaulys Bronius, then Paukštė Povilas, and after some time me because I had to transport potatoes with horses, . . . I could not find horses in the pasture. I saw that in his own homestead plot Jonaitis was using horses that I was assigned to take for transporting manure. When I approached him and requested the horses, he beat me up so [badly] that I was on a sick leave for six days. For about a month I felt pain in my chest and head. I thought hooligans have to be stopped once. I've got a testimonial about the battery [and] bruises from my doctors. I went to the Anykščiai police, showed [them] the [doctor's] note. The police officer read it. I went to the Court. An attorney wrote a statement. I gave it to the judge. . . . [He] read and [regretted that now he would have to] give [the hooligan] a year or two sentence in prison. It's a shame. "So, give fifteen days, not a year or two," [I suggested]. "We [the Court] cannot give fifteen days, I will resend it to the Comrades' Court," [the judge explained]. . . .

We got a notice to appear in the [Comrades'] Court. The judge of the Comrades' Court . . . listened to both the victim and the accused, [and] left to discuss the case. When he returned, he said Petkus Petras [the author of this letter] will get a fine of ten rubles. [It's] not clear why; he did not say. And who will punish the hooligans. . .? They will be punished by god after death.

Since he was not called to the Comrades' Court, during dances Jonas beat another young guy. I don't know his name, [it happened] up in Nokonys. . . .

It turns out that the court encourages [them] to beat people up. You can beat others and me [and the Court] will help if you need anything, a knife, an ax, or another gun. I can explain it—Jonaitis Pranas daughter Dana . . . is studying to become a prosecutor. That's why the Comrades' Court did not punish them. Connections helped, maybe money as well. . . . Let's talk openly. Is there any justice in the world, or not? There is no justice. There was no justice and there never will be. The masses describe it in all kinds of ways. Some say that justice was made up by the smart people, so the stupid will look for it. Others say that justice exists, but it is blind, it cannot see, still others say that justice is money, and a person is powerless if he does not have it. . . . Now I know that there is no justice, there has been no justice, and won't be any. Where did you see that the Court would defend hooligans? Petras Petkus, Anykščių region, May 1 kolkhoz, August 4, 1971.

If we sum up the vision of justice reconstructed from the *Broom* journalists' work with letters, it would be a society without cheaters, speculators, bribe givers or recipients, careerists, and thieves. All people would be employed and in good relations at work, divorced men would pay alimony for their children, men would drink responsibly, and nobody would share "bourgeois" values or act arrogantly.

All people would protect state property, work efficiently and responsibly. The leadership at workplaces would respect and protect their workers, while the workplace authorities would be responsive and accountable to citizens. This vision of a just society tells us that the *Broom*'s justice was primarily about fairness defined through the workplace and a collective. Public service relations in public spaces and good morals mattered as well. The *Broom* promoted this vision as well as the state's commitment to achieve this form of justice. It was not about fairness of the regime to its citizens, the accountability of the government and higher-ranking authorities, equal redistribution of resources, or equal rights.[98] In this context, returning to other scholars' arguments about letters promoting accountability and the legitimacy of the government, trust between citizens and the state, one could question whether the high numbers of letters themselves sent to state institutions are sufficient evidence that this policy of participation of citizens in state governance by writing letters of complaint worked.

The *Broom*'s satirical justice prevailed in the absence of a well-functioning legal and administrative system and ceased to exist in 1990 when Lithuania became an independent democratic state. A copy of one letter, written on October 7, 1990, and sent to the general prosecutor of the Lithuanian Republic and the *Broom*, illustrates the transformation of the satirical justice institution. The letter documented how salesclerks sold goods only to familiar people, while customers standing in line were told that new merchandise was not available anymore.[99] The letter writer explained that when she drafted a letter of complaint and collected signatures from others, salesclerks threatened to sue them because they undermined the clerks' dignity and honor. The letter writer reported that she was actually sued; she had to attend five court hearings, and received fines.[100] She later claimed in her letter to the general prosecutor and the *Broom* that justice is conditioned by relationships and corrupt courts. She regretted that she and the other complainants were being unjustly punished in the name of the Republic of Lithuania.[101] "We would like to know why laws have been passed, resolutions about fighting corruption, speculation? To deceive people? . . . Why did we suffer in deportation camps, prisons, so others would make fun of us even now?"[102] The *Broom* editors had no state-delegated authority to interfere anymore. Moreover, the magazine itself was sued for publications targeting authorities. While in Soviet times the *Broom* journalists in some cases were able to bring justice to ordinary people, without resources to win court cases and without political support they could not help them anymore. All cases had to be resolved in court, ending the magazine's thirty-year role as a justice arbiter. The *Broom*'s satirical justice institution did not survive into post-Soviet times.

In 1988 and 1989 the major satirical justice section "After the *Broom* Wrote," along with the publication of readers' letters, was still a regular feature in the *Broom*. In 1988 readers continued to write about lack of housing, complain about court decisions, express dissatisfaction about new fees for restroom use, or reflect on alcoholism or order in the city.[103] This section was discontinued in 1990. The disintegration of the institution of satirical justice illustrates that it was an institution of the authoritarian state: it depended on the state's support, promoted official visions of justice, and engaged readers for propaganda and prophylactic purposes. Readers had to ridicule fellow citizens for drinking or speculating, laugh at corrupt kolkhoz chairmen, criticize and moralize about drinking or hooliganism. As the next chapter illustrates, readers engaged in satirical justice and were active participants in the Soviet state satirical institution, but without an intent to build communism.

SOVIET DYSTOPIA

It cannot be worse. But it is!

—Jeronimas Laucius, 1990

People walk on wooden planks in flooded, muddy yards to safely reach apartment building entrances. In other yards, there are unfinished sidewalks and construction debris. Children play in playgrounds with broken wire fences and sandboxes without sand, and drive their bicycles over mud-washed roads in apartment housing districts. In parks, there are piles of garbage and leaking pipes discharging polluted water into rivers. On roads, there are deadly potholes and unreliable signs. This world is full of breakages and leakages: furniture breaks, apartment ceilings drip, a coat taken to the cleaners disappears, and new shoes lose their soles during the first walk. Water, mud, and garbage are everywhere (figure 8.1). This dystopian world emerges in people's complaint letters in the 1970s and early 1980s to the *Broom*.[1]

Dystopias are characterized by dehumanization, tyrannies, environmental disasters, and other aspects associated with a cataclysmic social decline. According to Michael D. Gordin, Helen Tilley, and Gyan Prakash (2010, 8), dystopia "is a utopia that has gone wrong." Utopia is about the future; it directs the present. Dystopia uncovers a dark reality; the "impulse or desire for a better future is usually present in each" (9). Like utopia, dystopia is not a comprehensive vision of reality. While the former projects an ideal that is usually impossible to attain, the latter exposes various breakages, leakages, dangers, and discontents (14). Gordin, Tilley, and Prakash, emulating the ideas of Karl Mannheim ([1929] 1991, 209), argue that histories of utopia and dystopia illuminate the "subjective positioning of historical agents. Tell me what you yearn for, and I will tell you who you are" (12). Thus, narrated materialities, such as muddy yards and deadly roads, are

FIGURE 8.1.   A store in Ukmergė is "unreachable without getting one's feet wet," wrote a reader from this city. The photo was taken and published in 1972, *Broom* no. 14, p. 15. Photo from the Lithuanian Archive of Literature and Art, LALA, 1973, f. 361, ap. 2, b. 240, l. 25.

biographical and political; they mediate the relationship between citizens, the public space, and the state.

The Soviet state promulgated utopian visions of the modern lifestyles of Soviet citizens living in the most progressive society and marching to a communist future. In July 1961, in a speech to the Central Committee, Nikita Khrushchev, first secretary of the CPSU (1953–1964), claimed that the next generation of Soviet people would live in a communist paradise. The Soviet Union would "rise to such a great height that, by comparison, the main capitalist countries will remain far below and way behind" (cited in Zubok 2009, 123). Under Leonid Brezhnev, ideas of progress in agriculture and industry, of socialism as the most advanced form of government, of people working to advance communism, and achievements of the celebrated working class continued to define Soviet modernity. Although without the revolutionary fervor common in Khrushchev's time (see Wolfe 2005), Brezhnev emphasized material welfare, growth of living standards, and social advancement.

This chapter inquiries into citizens' relations to Soviet modern materialities—their everyday encounters with objects and surroundings in public spaces in the 1970s and early 1980s, as described in their published and unpublished letters to the *Broom*. People's stories expressed dissociations from the Soviet project, disenchantment with Soviet modernity, and yearnings for a better future. As argued in the introduction, following Jacques Rancière, the reshaping of a sensory experience is at the core of politics itself. Politics, according to Rancière, "indeed, is not the exercise of, or struggle for, power. It is the configuration of a specific space, the framing of a particular sphere of experience, of objects posited as common and as pertaining to a common decision, of subjects recognized as capable of designating these objects and putting forward arguments about them" (Rancière 2009, 24). Politics is "an activity of reconfiguration of that which is given in the sensible" (Rancière and Panagia 2000, 115). In this context *Broom* readers were political actors putting forward arguments about their sensible experiences of Soviet materialities, challenging visions of Soviet modernity, and expressing a desire for something different.[2]

In their letters of complaint, citizens most often wrote about public spaces in their immediate, everyday surroundings, such as yards, children's playgrounds, parks, squares, streets, and roads. In these public spaces they most often noticed material aspects that made their lives unsafe (potholes in the roads), uncomfortable (flooded yards), or unpleasant (dumped garbage) (figure 8.2). Another group of commonly mentioned materialities was interconnected with their consumption experiences. Letter writers referred to stores, service shops, cafeterias, and canteens when complaining about furniture and household commodities, clothing, or food.[3] Many other spaces were public, including schools, workplaces, and theaters, but these were rarely the targets of complaint. People never wrote about theaters, and there were just a few letters about schools. The majority of letters about workplaces concerned relationships between the leadership and workers rather than Soviet materialities (see chapter 7). Readers' choice to write about yards, playgrounds, parks, roads, cafeterias, and service spaces was also dictated by the *Broom*, which extensively covered these topics in its pages.

The *Broom* published on Soviet materialities responding to Communist Party priorities to criticize various shortcomings that people encountered in society (see chapter 3). For the editors, publishing about garbage in public spaces, defective chairs, or poorly produced shoes was much safer than directly criticizing higher officials for corruption or other misdeeds (see chapter 7). Criticism of garbage piles, puddles, flooding, and muddy roads was published in the *Broom* as early as 1957 and became very prominent in the 1970s. As this chapter will show, this "safe" approach to Soviet materialities that presumably did not challenge the power of authorities (see chapter 7) produced powerful dystopian stories, which in turn expressed discontent reaching much beyond a particular garbage pile encountered in an apartment building yard. In some cases, the garbage pile became a metonym for the regime itself.

Readers' letters to the *Broom* were usually short, but sometimes they even exceeded ten pages. The longer letters might include additional information on

FIGURE 8.2.   A 1982 photo from the city of Trakai, titled "The future Trakai stadium 'shines' from far away." It was not published in the *Broom*. Photo from the Lithuanian Archive of Literature and Art, LALA, 1982, f. 361, ap. 2, b. 628, l. 9.

the writer's particular cause for discontent, as well as supporting documents or correspondence with other institutions testifying to how issues were addressed before the writer turned to the *Broom*. Some letter writers wrote and sent to the *Broom* feuilletons based on their encounters. Almost all the letters were written in Lithuanian. The letters from men were much more numerous, most likely because public issues were traditionally a male sphere of interest. In 1976, from several hundred archived letters to the *Broom*, about one-fifth were written by women. Although women and men wrote about all kinds of issues, men tended to address public-order issues, while women raised problems concerning their house, apartment building, or their apartment itself. Some writers, when addressing, for example, problems with their apartments, apartment building stairways, or basements, might send letters with multiple signatures.

Broom sought to publish pieces about different cities and regions of Lithuania, to represent its many geographic areas. Citizens from towns and villages wrote about unfinished construction projects or culture houses in disrepair, unattended collective farm machinery, and various wrongdoings, such as leaving twenty tons of carp to freeze on a fish farm during a cold winter.[4] In cities, problems were more diverse: people living in high-rise apartment blocks wrote about municipal and public order, their experiences in restaurants and cafeterias, stores, and service shops. Many issues were encountered similarly in both rural and urban areas: insufficient street lighting, broken sewers, and disorder in public spaces.

This chapter focuses on the experiences of public space and consumption from primarily *Broom* readers' perspectives. In the section "Materialities of Public Spaces" I analyze dystopian projections of public spaces encountered in everyday lives. The section "Everyday Objects of Discontent" analyzes consumption experiences in stores, canteens, and cafeterias. The last section, "Soviet Dystopia," shows that people wrote about "shortcomings" not as accidental, but as inseparable from everyday life. Letter writers questioned official Communist Party ideology about "shortcomings" and expressed a generalized critique of socialist everyday life. Negative depictions of socialist materialities encountered in public spaces communicated desires for a better future. Moreover, some letters implicitly or explicitly criticized the regime. The *Broom* censored letters and edited them in ways that muted direct criticism or anger toward the regime. However, editors and artists shared dystopian stories themselves and expressed them in satires and cartoons (see also chapter 6). Sometimes they generalized explicitly by stating that similar problems or conditions can be encountered in other cities. By routinely publishing critical readers' letters, satires, and cartoons, the *Broom* editors advanced arguments about everyday life as Soviet dystopia.

Soviet Materialities

In a well-known 1962 painting by Soviet artist Iurii Pimenov, titled *Wedding on Tomorrow Street*, newlyweds walk through a construction site amid cranes and rising apartment buildings. The bride, in a white dress and high heels, and the groom, in suit and tie and holding a bouquet, happily stroll on rough wooden planks over the mud into their new life in a new Soviet district. According to Susan Reid, "Soviet modernity, as represented in Pimenov's painting, is not something ready-made and finished, but is a work in progress" (Reid 2014, 87–88). The painting thus reflects on a process in the making—the party-state initiatives to pay greater attention to mass living standards, to build standardized and modern industrial-age living spaces (see Reid 2014). A Communist Party decree from July 31, 1957, launched an intensive program for mass-industrialized housing construction (89). The development of new districts of standard apartment blocks followed Lenin's utopian revolutionary experiment in living (see Boym 1994; Varga-Harris 2015). According to Susan Reid, Soviet modernity appeared as a "clean, bright, new world rising out of the swamp, in which the benefits of space-age science and technology were extended to the daily life of the masses" (2014, 89).

The Soviet modernization of Lithuania followed the model established in the first decades after the Bolshevik Revolution in Russia: requisition of land and forced collectivization, nationalization of private and church property, and economic restructuring based on the Soviet model.[5] Largely agricultural Lithuania became urbanized and industrialized during the Soviet era, but people often contrasted Soviet modernity to Western modernity to express their criticism of Soviet progress.[6] In the Soviet era, Lithuanian writers wrote about disruption of social relationships, traditional lifestyles, and Lithuanian villagers uprooted from their land (see, e.g., Granauskas 1988; Radzevičius [1979] 2008). According to Violeta Davoliūtė (2013), during the Soviet period, urbanization, collectivization, and land improvement led to the displacement of Lithuanian villagers from their rural homesteads to modern towns and traumatized them. During the perestroika movement in the late 1980s, political and cultural elites claimed that "the history of Lithuanian economic and political development would have paralleled Scandinavian countries if not for the Soviet annexation" (Klumbytė 2003, 284). Since independence, the post-Soviet Lithuanian government counts material and moral losses during the Soviet occupation in billions of dollars.[7]

Even if villagers or urban dwellers enjoyed new Soviet modern lifestyles, many encountered worrisome shortcomings on a daily basis. While in Pimenov's *Wedding on Tomorrow Street* newlyweds happily walk through a muddy construction site into the new future, for many readers of the *Broom*, the ruination of Soviet modernity foreclosed imagining a happy future (see figure 8.3). One man who had moved into a new cooperative apartment building wrote to the *Broom* in 1975, "In May 1974, a cooperative house was built here, and it was beautifully named 'Friendship.' This cooperative house was the first and most likely the last; nobody else will be willing to join cooperatives and friendships again." He reported that the ground-floor inhabitants had been flooded, clothes became moldy in closets, door handles fell off, there were no shower heads, and "at night, mice peek and laugh through holes in the floor. They say, you got what you deserve." Balconies are "like brown-and-white pied cows, one patch is brown, another white." A tractor crushes footbridges, which were made by the people themselves, and the tractor driver "sits in the tractor and laughs when schoolchildren get soaked in mud up to their waists when they go to school."[8] (The letter included thirty-five signatures.) Other complaints about newly built houses and their surroundings mentioned a variety of issues: windows could not be opened, water did not reach the highest floors, elevators were not working, the roof was damaged, streets were unpaved, pavement was destroyed. The everyday sensory experiences of Soviet materialities were humiliating, which starkly contrasted

FIGURE 8.3. On the way home in the city of Kaunas. Published in the *Broom*, 1974, no. 24, p. 15. Photo from the Lithuanian Archive of Literature and Art, LALA, f. 361, ap. 2, b. 265, l. 4.

with the smiling, modern citizens moving into new buildings presented in the official Soviet discourse.

Some images published in the *Broom* were staged, taken by *Broom* journalists, or changed to make a bigger impact. The image from the city of Ukmergė (figure 8.1) was retaken from a different perspective to make the puddle look like a "mere." The *Broom* published a short note next to the image: "A mere in the center of the city . . .," calling people to see this geographical novelty after a regular rain. In the "mere" a *Broom* artist drew a spouting whale. The original of another image with a man on planks (figure 8.3) portrayed the man in coat and hat and carrying a briefcase as in the original, but there was a woman with an umbrella in front of him, walking on the planks. A story published with this image narrated that the letter was signed by the cooperative chairs of six apartment building complexes in Partizanų Street in Kaunas. It stated that readers reported similar water and dirt issues in the cities of Tauragė and Alytus.

On October 29, 1969, dentist Irena Karkauskaitė sent a letter to the *Broom* together with her essay on everyday life along Kaunas Central Boulevard. She wrote that she had lived there for two years and had "suffered through it" while "thousands of people continue to suffer through this."[9] In her seven-page creative essay, which she claimed was based on facts, the woman writes how a family went to visit their friends in a new housing district: A woman named Konstancija, in a lace dress and lacquer shoes, and her husband, Petras, in his foreign-brand shoes, pack up their luggage and pick up a cake. In Kaunas they hire a taxi to take them to their Central Boulevard destination. Before entering Central Boulevard, the taxi driver announces, "Attention, we are entering Kaunas City Central Mud Place." Petras tries to object, citing facts from the media that Central Boulevard is paved, but the taxi driver only laughs sarcastically. When they arrive, they see piles of mud and pits with muddy water all around. They walk on planks, bricks, tin sheets, and pieces of old furniture over mud. Kostancija slips and steps into the mud. Her shoe gets stuck. On the same "monkey bridge" in front of them a drunk man appears, who falls into the mud and cannot get out. They see children fighting in the mud, a man yelling from the balcony at a seven-year-old child who is ordered to help a five-year-old get out of the mud. The couple decides to go back home right away, but when they reach a road and hail a taxi, the taxi driver refuses to give them a ride because of their dirty shoes and clothes. Women passing by advise them to wash their shoes in a cleaner puddle, so they can get into a taxi.[10] The *Broom* editors did not publish this piece. They wrote to the author that "such facts are common in every region, construction workers still cannot fix everything on time."[11] "Still" was added to their response later, after the original letter was written, most likely to indicate, following the Communist Party official discourse, that "enduring shortcomings" are temporary.

Children were often portrayed in Soviet media as the future of communist society. But like the children in Irena Karkauskaitė's essay, children in citizens' letters were reported having to cycle through muddy streets, or play in playgrounds with broken barbwire fencing, or in a sandbox without sand. One reader sent a photo of children on a playground in a Khrushchevite housing district, along with a comment that the playground "has been in ruins and, people say [sarcastically], when snowy winter comes, you will not be able to see this garbage."[12] One letter, written from the children's perspective, asked the *Broom* to "help us little ones to sweep trash and metal scrap" from the amusement park in the city of Palanga. "The Ferris wheel [has] not mov[ed] for two years. A train has stopped. Carousels are not moving either."[13] The *Broom* criticized disorder in another city park in a short, published note, "A Self-Service Carousel," ending with the ironic words, "Why do they need to fix a carousel if they [children] are having fun anyway, without elephants and horses."[14]

Readers complained to the *Broom* about various other parks, most often noticing garbage or polluted waters. One letter writer documented how the Nemunas riverside park in Kaunas had become an unsanitary garbage site where drunks gathered. The author included a satirical story about how a couple, going to listen to nightingales, end up navigating trash, stepping on a can of preserves, getting caught in wire, and stopping by a pipe that discharges polluted water into the river.[15]

A particular concern for letter writers was safety in public spaces. People had to walk home on unfinished sidewalks, avoid poorly covered holes, climb ruined stairs, or fear falling into an open sewage pit or walking under collapsing balconies (see figure 8.4). The photo with a collapsed balcony was published in the *Broom* with a short satirical essay—a dispute between residents from different Kaunas city streets, some from the Laisvės Avenue house No. 85 in the city center, and others from Prancūzų Street house No. 78, in a new housing district. Both sides disagreed on where it was better to live. In the city center, in a brick house, they had to heat the apartments with firewood, live under a damaged roof, and be wary of collapsing balconies and deep pits by the house. In the new district, residents experienced unreliable heating schedules, falling ceiling plaster, sinking floors, and lack of clean water in the wells. The essay concludes that actually the residents in the new housing district are in a better place, since the local government promised them to take care of everything only last year, while residents in the city center have been hearing promises for ten years. This ending might have implied that the new housing district residents could still hope that their

FIGURE 8.4. A collapsed balcony. Published in the *Broom*, 1976, no. 7, p. 15. Photo from the Lithuanian Archive of Literature and Art, LALA, 1976, f. 361, ap. 2, b. 367, l. 10.

apartment building will be fixed. At the same time it suggested that such an out-come was unlikely, since the other house had not been fixed for ten years.

In rare cases letter writers reported about accidents on the roads or mentioned murders. In one letter, a man wrote that because of an unsafe road, a young motorcyclist had died in his town.[16] Another person reported how a bus drove into a hole in the road, causing an accident in which one passenger's ribs were broken, a woman lost some of her teeth, other passengers were bruised, and the author suffered a concussion.[17] Other people complained about dark streets, and one letter recalled that there was a still-unsolved murder.[18]

Transportation service was another everyday nuisance. Road signs and bus schedules were not reliable, bus station waiting areas were unclean, with broken windows, and benches were missing (see box 8.1). In the small town of Kamajai, the bus randomly stopped at one of three different places. In a humorous story of how passengers tried to guess where the bus was going to stop on a particular day, one Kamajai resident wrote that it was a good exercise in winter to run from one place to another and treat oneself to a burst of energy.[19] Things could be worse, according to Pabališkiai residents: in their small town, the train often did not stop at all.[20]

Box 8.1. At the bus and train station

Dear editors,

   I was born and grew up in Rokiškis, and I would like to tell you about the hard-ships of this town, specifically about the bus and train station.

   In the station, every morning you can see drunk young people and other shady people. There are fights every day and passengers are often the victims. . . . In the station there is a police office, but it's usually closed. It's not a surprise then that there is so much hooliganism and crime.

   Dear editors, please use your "Broom" to punish Rokiškis's town authorities, who transformed the station into a beer bar.[21]

   An excerpt from a reader's letter, Utena, November 20, 1974.

In 1975, a journalist from Anykščiai wrote about his experiences: a man arrived at the bus station and had to guess whether the bus would run or not. Every day, five to seven buses do not depart from the station. Tickets are sold sometimes at the bus station, sometimes on the bus, sometimes nowhere. Conductors and drivers take money for themselves. In some cases, one waits for a couple of hours and then leaves on foot. Bus drivers sometimes leave for lunch and do not come back.[22] On May 23, 1975, the *Broom* published a report about a regional bus station: "In the bus station in Pasvalys a new fashion trend blew away all the benches. . . . Women, waiting for a bus, sit on bare ground. Charming, comfortable, but hippie-style is not [suitable] for their age."[23] Another letter invited the *Broom* to come to clean the bus station in Švenčionys. The author wrote about how a cleaner had swept the floor in such a way that "dust and cigarette butts landed in corners and under benches. . . . In the hall there was a cold draft coming from both doors with broken windows. . . . When a woman with two children came, she was thrilled to see a note on the door 'Mother's and child's room,' but the door was locked." The author invited the *Broom* to bring a cleaning cloth. It was signed, "With respect and a runny nose.—B.G."[24]

Depictions of public spaces questioned socialist modernity valorized in the newspapers and on television. The modern materialities of public spaces were presented as incomplete, disorderly, unsafe, an outcome of the authorities' and people's carelessness and neglect. The *Broom* reinforced the letters' discourse by only rarely pointing out in published articles that these were singular, "enduring shortcomings." Citizens' letters articulated a Soviet dystopia defined by debris and trash, flooding and mud, pollution and even death in public spaces.

Everyday Objects of Discontent

At the Twenty-Fourth Communist Party Congress in 1971, Leonid Brezhnev emphasized that the major task of a new five-year plan was to secure the growth of the material and cultural standards of people's lives (see Prybyla 1971, 227). The Soviet government embraced post-collectivist values by promoting private life and material consumption (Paretskaya 2012). It also presented consumption as a social right of its citizens (Klumbytė and Sharafutdinova 2012). Scholars of socialist Eastern Europe argue that socialist consumer appetites were stimulated by the insistence that under socialism the standard of living would constantly improve (Verdery 1996, 28). Socialist fashion journals, shop window displays, and a black market of Soviet and foreign goods shaped consumer desires and modern consumption expectations.

Readers' letters to the *Broom* reported on consumer experiences in terms of shortages, breakages, and various defects. One common theme was the poor quality of things, which often broke, and various production defects, such as shoes with buckles on the same side. The *Broom* wrote that instead of sending a letter, one reader brought to the *Broom*'s office "Red October" (Raudonasis spalis) shoes with buckles on the same side. The shoes, editors joked, illustrated how the Red October factory was expanding its production to include new styles.[25] Readers or other journalists brought various other user-unfriendly items, such as a spoon with a hole in its bowl.[26] Publishing a photo of this spoon, the *Broom* ironically wrote about the ingenuity of cafeteria leadership who ordered that holes be drilled in spoons to prevent customers from stealing them.[27] At the *Broom* editorial office, editors set up a museum of defective items.[28] In this museum they had a split metal ax; a tooth that had broken when a journalist bit a piece of chocolate candy with a "stone filling"; a harmonica that one could not blow; a piece of metal from a loaf of bread; and a piece of wire from a sausage.[29]

The letters from different factories to the *Broom*, which responded to readers' complaints about their production, mention candies with a piece of string, a raisin candy with a stone,[30] and cigarette packs lacking cigarettes.[31] Regarding the candy with a stone, the director of the Rūta confectionary factory responded that the raisins were received from foreign suppliers and had already been inspected by the Control Commission and therefore not reevaluated at the factory. They apologized for the incident and promised to control the quality of production more carefully and sort out raisins in the factory.[32] "Nuts are stored in bags," wrote the same factory director to the *Broom*, responding to another complaint, explaining that a piece of bag yarn had got into the cauldron where the candies were made. He reported that the administration discussed the reader's complaint and punished the workers who were in charge.[33]

One *Broom* issue included an investigative piece by journalist Ona Banadienė based on readers' letters on various shoe issues: in the summer you could get winter boots, but there were no summer shoes; factories continued to produce small-size shoes even if the average women's shoe size was considerably larger. Defects included newly produced shoe zippers that were broken, soles that were glued incorrectly, shoes that were sewn improperly, shoes with different-colored soles.[34] Banadienė writes that forty-one thousand pairs of shoes were returned to the P. Eidukevičius shoe factory because of various defects, and about the same number of pairs were also returned to the Elnias (Deer) enterprise.[35] Themes about substandard production were also common in *Broom* cartoons. One 1977 cartoon by V. Gorbačiovas portrays a man walking through the door in an orange suit jacket while two security guards exchange comments: "I think he stole a suit!" one guard says. "Impossible! What idiot would steal our products?" the other guard responds.[36] A 1981 cartoon by H. Vaigauskas juxtaposed official rhetoric about advances in the development of new production and the continuing lack of quality by showing two men in an office looking at examples of the newest products—shoes with heels attached to their front (see Bulota and Pakalnis 1984, 88).

In the "Following Readers' Letters" column, *Broom* journalist Vytautas Katilius wrote about things that broke: You have to wait for a refrigerator repairman for three days instead of going to work; in the evening you have to take your broken shoes back to the shoe repair shop even if they had been "fixed" in the morning. Shoddy kitchen stools broke because they were made using moist wood; the wood couldn't be dried because the equipment in the factory that was supposed to dry the wood didn't work, and it didn't work because the factory hadn't had a conveyer belt for several years. Like many others, Katilius thought that kitchen stools were not a trivial matter. They were symptomatic of everyday life in Soviet modernity: "Of course, a stool isn't a set of furniture or a refrigerator. It costs only a little more than five rubles. However, today the stool breaks, tomorrow your pocketknife, and after tomorrow . . . then we'll feel that all these small things become a big matter that poisons our blood, and [disrupts] normal work or rest" (Katilius 1981, 2–3).

Food and clothing were among the major objects of discontent reported in citizens' letters. Letters noted that restaurant and cafeteria food was cold or spoiled. One letter writer complained about an unclean cafeteria, with flies buzzing around, and a fly in the soup: "Is it so hard to get rid of flies, organize the space for a guest to have a delicious meal in a leisurely atmosphere?"[37] reflected the letter writer. Some letter writers complained about cafeteria staff who cheated customers by cutting the measure of sour cream or beer to make some money on the side.[38] They wrote about poor hygiene in food stores, as in a complaint from the city of Kapsukas, where at one store meat was being wrapped in old journal pages.[39] They also reported that there were no complaint books available in restaurants. As noted in a letter from the resort city of Palanga, where a complaint book was evidently available, leaving an entry did not change anything. Juozas Čepelė, who signed as the LSSR "honorary inventor" (Lith. *racionalizatorius*), complained that there were no prunes in the dish "beef with prunes," that the pancakes were cold, and that there was no variety in the dishes listed on the menu.[40] Another letter reported that extra water was added to the dough to make it heavier, and the bakers stole the flour. Everything that could be stolen was stolen: milk and vodka were diluted, and meat was mixed with bread to make meat patties. As with other examples, these complaints were not one-off, but symptomatic of consumption experiences.

Women shopping for clothing wrote letters about shops with little merchandise and poor-quality goods. They complained that they could not find clothing in their size or of good quality. Merchandise from reputable factories was difficult to find because people bought it as soon as it became available (Lith. *išgraibsto*).[41] In 1975, a woman from Vilnius wrote about bras and about men's shirts, vividly describing how men found collars "reaching up to their ears," while a woman wearing a bra "becomes an invalid" (Lith. *invalidas*), because one breast gets pushed under an arm and the other is pushed not up, but down.[42] She finished

her letter by including an ideologically correct statement emphasizing the desirability of socialist production over imported goods: "It's sickening to look for
imports. We can, and we have to produce well in our country, too."[43] In another
letter, two women asked the *Broom* where they could get size 39–40 winter boots:
"It is a major problem because I stopped at every store in the LSSR, and there are
no winter boots of this size. The shop assistants told me that there had not been
[shoes] of this size and never would be."[44] In the letter, the women hypothesized
that it was likely that this size shoe was sold from the storehouse for those who
had connections, because the stores carried only small-size shoes.[45] In the illegal
market, larger-size winter boots were reportedly sold for up to 180 rubles.[46] "We
ask you to help us solve this old problem. . . . [Authorities] have to think about
us, too, so we don't need to run from one place to another and beg shop assistants
for the right size shoes."[47]

Encounters with everyday objects such as furniture, food, and clothing exemplified the state's failure to live up to citizens' expectations of modern consumption, expectations generated by the state itself. The modern objects came with
defects, broke, were unusable, unattractive, of poor quality, or simply absent. As
with readers' experiences of modern materialities in public spaces, their letters
about modern objects told the story of Soviet dystopia.

Soviet Dystopia

Readers wrote about "shortcomings" not as accidental but as recurring aspects
of everyday life, not as a part, but as a totality, generalizing "shortcomings" as
intrinsic to the socialist regime and becoming its critics. The negative encounters
were continuous in time ("Nobody helps me," "I am tired of this") and repeti-
tive in space ("It is not only about people from the city of Mažeikiai," "In all of
the LSSR there are no larger-size winter boots"). Letter writers described their
sensory relations to materialities of public spaces ("We walked home in mud"),
articulating their dissatisfaction and humiliation, in this way expressing their
dissensus. Moreover, there was rarely a positive stance that would fulfill the ideological imperative of the Soviet utopian vision of an optimistic, future-looking
citizen. Temporality was different. Unlike in the abovementioned 1962 painting
by Soviet artist Iurii Pimenov, *Wedding on Tomorrow Street*, there was no beautiful and happy future, and the present was defined by disaffection, discontent,
and even suffering. The future looked bleak, and hopelessness was integral to
citizens' narratives.

In citizens' letters, the critique of their everyday encounters with Soviet
modernity was usually implicit and can be identified through allusions and hints.

Comments such as "I can't believe that in the era of spaceships, in our country you can't find glue to hold a shoe sole together" could have been a criticism of the socialist regime itself. In 1975, a man from the city of Telšiai complained that after he put on new shoes produced by the Red October factory, the sole came off. He considered who was to blame:

> First of all, winter is to blame: snow melted, moisture affected the glue, the sole fell off. "You're to blame," I hear my grandfather's voice. ["]We went to church with shoes over our shoulders, putting them on only in the churchyard["] . . . Red October is to blame, too, especially the packaging department. They could've included an instruction on how to wear shoes, or at least draw an umbrella on the box. Tradespeople are guilty, too; maybe they sold shoes produced for the Frank Kruk funeral parlor to living people.[48]

The letter writer advised Red October to start producing wooden shoes, "so they wouldn't wear out; they can use cheap material and will not need any glue."[49] In this way, he juxtaposed the quality of peasant shoes worn in the past with present-day, poor-quality Soviet products.

In some instances, the letter writers extended generalized critique to authorities and openly expressed their dissensus. Such generalized critique was censored by the *Broom*, which had to enforce the ideological position that all problems are past survivals and "enduring shortcomings." Residents of the city of Mažeikiai, for example, asked the *Broom* to help solve construction defects and unfinished work in their apartment building. They wrote, "We considered appealing to the Party Committee, the Executive Committee, however, it occurs [to us] that people who work there are so detached from ordinary people that they even eat their own 'Party' bread baked for them in the bread factory. Will they care about such small stuff? The 'Kremlin' built for them in the center of downtown is surrounded by green grass."[50] (This letter included sixteen signatures.) In another letter, a man swore at the Soviet government because he was not allowed to work as a taxi driver and in this way earn more money.[51] A journalist from Klaipėda, assigned to investigate the letter, wrote that this man complained to all institutions, including the CPSU CC and the USSR Council of Ministers. He speculated that the man might have a psychiatric disorder and decided to wait for confirmation from the health institution before investigating the case.[52]

Readers blamed "Lithuanians" or "Russians" for various vexations and afflictions. One reader wrote, "We live in a socialist society, as K. Marx said, it is the most just society, so why do brother Lithuanians deceive us?"[53] In another, anonymous, letter of 1984, a reader encouraged the *Broom* to name the actual culprits and say explicitly whether Russians liberated or occupied Lithuania:

> Our Dear beloved *Broom*,
> You have helped us for so many years, the deprived proletariat, you advise us, rearrange our existence.
> This time we appeal to you and ask you for advice, so we would not get lost in the crossroads of current times and would not stumble. Write in the *Broom*, don't be afraid: *Did Russians liberate us, or occupy us??*
> We will be waiting and waiting for the answer from the *Broom*, to purify our souls possessed by devils.
> The PROLETARIATS of Lithuania.[54] (emphasis in the original)

Another anonymous letter sent to the *Broom*, also in 1984, used the *Broom*'s fictional character Kindziulis to speak about the hypocrisy of Soviet ideology, Russian occupation, and Russification.

Kindziulis brought out old photos and described them:

> 1. Photo 1: Here I am in 1940 measuring and distributing land to small-holders to own it "forever." Hardworking people [Lith. *liaudis*] are happy, they even dance, they don't think that the biggest *kulak* [Rus., rich peasant]—the government—will take it away.[55]
> 2. Photo 2: Here is a banner: "Vilnius is ours, but we are [owned by] Russians."[56]
> 3. Photo 3: Lithuanians' homeland: from the Baltic to the Black Sea [reference to the Grand Duchy of Lithuania, in the fifteenth century the largest medieval state in Europe], from the river Nemunas to the river Pechora, right through Siberia [most likely a reference to Soviet deportations].
> 4. [Photo 4:] While implementing [school] program reforms it is important to expand and increase education of the Russian language in Lithuanian day care centers. We have to use a successful example with Prussians [reference to the vanished Baltic language and nation].
> 5. [Photo 5:] Purebred Lithuanian candidates to the Supreme Council: Svietlana Chochlanova, Kazimira Palevič, Nikolajus Dybenka and others [Slavic names, implying that Lithuania is ruled by foreigners].[57]
> For the *Broom*,
> Publish, if it is acceptable!!!

Broom journalist Albertas Lukša sent these last two letters to the KGB, which launched an investigation in search of their authors but was not able to find them. The first of these two is written in capital letters with grammatical mistakes, which might have been made on purpose. It is likely that the same person or people wrote these two letters, since both of them came from the city of Panevėžys in 1984. During an interview in 2017 in Liukonys village, Albertas Lukša reflected that it could have been a KGB provocation, which meant he could not ignore these letters and had to forward them to the KGB. Otherwise he could have been accused of concealing nationalistic anti-regime letters.[58]

Some readers compared a "bourgeois" or "capitalist" system with the socialist regime. Writing about glass-cutting shops in 1980, which were always closed in Kaunas, one man mentioned that "earlier you could just mention to a Jew that the wind broke a window. . . . Now workers who cut glass are overworked. . . . They are even afraid to speak without the orders from above."[59] Another reader moralized in his 1980 letter about pipeline drills left by workers, about their irresponsibility and carelessness and the hypocrisy of society, since children are sent to collect metal scrap, while huge pipeline drills are left in the field. He wants to remind readers of only one thing: that "in capitalist countries no manager would behave this way since it costs MONEY."[60]

Readers' letters and their creative experiments resonated with the themes of *Broom* feuilletons and satires. Vytautė Žilinskaitė, a leading Lithuanian satirist, in her feuilleton "A Secret of Immortality," published in the *Broom* in 1966, told a story about a new communal house: "A strange unbelievable rumor started spreading about our modern, communal house. The first year, when we just moved in, it was like any other house—maybe different in its dull appearance. But in a few years, it gained an original fame: the strangest stories started spreading about it. Stories were told that for eight years after it was built, nobody who lived in the house died. If somebody died, it was because of one's stupidity and recklessness. They did not die in the house" (Žilinskaitė 1966, 4).

The author humorously writes that the old people who had cancer did not die after the disease's fourth stage; they had already reached its nineteenth or even thirtieth stage, and were ready to reach even higher stages, leaving their doctors in awe. Sick and old people started to arrive at the house. Mothers with sick children begged residents to take their kids for a few days. Residents rented even their balconies, where people stayed in −30°C temperatures (−22°F). They had to pay three rubles—one ruble for bedsheets, and two for immortality. The author proceeds to write about hopeful scholars who administered surveys. Some scholars argued that immortality was due to bad sound isolation, which affected the brain. Continuous unbearable sounds made the nerves very resistant. Other scholars were convinced that bursting water and sewage pipes produce ultra-air waves, which positively affected the thyroid. According to a third group of scholars, polluted air currents from a factory nearby renewed lung cells and cleaned blood. The most serious hypothesis was about a cockroach infestation: if cock-roaches touch a human with their long antennae, an individual becomes immortal. A few dissertations were defended on this topic, the author claimed. Other rumors started spreading about relocating the residents and giving the house to people with major accomplishments. The story ends with disclosing the big secret of immortality, well known to its residents: how can a person die if a coffin cannot get through the entrance to the apartment?[61]

Just four years after Žilinskaitės's feuilleton was written, a photograph from 1971 (figure 8.5) sent to Bulota by a reader or a colleague shows how people came up with an inventive solution to get a coffin out of a new Khrushchevite apartment building. At the time, memorial services at churches were officially

FIGURE 8.5. A coffin containing the deceased is lowered from the second floor of a Khrushchevite apartment building. Unpublished photograph from 1971. Personal archive of *Broom* editor in chief Juozas Bulota. Courtesy of his son, Juozas Bulota.

disapproved of because of secularization campaigns (see Smolkin 2018; Putinaitė 2015), and funeral homes were not built until the mid-1970s and 1980s (see Drėmaitė 2014), so people had memorial services in their homes or workplaces.[62]

Similar feuilletons and satires, photos, and citizens' letters must have reinforced the notion of Soviet dystopia. Žilinskaitė's skillfully crafted feuilleton shaped emotional and moral worlds, encouraging people to think about housing and everyday life in a critical way. Its laughter was multidirectional: it criticized enduring shortcomings in Soviet society, including bad sound insulation, bursting pipes, and unsanitary conditions; it mocked the stupidity of immortality seekers and scholars; but it also criticized Soviet modern life and expressed a desire for difference. The house could be considered a metonym for the failures of the regime itself.

Some readers' letters indirectly asked questions about the legitimacy and functionality of the regime, about the obvious gap between, on the one hand, propagated values about the equality of working people, respect for ordinary people, and supposedly improving living conditions, and, on the other, their own everyday life experience. This gap between official language and experiential reality was addressed by unofficial jokes. Alexei Yurchak (1997) cites such jokes in his study of the late-socialist USSR:

> What is the most constant element of the Soviet system? [Answer:] Temporary problems.
>
> In what aspect is socialism better than other systems? [Answer:] In that it successfully overcomes difficulties which do not exist in other systems.
>
> How will the problem of lines in shops be solved in communism? [Answer:] There will be nothing left to line up for. (Yurchak 1997, 179)

Kateryna Yeremieieva and Vladimir Kulikov (2013), who studied the Soviet Ukrainian satire and humor magazine *Perets*, remind us that unofficial humor on consumption was much more critical and negative than what could be found in *Perets*. It addressed more important issues, such as allocation of apartments, cars, and dachas. In unofficial discourse, Soviet people are presented as "surviving" rather than consuming. A consumption-as-survival theme was not present in *Perets* (Yeremieieva and Kulikov 2013, 265). *Broom* readers rarely criticized allocation of apartments and never wrote about allocation of cars or dachas or consumption as survival. Writing to the *Broom*, readers indirectly knew what they could criticize and what could get published (see also chapter 7).

Explicit recognition of the gaps between the state's ideological discourse and everyday life experiences is not present in the *Broom* magazine. However, *Broom* satires, feuilletons, small humor pieces, and cartoons exposed these gaps through multidirectional laughter (chapter 6). Vytautas Žeimantas, a journalist at the *Truth* newspaper and LCP Central Committee vice chair of the Propaganda and Agitation Department from 1984 to 1988, remembered how *Broom* editors gathered and made decisions about what to include in the magazine. In their conversations they used Aesopian language and criticized socialism. At the *Truth*, nobody criticized socialism, according to him. At the *Broom* they did.[63] Bulota, the *Broom* editor in chief, was criticized by the Central Committee when it learned that a daily newspaper published by the American Lithuanians abroad mentioned that the *Broom* described Soviet reality quite accurately (*Šluota* 1991, 3). In perestroika-era public lecture notes, Bulota acknowledged that shortcomings were not decreasing, but increasing, in society.[64]

In her analysis of socialist materialities through the lens of interior living-space design in Hungary, Krisztina Fehérváry notes that utopian materiality was discredited by the 1970s: "Instead of realizing a modern, utopian society, the materialities of state-produced goods and housing became affectively aligned with the impersonal and bureaucratic state" (Fehérváry 2013, 5). Hungarian men and women "complained bitterly of having to endure the continuing abnormalities in everyday life, abnormalities that were generally tied to difficulties with transportation, provisioning, and living spaces." According to Fehérváry, "a life of civility, efficiency, and order," interconnected with being a different kind of person, embodying a fantasy of civilized personhood, was unreachable for Hungarians, who had to deal with "impossible schedules, late buses, insolent store clerks, and never-ending run-ins with bureaucracies" (230). Reported experiences of Soviet materialities in letters to the *Broom* encompassed similar encounters, and, as in Hungary, they indirectly encapsulated future desires of idealized everyday lives. Like in Hungary, the desired ideal was implicit: "a life of civility, efficiency and order," a life that was propagated in the government discourse and displayed in newspapers, fashion journals, and shop windows. Although people were not supposed to write openly about the West as a desirable ideal, some did, but the *Broom* censored any mention of Western materialities (see chapter 5).

For Western observers, the gray color of Eastern European materialities, according to Fehérváry, was indicative of people's lives "behind a dark, Iron Curtain, of enforced poverty and the fatigue of daily provisioning, of unsmiling salesclerks, scarce goods." For dissident intellectuals and émigrés, it "was iconic not so much of deprivation as of political repression" (1). Susan Reid, however, warns us that "we should not assume *a priori* that popular actions and ideals were inevitably in opposition to authoritative meanings and goals, including the project of socialist modernity (Reid 2014, 94). In Reid's perspective, complaining about the dark realities of Soviet socialism would not necessarily indicate opposition to Soviet modernity or the regime itself.

Letters to the *Broom* give a continuum of evidence, from some letter writers opposed to the regime, to others whose negativity was not necessarily a form of opposition. Interviews suggest that an enjoyment of new apartments coexisted with discontent about problems associated with them. The *Broom* data suggest that, in general, a prevalent discontent signaled dissociation from the Soviet utopian project, disenchantment with Soviet modernity, and yearning for a better future. While criticism of Soviet materialities may not indicate opposition to the regime, it was a political relation.[65] Letter writers reshaped their sensory experience, departing from Soviet utopian visions and transcending ideological prescriptions of future-looking critiques of "enduring shortcomings." *Broom* readers were political actors putting forward arguments about their sensory experiences of Soviet materialities, challenging Soviet modernity's vision with their stories of Soviet dystopia. They were political actors reframing Soviet history for the new future realized in the Singing Revolution of the late 1980s, which led to Lithuania's secession from the USSR.

REVOLUTION AND POST-AUTHORITARIAN LAUGHTER

Shortest joke: "COMMUNISM."

—*Broom*, 1991

On January 13, 1991, Soviet tanks rolled on the streets of Vilnius. People gathered by the TV tower and the Parliament. At night, fourteen civilians were killed, and hundreds were injured. Among them was a twenty-three-year-old girl with a zither (Lith. *kanklės*), a traditional Lithuanian folk string instrument. She came to sing, as many did during the long hours of protests. The Baltic revolutions were called the Singing Revolutions. That deadly night, the *Broom* no. 2 of 1991 was ready for printing. Its editors decided to publish an additional four-page newsletter titled *Red Genocide*. *Red Genocide* accused Mikhail Gorbachev, the general secretary of the Communist Party of the USSR, and the Soviet Army of civilian deaths and claimed that communist ideology was murderous: "Killing unarmed people—the Soviet Army honor!"; "[Gorbachev claimed] Referendum . . . fourteen [died] for independent Lithuania? It's not many!"; "Murderers do not have mothers—they are programmed, nurtured, and delivered to this world by communist ideology."[1] The *Broom* editors laughed at the fact that Gorbachev was awarded the Nobel Peace Prize in 1990.[2] The newsletter included a photo with USSR passports hanging on fence spears in Vilnius.[3] Lithuanians were declining Soviet citizenship. Three other special 1991 newsletters, dated January 14, 15, and 17, were published by the *Broom*. They addressed disinformation in Russia about January events in Lithuania; ridiculed communism; wrote about barricades and people's readiness to resist by the Parliament building; and included images of "bloodthirsty" Gorbachev next to Stalin.

It was not a Laughing Revolution, as in Egypt during the Arab Spring in 2011. In Lithuania, people recalled songs and poems, not laughter. But the *Broom* was an active supporter of the Sąjūdis (reform movement) and the Lithuanian revolution, a series of anti-Soviet, pro-independence protests, meetings, and encounters with Soviet armed forces that began in 1987.[4] Many of the *Broom* editors mentioned in this book, including Gediminas Astrauskas, Ona Banadienė, Andrius Cvirka, Albertas Lukša, Arvydas Pakalnis, Kęstutis Šiaulytis, Rytis Tilvytis, Česlavas Valadka, and contributing artists Fridrikas Samukas and Jonas Varnas, among others, were the authors of the January newsletters. At that time, they did not know when the next Soviet Army attack would take place. *Red Genocide* could have been their ticket to "see polar bears," as Lithuanians sarcastically joked about deportations to Gulag camps in the Arctic Circle. Citizens' strong support for Sąjūdis candidates in the spring of 1989 in the first elections to the USSR's Congress of People's Deputies; in the elections of February 24, 1990, to the Supreme Council of Lithuania; and for an independent Lithuania as a democratic republic at the referendum of February 9, 1991, indicates that many readers of the *Broom* would have gotten "polar bear" tickets as well.[5] How did thirty years of producing communist satire and humor end in anti-Soviet and anticommunist revolutionary laughter?

In 1985, Mikhail Gorbachev launched perestroika, a series of political and economic reforms hoping to revive the Soviet economy; and glasnost, a policy of transparency and openness, initiating open public criticism. Sąjūdis was founded on June 3, 1988. Sąjūdis and the Lithuanian Communist Party (LCP) were the major forces in the liberation movement. Sąjūdis, with its more radical inclinations toward liberation from the USSR and promotion of nationalist ideas, soon became a symbol of the struggle for independence (see Senn 2002).[6] The Supreme Council pronounced Lithuania an independent state on March 11, 1990.[7] As in other Eastern European states, many members of Sąjūdis were intellectuals, including representatives of the Lithuanian Academy of Sciences, members of the creative unions, and well-known artists and writers. During perestroika, Juozas Bulota, who had already retired from the *Broom*, wrote in his notes for a public lecture: "Perestroika brings big hopes, and we all desire they are fulfilled," and "We worked with a hope that times will change."[8] As the newsletter *Red Genocide* makes clear, the *Broom* editors were for Lithuania's independence. Another path, one not taken by the *Broom* editors, materialized in a new humor and satire magazine known as *Kranklys* (Raven), which between 1989 and 1992 published anti-Sąjūdis humor and pro-Soviet propaganda. The editor in chief of *Raven* was Leonas Kiauleikis, who worked at the *Broom* from 1956 to 1969 and who, according to the Lithuanian media, was a KGB agent (see chapter 1). None of the *Broom* editors published in *Raven*.

Following Sąjūdis agendas, from 1988 to 1991, *Broom* laughter promoted a new politics of virtue rooted in ideas of nationhood, freedom, and democracy.

The publication denounced Soviet oppression and violence. Political cartoons criticizing communism, the Soviet government, the Soviet Army, and the police increasingly populated the *Broom*'s pages. A 1990 cartoon by Gintautas Survila portrays a Soviet soldier carrying a banner that reads "Miru—Mir, A Nam Pobeda!" (Rus., Peace for the world, and victory for us!), ridiculing Soviet peace politics.[9] A 1991 cartoon by Vitalijus Suchockis shows a passerby walking toward a street corner, while behind the corner a peasant woman with a huge sickle and a worker with a big hammer wait to assault him.[10] A hammer and a sickle, the venerable emblem of the Soviet state and a symbol of communism, here symbolized a threat to life. Another 1991 cartoon, by Fridrikas Samukas, portrays a man waiting for a woman to get closer and then flashing her by opening his trench coat to show multiple Soviet medals on his shirt.[11] The medals, a pride of Soviet veterans, in the cartoon evoke danger and the threat of the Soviet state.

The *Broom* was no longer censored, even though Glavlit existed until 1990 and the KGB until 1991. Generally, anything could be published, as long as it did not undermine the *Broom*'s pro-independence agenda. The *Broom* incorporated many new topics previously forbidden by Soviet censorship, such as prostitution, drug addiction, or poverty. Editors also commented on new developments emerging during the revolutionary era, such as racketeering, inflation, or the monetary policy of coupons. The *Broom* discussed complicated property restitution rights, new taxes, emerging social stratification and business practices, and crimes. A cartoon by Fridrikas Samukas published in 1991 shows a man behind a street corner waiting for a passerby who approaches with two pieces of luggage and a cigarette in his mouth. In the next drawing, the passerby has been mugged and lies on the street, holding his luggage while the robber walks away smiling and smoking the cigarette he seized.[12] This cartoon was a commentary on widespread petty crimes and the everyday violence that occurred during the late 1980s and early 1990s transformations. Serious themes coexisted with casual articles and dark humor, sexual themes, and images of naked women's bodies, none of which could have passed Soviet censorship earlier. Nevertheless, the *Broom* continued to avoid obscene and very dark humor.

The archives and interviews illustrate that the *Broom*'s editors did not question Lithuania's independence. Moreover, in the magazine's pages they ridiculed those who did. However, during the revolutionary period, the *Broom* preserved its critical stance toward political, economic, and social realities. Since post-authoritarian laughter was also multidirectional, different audiences must have read the *Broom*'s humor in different ways: as a critique of the government, of transformations, of people's selfishness, or of other vices. In the September 1988 issue, Arvydas Pakalnis portrays people lined up toward a rising sun labeled "Tomorrow"; some are reading newspapers, others are talking.[13] Some audiences could see Pakalnis's cartoon as ridiculing false promises of the utopian future by Sąjūdis leaders, while Pakalnis most likely was laughing at euphoria about the promised future. On the cover of the February 1990 issue, artist Kęstutis Šiaulytis's cartoon comments on a harsh winter, referring to economic hardships. He depicts three beehives painted in flag colors of sovereign Lithuania, Latvia, and Estonia and covered by snow: "Comrades, let's get out the sugar we poured [into the beehives] in the fall for the bees, who is for?" Three men with buckets by the beehives were voting affirmatively.[14] At the time, sugar and other food products were rationed and sold for coupons. A 1991 cartoon by Juliusz Puchalski, republished from *Szpilki*, a Polish satire and humor journal, depicts a person asking for handouts and a man giving him money. The caption reads, "Of course it is better now [than in socialism]—now you can say that things are worse openly."[15] This cartoon was a commentary on economic hardships, suggesting that lives had not improved but that citizens had the freedom to say so. Like Šiaulytis's cartoon, it could have been generalized to criticize the revolution or the government. Others could have understood the cartoon as dark humor directed at critics of transformations.

During the revolutionary period, the *Broom* participated in establishing the new post-authoritarian justice regime in terms of the politics of memory and history rather than "enduring shortcomings." In 1990, the *Broom* wrote about Soviet deportations and the Gulag, forbidden topics in the pre-perestroika *Broom*. The *Broom* received letters in the late 1980s from readers who had never written to its editors before. Some of them reflected that they had not believed in socialist justice earlier but could now write to the *Broom*. Readers engaged questions of justice by discussing unresolved issues of Soviet occupation, World War II, and postwar violence, and by integrating voices of those silenced in Soviet times. The *Broom* editors did not send these letters to the KGB anymore. Changing perceptions of justice were among important factors that contributed to the disintegration of the institution of satirical justice, which was discontinued around 1990.

In 1990, many other jokes were openly anti-Soviet and anticommunist. A reader from the town of Švėkšna sent the *Broom* a joke about the Red Army:

> Once in a summer at the outskirts of Moscow kids herded sheep and goats by a highway. When the animals lay down, [the kids] collected dry dung bits and started playing. They put sheep dung bits in two long lines. In front of them they placed a big dung piece. . . . Stalin with his escort were passing by on the highway. They stopped and asked the kids what they were doing there.
>
> "We are playing the Red Army. Privates are in lines, and the Party leaders are in the front."
>
> "Sounds good. And where is Marshal Voroshilov?"

"Unfortunately, we could not find such a big piece of shit," the children regretted.[16]

If Bulota had received this joke during his tenure at the *Broom*, he would have had to forward it to the KGB for its ridicule of Stalin, the Red Army, and Marshal Voroshilov. The joke also contained other elements that Soviet political aesthetics rejected: obscene and low humor. I have never seen "shit" being mentioned in any readers' letters during Bulota's tenure.

The *Broom* also received letters that were critical of the revolution. A few readers claimed that the new system did not benefit them. In November 1989, one woman wrote that "it is hard to hear that we are moving backward rather than forward and that nothing good is promised for a worker."[17] The *Broom* did not publish her poem in which she expressed these concerns. Other readers blended Soviet sensibilities about equality with new realities: "It would be great if in independent Lithuania there was not only unity, but also equality in allocation of goods and we would not have to discuss the trade mafia."[18] Readers reprimanded the Parliament members for empty promises, corruption, inflation, and the disappearance of vinegar and matches from the stores.[19] In 1994, a reader suggested sending condoms to members of Parliament (the letter did not provide explanation). Various swear words and obscene language became common in letters to the *Broom*. Post-authoritarian political aesthetics did not require Soviet-era language purity (see chapter 5). Moreover, some readers sent antisemitic and anti-Asian jokes, which I had never seen in the pre-1985 *Broom* archives. The editors did not publish these jokes.

The question of why the Soviet Union collapsed has fascinated Sovietologists since 1991. Alexei Yurchak argues that the last Soviet Russian generation in Leningrad perceived the Soviet system as permanent and immutable and experienced its collapse as unexpected. In Yurchak's terms, "The system's collapse had been unimaginable before it began," and was quickly followed by excitement and readiness to participate in the transformation (Yurchak 2006, 1). In the case of Russia, "Everything was forever, until it was no more," as the title of Yurchak's book tells us. Looking back at Soviet times, many Lithuanians claim that the collapse was imminent, only a matter of time. Divergent memories among Russian and Lithuanian interlocutors indicate different positionality toward history in post-Soviet times. But unlike Yurchak's interlocutors (see chapter 1), nobody—not even the highest authorities I interviewed—claimed to feel proud of having been a Soviet person. Goda Ferensienė, who worked in the literary division of the *Broom* in the 1960s and was married to the LCP CC secretary Algirdas Ferensas, argued that they were free, indicating that Lithuanians did not perceive themselves as "Soviet" (see Klumbytė 2014). Archival data suggests that perceptions of the Soviet system as destined to fail might have been shared among some editors and readers. A sense of the imminence of collapse, often implied rather than explicit because of censorship, is prevalent in some readers' dystopian stories discussed in chapter 8.

I argue that the *Broom*, with its criticism of Soviet everyday life, contributed to making the revolution imaginable. The rhetoric of Lithuanian revolution was founded on a strong criticism of socialism present in the *Broom* as criticism of social and economic issues, everyday discontent, and experiences of social injustices.[20] The critical anti-Soviet, antiestablishment, and pro-Western discourse, part of *Broom*'s multidirectional laughter, was a medium of national interrelation integral to the mobilization of people and legitimation of the movement for independence (see Klumbytė 2013; cf. Kubik 1994 on Poland). A popular discourse posits the Lithuanian revolution as a rebirth of the nation; I suggest that satirical and humorous stories expressing editors' and readers' dissensus and circulating in the public space made the sovereign nation imaginable.[21]

A notorious collective monograph, *Sąjūdžio ištakų beieškant* (In search of Sąjūdis origins), edited by Ainė Ramonaitė and Jūratė Kavaliauskaitė, develops a concept of *independent society* to expand the popular understanding of opposition in Lithuania as a direct dissident confrontation with the regime to include a variety of indirect challenges of official ideology and institutions through an informal network of activities. The authors argue that networks of various cultural circles and professional groups—including an ethnocultural movement, hippie and punk subcultures, scientists' clubs, Catholic opposition, and heritage preservation enthusiasts, among others—explain the rise of Sąjūdis (Ramonaitė and Kavaliauskaitė 2011).[22] However, Sąjūdis mobilized many new people who had not been active in informal civic networks (Ramonaitė and Kavaliauskaitė 2011). Vilius Ivanauskas (2017), on the contrary, contends in his study of Soviet-era cultural elites in Lithuania that "alternative spheres" existed within the official space and created a "legal zone of disobedience." This book contributes to these studies by illustrating that officially sanctioned and censored laughter was a site of banal opposition and dissensus. In my approach, this opposition was neither "informal," "independent," nor "alternative" engagements with power; banal opposition and dissensus were intrinsic to the Soviet governance regime at the periphery and transformed into pro-independence opposition during the Lithuanian revolution.

The *Broom* did not survive long in post-Soviet times. In 1991, the *Broom* became an independent legal entity—*Šluota* Ltd. Because of financial issues in 1994, the *Broom* was not published regularly. The magazine became a humor newspaper in 1995. It published fourteen issues in 1994, seventeen in 1995, and twelve in 1996. In 1998, the last issue of the *Broom* came out, after which the publication closed.[23] The era of sovereignty coincided with the rise of digital media and the decline of print media. Caricature lost its appeal to the public in a new information market saturated with illustrated newspapers and magazines, comic books, and advertisement catalogs. Moreover, alternative venues for political participation during the Lithuanian revolution included protest actions, meetings, public discussions, and uncorrupted voting. Laughing at cartoons, creating satires, or writing complaint letters became a limited form of political participation when people could protest on the streets or use the internet for criticism. Moreover, artists and satirists had to find a new political language in a changing society. In 2008, satirist Jurgis Gimberis reflected on the new limits of post-authoritarian laughter: "Big hopes. Sacred things. Sacred slogans. There was no place for laughter, critique, satire. How can you cut the branch on which you sit?" (see Kauzonas 2008). Andrius Cvirka, a leading *Broom* artist in the 1970s and 1980s, stopped drawing entirely.[24] Jonas Varnas had to reinvent himself and became a contributing artist to some major Lithuanian newspapers. Kęstutis Šiaulytis, one of the youngest *Broom* artists, who joined the magazine at twenty-five years old in 1978, rediscovered himself in new genres and new opportunities: painting, creating a blog, and drawing caricatures of people at various events.[25]

The disintegration of the institution of satirical justice illustrates the interdependence of the authoritarian state and satire. As argued in chapter 7, the institution of satirical justice was rooted in Communist Party ideologies of media propaganda, public criticism, and prophylactic disciplining. Satirical justice reaffirmed the authority of the state and served a preventive and propaganda role. Soviet media, including the *Broom* magazine, complemented functions of other institutions, such as Comrades' Courts, which were instruments of persuasion and propaganda and had minor coercive power to punish wrongdoers. According to Communist Party ideology, the state had to die out and crime would gradually disappear; official law enforced by the state as an instrument of coercion had to become unnecessary (see Berman and Spindler 1963; Kareniauskaitė 2017). In Soviet times, neither courts nor media were independent from the state. The Communist Party leadership could influence court decisions and media profiles. Under a democracy, which recognizes the rule of law and human rights, as well as accountability under the law of the government and citizens, the institution of satirical justice could not survive. Investigative journalism became a subject of libel suits; the *Broom* did not have funding to defend itself in court. Without the backing of the government and resources to hire good attorneys, *Broom* editors could not win lawsuits. Courts replaced media institutions, which stopped functioning as justice arbitrators. Moreover, in the market economy, satirical disciplining was not needed; employers could fire workers for poor performance rather than shame them into improvement. Employees could sue employers if their rights were violated.

After the collapse of the Soviet Union, not only were state-sponsored jokes gone, but unofficial jokes vanished, too. In their article on unofficial jokes, "'What

Happened to Jokes?': The Shifting Landscape of Humor in Hungary," Martha Lampland and Maya Nadkarni note that since 1989, "commentators on both sides of the Atlantic have mourned the death of jokes in post-socialist societies" (Lampland and Nadkarni 2016, 449). They conclude that jokes as an intimate form of political criticism did disappear because of changing social relations, socialization patterns, and other reasons, but humor did not vanish (Lampland and Nadkarni 2016). In Lithuanian TV and radio broadcasts, the incorporation of more open and spontaneous communication and the evolving genre of talk shows contributed to an increased frequency of laughter (Aleksandravičiūtė and Vaicekauskienė 2012). The new post-Soviet laughter is not necessarily funny to former *Broom* editors and readers. Former *Broom* artists and writers rationalize that in post-Soviet times, there is no intellectual humor, which defined the Soviet era. Kęstutis Šiaulytis argues that the *Broom* was "a publication of a sophisticated humor culture. Now if people laugh, they most often laugh at all kinds of nonsense" (see Šileika 2003). Pre-perestroika Soviet *Broom*'s laughter did exclude dark, vulgar, and obscene themes common in post-Soviet times. It was also satirical—critical and moralizing, purposeful rather than entertaining laughter. Some of this laughter was sophisticated, especially that with Aesopian messages. But it rarely addressed complex aesthetic or philosophical matters; abstract and ambiguous humor was not welcome in the *Broom*. Moreover, it had to appeal to ordinary people rather than intellectuals, making artists' engagement with intellectual humor limited. It may seem paradoxical that in Soviet times artists embraced foreign, dark, and entertaining humor, while they now argue against "all kinds of nonsense" and long for more sophisticated humor. Both positions, though, should be understood in their historical contexts.

In the post–Cold War era, laughter continues to be a form of political participation in different authoritarian states. We can observe similar dynamics to those in Soviet Lithuania: the use of humor for statecraft and as a propaganda tool; prohibition of humorous portrayals of the leaders or the regime itself; the presence of Aesopian language; and censorship. In Vietnam, a Marxist-Leninist one-party socialist republic, government officials cannot be portrayed realistically, and caricatures of Vietnamese national leaders largely do not exist (Ho 2019). Like in the former Soviet Lithuania, in Vietnam the most prevalent target is a bureaucrat commonly portrayed as a greedy, corrupt government official (Ho 2019). Katy Pearce and Adnan Hajizada (2014) argue that in Azerbaijan, an authoritarian semi-presidential republic, nobody can criticize and insult the first family. Personal and family honor is of great importance, and honor serves as a disciplining tool.

As in Soviet times, it is likely that some authoritarian regimes tolerate satire and humor. Lisa Wedeen, for example, notes that edgy political satire contributed to nourishing the image of benevolent dictatorship in public, supporting the regime's self-presentation as a kinder, gentler form of autocracy (Wedeen 2019, 51). In her opinion, under the first decade of Syrian president Bashar al-Assad's rule (2000–2010), comedy worked as an "incubator for oppositional consciousness, a testing ground for novel ways to experience and claim the 'us' of collective action" (50). As Syrian examples illustrate, laughter was multidirectional, "reproducing attitudes central to politics" (55), as well as promoting oppositional thinking. Julie Hemment (2015; forthcoming) shows that in authoritarian Russia under Vladimir Putin, memes and jokes are directed not only at local audiences but also circulate internationally. Through media and spectacle, as in the case of Russian spy Anna Chapman's sexualized images, they criticize a "popularly defined Western liberalism" (Hemment 2015, 167), "commodified and sexualized U.S. media culture" (171), and incite a Western feminist response. By targeting and involving audiences outside Russia, I would argue, multidirectionality acquires global and geopolitical forms.[26]

In democratic states, laughter prevails as a politics of virtue and is integral to political participation. Post-Soviet laughter during the 2008 parliamentary elections has been an affective and moral critique of mainstream politics, expressing dissensus. The Lithuanian National Resurrection Party (NRP) employed humor to gain victory in the Lithuanian elections of 2008. It garnered 15 percent of the total vote and finished second, to become the second-largest coalition partner and receive important government positions (Klumbytė 2014). Lithuanian carnivalesque politics was a form of political opposition as well as a future-oriented process of change (Klumbytė 2014). Like socialist jokes, post-Soviet laughter exposed the gap between the official representational system and everyday life (see Boyer and Yurchak 2010). The NRP's critical humor revealed incongruities between, on the one hand, the official political elite discourse, with its futuristic narrations of history in the idioms of nationhood, modernity, progress, the welfare state, and Europeanization, and, on the other hand, the experiential reality of some people (cf. Boyer and Yurchak 2010). These elections illustrate that post-Soviet neoliberal regimes have their own power structures and their own predicaments.

In her analysis of the satirical activism of "Billionaires for Bush," a political street theater organization active during the 2000 and 2004 US presidential elections, Angelique Haugerud (2013) emphasizes the transformative power of such activism, which "can be a vital step in helping to destabilize political categories, reframe debates, introduce new ideas and norms, rewrite discourse, and build new political communities" (126). The 2010 elections in Brazil, in which an actual clown was elected to the National Congress; the Five Star Movement in Italy, with the victory of comedian Beppe Grillo in parliamentary elections in 2012 (see Molé 2013); comedians gaining mayoral office in Iceland in 2010 (see Boyer 2013); and a comedian winning the presidency in Ukraine are among a few examples of how laughter functions as a form of political mobilization and participation in democratic regimes (see Klumbytė 2014).

During a 2017 event at the Martynas Mažvydas National Library of Lithuania, "Vanished Laughter," devoted to the *Broom*, Jonas Varnas joked that every time *Broom* caricaturists organized a collective photo by a monument, the monument got demolished afterward.[27] In 1990, *Broom* artists and contributors gathered by the most significant Soviet monument—that of Lenin—in front of the KGB headquarters in the central square in Vilnius (figure 9.1). A determined-looking Lenin was pointing in one direction, while the posing group all pointed the opposite way.[28] In 1991, Lenin's grand project of a communist state—the Soviet Union—collapsed. Lenin's statue and projects of "red laughter" landed in the dustbin of history. The *Broom* published its shortest joke: "Communism."[29]

FIGURE 9.1.   Lithuanian cartoonists in 1990. The statue of Lenin was razed at his knees and demolished on August 23, 1991, the anniversary of the signing of the Molotov-Ribbentrop Pact, which divided Europe, by the USSR and Nazi Germany in 1939. Photo by Jonas Jakimavičius. *Literatūra ir menas* archive. Courtesy of Jonas Jakimavičius and Darius Pocevičius.

LOST LAUGHTER AND AUTHORITARIAN STIGMA

It is April 28, 2017. I stand on a podium to lead an event at the Martynas Mažvydas National Library of Lithuania, "Vanished Laughter," devoted to the *Broom*. It was my idea to bring former *Broom* artists and journalists all together again. My heart is beating faster as Kęstutis Šiaulytis, Jonas Varnas, Albertas Lukša, and Romas Palčiauskas enter through the door of the hall. I could always recognize artist Kęstutis Šiaulytis from his large frizzy head of hair. Comic strip author Romas Palčiauskas was with a walking stick and his warm smile. Journalist Albertas Lukša looked serious every time I met him. Artist Varnas walked in with an angel amulet, almost a foot in height, hanging from his neck by a blue string. All of them were part of the significant state project of creating Soviet laughter. Their voices are part of this book. Some other artists, writers, and journalists were too weak to come. Andrius Deltuva left this world a month before the event. Romualdas Lankauskas and Algirdas Radvilavičius would leave it soon after.

As the event commenced, nostalgia for lost *Broom* laughter pervaded the room. Šiaulytis, Varnas, Lukša, and Šniukas argued for the need to revive the *Broom*.[1] They recalled the high reputation and popularity of this magazine in Soviet times. Lukša noted that "the *Broom* in Soviet times brought as much profit as a kolkhoz farm." Šiaulytis praised the *Broom* as the most modern and experimental magazine in the Soviet Union, which introduced comic strips and modernized graphic art.[2] He mentioned that he knew that times would change and stressed that the *Broom* created the *Lithuanian* graphic art tradition. Šiaulytis spoke of the popularity of the *Broom* and restrictions on its subscription. If there were no limits, he argued, the *Broom*'s circulation might have reached two or three hundred thousand; all Lithuania might have read it (Šiaulytis 2017). Varnas said he missed the lively culture of cartoonists who were united around the *Broom*. He recalled various jokes from his Soviet experience. In 1968 they created a Cartoonists' Union. The center was the *Broom*; it paid for artists' travel to the April Fools' Day gathering and other events in the fall. Artists also collected funds among themselves for these events. Mečislovas Ščepavičius had a briefcase with a fake revolver to persuade people to pay debts. Debtors ran when they saw him. Artists drank part of the money away. Other funds were used to prepare cartoons for foreign exhibits. Varnas related a story of how he once decided to give a New Year's gift to his friend the cartoonist Fridrikas Samukas and subscribed him to the newspaper *Kyrgyzstan Uzbekistan*. An average Lithuanian citizen knew very little about distant Central Asian republics, despite Soviet ideology about the friendship of all Soviet peoples. It was a cheap daily publication. Samukas complained about it—"what kind of a moron subscribed it for me? I went to the post office to end its delivery, and they said that I couldn't." He received *Kyrgyzstan Uzbekistan* the entire year.[3]

The post-Soviet nostalgia for the *Broom*'s laughter prevalent at the event indicated artists' positionality in post-Soviet society. That positionality was interconnected with the *Broom* editors' loss of social prestige associated with their former employment at a highly regarded popular magazine. As "workers at the Soviet ideological front," *Broom* editors had enjoyed relative power and freedom to authorize certain forms of laughter; they had status and recognition. Soviet times marked the epitome of their work life, creative careers, and popularity. The post-Soviet nostalgia for *Broom* laughter is also a reflection of dissociation from new post-Soviet communities of laughter that do not reflect their generational experiences. Importantly, in their nostalgia for lost laughter, they reclaim recognition in the society where Soviet-era art and writing have been generally ignored or devalued.

My presentation, "Vanished Laughter: Politics of Secrecy in the *Broom*," focused on various artistic strategies used to hide meanings in cartoons, as well as censorship of the *Broom*. I discussed one side of multidirectional laughter—the opposition—glossing over the story of how the *Broom* perpetuated CP ideology. There was a feeling that everybody knew what was unsaid—*Broom*'s CP agendas and the editors' complex implication into Soviet history. Our silence was part of the post-Soviet predicament, which required distancing from the Soviet past, denouncing the Communist Party banned since 1991, and aligning with national ideologies, centering on resistance, democracy, and Europeanness.[4]

As implicated subjects, some *Broom* editors, artists, and journalists have been vulnerable to authoritarian stigma, a negative association with "collaborators" of the Soviet government, for their work at the Soviet humor propaganda magazine.

Almost half of them were members of the Communist Party, which the right-wing parties in post-Soviet Lithuania have proposed become recognized as a criminal organization. There are over seven hundred pages of *Broom* Communist Party Primary Organization reports, which outline the *Broom* editors' work in building communism. The fictionality and factuality of these reports require further research. None of the reports can be read without paying attention to the specific political conditions in which they were created. Although editors engaged Communist Party ideology and slogans to speak about their work, *Broom* political laughter was multidirectional. This laughter, the *Broom* editors' memories, and private archives testify that PPO reports were documents of bureaucratic showcasing written with a particular audience in mind. While PPO documents reflect how Communist Party ideology influenced the *Broom* editors' work, they tell very little about the multidirectional laughter that defined the magazine.

The authoritarian stigma is more than blaming—it devalues work and achievements in Soviet times. In 2021 the monument of Petras Cvirka, the father of Andrius Cvirka, was removed from one of the major squares of Vilnius. P. Cvirka, according to the Genocide and Resistance Research Centre of Lithuania, "actively collaborated with the Soviet occupational government structures," and his involvement "caused considerable harmful effects for the Lithuanian state and the destiny of its citizens" (BNS 2021). In post-Soviet times the monument cast a different shadow on Andrius Cvirka: the shadow of his father as a "collaborator" with the Soviet regime. This shadow tarnishes Petras Cvirka's literary contributions. *Broom* artists rarely mention the awards they received in the Soviet Union exhibition *Satire in the Struggle for Peace*. They often see the entire collection of their political cartoons, even if they are examples of multidirectional laughter, as valueless artifacts of the Soviet regime's history.

In 1982, as if envisioning the end of Soviet laughter, *Broom* contributor Zenonas Šteinys drew a cartoon—the last supper of the Lithuanian cartoonists (figure 10.1). This cartoon mimics Leonardo da Vinci's famous late fifteenth-century mural painting *The Last Supper*. Juozas Bulota, at the far right of the drawing, wearing glasses, is looking over the supper. Jonas Varnas is standing in the middle. Šiaulytis, Cvirka, Deltuva, Samukas, Pakalnis, Beresniovas—artists mentioned in this book—and others are gathered at the table.

The *Broom* editors did not know that this cartoon would look like a celebration of the end of Soviet laughter many years later. Bulota would retire in three years, and the *Broom* would change editors in chief several times, until it would cease to exist as a Soviet institution (see post scriptum). Those who were gathered at the table and others mentioned in this book most likely would disagree with me for calling this laughter "Soviet" and placing it within the conceptual context of authoritarianism. "Soviet" implies contextualization of the *Broom*'s

FIGURE 10.1.   Zenonas Šteinys's cartoon mimics Leonardo da Vinci's *Last Supper*. 1982. Personal archive of editor in chief Juozas Bulota. Courtesy of (son) Juozas Bulota.

political history within Soviet history, while "authoritarian" suggests contextualization within studies of nondemocratic states. I use these concepts to refer to political regimes, without an intention to imply any authoritarian stigma. I hope this book will help articulate the complexities of Soviet authoritarianism and political participation in this system beyond the notions of collaboration and complicity. I did not use the term "Soviet laughter" at the event at the National Library. The gathering was meant to celebrate the *Broom* editors' work and the *Broom*'s legacy. In that context, using "Soviet laughter" and "authoritarianism" would have reinvoked authoritarian stigma.

When the event at the National Library was over, I thought to myself, what would this book be like if the Soviet Union never collapsed? It was a question about the bias of the current time. I had integrated many different perspectives, from communists' voices at the Primary Communist Party Organization meetings, recollections of the Central Committee leaders, to claims by *Broom* editors that they had been relatively free to create what they wished. Nevertheless, this book, by the nature of the object of its study and the questions raised, is about a collapsed authoritarian regime. The answer to my own question is rather simple: if the Soviet Union had not collapsed, this project would never even have been conceived in my mind.

This book, I hope, will contribute to several strands of scholarly literature. First, it explores authoritarianism by inquiring into intimate and everyday experiences of power. Studies of authoritarianism usually center on sham elections, violence, and the curtailment of freedoms as defining institutional features of authoritarian regimes (see Roudakova 2017). Natalia Roudakova, who studied Soviet journalism, notes that there are far fewer studies on cultural practices that helped to consolidate authoritarianism (159). These cultural practices tend to be conceptualized through the lens of resistance, or taking place despite the state (see, e.g., Yurchak 2006, 8–9). Moreover, while the dehumanizing effects of authoritarian systems are well known, it is rarely asked how authoritarian systems institutionalize meaningful practices that have a popular appeal. This book contributes to these explorations of intimate experiences of power—laughing and meaning-making at the everyday level, as well as state attempts to shape citizens into its subjects through popular culture. By exploring the Soviet experiment to create Soviet laughter in a newly acquired territory, this book shows that power can be commonplace, that embracing Soviet power can coexist with opposition, and that state power can become an intimate and even meaningful experience integrated into people's lives. Thus, it is imperative to understand how authoritarianism functions for prolonged periods in the form of cultural practices and everyday phenomena.

Second, this book develops the analytics of *multidirectional laughter*, which incorporates both propaganda and oppositional humor. I show that the analytical lens of official and unofficial humor is not useful in the case of the *Broom*, since many cartoons and satires both affirmed state power and Communist Party ideology *and* integrated oppositional messages. The critique of shortcomings that the Communist Party initiated through the means of this satire and humor magazine, in order to progress to the communist future, became a source of dissensus mobilized during the nationalist movement of the late 1980s. The concept of *political intimacy*, which I develop in this study, is also central to an understanding of Soviet authoritarianism, since multidirectional laughter could not have prevailed without trust and coexistence among editors, censors, and Communist Party authorities.

Third, this book makes several contributions to Soviet western periphery studies. Studies of the Soviet Union, unless they focus on different republics or regions, often gloss over the diversity of "Sovietness." The Lithuanian *Broom*, Latvian *Dadzis*, and Estonian *Pikker* were very different magazines from *Krokodil*, although they all constituted examples of Soviet laughter. Moreover, this study sidesteps postcolonial studies that underscore victimization and colonial identities in the Soviet western periphery. A concept introduced in this book—*antagonistic complicity*—contributes to understanding how an alternative form of agency, unrelated to the status of a victim or a colonizer, develops under the occupational regime. The concept of *satirical justice* reconceptualizes approaches to Soviet citizen letters by suggesting that complaining to the state was an institution grounded in authoritarian state structures. Satirical justice reaffirmed social injustices, even if it provided for participation and limited accountability. The approach to censorship through the lens of *censorial indistinction* revisits the popular understanding of Soviet ideological censorship as a form of oppression by arguing that ideological censorship was an inconsistent, fluctuating, and relational practice.

By showing the details of how Soviet laughter was produced in Lithuania, this project reveals the intimate statecraft directed at constructing everyday lives and everyday sociality. This book illustrates how imperial peripheries are unstable and their governance is limited. It also reveals that laughter in its multiple genres (graphic satire, satirical readers' letters, published feuilletons and jokes) is intrinsically political and transformative. This book shows that authoritarianism is a statecraft of the everyday and a project of engineering intimate lives. As a lived reality it exists in multiple stories people tell each other about themselves in jokes, cartoons, and satires.

Did laughter serve the Bolshevik cause and later the agendas of the Communist Party? Can authoritarian states use laughter as a tool of statecraft to engage citizens to laugh with them? This book argued that the authoritarian state succeeded to some extent, even though ultimately it failed. In Lithuania, laughter primarily served as a tool of ideological socialization, promoting everyday Soviet values, such as disdain for materialism, rather than anti-Western propaganda. Moreover, the periphery, as argued in this book, was a site of contested Sovietness, owing to its history of sovereignty, the violence of World War II and the postwar era, religious and linguistic differences, Lithuanian minority status, and closeness to the West. Since laughter is ambiguous and contextual, readers of the *Broom* often laughed at the state rather than with it.

My last interview for this book was with journalist Česlovas Juršėnas, the former chair of the Press, TV, and Radio Division at the LCP CC Propaganda and Agitation Department. We met at the Parliament, the former building of the Highest Council of the Lithuanian Soviet Socialist Republic. All the time during my research I wondered why the state allowed satire and humor. Didn't the Central Committee members know about the dangers of humor to the government? Juršėnas was among the Central Committee authorities who oversaw Lithuanian media. He said that some Central Committee authorities were more insightful than others. "In the *Broom*, [authors] were allowed to be more critical than in other journals. We can relatively say, it was their task, but without transgressing [certain] boundaries. The *Broom* was not anti-Soviet or dangerous," Juršėnas said.[5] I was happy to see he was partly wrong. The *Broom* was not anti-Soviet, but it *was* dangerous. *Broom* artists, journalists, writers, and readers all humanized authoritarian laughter by turning it into a wry smile at the state.

Notes

INTRODUCTION

1. This episode with Juozas Bulota is reconstructed from the recollections of his son, also named Juozas Bulota. Interview with journalist Juozas Bulota, the editor in chief's son, July 19, 2018, Vilnius. In the book, cited interviews and personal communication between me and "Juozas Bulota" refer to the son of the editor in chief. "Personal archive of Juozas Bulota" refers to the archive containing the papers of the former editor in chief, now in the possession of his son.

2. The *Broom* magazine originated in 1934. See chapter 1 for more detailed information about the prehistory of the Soviet *Broom*.

3. Although Bulota retired in 1985, he continued to meet with readers as a former *Broom* editor in chief and writer.

4. The concepts of "editors," "journalists," "writers," and "artists" overlap in some cases. All artists, journalists, and writers who worked at the *Broom* were "editors," since they were members of the *Broom* editorial board. Some journalists focused on investigative journalism and wrote fact-based feuilletons or pieces on readers' letters. Others wrote both creative pieces and factual reports and could be considered writers and journalists. There were many writers and artists who contributed to the *Broom* but were not members of the editorial board. In this book *Broom* artists, journalists, and writers are referred to as editors or called *Broom* artists, journalists, and writers.

5. Denis Kozlov makes a parallel argument about Soviet literature by claiming that it served as an important venue for social commentary in the absence of other mechanisms of legitimate political expression (2013, 2). According to Kozlov, literature was a lens "through which an individual saw, interpreted, and interacted with the outside world" (26). Laughter, in my perspective, too, was a form of self-expression, social communication, aesthetic engagement, and political commentary.

6. The term "institution" in the case of "laughter as an institution" or "institution of complaints" refers to social phenomena that are, as Andreas Glaeser argued, "seemingly self-same across time" (2011, 33). They are "articulations of a multiplicity of intentions, deep motivations, as well as of systematically recurring unintended consequences" (34).

7. Jonas Lenkutis is the editor in chief of sluota.lt, published online since 2001. See http://www.sluota.lt/index.html.

8. The ideological formula endorsed by the official Communist Party discourse was "shortcomings that we still keep encountering" (Rus. *vse eshche vstrechaiushchiesia nedostatki*, Lith. *dar vis pasitaiko trūkumų*).

9. Anatoly Lunacharsky worked on the book manuscript provisionally titled "Laughter as a Weapon in Class Struggle," which he did not finish (see Gérin 2018). On ideological and institutional changes that shaped Soviet satire after the Revolution see Gérin (2018). See Oushakine (2012) for the discussion of the 1920s–1950s public debates about the nature and purpose of distinctively "Soviet" laughter and comedy.

10. In this book "laughter" is an umbrella term that incorporates textual (humor, satire), participatory (reading, creating humor, and laughing), affective (expressing content, indignation, shame, joy), performative (involving elements of carnival, theater), and moral (conveying condemnation, critique, praise) aspects. Annie Gérin (2018, 7) reminds

us that Russian *smekh* (laughter) was "the word used most widely in Soviet theoretical and critical writings in the 1920s and 1930s." Similarly, Lithuanian *juokas* (laughter) is a very broad term, which entails actual laughing, as the expression of contentment, joy, or cheerfulness, as well as play, wittiness, joke, or humiliation (*Lietuvių kalbos žodynas* 2018). See also Vidugirytė (2012).

11. Bulota might have copied a note from another source, not necessarily Brezhnev's book. Personal archive of Juozas Bulota.

12. Undated lecture notes. Personal archive of Juozas Bulota.

13. Some facts illustrate that after World War II authorities took into account different audiences in Soviet peripheries. In Soviet Ukraine, the satire and humor magazine *Perets* was published in two versions. The western regions, with newly incorporated formerly Polish lands after the war, received a different version from the rest of the country until 1951. *Perets* for western Ukraine carried negative propaganda against Polish fascist and bourgeois nationalists (Yeremieieva 2018). *Perets* for the rest of the country included criticism of minor domestic shortcomings, considered to be still inappropriate for the new western regions (Yeremieieva 2018).

14. The popularity of Ukrainian *Perets* grew exponentially from the mid-1960s to the 1980s, when it started to decline. At the magazine's peak in the late 1970s, over three million copies were published (see Yeremieieva 2018, 184). *Krokodil* had circulation growth of between four hundred thousand and two million between 1954 and 1964 (Etty 2019, 10). *Krokodil*'s circulation was smaller than "only a few of the national newspapers and magazines by 1968" (10). Pehowski (1978, 729) claims that *Krokodil* had 90 percent subscription readers, with 10 percent sold at newsstands. In Lithuania *Krokodil* did not have a high circulation.

15. According to the official publication records, in 1971 there were 120,082 copies published. High publication numbers persisted throughout the 1980s. In 1986, publication rates were still as high as 112,053. The numbers decreased in the late 1980s and early 1990s.

16. According to the 1989 population census there were 3.67 million inhabitants in Lithuania (Maslauskaitė et al. 2006, 9).

17. Marian Pehowski makes a similar point about *Krokodil* in the 1970s—*Krokodil* made 20 million rubles annually, which helped support some of the less popular *Pravda* periodicals (Pehowski 1978, 730). In 1958, the *Broom* received subsidies from the government, as stated in Juozas Bulota's report to the Central Committee of the LCP Agitation and Propaganda Department of 1958. Personal archive of Juozas Bulota.

18. Former editor in chief Juozas Bulota, in an interview with him in 1991, confirms that the *Broom* was a profitable magazine (*Šluota* 1991).

19. On *Krokodil*'s transmediality—that is, the dispersal of its content across different media—see Etty (2019, chapter 5).

20. Jonas Varnas (2017) argued that the first cartoon exhibition took place in 1968.

21. Juozas Bulota's report to the Central Committee of the LCP Agitation and Propaganda Department of 1958. Personal archive of Juozas Bulota. For many years only two artists were *Broom* editorial staff members, employed at the magazine. In this book they are called "*Broom* artists"; others are called "contributors."

22. On KVN, Klub Veselykh i Nakhodchivykh (Club of the cheerful and inventive), a Soviet-bloc comedy group, see Garey (2020). Amy Garey illustrates that comedy shows were supported as well as censored and even banned by the state; they were ideologically conservative as well as politically subversive, both grassroots phenomenon and media spectacle.

23. In Soviet Lithuania, cartoons were published in a weekday *Komjaunimo tiesa* (Communist youth truth); a culture weekly *Literatūra ir menas* (Literature and art); a culture monthly *Kultūros barai* (Culture sector); a tri-weekly newspaper *Valstiečių laikraštis*

(Peasants' newspaper); a monthly magazine *Jaunimo gretos* (Ranks of the youth); a monthly magazine *Švyturys* (Beacon); a monthly youth journal *Nemunas* (Nemunas); a monthly agriculture science and achievements journal *Žemės ūkis* (Agriculture); a monthly horticulture journal *Mūsų sodai* (Our gardens); and others.

24. Other special publications with popular jokes, such as the books *Čia priėjo Kindziulis* (Here came Kindziulis) and *Šluotos kalendorius* (*Broom* calendar), were produced in the 1970s and 1980s. *Čia priėjo Kindziulis* was a collection of short dialogues, which ended with the character Kindziulis approaching speakers with a resolution. Both *Čia priėjo Kindziulis* and *Šluotos kalendorius* were very popular among *Broom* readers and were translated and published in other Soviet republics and Eastern Bloc countries.

25. At workplaces and schools, employees and schoolchildren were required to subscribe to Soviet newspapers, magazines, and journals. The *Broom* was one of the magazines people could subscribe to. According to Kęstutis Šiaulytis (2017), since the *Broom* was so popular, quotas were imposed on the *Broom* subscription, so people had to sign up for other magazines or newspapers.

26. Specifically, I heard people quoting jokes about Kindziulis, a character in the popular Kindziulis jokes series published during Soviet times. In 2020, these jokes were still published by the *Broom* online.

27. These authors were at the margins of their discipline. In the 1970s and 1980s the field was strongly influenced by historians, such as Robert Conquest, Richard Pipes, and Martin Malia, writing within the totalitarian framework. For a broader discussion see Klumbytė and Sharafutdinova (2012). For a discussion of revisionism see *Slavic Review* 67, no. 3 (2008), and Fitzpatrick (2008).

28. Studies of late socialism explored youth and popular culture (Zhuk 2010; Yurchak 2006), the Soviet film industry (First 2015), nonconformist movements (Fürst 2021), consumption (Chernyshova 2013), and the new middle classes (Paretskaya 2012).

29. On jokes in Eastern Europe see Rehak (2019) and Lampland and Nadkarni (2016).

30. Since my concept of "political" is linked to Rancière, for me it is imperative to think in dialogue with his ideas. My aim, however, is not to directly apply Rancière's theory to analysis of authoritarian laughter but to use some of his insights on politics and dissensus to interpret a Soviet Lithuanian case.

31. While many studies on laughter or the carnivalesque focus on reactive powers of humor, Gerald Creed (2011) emphasizes its transformative potential by discussing the constitution of community through conflict in Bulgarian mummer (*kukery*) carnivalesque rituals.

32. I analyze how everyday sentiments are translated into political action in my article on post-Soviet humor; see Klumbytė (2014).

33. The Lithuanian language is an Indo-European Baltic language, distinct from Slavic languages. According to the 2011 census, 77 percent of the population of Lithuania identified itself as Roman Catholic (Official Statistics Portal 2013).

34. Lithuania's Fight for Freedom Movement sought to restore Lithuania as an independent democratic state. The armed resistance at peak size involved 0.5 to 1 percent of the total population, comparable to the peak Viet Cong strength in South Vietnam (discounting the North Vietnamese supplements) (Misiunas and Taagepera 1983, 81).

35. The Lithuanian criminal code recognizes dual—Nazi and Soviet—genocide. Different from the United Nations Convention, Lithuanian "genocide" law recognizes genocide against social and political groups. According to the Criminal Code of the Republic of Lithuania, Soviet-era deportations and suppression of the armed resistance constituted genocide, acts committed with an intent to physically destroy, in whole or in part, a "national, ethnic, racial, religious, social or political group" (Lietuvos Respublikos Baudžiamasis Kodeksas 2020).

36. On different approaches to the Soviet and the national see Nerija Putinaitė (2015). Amanda Swain's work on the self-immolation of Romas Kalanta and youth protest movements in Kaunas, Lithuania, also transcends the national/Soviet dichotomy by contextualizing youth protests within the broader youth movements (Swain 2015).

37. On demographic changes in villages in southeast Lithuania see Stravinskienė (2016).

38. In 2000, the Lithuanian government estimated that the material loss due to Soviet occupation amounted to US$20 billion.

39. Kęstutis Šiaulytis, interview with the author, August 8, 2013, Vilnius.

40. On conceptualizations of forms of opposition among different social groups or strata see Rytis Bulota (2011), Klumbys (2008), Ramonaitė (2015b).

41. On satirical images of freedom in the *Broom* in 1989 see Grigaliūnas (2013).

42. Jonas Varnas, interview with the author, July 2009, Vilnius.

43. Varnas did not remember the author of this cartoon.

44. *Broom* contributing artist Algirdas Radvilavičius, in our interview on July 12, 2014, in Kaunas, mentioned that Bulota went to Moscow with sausages. Radvilavičius mentioned him taking smoked eel and vodka when an issue with cartoons with naked women in the foreign humor section was published. Algirdas Radvilavičius, interview with the author, May 31, 2017, Kaunas.

45. See Michael Herzfeld ([1997] 2016, chapter 2) for a discussion of the use of the concept *cultural intimacy* in works on different societies and cases; Neofotistos's (2010) review and insights on critical engagements with the concept of cultural intimacy; and case studies on cultural intimacy and mass meditation (Shryock 2004), public intimacy (Soysal 2010), and cultural intimacy and complaisance (Jung 2010).

46. On notions of "ordinary people" and common sociality in the former Yugoslavia see Helms (2007, on Bosnia), Neofotistos (2012, chapter 4, on Macedonia).

47. The importance of connections in the Soviet Union and socialist Eastern Europe has been widely studied; see, e.g., Berdahl (1999), Ledeneva (1998), Praspaliauskienė (2022).

48. Emil Draitser (2021, 97), a Soviet Jewish satirist, writing about Soviet Ukraine and Russia, argues that in the 1960s he was unemployable at a press because he was Jewish and not a party member.

49. Some examples of historical anthropology include Grant (1995), Buck Quijada (2019), Rogers (2009), Ssorin-Chaikov (2003), Verdery (2003, 2011), Yurchak (2006).

50. Juozas Bulota, the son of the editor in chief, pers. comm., July 30, 2019, Vilnius.

51. The event was co-organized and hosted by Dalia Cidzikaitė and the Martynas Mažvydas National Library staff.

52. On Russian *Novyi mir* (New world) and its relative independence, or "permitted dissent," see D. Kozlov (2013).

53. On *Krokodil* see also Draitser (2021), Frazer (2000), Kozin (2009), Low (1950), Pehowski (1978), Pyanov et al. (1989), and *Istoriia glazami Krokodila* (2015).

54. On Ukrainian *Perets* see Yeremieieva (2018) and Yekelchyk (2006); on Estonian *Pikker* (Lightning) see Lõhmus (2012).

1. BANALITY OF SOVIET POWER

1. The description of Dita's childhood is based on her memoir and interviews by the author with Dita Lomsargytė-Pukienė on July 10 and July 18, 2018, in Vilnius. See Lomsargytė-Pukienė (2004, 72) for her recollections of Sunday morning, June 22, 1941.

2. More than 95 percent of Lithuanian Jews were killed, more than 80 percent of whom were killed in Lithuania (Anušauskas et al. 2005, 222). On the Holocaust in Lithuania see, e.g., Dieckmann and Sužiedėlis (2006).

3. Lomsargytė-Pukienė does not mention bombers in her book. I believe Dita and Andrius both described the same event during my interviews with them. Both described how the Nazi occupation started in Kaunas, and each referred to Freda.

4. Andrius Cvirka, interview with the author, July 5, 2014, Zarasai, Lithuania.

5. See Krylova (2000) for discussion of forms of agency in Soviet studies.

6. Cvirka interview.

7. For a critique of Arendt's approach see Cesarini (2006) and Lipstadt (2011).

8. The *Broom* editorial staff, with the exception of poet Algirdas Skinkys, who worked only briefly at the magazine, are not known to have participated in any violent acts. Before the *Broom* was founded in 1948, Skinkys and another poet, Kostas Kubilinskas, infiltrated the Lithuanian armed resistance base, killed its leader, and betrayed others to the Soviet State Security (Kondratas 2021).

9. Rothberg emphasizes that "contexts of injustice are multiple and often contradictory, and that categories such as 'perpetrator,' 'victim,' and 'implicated subject' are abstractions that serve analytical purposes but do not describe human essences. That is, it is best to think of the implicated subject (not to mention the victim and the perpetrator) as a position that we occupy in particular, dynamic, and at times clashing structures and histories of power; it is not an ontological identity that freezes us forever in proximity to power and privilege" (Rothberg 2019, 8).

10. On "implication" as a new moral category that calls for political responsibility on a broader scale than narrower legalistic categories of historical violence see Rothberg (2019, chapter 3).

11. On Lithuanian leftist intellectuals and their support of the Soviet regime in the 1930s see Tamošaitis (2010).

12. Juozas Bulota, the son of the editor in chief, noted that his father never spoke about any support to Soviet partisans and, if asked, claimed to have had no option when they knocked on the door. Juozas Bulota, pers. comm., June 24, 2021.

13. While editor in chief Bulota was recognized as a Soviet partisan liaison during the years 1942–1944 (*Tarybų Lietuvos enciklopedija* 1985), this fact had never been invoked at the *Broom* PPO meetings until the 1975 meeting commemorating the thirtieth anniversary of the Soviet victory in World War II. See the Lithuanian Special Archive (hereafter cited in notes as LSA), f. 15020, ap. 1, b. 11, l. 10. On Bulota's life see also Šniukas (2018).

14. Article "Mano pirmieji žingsniai *Eltoje*," December 26, 1967. Personal archive of Juozas Bulota. In an interview with him in 1991, Bulota mentioned that it was important that his uncle Andrius Bulota and his wife were killed by Nazis (*Šluota* 1991, 3).

15. Elena Kurklietytė Bubnienė, interview with the author, July 18, 2018, Vilnius. Zimanas was Jewish and an orthodox communist, who was remembered bitterly by some Lithuanian cultural elites (see, e.g., Baltušis 2019).

16. Thirteen-year-old Donata worked as a nanny in Siberia, looking after two other little children. This family was invited by Sofija Kymantaitė to come back to join an ensemble in Pereslavl' since actors were needed. "It was a miracle," recalled Donata, that they were allowed to leave in 1943. Later they returned to Lithuania. Donata stayed with this family until adulthood, since her real family escaped from Siberia only later and lived in Lithuania illegally. Donata Bulotienė, interview with the author, June 24, 2018, Mardasavas, Lithuania.

17. Before his second marriage, Bulota, like many other Soviet cultural elites, traveled to capitalist countries. He visited Italy, Finland, France, and Greece. Throughout his career he visited many Eastern European countries (data from Juozas Bulota's personal archive and editor in chief's son Juozas Bulota, pers. comm., July 30, 2019).

18. Juozas Bulota, pers. comm., July 19, 2018, Vilnius.

19. Juozas Bulota, pers. comm., July 19, 2018, Vilnius.

20. In his autobiographical novel, which merged autobiographical and fictive elements, Sadaunykas used pseudonyms for people, many of whom are identifiable, and called the *Broom* the *Thorn*.

21. Perestroika-era lecture notes for delivery of a public lecture prepared by Bulota himself. Personal archive of Juozas Bulota.

22. Juozas Bulota, pers. comm., July 19, 2018, Vilnius.

23. Bulotienė interview.

24. Dita Lomsargytė-Pukienė, interview with the author, July 10, 2018, Vilnius.

25. Lomsargytė-Pukienė interview.

26. See a LCP CC report no. 35 of September 3, 1956. LSA, f. 1771, ap. 191, b. 124, l. 18.

27. In Lithuanian "Nuo 1956 m. spalio 20 d. pradedu eiti 'ŠLUOTOS' redaktoriaus pareigas." Juozas Bulota personal archive.

28. In Juozas Bulota's personal archive there are the following hiring orders signed by him: Order No. 2 of October 31, 1956, for Regina Kučaitė for a one-month probation period as a secretary-typist; Rytis Tilvytis and Algimantas Pabijūnas, for a one-month probation period as literary editors; and Vytautas Kaušinis for a one-month probation period as an artist. Order No. 3 of November 1, 1956, noted the hiring of Juozas Buivydas as an art editor. This same order had a handwritten note that the *Broom* editorial office should consist of J. Bulota, the editor in chief; P. Pukys, a deputy editor; and T. Tilvytis, A. Gricius, N. Petrulis, J. Baltušis, and S. Krasauskas—the editorial board members. With Order No. 4 of November 12, 1956, Bulota hired Vytautas Mačinskas as a managing editor and Aleksandras Vitulskis as an artist for a probation period of one month. With Order No. 5 of November 14, 1956, he hired Povilas Pukis as a deputy editor and dismissed Vytautas Kaušinis (because of his transfer to another magazine, *Soviet Woman*). Order No. 6 of November 14, 1956, recorded the hire of Leonas Kiauleikis as a literary editor. The next year Antanas Pakalnis was hired as a literary editor (Order No. 1, January 15, 1957) and fired less than two weeks later (Order No. 2, January 28, 1957) because he did not pass the probation period (Lith. *kaip neišlaikiusį bandomojo laiko*). Elena Kurklietytė was hired as a literary editor on March 15, 1957 (Order No. 3); Sofija Liugailienė as an artist on March 27, 1957 (Order No. 4). Vitulskis quit his work on June 1, 1957 (Order No. 6 of May 27, 1957). Jonas Sadaunykas was hired as an executive secretary on May 30, 1957 (Order No. 7). Vlada Černiauskaitė was hired as an artist on December 10, 1956 (Order No. 8). She was dismissed on January 28, 1957, by her request (Order No. 2). Algirdas Šiekštelė was hired as an artist on June 7, 1957 (Order No. 9). Order No. 10 of June 14, 1957, stated that Algimantas Pabijūnas was dismissed by his request. For a list of artists and writers who collaborated in the *Broom* from 1956 to 1984 see Juozas Bulota, "*Šluotai—50*."

29. Albertas Lukša, interview with the author, July 30, 2019, Liukonys, Lithuania.

30. Juozas Bulota's 1958 report to the LCP CC Propaganda and Agitation Department. Personal archive of Juozas Bulota.

31. On Soviet and Lithuanian trajectories in the poetry of Justinas Marcinkevičius see Putinaitė (2015, 2019).

32. Lithuanian Archive of Literature and Art (hereafter cited in notes as LALA), f. 361, ap. 1, b. 81, l. 2.

33. Juozas Bulota, interview with the author, July 19, 2018, Vilnius. In his father's personal archive are some photos and documents illustrating the visit of *Krokodil* editors to the *Broom*.

34. Bulota interview, July 19, 2018, Vilnius.

35. Juozas Bulota's perestroika-era lecture notes for delivery of a public lecture. Personal archive of Juozas Bulota.

36. Sąjūdis was founded in support of Mikhail Gorbachev's perestroika. Almost half of the Sąjūdis initiative's group members were members of the Communist Party. With its

inclination toward secession from the USSR and promotion of nationalist ideas, Sąjūdis soon became a symbol of the struggle for independence (see Senn 2002).

37. Perestroika-era lecture notes for delivery of a public lecture prepared by Bulota himself. Personal archive of Juozas Bulota.

38. Juozas Bulota, pers. comm., June 18, 2018, Vilnius.

39. Bulota interview.

40. The description of Sadaunykas's childhood and youth is based on his autobiographical novel, written in 1987–1989 and published in 2002. See pages 13–15 on his childhood and youth.

41. Juodzevičius (2003) lists Jonas Sadaunykas, a teacher from Utena, as a political prisoner.

42. Romualdas Lankauskas, pers. comm., August 31, 2016.

43. In Lithuanian *geriausiai apsimetinėjo komunistu*. Kęstutis Šiaulytis, interview with the author, June 19, 2014, Vilnius.

44. Šiaulytis interview.

45. During interviews interlocutors usually used the term "Stalinist" when they emphasized connections to Stalin's period or named somebody who was an orthodox communist, a literal follower of communist ideology and Communist Party principles.

46. Kęstutis Šiaulytis, pers. comm., April 2, 2020.

47. Jonas Sadaunykas's postcard to Juozas Bulota on his seventieth birthday, May 20, 1988, Vilnius. Personal archive of Juozas Bulota.

48. Lukša interview.

49. Lukša interview.

50. Albertas Lukša said he was fifteen or sixteen years old. Lukša interview.

51. Lukša interview.

52. Lukša interview.

53. Albertas Lukša claimed that he joined the *Broom* most likely in 1959, or even 1960. Lukša interview. He worked at the *Broom* for thirty-six years.

54. Teofilis Tilvytis's biography and creative work have been discussed by Areška (1988).

55. Lomsargytė-Pukienė interview.

56. Romas Palčiauskas, interview with the author, July 29, 2014, Vilnius.

57. Kęstutis Šiaulytis, pers. comm., undated.

58. Throughout the chapters I use text boxes to include examples from research or archives, cite some interview data, provide contextual information, or my own reflections on the research process.

59. Kurklietytė Bubnienė interview.

60. Romualdas Lankauskas, interview with the author, August 14, 2016, Vilnius.

61. Lankauskas interview.

62. The fact of collaboration with the KGB was established by the Lithuanian Lustration Commission (see Šliažienė 2005). One of the *Broom*'s contributors confirmed that Kiauleikis was a KGB agent when he worked at the *Broom*. I was not able to find any evidence about this collaboration in the Lithuanian KGB archives.

63. Vytautas Žeimantas, interview with the author, June 25, 2019, Vilnius.

64. Žeimantas interview.

65. Kęstutis Šiaulytis, pers. comm., undated.

66. See Semenov (1982, 18–21) on founding of *Krokodil*.

67. In the interwar period artists studied in France, Italy, and Germany. They were also influenced by Russian artists, especially through the art of Mstislavas Dobužinskis. On art and graphic art specifically in interwar Lithuania see Jankevičiūtė (2008, 2016) and *Lietuvos dailės istorija* (2002).

68. See Juozas Bulota, "*Šluotai—50*," Bulota's typed lecture dated September 12, 1984. Personal archive of Juozas Bulota.

69. *Wooden Clog*, 1940, no. 51, p. 1.

2. POLITICAL INTIMACY

1. In Lithuanian, "'Šluotos' žurnalo darbuotojų įsipareigojimai Spalio socialistinės revoliucijos švenčių proga."

2. I assume that Bytautas told Bulota about the proclamation, and Bulota called the KGB. It is unlikely that another, lower-ranking editor would have called the KGB without informing Bulota.

3. The report from the meeting of Bytautas's case on April 6, 1972, provides only a short mention of the KGB operative's visit. See LSA, f. 15020, ap. 1, b. 10, l. 9. See documents and discussion of Bytautas's case at LSA, f. 15020, ap. 1, b. 10, ll. 8–22, and the follow-up reports on ll. 43–46, 71, 84, 100. The "case of Bytautas" is reconstructed based on PPO reports. *Broom* editors did not remember this case.

4. Yurchak argues that *stiob* shared some elements with Bakhtin's notion of carnivalesque parody, and thus it was not simply a form of resistance, because it involved a feeling of affinity and warmth toward authoritative symbols (2006, 250). Some of the former *Broom* editors did not think the proclamation was against the regime or ideological discourse. It could have been self-mocking laughter. The data I gathered on the *Broom* do not provide evidence that "affinity" and "warmth" described editors' relation to the bureaucratic or CP language used in the proclamation (see chapter 3).

5. At the PPO meetings editors did not discuss financial questions, with the exception of honoraria to the activists who helped with journalistic investigations.

6. LSA, f. 15020, ap. 1, b. 10, l. 9.

7. LSA, f. 15020, ap. 1, b. 10, l. 9.

8. LSA, f. 15020, ap. 1, b. 10, l. 9.

9. LSA, f. 15020, ap. 1, b. 10, ll. 9–10.

10. LSA, f. 15020, ap. 1, b. 10, l. 12.

11. LSA, f. 15020, ap. 1, b. 10, l. 12.

12. LSA, f. 15020, ap. 1, b. 10, l. 44.

13. LSA, f. 15020, ap. 1, b. 10, ll. 44–45.

14. LSA, f. 15020, ap. 1, b. 10, l. 45.

15. LSA, f. 15020, ap. 1, b. 10, l. 45.

16. LSA, f. 15020, ap. 1, b. 10, l. 46.

17. LSA, f. 15020, ap. 1, b. 10, l. 100.

18. Kęstutis Šiaulytis, interview with the author, June 19, 2014, Vilnius.

19. LSA, f. 15020, ap. 1, b. 10, l. 84.

20. In perestroika-era public lecture notes, Juozas Bulota mentions that the *Broom* was published without his signature for twenty years. Personal archive of Juozas Bulota.

21. *Krokodil* contributed many antisemitic caricatures to the "cosmopolitanism" campaign (against foreigners and "rootless cosmopolitans," a code word for Jews) during the so-called Zhdanovshchina, 1946–1953 (see Alaniz 2010, 62).

22. Dita Lomsargytė-Pukienė, interview with the author, July 10, 2018, Vilnius.

23. Personal archive of Dita Lomsargytė-Pukienė. In the anonymous letter Dita is called "S. Petkevičienė." Bulota calls her "Silvija P." in his letter. Dita was renamed to Silvija when her mother and her stepfather Lithuanized her name (see chapter 1). "Lomsargytė-Petkevičienė" was her last name after her first marriage.

24. Dovainis was one of the pen names used by Bulota.

25. LSA, f. 15020, ap. 1, b. 4, l. 6.

26. LSA, f. 15020, ap. 1, b. 10, l. 2.

27. LSA, f. 15020, ap. 1, b. 11, l. 31. On the collective and the individual in Russia, party rituals, mutual surveillance, and criticism see Kharkhordin (1999).

28. LSA, f. 15020, ap. 1, b. 13, l. 16.

29. LSA, f. 15020, ap. 1, b. 13, l. 28.

30. LSA, f. 15020, ap. 1, b. 13, l. 17.

31. LSA, f. 15020, ap. 1, b. 12, l. 23.

32. E.g., LSA, f. 15020, ap. 1, b. 10, l. 91.

33. Martha Lampland's comments on this manuscript, pers. comm., July 10, 2021.

34. Juozas Bulota, interview with the author, July 19, 2018, Vilnius.

35. A note about taking a taxi to Vilnius most likely refers to the 1960s. According to Kęstutis Šiaulytis, because of later editorial board changes in Latvia, Lithuania, and Estonia, these gatherings were discontinued, even if close relationships between some people continued.

36. Kęstutis Šiaulytis, interview with the author, August 17, 2013. Pilies Alley was renamed Bernardinų Street in the post-Soviet period.

37. Andrius Cvirka, interview with the author, July 5, 2014, Zarasai, Lithuania.

38. E.g., LSA, f. 15020, ap. 1, b. 1, 3, 4, 5, 6, 7, 10.

39. Romas Palčiauskas, interview with the author, July 29, 2014, Vilnius.

40. On cognac as a form of recognition in post-Soviet Russia see Patico (2002). On moonshine as economic exchange and social status medium see Rogers (2009, chapter 5).

41. Lomsargytė-Pukienė interview.

42. A note dated May 20, 1977. Personal archive of Juozas Bulota.

43. LSA, f. 15020, ap. 1, b. 14, l. 31.

44. LSA, f. 15020, ap. 1, b. 14, ll. 29–30.

45. LSA, f. 15020, ap. 1, b. 14, l. 30.

46. *Broom*, 1966, no. 1, p. 5. Comrades' Courts were volunteer tribunals established in enterprises, apartment buildings, universities, collective farms, and elsewhere after the 1959 Soviet criminal law reform (Berman and Spindler 1963, 842). Comrades' Courts could impose a small fine, recommend eviction from an apartment, temporary demotion to a lower-paying job, etc. (842). They had to perform a persuasive rather than a coercive function and illustrate an increase in informal and popular mechanisms of self-governance (842).

47. Andrius Cvirka, interview with the author, July 7, 2014, Zarasai, Lithuania.

48. The episode with Andrius Cvirka and Sadaunykas at the drunk tank could have happened between 1972 and 1984.

49. LSA, f. 15020, ap. 1, b. 14, l. 33.

50. Albertas Lukša, interview with the author, July 29, 2015, Liukonys, Lithuania. Lukša did not remember when this happened. It is likely that it was when Lionginas Šepetys was the LCP CC secretary and Bulota was still the editor in chief, that is, between 1976 and 1985.

51. Vytautas Žeimantas, interview with the author, June 25, 2019, Vilnius.

52. Česlovas Juršėnas, interview with the author, August 1, 2019, Vilnius. Juršėnas's statement most likely describes the *Broom* in the 1970s and 1980s.

53. Albertas Lukša, interview with the author, July 30, 2019, Liukonys, Lithuania.

54. Lukša interview, July 30, 2019. In Soviet times homosexuality was criminalized and concealed from the public. In the 2010s the LGBTQ+ community was growing, although it lacked wide popular support. Since sharing a bed with another man in the 2010s might indicate homosexual relations, Lukša makes a comment to deny that there were any.

55. Albertas Lukša, interview with the author, August 5, 2017, Liukonys, Lithuania.

56. Algirdas Radvilavičius, interview with the author, July 12, 2014, Kaunas.

3. THE SOVIET PREDICAMENT

1. Albertas Lukša's biography is discussed in more detail in chapter 1.

2. Kęstutis Šiaulytis, interview with the author, May 8, 2015, Vilnius.

3. Kęstutis Šiaulytis, interview with the author, June 19, 2014, Vilnius.

4. Vytautas Žeimantas, interview with the author, June 25, 2019, Vilnius.

5. Žeimantas interview.

6. Journalist Aleksei Adzhubei, Khrushchev's son-in-law and editor in chief of the Soviet newspaper *Izvestiia*, was known to claim that his main ideal was to "help the person. Not humanity. Not class. Not the republic, not even the country" (Wolfe 2005, 44). On Soviet journalists' imperative to help ordinary people see also Roudakova (2017).

7. The first Party Organization meeting report, available in the LSA collections, notes that all communists and all editorial staff participated in the meeting of May 10, 1960. The four Communist Party members were Juozas Bulota, Leonas Kiauleikis, Jonas Sadaunykas, and Antanas Rudzinskas. Rytis Tilvytis and Albertas Lukša joined the *Broom* PPO after being accepted into the Communist Party in 1962.

8. PPO annual assessment meetings were called "assessment electoral" meetings in official PPO reports. At these meetings *Broom* CP members elected a new PPO secretary and a PPO associate secretary.

9. Albertas Lukša, interview with the author, July 29, 2015, Liukonys, Lithuania.

10. From 1960 to 1979, the period for which PPO archival data exist, there were never more than eight CP members at the *Broom*.

11. See, e.g., LSA, f. 15020, ap. 1, b. 10, l. 58. Sadaunykas's words in the epigraph are from the PPO meeting in 1972. See LSA, f. 15020, ap. 1, b. 10, l. 2.

12. See LSA, f. 15020, ap. 1, b. 12, ll. 21–24.

13. Kęstutis Šiaulytis, interview with the author, August 8, 2013, Vilnius.

14. Šiaulytis interview, June 19, 2014.

15. Šiaulytis interview, May 8, 2015.

16. LSA, f. 15020, ap. 1, b. 10, l. 57.

17. At the PPO annual meeting in October, Rytis Tilvytis claimed that before October the PPO met eight times, which is not enough. According to Tilvytis, some meetings were not recorded because there were only three out of five CP members present (others were absent because of illness and hospitalization). LSA, f. 15020, ap. 1, b. 10, l. 131.

18. On the lack of effective political education see LSA, f. 15020, ap. 1, b. 10, l. 130. On the need for serious attitude to political education see LSA, f. 15020, ap. 1, b. 12, l. 22. On the importance of control see LSA, f. 15020, ap. 1, b. 12, l. 22; LSA, f. 15020, ap. 1, b. 11, l. 13; LSA, f. 15020, ap. 1, b. 10, ll. 91, 116, 118.

19. See, e.g., LSA, f. 15020, ap. 1, b. 11, l. 30.

20. LSA, f. 15020, ap. 1, b. 11, l. 19.

21. See, e.g., LSA, f. 15020, ap. 1, b. 10, l. 116; LSA, f. 15020, ap. 1, b. 10, l. 91.

22. See LSA, f. 15020, ap. 1, b. 14, ll. 45–46.

23. LSA, f. 15020, ap. 1, b. 15, l. 46.

24. LSA, f. 15020, ap. 1, b. 11, l. 33.

25. LSA, f. 15020, ap. 1, b. 10, ll. 133–34.

26. LSA, f. 15020, ap. 1, b. 11, l. 8.

27. LSA, f. 15020, ap. 1, b. 11, l. 2.

28. LSA, f. 15020, ap. 1, b. 11, l. 7; LSA, f. 15020, ap. 1, b. 11, l. 11.

29. LSA, f. 15020, ap. 1, b. 11, l. 7.

30. See Lukša's report of April 28, 1975. LSA, f. 15020, ap. 1, b. 11, ll. 6–9. See P. Raščius's personal statement, LSA, f. 15020, ap. 1, b. 12, l. 2. LSA, f. 15020, ap. 1, b. 10, l. 91.

31. On archival genres of secrecy and forms of knowledge see Verdery (2014, 2018), Krakus (2015), Krakus and Vatulescu (2019).

32. See LSA, f. 15020, ap. 1, b. 3, l. 18.

33. LSA, f. 15020, ap. 1, b. 1, l. 12.

34. LSA, f. 15020, ap. 1, b. 1, l. 17.

35. LSA, f. 15020, ap. 1, b. 12, l. 25.

36. LSA, f. 15020, ap. 1, b. 13, l. 8.

37. LSA, f. 15020, ap. 1, b. 9, l. 67.

38. LSA, f. 15020, ap. 1, b. 10, l. 77.

39. LSA, f. 15020, ap. 1, b. 9, l. 101.

40. LSA, f. 15020, ap. 1, b. 10, l. 108.

41. LSA, f. 15020, ap. 1, b. 10, l. 112.

42. Šiaulytis interview, June 19, 2014.

43. *Broom*, 1973, no. 5. A similar cartoon by N. Lisogorski was published in *Krokodil*, 1963, no. 6.

44. *Broom*, 1965, no. 5, p. 9.

45. For other work-related themes see May 26, 1978, report. LSA, f. 15020, ap. 1, b. 14, ll. 15–17.

46. See Rimantas Baldišius's cartoon in *Broom*, 1985, no. 5, p. 2.

47. On state policy and different spheres of consumption see Chernyshova (2013), Oushakine (2014), Siegelbaum (2008), Tsipursky (2016).

48. *Broom*, 1977, no. 19, p. 2. Many short anecdotes in the *Broom* are cited without an author.

49. *Broom*, 1981, no. 1, p. 7.

50. I used some of the examples discussed in the section "Soviet ideology of everyday life" in Klumbytė (2012). See Field (2007) on private life and communist morality under Khrushchev.

51. I discussed *Broom* moral agendas in detail in Klumbytė (2012).

52. LSA, f. 15020, ap. 1, b. 12, ll. 7–9.

53. I thank Rima Praspaliauskienė for drawing my attention to this point.

4. CENSORIAL INDISTINCTION

1. Glavlit had different names—from 1953 to 1966 it was called the Main Administration for the Protection of State and Military Secrets in the Press; after 1966 it was renamed the Main Administration for the Protection of State Secrets in the Press under the USSR Council of Ministers (see Ermolaev 1997, 182). See Streikus (2018) on the history of Glavlit in the USSR and Lithuania.

2. Adomas Subačius (1928–2018), interview with the author, October 2, 2016, Antagavė, Lithuania.

3. The state secrets included data on the USSR military; addresses, names, and ranks of military personnel; numbers of draftees to the Soviet Army; defense industry objects, their functioning and location; prisons and camps; transport and communication questions; information about airports, railways, and strategic roads; various strategic factories, factory plans, production plans, and output; scientific industry questions; oil industry; the number of *druzhiny* (Rus., people's voluntary patrols) in the border region; negative information about air pollution; dangerous chemicals in agricultural products that affected people's health; statistical information about various diseases; health care questions, including developments like disease outbreaks; city maps; government resorts; unpublished Communist Party and government decrees; and drug users (see *Perechen'* 1976). Some of these secrets were related to ideological positions: disease outbreaks could not occur in a socialist society, or there could be no drug users in the USSR; such issues would undermine the image of the Soviet Union. Other secrets, like

roads on maps or scientific industry secrets, had to be hidden because of Cold War defense concerns.

4. Lankauskas was a writer and briefly worked at the *Broom* in the 1960s. Romualdas Lankauskas, interview with the author, August 14, 2016, Vilnius.

5. Jonas Varnas, interview with the author, July 2009, Vilnius.

6. See also Herman Ermolaev's analysis of Brezhnev-period censorship. Ermolaev argues that even if censorship was strengthened after 1968, it lacked strict consistency (1997, chapter 5).

7. The full title of *Perechen'* is *Perechen' svedenii, zapreshchennykh k opublikavoniiu v otkrytoi pechati, peredachakh po radio i televideniiu* . . . (The List: Information forbidden to be published in the open press, radio, and television broadcasts).

8. Estonian media scholar Epp Lauk notes (1999, 22) that in Estonian the word *censorship* was not published in a newspaper until as late as 1987.

9. Vladimiras Beresniovas, interview with the author, July 20, 2014, Kaunas.

10. During the authoritarian regime of President Antanas Smetona (1926–1940), all print material had to be approved by a censorship committee (Kelertas 2007). On censorship in Lithuania between 1918 and 1940 see Glosienė (1993); Papaurėlytė (1999, 2003); Riaubienė (2005); Vaišnys (1999). On Soviet censorship in Lithuania see Gudaitis (2010); Kelertas (2007); Sabonis and Sabonis (1992); Sėdaitytė (2017); Streikus (2018).

11. In the Soviet Union, Glavlit was founded in June 1922 to coordinate and centralize censorship functions in the Soviet state. On Glavlit in the USSR see Goriaeva (2009); Fedotova (2009); Kassof (2015).

12. On the thaw period's liberalization of censorship and resuming control by Glavlit see Streikus (2004, 45–46). On suppression of satire and Zhdanovshchina in Ukrainian culture see Yekelchyk (2006).

13. Simon Huxtable (2018) argues that post-1953 journalism reflected the broader cultural politics of the post-Stalin period that ended after the Czechoslovakian crisis of 1968. On post-1953 journalism in Russia see Huxtable (2018).

14. LSA, f. 15020, ap. 1, b. 10, l. 23.

15. LSA, f. 15020, ap. 1, b. 10, l. 23.

16. In the 1960s, almost every year in Glavlit PPO reports it is argued that work with presses should be strengthened. In 1968, Glavlit monitored forty magazines, journals, and bulletins; in 1971, it monitored thirty-eight; in 1976, forty-three; in 1981, it monitored forty-six; and in 1982, forty-nine. Some of the often-censored magazines, which were censored more often than the *Broom*, included *Pergalė* (Victory), *Jaunimo gretos* (Ranks of the youth), *Kultūros barai* (Culture sector), and *Nemunas* (Nemunas).

17. From 1964 to 1974, Glavlit censors complain that there were not enough censors. See, e.g., the protocol of LSSR Glavlit PPO meeting of February 23, 1965, LSA, f. 7759, ap. 2, b. 9, l. 10. In 1976, it is reported that the cadre problem is "practically solved." See also Streikus (2018, 101).

18. Censors' errors discussed at the Glavlit meetings were to be reported to Moscow. Some errors were not sent to Moscow, which was critically reflected upon in some Glavlit PPO reports; see, e.g., LSA, f. 7759, ap. 2, b. 8, ll. 9–12.

19. See censors' memoirs in Sabonis and Sabonis (1992). According to Streikus (2018, 101), cadre fluctuation stabilized and salaries increased in the mid-1970s.

20. Lithuanian Central State Archive (hereafter cited in notes as LCSA), f. R-522, ap. 2, b. 28, ll. 38–41.

21. See LSA, f. 7759, ap. 2, b. 5, ll. 13–25.

22. LSA, f. 7759, ap. 2, b. 11, l. 26.

23. LSA, f. 7759, ap. 2, b. 5, l. 24.

24. LSA, f. 7759, ap. 2, b. 5, l. 23.

25. LSA, f. 7759, ap. 2, b. 11, l. 25. Artist Andrius Cvirka, who worked at the *Broom* from the 1960s to the 1980s, recalled that Glavlit censors missed many things because of lack of knowledge. Andrius Cvirka, interview with the author, July 5, 2014, Zarasai, Lithuania. See also Vilius Ivanauskas (2014, 655–56) for his discussion of limited censorship in Lithuania.

26. LSA, f. 7759, ap. 2, b. 11, l. 26.

27. See, e.g., LSA, f. 7759, ap. 2, b. 3. l. 15v.

28. LSA, f. 7759, ap. 2, b. 9, l. 8.

29. Varnas interview. Most likely Varnas refers to the post-1976 period.

30. See, e.g., LCSA, f. R-522, ap. 2, b. 33, l. 10.

31. LCSA, f. R-522, ap. 2, b. 172, l. 14.

32. Varnas most likely was talking about the 1970s and 1980s.

33. LCSA, f. R-522, ap. 2, b. 88, l. 6.

34. LCSA, f. R-522, ap. 2, b. 88, l. 6.

35. LCSA, f. R-522, ap. 2, b. 88, l. 6.

36. LCSA, f. R-522, ap. 2, b. 42, l. 16.

37. LCSA, f. R-522, ap. 2, b. 29, l. 20 (185).

38. LCSA, f. R-522, ap. 2, b. 88, l. 4.

39. LCSA, f. R-522, ap. 2, b. 88, l. 7.

40. LCSA, f. R-522, ap. 2, b. 33, l. 17.

41. LCSA, f. R-522, ap. 2, b. 33, l. 17.

42. LCSA, f. R-522, ap. 2, b. 195, l. 8.

43. LCSA, f. R-522, ap. 2, b. 195, l. 8.

44. LCSA, f. R-522, ap. 2, b. 33, l. 19.

45. LCSA, f. R-522, ap. 2, b. 37, l. 24.

46. LCSA, f. R-522, ap. 2, b. 37, l. 24.

47. There is little known about the censoring of *Krokodil*. John Etty (2019, 111) writes that during the almost seventy years of the publication's history, *Krokodil* staff fell victim to political repression on a few occasions, but the magazine was the subject of LCP Central Committee decrees on only four occasions.

48. There might have been another undocumented case (see chapter 6).

49. Česlovas Juršėnas, interview with the author, August 1, 2019, Vilnius.

50. I summarize information presented in two Glavlit reports of 1968, namely, M. Slizevičius's "Report on Republic Censorship Organs Inspection Remarks on Print Media Publications" (LCSA, f. R-522, ap. 2, b. 88, ll. 2–8; this report discussed the *Broom* on pages 2–3), and M. Slizevičius's "Report on Some Works Placed in the *Broom* Magazine" (LCSA, f. R-522, ap. 2, b. 88, ll. 25–29).

51. LCSA, f. R-522, ap. 2, b. 88, l. 26.

52. LCSA, f. R-522, ap. 2, b. 88, l. 26.

53. LCSA, f. R-522, ap. 2, b. 88, l. 2.

54. LCSA, f. R-522, ap. 2, b. 88, ll. 2–3.

55. I thank Stephen Norris for drawing my attention to this hidden message.

56. See the poem in LCSA, f. R-522, ap. 2, b. 88, l. 3.

57. LCSA, f. R-522, ap. 2, b. 88, l. 26.

58. On puritanical censorship in Soviet history see Ermolaev (1997). Erotic and sexual themes are censored in democratic countries as well; see Freedman (2012) and Mazzarella (2013).

59. LCSA, f. R-522, ap. 2, b. 88, l. 29.

60. LCSA, f. R-522, ap. 2, b. 88, l. 29.

61. LCSA, f. R-522, ap. 2, b. 88, l. 28.

62. The ad was published in the *Broom*, 1968, no. 20, p. 3.

63. LCSA, f. R-522, ap. 2, b. 88, ll. 26–27. Author's translation.

64. LCSA, f. R-522, ap. 2, b. 88, ll. 27–28. Author's translation.

65. Vilnius Glavlit annual report for 1957, LCSA, f. R-522, ap. 2, b. 29, l. 22.

66. Vilnius Glavlit annual report for 1958–1959, LCSA, f. R-522, ap. 2, b. 37, l. 25.

67. Vilnius Glavlit annual report for 1960, LCSA, f. R-522, ap. 2, b. 43, l. 23.

68. LSA, f. 7759, ap. 2, b. 4, l. 61.

69. LSA, f. 7759, ap. 2, b. 4, l. 61.

70. LSA, f. 7759, ap. 2, b. 4, l. 61.

71. Vilnius Glavlit annual report for 1963, LCSA, f. R-522, ap. 2, b. 56, l. 9.

72. Vilnius Glavlit annual report for 1966, LCSA, f. R-522, ap. 2, b. 76, l. 5.

73. Vilnius Glavlit annual report for 1966, LCSA, f. R-522, ap. 2, b. 76, l. 6.

74. LCSA, f. R-522, ap. 2, b. 88, l. 2.

75. LCSA, f. R-522, ap. 2, b. 88, ll. 2–3.

76. LCSA, f. R-522, ap. 2, b. 88, l. 3.

77. LCV, f. R-522, ap. 2, b. 88, ll. 28–29.

78. LCSA, f. R-522, ap. 2, b. 88, l. 29.

79. LCSA, f. R-522, ap. 2, b. 88, l. 26.

80. LCSA, f. R-522, ap. 2, b. 88, ll. 27–28.

81. LCSA, f. R-522, ap. 2, b. 88, l. 29.

82. Vilnius Glavlit annual report for 1970, LCSA, f. R-522, a. 2, b. 104, l. 20.

83. Vilnius Glavlit report to LCP CC, May 5, 1970, LCSA, f. R-522, ap. 2, b. 100, l. 18.

84. Vilnius Glavlit annual report for 1979, LCSA, f. R-522, ap. 2, b. 175, l. 4.

85. Vilnius Glavlit annual report for 1983, LCSA, f. R-522, ap. 2, b. 205, l. 3.

86. Vilnius Glavlit annual report for 1983, LCSA, f. R-522, ap. 2, b. 205, l. 3.

87. Vilnius Glavlit annual report for 1970, LCSA, f. R-522, a. 2, b. 104, l. 20. See chapter 6 for a detailed discussion.

88. Vilnius Glavlit report to LCP CC, May 5, 1970, LCSA, f. R-522, ap. 2, b. 100, l. 18.

89. LCSA, f. R-522, ap. 2, b. 175, l. 4.

90. LCSA, f. R-522, ap. 2, b. 205, l. 3.

91. LSA, f. 15020, ap. 1, b. 11, l. 37. J. Kunčinas's "Kaunas Resident X in Vilnius, Vilnius Resident X in Kaunas" was published in the *Broom*, 1975, no. 18.

92. Valaitis's poem was published in the *Broom*, 1975, no. 18. LSA, f. 15020, ap. 1, b. 11, l. 37.

93. LSA, f. 15020, ap. 1, b. 15, l. 22.

94. LSA, f. 15020, ap. 1, b. 15, l. 22.

95. Andrius Deltuva, phone conversation with the author, April 1, 2016.

96. Algirdas Radvilavičius, interview with the author, July 12, 2014, Kaunas.

97. Kęstutis Šiaulytis, pers. comm., summer 2011, Vilnius.

98. Many studies of humor emphasize ambiguity as a defining category of humor; see Bahktin (1984); Goldstein (2012); Haugerud (2013).

99. Kęstutis Šiaulytis, interview with the author, June 19, 2014, Vilnius.

100. *Broom*, 1981, no. 1, cover.

101. On the Aesopian language in Lithuania or other Baltic states see Jevsejevas (2014); Jurgutienė and Satkauskytė (2018); Kelertas (2007); Kirss (1994); Klivis (2010); Klumbys (2016); Kmita (2015); Satkauskytė (2018).

102. Radvilavičius interview.

103. Radvilavičius interview.

104. Žilinskaitė, interview with the author, May 13, 2017, Vilnius.

105. Žilinskaitė interview.

106. LSA, 1973, f. 15020, ap. 1, b. 10, l. 74.

107. Šarūnas Jakštas, interview with the author, July 2009, Vilnius.

108. Varnas interview.

109. Kęstutis Šiaulytis, interview with the author, August 7, 2013, Vilnius.

110. Lankauskas interview.

111. Lankauskas interview.

112. In Lithuanian, "Jam jaunieji per jauni, o senieji per seni. Vienas pėdina gatve— pats didesnis už save." Elena Kurklietytė Bubnienė, interview with the author, July 18, 2018, Vilnius.

113. On writers' resistance to censorship in Russia in the 1965–1984 period see Ermolaev (1997, 219–21).

5. POLITICAL AESTHETICS

1. In the USSR the transfer of print media censorship to editorial boards took place in the early 1930s (see Streikus 2018, chapter 1).

2. Cited in G. Astrauskas's response to one of the authors. See LALA, f. 361, ap. 2, b. 204, l. 456–57.

3. In the 1970s and 1980s, some artists were interested in publishing more of their work because of honoraria, which supplemented their salaries.

4. In LALA archives I found several submissions from Ukraine and Russia in Russian.

5. LALA, f. 361, ap. 2, b. 204, l. 458.

6. LALA, f. 361, ap. 2, b. 204, l. 458.

7. Jeronimas Laucius, interview with the author, June 28, 2019, Vilnius.

8. Laucius interview.

9. Laucius interview.

10. Laucius interview.

11. Originally the aphorism was published in Soviet times in the *Broom*. Jeronimas Laucius, the author, claimed that the aphorism was not against the regime, but against people's actions. Laucius interview.

12. Laucius interview.

13. The number of rejected works might be even higher, since some manuscripts were returned to authors and not saved in the *Broom* archives.

14. LALA, f. 361, ap. 2, b. 204, l. 138.

15. LALA, f. 361, ap. 2, b. 204, l. 388.

16. LALA, f. 361, ap. 2, b. 204, l. 159.

17. See, e.g., LALA, f. 361, ap. 2, b. 205, l. 376.

18. Undated reader's note to Juozas Bulota. Personal archive of Juozas Bulota.

19. LALA, f. 361, ap. 2, b. 33, l. 9.

20. LALA, f. 361, ap. 2, b. 620, l. 72.

21. LALA, f. 361, ap. 2, b. 205, l. 231.

22. LALA, f. 361, ap. 2, b. 622, l. 68. The specific reasons why authors' submissions were rejected were similar in the 1960s, 1970s, and 1980s.

23. From a speech during a meeting between the party and the government and literature and art specialists, March 8, 1963. Cited in *1934–1964 "Šluota." Karikatūros* 1964.

24. Albertas Lukša, interview with the author, August 5, 2017, Liukonys, Lithuania.

25. LALA, f. 361, ap. 2, b. 8, l. 155.

26. LALA, f. 361, ap. 2, b. 8, l. 154.

27. Teachers twisting students' ears, hitting them with a magazine or a ruler, or yelling was remembered by interlocutors in their forties and fifties during interviews in 2016. Even if people did not have such memories, they responded affirmatively in general—it could have happened. Naudžiūnienė (2021) argues that based on her research in different cities and towns of Lithuania, physical punishment in Soviet schools was rarely mentioned

by respondents who were schoolchildren in the Soviet era; at the same time they considered it normal and did not question it.

28. LALA, f. 361, ap. 2, b. 205, l. 180.

29. LALA, f. 361, ap. 2, b. 33, l. 39.

30. LALA, f. 361, ap. 2, b. 33, l. 63.

31. LALA, f. 361, ap. 2, b. 535, l. 72.

32. *Broom* text, LALA, 1972, no. 21, f. 361, ap. 2, b. 651, l. 29.

33. *Broom* text, LALA, 1975, no. 5, f. 361, ap. 2, b. 316, l. 37.

34. All examples in this paragraph are from a lecture delivered at a meeting with satirists (no other detail provided). Personal archive of Juozas Bulota.

35. Albertas Lukša, interview with the author, July 29, 2015, Liukonys, Lithuania.

36. LALA, the *Broom* text, 1971, no. 21, f. 361, ap. 2, b. 200, l. 3.

37. LALA, the *Broom* texts, 1973, no. 8–12, f. 361, ap. 2, b. 258c, l. 236.

38. LALA, *Broom* text, 1970, no. 1, f. 361, ap. 2, b. 134, l. 35.

39. LALA, *Broom* text, 1964, no. 19, f. 361, ap. 2, b. 2, l. 16.

40. LALA, *Broom* text, 1971, no. 11, f. 361, ap. 2, b. 190, l. 76.

41. LALA, *Broom* text, 1975, no. 5, f. 361, ap. 2, b. 316, l. 27.

42. LALA, *Broom* text, 1977, no. 10, f. 361, ap. 2, b. 382, l. 97.

43. LALA, *Broom* text, 1975, no. 5, f. 361, ap. 2, b. 316, l. 78.

44. LALA, f. 361, ap. 2, b. 8, l. 154 on teachers; LALA, f. 361, ap. 2, b. 205, l. 180, on a TV editor.

45. LALA, *Broom* text, 1975, no. 5, f. 361, ap. 2, b. 316, l. 13 (previously 39).

46. LALA, f. 361, ap. 2, b. 8, l. 20.

47. LALA, f. 361 ap. 2, b. 108, l. 102.

48. LALA, *Broom* text, 1967, no. 15, f. 361, ap. 2, b. 73, l. 69.

49. LALA, *Broom* text, 1977, no. 10, f. 361, ap. 2, b. 382, l. 10.

50. LALA, *Broom* text, 1971, no. 21, f. 361, ap. 2, b. 200, l. 13.

51. LALA, f. 361, ap. 2, b. 534, l. 11.

52. *Broom* text, LALA, 1983, no. 24, f. 361, ap. 2, b. 657, ll. 71–72.

53. *Broom* text, LALA, 1977, no. 10, f. 361, ap. 2, b. 382, l. 10.

54. *Broom* text, LALA, 1964, no. 19, f. 361, ap. 2, b. 2, l. 34.

55. LALA, f. 361 ap. 2, b. 108, l. 102.

56. *Broom* text, LALA, 1965, no. 6, f. 361, ap. 2, b. 14, l. 10.

57. The reference to the pig is not clear in the Lithuanian version.

58. *Broom* text, LALA, 1965, no. 6, f. 361, ap. 2, b. 14, l. 10. The letter appeared in *Broom* no. 6, p. 7.

59. Kęstutis Šiaulytis, pers. comm., undated.

6. MULTIDIRECTIONAL LAUGHTER

1. The cartoon is known as Cheremnykh and Deni's cartoon, since in 1920 Victor Nikolaevich Deni redrew Mikhail Cheremnykh's 1918 drawing. For the discussion of the iconography of Cheremnykh and Deni's poster see Bonnell (1996, 117–18).

2. The details of this event are lacking. It must have been somebody from the *Broom* or the printing house who noticed the "sedition."

3. Andrius Cvirka, interview with the author, August 4, 2015, Antalieptė, Lithuania. The official number of the circulation of this issue was 114,082.

4. Cvirka referred to images of Vladimir Krikhatskii's *Lenin at the First Subbotnik.* Krikhatskii's painting depicts the first *subotnik* (Rus., volunteer unpaid work on Saturdays) held on May 1, 1920. Andrius Cvirka, pers. comm., April 16, 2016.

5. LSA, f. 15020, ap. 1, b. 9, l. 5.

6. LSA, f. 15020, ap. 1, b. 11, l. 38.

7. Interview with Andrius Cvirka, July 5, 2014, Zarasai, Lithuania.

8. LSA, f. 15020, ap. 1, b. 12, ll. 22–23.

9. LSA, f. 15020, ap. 1, b. 14, l. 37.

10. LSA, f. 15020, ap. 1, b. 14, l. 33

11. LSA, f. 15020, ap. 1, b. 14, l. 37.

12. LSA, f. 15020, ap. 1, b. 15, l. 8.

13. LSA, f. 15020, ap. 1, b. 15, l. 12.

14. The PPO archival documents end in 1979. In 1979 Pakalnis was complimented for his initial attempts to raise *Broom* graphic art's political profile. During interviews, artists did not identify the 1980s as a different time in *Broom*'s political history, so it is unlikely that Pakalnis improved the ideological profile of its artistic work. See the annual PPO report for 1979, esp. LSA, f. 15020, ap. 1, b. 15, ll. 1, 35.

15. Cvirka interview, July 5, 2014.

16. Cvirka interview, July 5, 2014.

17. Vladimiras Beresniovas, interview with the author, July 20, 2014, Kaunas.

18. Kęstutis Šiaulytis, interview with the author, May 8, 2015, Vilnius.

19. Kęstutis Šiaulytis, pers. comm., undated.

20. *Broom* editors often used both terms "anti-imperialist" and "antireligious" to refer to political cartoons. They used the term "antireligious cartoons" much more often than "atheistic propaganda."

21. LSA, f. 15020, ap. 1, b. 4, l. 3.

22. LSA, f. 15020, ap. 1, b. 9, ll. 6–7.

23. LSA, f. 15020, ap. 1, b. 9, l. 6.

24. See, for example, LSA, f. 15020, ap. 1, b. 5, l. 2; LSA, f. 15020, ap. 1, b. 9, ll. 102, 118–19.

25. On obligations to attend various seminars for political education see LSA, f. 15020, ap. 1, b. 10, l. 59 and LSA, f. 15020, ap. 1, b. 14, ll. 13–14.

26. LSA, f. 15020, ap. 1, b. 15, l. 12.

27. On modernism in art in Soviet Lithuania see *Lietuvos dailės istorija* (2002) and Lubytė (1997, 2019).

28. On the discussion of *Broom* awards for artists and contributors and publication of their cartoons in other Soviet and socialist magazines see LSA, f. 15020, ap. 1, b. 9, l. 35.

29. For example, in 1977, the fourteen most active artists who contributed to the *Broom* participated in the international exhibit *Satire in the Battle for Peace* in Moscow. Two artists received prizes, while the *Broom* received a certificate of honor from the Soviet Peace Defense Committee. LSA, f. 15020 (1), b. 13, l. 25. In 1975, Arvydas Pakalnis participated in the international cartoon exhibition in Gabrovo, Bulgaria, and received prizes. LSA, f. 15020 ap. 1, b. 11, l. 29.

30. LSA, f. 15020, ap. 1, b. 10, ll. 117–18.

31. In the dictionary *Dabartinės lietuvių kalbos žodynas* (2015), *banalus* means "visiems žinomas, nuvalkiotas," that is, "known to everyone, commonplace, overused."

32. Kęstutis Šiaulytis, interview with the author, August 8, 2013, Vilnius, and Kęstutis Šiaulytis, pers. comm., January 6, 2020.

33. Jonas Varnas, interview with the author, July 2009, Vilnius.

34. Kęstutis Šiaulytis, pers. comm., January 6, 2020.

35. Cartoons discussed in this chapter can be accessed at https://wordpress.com/page/neringaklumbyte.com/29.

36. Etty also notes that *Krokodil* was multivoiced, a "site of ongoing, subtle, and serio-comic critical counter-commentaries on Soviet orthodoxies and political policy" (2019, 99). Etty proposes to see *Krokodil* as a "Menippean satire, according to Bakhtin's definition, and a 'politcarnival' (Brandist 1996, 69) development in a long Russo-European

satirical tradition" (2019, 99). Although Etty claims that some cartoons bordered on the subversive, he does not argue that they were against the regime itself.

37. Some *Broom* cartoons, especially in the 1950s and early 1960s, were overtly propagandistic. In the late 1960s and 1970s artists were fascinated with collages, photo-reports, and other experiments, which are not discussed in this chapter.

38. Andrius Cvirka, interview with the author, June 20, 2015, Zarasai, Lithuania.

39. See, e.g., LSA, f. 15020, ap. 1, b. 10, l. 53.

40. *Broom*, 1970, no. 3, front cover.

41. In general, men were lampooned in the *Broom* far more than women. Directors, bureaucrats, fishermen, drunks, and assorted clerks are uniformly men.

42. *Broom*, 1967, no. 18, p. 10.

43. LALA, f. 361, ap. 1, b. 109, l. 6.

44. Kęstutis Šiaulytis, pers. comm., February 13, 2022.

45. LSA, 15020, ap. 1, b. 12, l. 6.

46. Kęstutis Šiaulytis, pers. comm., undated.

47. *Broom*, 1972, no. 9, back cover.

48. *Broom*, 1972, no. 2, back cover.

49. S. Malahovas's cartoon, reprinted from *Pikker*, the *Broom*, 1972, no. 11, back cover.

50. *Broom*, 1972, no. 3, back cover.

51. Kęstutis Šiaulytis, interview with the author, August 5, 2015, Vilnius.

52. *Broom*, 1971, no. 12, back cover.

53. See back covers of *Broom*, 1972, no. 3, 11, 12, 14, 15, 16; *Broom*, 1965, no. 11, 16; *Broom*, 1966, no. 4, 6, 16, 17.

54. *Broom*, 1972, no. 15, back cover.

55. Cartoon by G. Kunickis, *Broom*, 1965, no. 5, back cover.

56. Cartoon by Algirdas Šiekštelė, *Broom*, 1966, no. 8, front cover.

57. Cartoons by G. Kunickis and A. Šiekštelė can be accessed at https://wordpress.com/page/neringaklumbyte.com/29.

58. The cartoon was published in the *Broom*, 1988, no. 20, p. 13.

59. Cartoon by Algirdas Radvilavičius, *Broom*, 1972, no. 19, back cover.

60. Cartoon by Algirdas Radvilavičius, *Broom*, 1969, no. 11, p. 7.

61. I thank Stephen Norris (pers. comm., August 25, 2020) for drawing my attention to critiques of racism in *Krokodil*.

62. *Broom*, 1977, no. 2, back cover.

63. See, e.g., LSA, f. 15020, ap. 1, b. 9, ll. 8–9.

64. Andrius Deltuva, interview with the author, Kaunas, July 13, 2014.

65. LSA, f. 15020, ap. 1, b. 15, l. 12. Higher honoraria were given intermittently; some artists remembered receiving higher honoraria in the 1970s.

66. Kęstutis Šiaulytis, pers. comm., undated.

67. Algirdas Radvilavičius, interview with the author, July 12, 2014, Kaunas.

68. Radvilavičius interview.

69. LSA, 15020, ap. 1, b. 4, l. 2.

70. LSA, f. 15020, ap. 1, b. 3, l. 6.

71. LSA, f. 15020, ap. 1, b. 10, ll. 105–6.

72. Jonas Varnas, interview with the author, July 2009, Vilnius.

73. Radvilavičius interview.

74. Radvilavičius interview.

75. Radvilavičius interview.

76. LSA, f. 15020, ap. 1, b. 10, l. 85.

77. LSA, f. 15020, ap. 1, b. 10, l. 85.

78. The *Broom* also published cartoons from other Eastern European socialist states, such as Czechoslovakia, Poland, and East Germany. Eastern Bloc humor was perceived

as superior to Lithuanian by readers and artists alike. It could sometimes be referred to as foreign humor, or published in a foreign humor section together with cartoons from Western countries.

79. Kęstutis Šiaulytis, pers. comm., January 6, 2020.

80. *Broom*, 1972, no. 9, p. 14.

81. *Broom*, 1971, no. 21, p. 14.

82. *Broom*, 1972, no. 3, p. 14.

83. Soviet-West opposition became pronounced during the liberation movement. "Soviet" was associated with the "East," and "nation" with the "West." While the "West" referred to Christian values, civilization, and European tradition, the "East" and "Soviet" were related to evil, totalitarian, and uncivilized empire (Klumbytė 2013, 284).

84. These cartoons were published in 1977. *Broom*, 1971, no. 12, p. 15; *Broom*, 1972, no. 19, p. 14. Source: German *Pardon* magazine. *Broom*, 1972, no. 6, p. 14. Source: German *Stern* magazine.

85. Kęstutis Šiaulytis, pers. comm., undated.

86. The source of the cartoon, as in many other cases, is not identified. Since the name is Huggins, it might have been English or American humor. *Broom*, 1965, no. 16, p. 15.

87. LALA, f. 361, ap. 2, b. 160, pages unspecified.

88. LALA, f. 361, ap. 2, b. 160, l. 164.

89. Kęstutis Šiaulytis, pers. comm., January 6, 2020.

90. Perestroika-era public lecture notes. Personal archive of Juozas Bulota.

91. Notes for meeting with readers. Personal archive of Juozas Bulota.

92. Published in *Broom*, 1968, no. 14, p. 15.

93. In one of his speeches during the perestroika era, Juozas Bulota had a note to say, "Here it is, the decadent West!" (Lith. *Štai jie, supuvę Vakarai!*), and in another place, "Here it is, America!" which most likely refers to the same image. Personal archive of Juozas Bulota.

94. Juozas Bulota, interview with the author, July 19, 2018, Vilnius.

95. *Broom*, 1972, no. 2, p. 14.

96. *Broom*, 1972, no. 17, p. 14.

97. Cvirka interview, June 20, 2015.

98. Cvirka interview, June 20, 2015.

99. While comic strips were disapproved of, Alaniz (2010) argued that they prevailed in Soviet children's literature, underground works, and the Russian diaspora during late socialism. During World War II they prevailed in the propaganda poster (Alaniz 2010).

100. According to Romas Palčiauskas he worked at the *Broom* from 1961 to 1967. Romas Palčiauskas, interview with the author, July 29, 2014, Vilnius.

101. A few comic strips appeared before 1966 and after 1981. Nevertheless, the *Broom* was known primarily for the *Jack and Bobby* series. From 1988 to 1991 comic strips were published regularly in the *Broom* again.

102. Palčiauskas interview.

103. I thank Stephen Norris (pers. comm., August 25, 2020) for the note about the Kennedy brothers.

104. Romas Palčiauskas, conversation with the author, July 9, 2021, Vilnius.

105. *Broom*, 1966, no. 23, p. 14.

106. *Broom*, 1968, no. 14, p. 16.

107. Palčiauskas interview.

108. A speech by Juozas Bulota delivered in Moscow at the celebration of the fiftieth anniversary of *Krokodil*, 1972. Personal archive of Juozas Bulota.

109. Sadaunykas considered publishing comic strips with cartoonist Vitalijus Suchockis. LSA, f. 15020, ap. 1, b. 10, l. 118.

110. LSA, f. 15020, ap. 1, b. 10, l. 128.

111. LSA, f. 15020, ap. 1, b. 10, l. 119.

112. LSA, f. 15020, ap. 1, b. 11, l. 2.

113. Palčiauskas interview.

114. Palčiauskas interview.

115. Kęstutis Šiaulytis, pers. comm., January 6, 2020.

116. Kęstutis Šiaulytis, pers. comm., January 6, 2020.

117. Palčiauskas interview.

118. Palčiauskas interview.

119. Comment on *Jack and Bobby* by Donatas (September 21, 2015) on Lithuanian comic strips web page. See http://komiksai.com/rastai.php?sub=2&s=126.

120. Juršėnas specifically referred to Juozas Baltušis, a Lithuanian writer, whose Soviet-era diaries were published in 2019 (see Baltušis 2019).

121. *Broom*, 1975, no. 4, p. 5.

122. Bulota interview.

123. According to Ronald Reagan, in the late 1980s he had a hobby collecting jokes about the Soviet Union. Stories like this were coming to the president from the Central Intelligence Agency, foreign dignitaries, and a Soviet *émigré* comedian in Los Angeles (see Roberts 1987).

7. SATIRICAL JUSTICE

1. The description of Siudikaitė's case is based on her 1977 and 1979 letters to the *Broom* (LALA, f. 361, ap. 2, b. 404, ll. 7–11; LALA, f. 361, ap. 2, b. 495, ll. 34–40), reporting about her case in the *Broom* (1977, no. 13, pp. 2, 3, and 1977, no. 19, p. 15), and the *Broom*'s correspondence with different institutions (LALA archives).

2. *Komunistinio darbo spartuolė* refers to a hardworking worker who achieves production records, otherwise demonstrates mastery of work skills, and is a model for success on the shop floor.

3. LSA, f. 15020, ap. 1, b. 13, l. 43.

4. LALA, f. 361, ap. 2, b. 495, ll. 36–37.

5. Juozas Bulota, "'Šluotai'—50." Personal archive of Juozas Bulota.

6. On governing Soviet journalism see Wolfe (2005) and Roudakova (2017).

7. There are very few studies of complaint writing in interwar Lithuania. See Petrauskaitė (2006) on citizens' complaints to the army.

8. Resolution No. 2534-VII of April 12, 1968. See Ukaz Prezidiuma Verkhovnogo Soveta SSSR 1968.

9. A related right was stated in Article 49: "Every citizen of the USSR has the right to submit proposals to state bodies and public organizations for improving their activity, and to criticize shortcomings in their work. Officials are obliged, within established time limits, to examine citizens' proposals and requests, to reply to them, and to take appropriate action. Persecution for criticism is prohibited. Persons guilty of such persecution shall be called to account" (Constitution of the Union of Soviet Socialist Republics, 1977). In 1978–1979 a Letters Department was created in the CPSU Central Committee Secretariat to analyze citizens' letters. It prepared summaries and reports for the Politburo and the Secretariat (see Slider 1985, 211).

10. In 1976, 1980, and 1981 other resolutions regarding work with letters were passed. See White (1983, 45–46) for CPSU CC resolutions regarding communication with citizens.

11. For example, in 1963, the *Broom* received 2,234 letters, 230 of which were published (LSA, f. 15020, ap. 1, b. 6, l. 1). In 1977, from January 1 to December 1, readers sent 2,217 letters (LSA, f. 15020, ap. 1, b. 13, l. 46). According to Pehowski (1978, 730), *Krokodil* received an average of five hundred letters a day. Shabad (1964) claims that in the early

1960s *Krokodil* received four hundred to six hundred letters a day and a total of about one hundred thousand a year.

12. Jonas Bulota (1964), no page numbers provided.

13. LSA, f. 15020, ap. 1, b. 13, l. 46. Juozas Bulota in his note to the LCP CC Propaganda and Agitation Department claims that in every issue they used three to five readers' letters, for important investigative articles. Personal archive of Juozas Bulota, undated document, p. 7. The numbers of the letters received in the early and mid-1980s should have been similar.

14. Albertas Lukša, interview with the author, August 5, 2017, Liukonys, Lithuania.

15. Juozas Bulota's note to the LCP CC Propaganda and Agitation Department, undated, p. 1. Personal archive of Juozas Bulota.

16. On studies of complaints that emphasize contacts with the masses see Livshin and Orlov (1998, on the period of 1917–1927); on the importance to control bureaucrats see Kozlov (1997, on the period of 1944–1953), or to solve legal and citizen welfare questions see Bittner (2003, on the post-Stalinist period). Other authors relate denunciations and complaints to the search for justice (Fitzpatrick 1996b on the 1930s), or a form of citizen rights protection (Galmarini 2014, 2016, on the period of 1917–1950; Hilton 2009, on the late NEP (New Economic Policy) in the absence of the rule of law.

17. See Alexopoulos (1999) on letters to authorities under Stalin. Golfo Alexopoulos argues that by denouncing others they became participant agents in the system of repression. On popular denunciation as a form of participation see also Fitzpatrick (1996b).

18. The archives of correspondence with different journalists and activists, regular contributors to the *Broom*, about checking the facts include documents from 1961 to 1976. During all these years the honorarium was five rubles.

19. In Lithuanian "Plevėsų kampelis," "Brokdarių karuselė," "Pagal skaitytojų laiškus," "Mums laiškelį rašė," "Apginkime nuskriaustuosius," "Būta—nepramanyta."

20. In Lithuanian "Raiti ant šluotos," "Mes atsakome į skaitytojų paklausimus," "Reporteris ieškos šiukšlių," and "Aš noriu Tave iššluoti!"

21. This section in Lithuanian is called "Atsirašinėtojų užpečky." "Atsirašinėtojas" refers to bureaucrats who write letters back to the *Broom* without actually addressing raised issues. "Užpečkis" refers to the part of an old-fashioned (clay or stone) stove used in villages, where people could sleep.

22. LSA, f. 15020, ap. 1, b. 5, l. 24.

23. LSA, f. 15020, ap. 1, b. 14, ll. 25, 27.

24. See, for example, LSA, f. 15020, ap. 1, b. 14, ll. 5, 7.

25. LSA, f. 15020, ap. 1, b. 5, ll. 11–12.

26. LSA, f. 15020, ap. 1, b. 7, l. 8.

27. LSA, f. 15020, ap. 1, b. 4, l. 24. On themes in the Primary Party Organization prospective plans see also chapter 3.

28. LSA, f. 15020, ap. 1, b. 11, l. 6.

29. LSA, f. 15020, ap. 1, b. 13, l. 46.

30. According to the LSA Committee for State Security (KGB) documents, two articles were published in the *Broom* based on the KGB material in 1985. One was on mismanagement of socialist property in the Lelija (Lily) factory. See K-18, ap 1, b. 21, l. 109, and K-18, ap. 1, b. 21, l. 136. There was no direct collaboration between the *Broom* and the KGB. Most likely, upon request from the KGB, LCP organs asked the *Broom* to publish the material. Česlovas Juršėnas, interview with the author, August 1, 2019, Vilnius.

31. LSA, f. 15020, ap. 1, b. 1, l. 23.

32. See, e.g., the discussion on effectiveness, LSA, f. 15020, ap. 1, b. 12, l. 23, and A. Lukša's report "On the effectiveness of material published in the *Broom*," LSA, f. 15020, ap. 1, b. 13, ll. 35–46.

33. LYA, f. 15020, ap. 1, b. 13, l. 35.

34. LSA, f. 15020, ap. 1, b. 13, l. 35.

35. LSA, f. 15020, ap. 1, b. 13, l. 35.

36. LSA, f. 15020, ap. 1, b. 13, l. 38.

37. LSA, f. 15020, ap. 1, b. 13, l. 40.

38. LSA, f. 15020, ap. 1, b. 13, ll. 37–38.

39. LSA, f. 15020, ap. 1, b. 13, ll. 43–44. See also *Broom*, no. 4, pp. 2–3.

40. LSA, f. 15020, ap. 1, b. 13, l. 37.

41. LSA, f. 15020, ap. 1, b. 13, l. 38.

42. LSA, f. 15020, ap. 1, b. 13, l. 36.

43. LSA, f. 15020, ap. 1, b. 13, l. 37.

44. LSA, f. 15020, ap. 1, b. 13, l. 40.

45. LSA, f. 15020, ap. 1, b. 13, l. 40.

46. LSA, f. 15020, ap. 1, b. 13, l. 44. See also *Broom*, 1977, no. 19, p. 2.

47. LALA, f. 361, ap. 1, b. 94, l. 5.

48. LALA, f. 361, ap. 1, b. 92, l. 76.

49. LALA, f. 361, ap. 2, b. 207, l. 254.

50. LALA, f. 361, ap. 2, b. 541, l. 16.

51. LALA, f. 361, ap. 2, b. 541, l. 16.

52. In a few cases readers sent letters criticizing *Broom* editors, e.g., LALA, f. 361, ap. 2, b. 207, l. 278; blaming the *Broom*, e.g., LALA, f. 361, ap. 2, b. 207, l. 278; or even threatening the *Broom* editors, e.g., LALA, f. 361, ap. 2, b. 541, l. 18. Some readers complained that they were unfairly described in the *Broom*, e.g., LALA, f. 361, ap. 2, b. 207, l. 278. A few readers claimed that they had never written to the *Broom*, that somebody else did, using their names. They asked to find out who did it and open a lawsuit, e.g., LALA, f. 361, ap. 2, b. 303, l. 49.

53. LALA, f. 361, ap. 2, b. 303, l. 13.

54. See LALA, f. 361, ap. 2, b. 302, ll. 68–69v.

55. LALA, f. 361, ap. 2, b. 303, l. 25.

56. LALA, f. 361, ap. 2, b. 304, l. 55.

57. LALA, f. 361, ap. 2, b. 541, l. 16.

58. A view of crime, alcoholism, drug abuse, or domestic violence as bourgeois remnants was integrated into the legal education in late-Soviet Lithuania (see Kareniauskaitė 2017, 237).

59. See Roudakova (2017) on Soviet journalism as a forum for truth seeking and truth telling.

60. "To LSSR Health Care Minister Cmde. Dirsė," September 15, 1958, in LCVA, f. R-769, ap. 1, b. 1429, l. 6. The letter does not specify facts; Tomas Vaiseta discusses it in the context of concealed sexual violence in the Vilnius psychiatric hospital.

61. See the letter from the psychoneurological hospital, LALA, f. 361, ap. 1, b. 92, l. 126.

62. LSA, f. 15020, ap. 1, b. 11, l. 19.

63. Juozas Bulota's note to the LCP CC Propaganda and Agitation Department, undated, p. 5. Personal archive of Juozas Bulota.

64. Juozas Bulota's note to the LCP CC Propaganda and Agitation Department, undated, p. 7. Personal archive of Juozas Bulota.

65. Tomkus was a controversial figure. In his memoir *Taranas* he describes cases of manipulating people and lying in order to get critical information, which violated the *Broom* editors' journalistic ethics, even if he disclosed the corrupt system itself (Tomkus 1988).

66. Albertas Lukša, interview with the author, July 29, 2015, Liukonys, Lithuania.

67. Vytautė Žilinskaitė, interview with the author, April 29, 2017, Vilnius.

68. LSA, f. 15020, ap. 1, b. 13, ll. 23–24.

69. Vladimir A. Kozlov (1997, 147) argues that for Russian bureaucrats the "biggest risk lay not in breaking the laws themselves but in losing their 'sense of proportion,' their 'feeling for their turf,' their knowledge of what they could and could not get away with."

70. Vorobjovas's cartoon appeared in the *Broom*, 1985, no. 6, p. 5.

71. Elena (b. 1935), interview with the author, May 10, 2017, Klaipėda, Lithuania. Her family were Lutherans. Elena identified as Lithuanian.

72. Elena recalled that the shop most likely was called Geležinkelio, and it could have been in 1956 or 1957. I was not able to find the mention of the shop in the *Broom*.

73. See LSA, f. 15020, ap. 1, b. 11, l. 8.

74. Juozas Bulota, interview with the author, July 19, 2018, Vilnius.

75. LSA, f. 15020, ap. 1, b. 13, ll. 23–24.

76. LSA, f. 15020, ap. 1, b. 13, l. 39.

77. LALA, f. 361, ap. 1, b. 94, l. 7.

78. LALA, f. 361, ap. 1, b. 94, l. 7.

79. LALA, f. 361, ap. 1, b. 94, l. 10.

80. LALA, f. 361, ap. 1, b. 94, l. 27.

81. LALA, f. 361, ap. 1, b. 92, ll. 103–4. On readers' graphomania as a practice of obsessive writing in Soviet Russia see Boym (1994, 168–214).

82. LSA, f. 15020, ap. 1, b. 13, l. 39.

83. LCSA, Internal Affairs Ministry fond, l. 84.

84. LCSA, Internal Affairs Ministry fond, l. 215.

85. LCSA, Internal Affairs Ministry fond, l. 215.

86. The story was narrated by Liudmila Paškevičienė, written by Andrius Gelvaitis (1977).

87. *Broom* 1971, no. 21, p. 7.

88. *Broom* 1971, no. 21, p. 7.

89. LALA, f. 361, ap. 2, b. 543, l. 24. Published in *Broom*, 1980, no. 14, p. 6.

90. The photo of E. Trinkūnaitė and the message about her were published in the *Broom*, 1980, no. 14, pp. 6–7.

91. *Broom*, 1965, no. 18, pp. 8–9.

92. *Broom*, 1972, no. 5, p. 15.

93. LSA, f. 15020, ap. 1, b. 13, l. 37.

94. LALA, f. 361, ap. 1, b. 90, l. 53.

95. LALA, f. 361, ap. 1, b. 91, ll. 74, 75.

96. LALA, f. 361, ap. 1, b. 91, ll. 74, 75.

97. LALA, f. 361, ap. 2, b. 207, pp. 15–16. The letter has many grammatical and syntax errors. The names in this version are changed.

98. See Vaiseta (2014, 305–6) for discussion of letters sent to workplaces. They are very different from letters sent to the *Broom*, since in letters to workplaces people wrote about their spouses' love affairs, violence in the family, drinking at home, or disagreements with relatives.

99. LALA, f. 672, ap. 1, b. 24, ll. 27–29v.

100. LALA, f. 672, ap. 1, b. 24, ll. 27–29v.

101. LALA, f. 672, ap. 1, b. 24, ll. 27–29v.

102. LALA, f. 672, ap. 1, b. 24, 29v.

103. See, e.g., LALA, f. 361, ap. 2, b. 762.

8. SOVIET DYSTOPIA

1. The primary data in this chapter are citizens' complaint letters to the *Broom* in the period 1971–1982, 4,828 pages of archival materials preserved in the Lithuanian Archive of Literature and Art (LALA, f. 361, ap. 2).

2. See Jessica Greenberg (2014) on disappointment as a form of political participation in democratic Serbia. Similar dystopian visions have been recorded in women's laments during perestroika (Ries 1997), memoirs (Lebow 2014), films (Fedorova 2014), and letters sent to various state institutions (Bogdanova 2021; Kozlov 1997).

3. There was also a large group of letters in which people directly complained about salesclerks, supervisors at work, and village or city authorities. The letters are discussed in chapter 7.

4. LALA, f. 361, ap. 2, b. 207, ll. 174–75.

5. On economic development in Lithuania see Vaskela (2014); Grybkauskas (2011); Misiunas and Taagepera (1983).

6. See, e.g., diaries by Juozas Baltušis (2019) and a memoir by Silvija Lomsargytė-Pukienė (2004).

7. For a discussion see Marcinkevičius (2020).

8. LALA, f. 361, ap. 2, b. 302, ll. 6–7.

9. LALA, f. 361, ap. 2, b. 133, l. 81.

10. LALA, f. 361, ap. 2, b. 133, ll. 82–85.

11. LALA, f. 361, ap. 2, b. 133, l. 80.

12. LALA, f. 361, ap. 2, b. 304, l. 144. This photo most likely was not published in the *Broom*.

13. LALA, f. 361, ap. 2, b. 301, ll. 144–45.

14. The original is available at LALA, f. 361, ap. 2, b. 306, l. 27. Published in the *Broom*, 1975, no. 21, p. 7.

15. LALA, f. 361, ap. 2, b. 207, ll. 17–21.

16. LALA, f. 361, ap. 2, b. 301, ll. 13–14.

17. LALA, f. 361, ap. 2, b. 303, ll. 155–55v.

18. LALA, f. 361, ap. 2, b. 542, l. 107.

19. *Broom*, 1970, no. 3, p. 13.

20. *Broom*, 1980, no. 4, p. 15.

21. LALA, f. 361, ap. 2, b. 262, l. 31.

22. LALA, f. 361, ap. 2, b. 301, ll. 38–44.

23. *Broom*, 1975, no. 13, p. 15. I published this image in Klumbytė (2017). The original is available at LALA, f. 361, ap. 2, b. 306.

24. LALA, f. 361, ap. 2, b. 207, l. 79.

25. Published in the *Broom*, 1977, no. 17, p. 15. The original is available at LALA, f. 361, ap. 2, b. 405, l. 9.

26. The original image is at LALA, f. 361, ap. 2, b. 496, l. 31. Published in the *Broom*, 1979, no. 24, p. 15.

27. Published in the *Broom*, 1979, no. 24, p. 15.

28. "*Šluotai*—50." Bulota's typed lecture dated September 12, 1984. Personal archive of Juozas Bulota.

29. "*Šluotai*—50." Bulota's typed lecture dated September 12, 1984. Personal archive of Juozas Bulota. A. Lukša remembered the sausage with a piece of wire. Albertas Lukša, interview with the author, July 30, 2019, Liukonys, Lithuania.

30. LALA, f. 361, ap. 1, b. 92, ll. 43–44, 65.

31. LALA, f. 361, ap. 1, b. 92, l. 163.

32. LALA, f. 361, ap. 1, b. 92, ll. 43–44, 65.

33. LALA, f. 361, ap. 1, b. 92, ll. 65.

34. Ona Banadienė, *Broom*, 1980, no. 1, p. 6.

35. Ona Banadienė, *Broom*, 1980, no. 1, p. 6.

36. *Broom*, 1977, no. 1, p. 5.

37. LALA, f. 361, ap. 2, b. 301, no page provided.

38. LALA, f. 361, ap. 2, b. 302, l. 68v.

39. *Broom*, 1965, no. 5, p. 14.

40. LALA, f. 361, ap. 2, b. 302, ll. 235–37.

41. See, e.g., LALA, f. 361, ap. 2, b. 303, ll. 121–23.

42. LALA, f. 361, ap. 2, b. 303, ll. 121–22v.

43. LALA, f. 361, ap. 2, b. 303, ll. 121–22v.

44. LALA, f. 361, ap. 2, b. 541, l. 66.

45. LALA, f. 361, ap. 2, b. 541, ll. 66–66v.

46. LALA, f. 361, ap. 2, b. 541, l. 66v.

47. LALA, f. 361, ap. 2, b. 541, l. 66v.

48. LALA, f. 361, ap. 2, b. 302, ll. 42–44a. "Frank Kruk" refers to a satirical Lithuanian novel by Petras Cvirka ([1934] 2016).

49. LALA, f. 361, ap. 2, b. 302, l. 43a.

50. LALA, f. 361, ap. 2, b. 541, ll. 6–7.

51. The letter was described by a journalist from the newspaper *Soviet Klaipėda*, who was assigned to investigate the case for the *Broom*. LALA, f. 361, ap. 1, b. 123, l. 15.

52. LALA, f. 361, ap. 1, b. 123, l. 15.

53. LALA, f. 361, ap. 2, b. 207, l. 270.

54. LSA, f. K-18, ap. 1, b. 630, ll. 9–2 [*sic*]. I published an image of this letter in Klumbytė (2017).

55. *Kulak* refers to rich peasants, whose land was nationalized and redistributed in Soviet times to poor peasants or smallholders. However, in the USSR in many cases the term was applied to smallholders or even poor peasants (cf. Fitzpatrick 1994).

56. "Vilnius is ours" refers to the USSR's redrawing of the map in 1939 when Vilnius and its region became part of Lithuania again. It was a Polish territory from 1920 to 1939.

57. LSA, f. K-18, ap. 1, b. 630, ll. 6–2 [*sic*].

58. Albertas Lukša, interview with the author, August 5, 2017, Liukonys, Lithuania.

59. LALA, f. 361, ap. 2, b. 542, l. 63. A few readers' letters invoke "Jews" in a stereotypical way, indexing ethnic differences between Lithuanians and Jewish people. While antisemitism prevailed in Soviet Lithuania after World War II (during which over 95 percent of Lithuania's Jewish population was killed), it is difficult to say whether invoking "Jews" in letters also indicates antisemitism.

60. LALA, f. 361, ap. 2, b. 542, ll. 57–58.

61. The content of the story is based on Žilinskaitė (1966).

62. On funeral home planning and policy in Soviet times see Drėmaitė (2014).

63. Vytautas Žeimantas, interview with the author, June 25, 2019, Vilnius.

64. Personal archive of Juozas Bulota.

65. See also Jessica Greenberg (2014) on disappointment as a new ethical and affective knowledge, a form of political participation integral to democracy-building in the case of student activism after the mass protests of October 2000 in Serbia.

POST SCRIPTUM

1. Special newsletter *Red Genocide*, January 13, 1991, published by the *Broom*.

2. The Nobel Prize was awarded to Gorbachev for "his leading role in the peace process [leading to] dramatic changes . . . in the relationship between East and West" (Nobel Prize 1990).

3. Special newsletter *Red Genocide*, January 13, 1991.

4. For a detailed analysis of events in Lithuania since Gorbachev came to power see Senn (2002). In Lithuania, this period is usually referred to as Sąjūdis, the "movement," rather than a "revolution." There was no armed overthrow of the government, but instead a civilian resistance leading to a radical change of the system and the government, as well as Lithuania's independence. On nationalism and political community building in the

Baltic States after the collapse of the USSR see Budrytė (2005). See also Suziedelis et al. (1989).

5. At the referendum of February 9, 1991, three-quarters of the citizens of Lithuania voted in favor of an independent democratic republic as the form of the Lithuanian state.

6. In the Sąjūdis provisional program of June 13, 1988, the assertion of political independence was not stated (Senn 2002, 255). In the beginning Sąjūdis tended to conform to the discursive boundaries provided by perestroika (Senn 2002, 255). A more radical pro-independence political force than Sąjūdis was the Lietuvos Laisvės Lyga (Lithuanian Freedom League) (see Senn 2002).

7. After the unsuccessful Communist coup in Moscow on August 19–21, 1991, the independence of Lithuania was internationally recognized. The United States recognized the restoration of Lithuania's independence on September 2, 1991. (The US had never recognized the annexation of the three Baltic states.) The USSR recognized Lithuania's independence on September 6, 1991. On September 17, 1991, Lithuania became a member of the United Nations.

8. Perestroika-era lecture notes for delivery of a public lecture prepared by Bulota himself. Personal archive of Juozas Bulota.

9. *Broom*, 1990, no. 4, p. 3.

10. *Broom*, 1991, no. 16, p. 10.

11. *Broom*, 1991, no. 14, p. 3.

12. *Broom*, 1991, no. 5, p. 18.

13. *Broom*, 1988, no. 18, cover.

14. *Broom*, 1990, no. 3, cover.

15. *Broom*, 1991, no. 3, p. 18.

16. LALA, f. 361, ap. 2, b. 821, l. 28. The joke most likely was not published.

17. LALA, f. 361, ap. 2, b. 821, l. 77.

18. LALA, f. 361, ap. 2, b. 823, l. 35.

19. LALA, f. 672, ap. 1, b. 23.

20. On Singing Revolutions see Šmidchens (2014). On laughter's mobilizing power see, e.g., Emmerson (2017). The literature that speaks about laughter as a weapon of propaganda often assumes laughter's mobilizing potential (see, e.g., Gérin 2018; Norris 2013; Wolf 2017). See also Daina Stukuls Eglitis (2002), who asserts that people in Latvia became disenchanted with communist utopian promises and sought "normality" in the 1980s.

21. On related approaches in nationalist and ethnic conflict studies see, e.g., Bringa (1995); Brubaker et al. (2006); Hayden (2013); Neofotistos (2012).

22. See also Ramonaitė (2015b) and Ramonaitė, Kavaliauskaitė, and Klumbys (2015).

23. See LALA, f. 672, ap. 1, Rūta Mielkutė "UAB 'Šluota' archyvinio fondo pratarmė," June 11, 2001, Vilnius. No page numbers provided.

24. Andrius Cvirka, interview with the author, July 24, 2016, Antalieptė, Lithuania.

25. See Kęstutis Šiaulytis blog, http://kestutis-galerija.blogspot.com/.

26. Another example of global multidirectional laughter would be the magazine *Molla Nasreddin*, a satirical Azeri periodical, published from 1906 to 1931, which addressed different audiences in different periods of its publication (see Grant 2020). The journal offered inspiration to other satirists, from the Balkans to Iran and Serbia (*Molla Nasreddin* 2017).

27. These photos by the monument were for an April 1 cartoon catalog (Varnas 2017).

28. Pocevičius (2018, 575) mentions that when the monument was opened in 1952, some people joked that Lenin was pointing to the Tauro Ragas brewery, others that he was indicating the KGB headquarters.

29. *Broom*, 1991, no. 24, p. 18.

CONCLUSION: LOST LAUGHTER AND AUTHORITARIAN STIGMA

1. The event included presentations on the *Broom* by Kęstutis Šiaulytis, former *Broom* artist and editor; Romas Palčiauskas, former *Broom* artist and the creator of famous Lithuanian comic strips; Albertas Lukša, journalist and chair of the *Broom* Letters Department; Jonas Varnas, contributing artist; and Domas Šniukas, journalist and editor of the *Truth* and *Literature and Art*. Kęstutis Šiaulytis and Albertas Lukša were editors in chief of the *Broom* after Juozas Bulota retired. Short videos of the event (in Lithuanian) by Giedrius Subačius are available at https://vimeo.com/215490915 and https://vimeo.com/215879279.

2. On other occasions Kęstutis Šiaulytis would recognize that the Estonian *Pikker* was the most modern satire and humor magazine in the USSR.

3. The story is based on Varnas (2017).

4. I thank Julie Hemment for drawing my attention to, in her words, the "contemporary predicament."

5. Česlovas Juršėnas, interview with the author, August 1, 2019, Vilnius.

References

Adams, Bruce. 2005. *Tiny Revolutions in Russia: Twentieth-Century Soviet and Russian History in Anecdotes*. New York: Routledge.

Alaniz, José. 2010. *Komiks: Comic Art in Russia*. Jackson: University Press of Mississippi.

Aleksandravičiūtė, Skaistė, and Loreta Vaicekauskienė. 2012. "Juokai juokais, bet šiandien juokiamės daugiau ir kitaip: Juokais kaip TV ir radijo diskurso bruožas 1960–2010 metais." *Darbai ir dienos* 58:283–95.

Alexopoulos, Golfo. 1999. "Defense Testimony and Denunciation under Stalin." *Law & Social Inquiry* 24 (3): 637–54.

Annus, Epp. 2018. *Soviet Postcolonial Studies: A View from the Western Borderlands*. London: Routledge.

Anušauskas, Arvydas. 2012. *Teroras 1940–1958 m*. Vilnius: Versus aureus.

Anušauskas, Arvydas, et al. 2005. *Lietuva 1940–1990: Okupuotos Lietuvos istorija*. Vilnius: Lietuvos gyventojų genocido ir rezistencijos tyrimo centras.

Anušauskas, Arvydas, Juozapas Romualdas Bagušauskas, Česlovas Bauža, Danutė Blažytė, Vitalija Ilgevičiūtė, Vanda Kašauskienė, and Algimantas Liekis. 2000. *Lietuvos suvereniteto atkūrimas 1988–1991 metais*. Vilnius: Diemedžio leidykla.

Aputis, Juozas. 2007. Presentation at the Turin book fair. May 11. Giedrius Subačius video. https://vimeo.com/84234600.

Arendt, Hannah. 1951. *The Origins of Totalitarianism*. New York: Schocken.

——. (1963) 2006. *Eichmann in Jerusalem: A Report on the Banality of Evil*. London: Penguin.

Areška, Vitas. 1988. *Teofilis Tilvytis*. Kaunas: Šviesa.

Arkhipova, Aleksandra, and Mikhail Mel'nichenko. 2008. *Anekdoty o Staline: Teksty, kommentarii, issledovaniia*. Moscow: O.G.I.

Bakhtin, Mikhail. 1984. *Rabelais and His World*. Translated by Hélène Iswolsky. Bloomington: Indiana University Press.

Baltušis, Juozas. 2019. *Juozas Baltušis. Vietoj dienoraščio. 1970–1975*. Vol. 1. Edited by Antanas Šimkus. Vilnius: Lietuvos rašytojų sąjungos leidykla.

Barker, Adele Marie. 1999. Introduction to *Consuming Russia: Popular Culture, Sex, and Society since Gorbachev*, edited by Adele Marie Barker, 243–65. Durham, NC: Duke University Press.

Berdahl, Daphne. 1999. *Where the World Ended: Re-unification and Identity in the German Borderland*. Berkeley: University of California Press.

Berman, Harold J., and James W. Spindler. 1963. "Soviet Comrades' Courts." *Washington Law Review* 38 (4): 842–910.

Bittner, Stephen V. 2003. "Local Soviets, Public Order, and Welfare after Stalin: Appeals from Moscow's Kiev Raion." *Russian Review* 62:281–93.

Blium, Vladimir. 1929. "Vozroditsia li satira?" *Literaturnaia gazeta*, May 27.

BNS. 2021. "Kaune aiškinamasi, kam priklauso Cvirkos paminklas." BNS, September 25. https://www.delfi.lt/news/daily/lithuania/kaune-aiskinamasi-kam-priklauso-cvirkos-paminklas.d?id=88279065.

Bogdanova, Elena. 2021. *Complaints to the Authorities in Russia: A Trap between Tradition and Legal Modernization*. Abingdon, UK: Routledge.

Bonnell, Victoria E. 1996. "The Leader's Two Bodies: A Study in the Iconography of the 'Vozhd.'" *Russian History* 23 (1/4): 113–40.

Boyer, Dominic. 2012. "Postcard from Berlin: Rethinking the Juncture of Late Socialism and Late Liberalism in Europe." In *Soviet Society in the Era of Late Socialism, 1964–85*, edited by Neringa Klumbytė and Gulnaz Sharafutdinova, 203–14. Lanham, MD: Lexington Books.

——. 2013. "On Happiness and Politics: Jón Gnarr's Best Party (2009–2013)." *Perspectives on Europe* 43 (2): 21–28.

Boyer, Dominic, and Alexei Yurchak. 2010. "American Stiob: Or, What Late-Socialist Aesthetics of Parody Reveal about Contemporary Political Culture in the West." *Cultural Anthropology* 25 (2): 179–221.

Boym, Svetlana. 1994. *Common Places: Mythologies of Everyday Life in Russia*. Cambridge, MA: Harvard University Press.

Brandist, Craig. 1996. *Carnival Culture and the Soviet Modernist Novel*. Houndmills, UK: Macmillan.

Brezhnev, Leonid I. 1978. *Malaia zemlia*. Moscow: Politizdat.

Bringa, Tone Rand. 1995. *Being Muslim the Bosnian Way: Identity and Community in a Central Bosnian Village*. Princeton, NJ: Princeton University Press.

Brubaker, Rogers, Margit Feischmidt, Jon Fox, and Liana Grancea. 2006. *Nationalist Politics and Everyday Ethnicity in a Transylvanian Town*. Princeton, NJ: Princeton University Press.

Buck Quijada, Justine. 2019. *Buddhists, Shamans, and Soviets: Rituals of History in Post-Soviet Buryatia*. New York: Oxford University Press.

Budrytė, Dovilė. 2005. *Taming Nationalism: Political Community Building in the Post-Soviet Baltic States*. London: Routledge.

——. 2011. "'We Did Not Keep Diaries, You Know': Memories of Trauma and Violence in the Narratives of Two Former Women Resistance Fighters." *Lituanus* 57 (3): 59–71.

Bulota, Jonas. 1964. "Juoko ginklu." In *1934–1964 "Šluota." Karikatūros*. Vilnius: LKP CK Laikraščių ir žurnalų leidykla.

——. 1984. "'Šluotos' Kelias." In *Šluota*, edited by Juozas Bulota and Arvydas Pakalnis, 5–9. Vilnius: Mintis.

Bulota, Juozas. 1965. "Vėl tas sienlaikraštis . . . " *Agitatorius*, July 2.

Bulota, Juozas, and Arvydas Pakalnis, eds. 1984. *Šluota*. Vilnius: Mintis.

Bulota, Rytis. 2011. "Visuomeninės nuostatos ir (nepastebima) rezistencija Kaune vėlyvuoju sovietmečiu." *Sociologija. Mintis ir veiksmas* 2 (29): 244–58.

Bytwerk, Randall L. 1988. "Official Satire in Propaganda: The Treatment of the United States in the GDR's *Eulenspiegel*." *Central States Speech Journal* 39 (3&4): 304–14.

Cesarani, David. 2006. *Becoming Eichmann: Rethinking the Life, Crimes, and Trial of a "Desk Murderer"*. Cambridge, MA: Da Capo.

Chernyshova, Natalya. 2013. *Soviet Consumer Culture in the Brezhnev Era*. London: Routledge.

Clegg, Cyndia Susan. 1997. *Press Censorship in Elizabethan England*. Cambridge: Cambridge University Press.

Constitution of the Union of Soviet Socialist Republics. 1977. http://www.departments.bucknell.edu/russian/const/77cons02.html#chap07.

Creed, Gerald. 2011. *Masquerade and Postsocialism: Ritual and Cultural Dispossession in Bulgaria*. Bloomington: Indiana University Press.

Cvirka, Petras. (1934) 2016. *Frank Kruk: Or, the Undertaker Pranas Krukelis*. Translated by Elizabeth Novickas. Flossmoor, IL: Pica.

Dabartinės lietuvių kalbos žodynas. 2015. Lietuvių kalbos išteklių informacinė sistema. https://lkiis.lki.lt/.

Davoliūtė, Violeta. 2013. *The Making and Breaking of Soviet Lithuania: Memory and Modernity in the Wake of War*. London: Routledge.

Davoliūtė, Violeta, and Tomas Balkelis, eds. 2012. *Maps of Memory: Trauma, Identity and Exile in Deportation Memoirs from the Baltic States*. Vilnius: Lietuvių literatūros ir tautosakos institutas.

Deranty, Jean-Philippe. 2003. "Jacques Rancière's Contribution to the Ethics of Recognition." *Political Theory* 31 (1): 136–56.

Dieckmann, Christoph, and Saulius Sužiedėlis. 2006. *Lietuvos žydų persekiojimas ir masinės žudynės 1941 m. vasarą ir rudenį*. Vilnius: Margi raštai.

Dimitrov, Martin K. 2014a. "Tracking Public Opinion under Authoritarianism: The Case of the Soviet Union during the Brezhnev Era." *Russian History* 41 (3): 329–53.

———. 2014b. "What the Party Wanted to Know: Citizen Complaints as a 'Barometer of Public Opinion' in Communist Bulgaria." *East European Politics and Societies* 28 (2): 271–95.

Douglas, Mary. 1991. "Jokes." In *Rethinking Popular Culture*, edited by Chandra Mukerji and Michael Schudson, 291–310. Berkeley: University of California Press.

Draitser, Emil. 2021. *In the Jaws of the Crocodile: A Soviet Memoir*. Madison: University of Wisconsin Press.

Drėmaitė, Marija. 2014. "Sovietinė ritualinė architektūra—santuokų ir laidotuvių rūmai Lietuvoje." *Acta Academiae Artium Vilnensis* 73:47–64.

Drilinga, Antanas. 2005. *Aš juos mylėjau: Atsiminimai*. Vilnius: Gairės.

Eglitis, Daina Stukuls. 2002. *Imagining the Nation: History, Modernity, and Revolution in Latvia*. University Park: Penn State University Press.

Elon, Amos. 2006. "Introduction: The Excommunication of Hannah Arendt." In *Eichmann in Jerusalem: A Report on the Banality of Evil*, by Hannah Arendt, vii–xxiii. London: Penguin.

Emmerson, Phil. 2017. "Thinking Laughter beyond Humour: Atmospheric Refrains and Ethical Indeterminacies in Spaces of Care." *Environment and Planning* 49 (9): 2082–98.

Ermolaev, Herman. 1997. *Censorship in Soviet Literature, 1917–1991*. Lanham, MD: Rowman & Littlefield.

Etty, John. 2019. *Graphic Satire in the Soviet Union: Krokodil's Political Cartoons*. Jackson: University Press of Mississippi.

Fainberg, Dina, and Artemy M. Kalinovsky, eds. 2016. *Reconsidering Stagnation in the Brezhnev Era: Ideology and Exchange*. Lanham, MD: Lexington Books.

Fedorova, Milla. 2014. "'Give Me the Book of Complaints': Complaint in Post-Stalin Comedy." *Laboratorium* 6 (3): 80–92.

Fedotova, O. O. 2009. *Politychna tsenzura drukovanykh vydan' v USRR—URSR (1917–1990 rr.)*. Kyiv: Parlaments'ke vydavnytstvo.

Fehérváry, Krisztina. 2013. *Politics in Color and Concrete: Socialist Materialities and the Middle Class in Hungary*. Bloomington: Indiana University Press.

Feshbach, Murray, and Alfred Friendly Jr. 1992. *Ecocide in the USSR: Health and Nature under Siege*. New York: Basic Books.

Field, Deborah A. 2007. *Private Life and Communist Morality in Khrushchev's Russia*. New York: Peter Lang.

First, Joshua. 2015. *Ukrainian Cinema: Belonging and Identity during the Soviet Thaw.* London: Bloomsbury.

Fitzpatrick, Sheila. 1996a. "Signals from Below: Soviet Letters of Denunciation of the 1930s." *Journal of Modern History* 68 (4): 831–66.

———. 1996b. "Supplicants and Citizens: Public Letter Writing in Soviet Russia in the 1930s." *Slavic Review* 55 (1): 78–105.

———. 2008. "Revisionism in Retrospect: A Personal View." *Slavic Review* 67 (3): 682–704.

Frazer, Erica Lee. 2000. "Masculinity and the Sexual Politics of Self and Other in Soviet Political Cartoons, 1945–1955." MA thesis, University of British Columbia.

Freedman, Leonard. 2012. "Wit as a Political Weapon: Satirists and Censors." *Social Research* 79 (1): 87–112.

Freud, Sigmund. 1976. *Jokes and Their Relation to the Unconscious.* Translated by James Strachey. New York: Penguin Books.

Friedrich, Carl J., and Zbigniew K. Brzezinski. 1956. *Totalitarian Dictatorship and Autocracy.* Cambridge, MA: Harvard University Press.

Fürst, Juliane. 2021. *Flowers through Concrete: Explorations in Soviet Hippieland.* Oxford: Oxford University Press.

Galmarini, Maria Cristina. 2014. "Deviant Subjects, Rights, and the Soviet Moral Economy of Justice (1917–1950)." *Perspectives on Europe* 44 (1): 39–47.

———. 2016. *The Right to Be Helped: Entitlement, Deviance, and the Soviet Moral Order.* DeKalb: Northern Illinois University Press.

Garey, Amy. 2020. "The People's Laughter: War, Comedy, and the Soviet Legacy." PhD diss., University of California, Los Angeles.

Gelvaitis, Andrius. 1977. "Pavargusiųjų prieglauda." *Šluota,* no. 15: 5.

Gérin, Annie. 2018. *Devastation and Laughter: Satire, Power, and Culture in the Early Soviet State, 1920s–1930s.* Toronto: University of Toronto Press.

Girnius, Kęstutis K. 2016. "Pasipriešinimas, prisitaikymas, kolaboravimas." *Naujasis Židinys-Aidai* 5:268–79. https://nzidinys.lt/wp-content/uploads/2018/09/1996-05.pdf.

Glaeser, Andreas. 2011. *Political Epistemics: The Secret Police, the Opposition, and the End of East German Socialism.* Chicago: University of Chicago Press.

Glosienė, Audronė. 1993. "Knygų leidyba ir platinimas Lietuvoje 1918–1940 metais." PhD diss., Vilnius University.

Goldstein, Donna. 2003. *Laughter Out of Place: Race, Class, Violence, and Sexuality in a Rio Shantytown.* Berkeley: University of California Press.

Goldstein, Robert Justin. 2012. "Censorship of Caricature and the Theater in Nineteenth-Century France: An Overview." *Yale French Studies* 122:14–36.

Gordin, Michael D., Helen Tilley, and Gyan Prakash, eds. 2010. *Utopia/dystopia: Conditions of Historical Possibility.* Princeton, NJ: Princeton University Press.

Goriaeva, Tat'iana M. 2009. *Politicheskaia tsenzura v SSSR, 1917–1991 gg.* Moscow: Rossiiskaia politicheskaia entsiklopediia (ROSSPEN).

Granauskas, Romualdas. 1988. *Gyvenimas po klevu.* Vilnius: Vaga.

Grant, Bruce. 1995. *In the Soviet House of Culture: A Century of Perestroikas.* Princeton, NJ: Princeton University Press.

———. 2020. "Satire and Political Imagination in the Caucasus: The Sense and Sensibilities of *Molla Nasreddin.*" *Acta Slavica Iaponica* 40:1–17.

Greenberg, Jessica. 2014. *After the Revolution: Youth, Democracy, and the Politics of Disappointment in Serbia.* Stanford, CA: Stanford University Press.

Grigaliūnas, Modestas. 2013. "Negalėtumėte pasakyti, kokia maždaug mūsų vėliava? Satyriniai *laisvės* vaizdiniai 1989 m. *Šluotos* žurnale kaip atgimstančios tautos autoironija." *Acta humanitarica universitatis Saulensis* 16:148–64.

Grushin, Boris. 2003. *Chetyre zhizni Rossii v zerkale oprosov obshchestvennogo mneniia: Epokha Brezhneva*. Moscow: Progress-Traditsiia.

Grybkauskas, Saulius. 2011. *Sovietinė nomenklatūra ir pramonė Lietuvoje 1965–1985 metais*. Vilnius: Lietuvos istorijos institutas.

——. 2016. *Sovietinis "generalgubernatorius": Komunistų partijų antrieji sekretoriai Sovietų Sąjungos respublikose*. Vilnius: Lietuvos istorijos institutas.

Gudaitis, Leonas. 2010. "Uždusinti žodžiai: Sovietinė cenzūra pokario metais." *Metai* 5–6: 93–109. http://www.tekstai.lt/zurnalas-metai/6055-leonas-gudaitis-uzdusinti-zodziai-sovietine-cenzura-pokario-lietuvoje?catid=575%3A2010-m-nr-5-6-geguze-birzelis.

Halfin, Igal. 1999. *From Darkness to Light: Class, Consciousness, and Salvation in Revolutionary Russia*. Pittsburgh: University of Pittsburgh Press.

——. 2003. *Terror in My Soul: Communist Autobiographies on Trial*. Cambridge, MA: Harvard University Press.

Hall, Kira, Donna Meryl Goldstein, and Matthew Bruce Ingram. 2016. "The Hands of Donald Trump: Entertainment, Gesture, Spectacle." *Journal of Ethnographic Theory* 6 (2): 71–100.

Haugerud, Angelique. 2013. *No Billionaire Left Behind: Satirical Activism in America*. Stanford, CA: Stanford University Press.

Havel, Václav. 1978. *The Power of the Powerless*. International Center on Nonviolent Conflict. https://www.nonviolent-conflict.org/wp-content/uploads/1979/01/the-power-of-the-powerless.pdf.

Hayden, Robert M. 2013. *From Yugoslavia to the Western Balkans: Studies of a European Disunion, 1991–2011*. Leiden: Brill.

Hellbeck, Jochen. 2006. *Revolution on My Mind: Writing a Diary under Stalin*. Cambridge, MA: Harvard University Press.

Helms, Elissa. 2007. "'Politics Is a Whore': Women, Morality and Victimhood in Post-war Bosnia-Herzegovina." In *The New Bosnian Mosaic: Identities, Memories and Moral Claims in a Post-war Society*, edited by Xavier Bougarel, Elissa Helms, and Ger Duijzings, 235–54. Burlington, VT: Ashgate.

Hemment, Julie. 2015. *Youth Politics in Putin's Russia: Producing Patriots and Entrepreneurs*. Bloomington: Indiana University Press.

——. Forthcoming. "Satirical Strikes and Deadpanning Diplomats: *Stiob* as Geopolitical Performance in Russia-US Relations."

Herzfeld, Michael. (1997) 2005. *Cultural Intimacy: Social Poetics in the Nation-State*. New York: Routledge.

——. (1997) 2016. *Cultural Intimacy: Social Poetics and the Real Life of States, Societies, and Institutions*. New York: Routledge.

Hile, Rachel E. 2017. *Spenserian Satire: A Tradition of Indirection*. Manchester: Manchester University Press.

Hilton, Marjorie. 2009. "The Customer Is Always Wrong: Consumer Complaint in Late-NEP Russia." *Russian Review* 68:1–25.

Ho, Tung M. 2019. "Representation of Corruption in Vietnam's Contemporary Mass Media: Insights from Satirical Cartoons." *SocArXiv*, February 1. https://doi.org/10.31235/osf.io/a92mk.

Huxtable, Simon. 2018. "Making News Soviet: Rethinking Journalistic Professionalism after Stalin." *Contemporary European History* 27 (1): 59–84.

Istoriia glazami Krokodila. XX vek. Liudi. Sobitiia. Slova. 1957–1979. 2015. Moscow: Pareto.

Ivanauskas, Vilius. 2010. "Sovietinis režimas ir kultūrinės nomenklatūros kaita vėlyvuoju sovietmečiu Lietuvoje. Rašytojų aplinkos atvejis." *Politologija* 4:53–84.

——. 2014. "'Engineers of the Human Spirit' during Late Socialism: The Lithuanian Union of Writers between Soviet Duties and Local Interests." *Europe-Asia Studies* 66 (4): 645–65.

——. 2015. *Įrėminta tapatybė: Lietuvos rašytojai Tautų draugystės imperijoje*. Vilnius: Lietuvos istorijos institutas.

——. 2017. "Menininkų rateliai ir kitoniška laikysena: Nuo Chruščiovo laikų iki Sąjūdžio." In *Sąjūdžio ištakų beieškant: Nepaklusniųjų tinklaveikos galia*, edited by Jūratė Kavaliauskaitė and Ainė Ramonaitė, 98–131. Vilnius: Baltos lankos.

Jankevičiūtė, Giedrė. 2008. *Lietuvos grafika 1918–1940*. Vilnius: E. Karpavičiaus leidykla.

——. 2016. *Telesforas Kulakauskas 1907–1977*. Vilnius: Vilniaus grafikos meno centras.

Jevsejevas, Paulius. 2014. "Ezopo kalba: Turinio nušalinimas, visuomeninė stereotipija, tekstinė esatis." *Acta Academiae Artium Vilnensis* 73:141–56.

Jung, Yuson. 2010. "The Inability Not to Follow: Western Hegemonies and the Notion of 'Complaisance' in the Enlarged Europe." *Anthropological Quarterly* 83 (2): 317–53.

Juodzevičius, Balys. 2003. *Laisvės kaina*. Utena, Lithuania: Utenos spaustuvė.

Jurašas, Jonas. 1977. Jurašas's testimony at the 1975 International Sakharov Hearings held in Copenhagen. *Lituanus* 23 (2). http://www.lituanus.org/1977/77_2_05. htm.

——. 1987. "Jonas Jurašas." *Baltic Forum* 4 (1): 18–27.

Jurgutienė, Aušra, and Dalia Satkauskytė, eds. 2018. *The Literary Field under Communist Rule*. Boston: Academic Studies.

Kalėda, Algis. 1984. *Lietuvių tarybinė satyra: Meniškumo ir socialinio kryptingumo klausimai* (Medžiaga lektoriui). Vilnius: Žinija.

Kareniauskaitė, Monika. 2017. "Crime and Punishment in Lithuanian SSR." PhD diss., Vilnius University and Lithuanian Institute of History.

Kassof, Brian. 2015. "Glavlit, Ideological Censorship, and Russian-Language Book Publishing, 1922–38." *Russian Review* 74:69–96.

Katilius, Vytautas. 1981. "Didelės smulkmenos." *Šluota*, no. 1: 2–3.

Kauzonas, Ferdinandas. 2008. Interview with Jurgis Gimberis, "Kaip mudviem su J. Gimberiu nepavyko." *Respublika*, April 3. http://www.kamane.lt/lt/atgarsiai/ literatura/litatgarsis231.

Kavaliauskaitė, Jūratė. 2011. "Tarp prigimties ir tautos: Žaliųjų pirmeiviai sovietmečio Lietuvoje." In *Sąjūdžio ištakų beieškant: Nepaklusniųjų tinklaveikos galia*, edited by Jūratė Kavaliauskaitė and Ainė Ramonaitė, 214–67. Vilnius: Baltos lankos.

Kelertas, Violeta. 2006. *Baltic Postcolonialism*. Amsterdam: Rodopi.

——. 2007. "Strategies against Censorship in Soviet Lithuania: 1944–90." *Comparative History of Literatures in European Languages* 22:125–34.

Kharkhordin, Oleg. 1999. *The Collective and the Individual in Russia: A Study of Practices*. Berkeley: University of California Press.

Kirss, Tiina. 1994. "The Censor's Apprentice: Allegory and Aesopian Discourse in Twentieth-Century Estonian and European Texts." PhD diss., University of Michigan.

Klivis, Edgaras. 2010. "Ardomasis prisitaikymas: Cenzūra ir pasipriešinimo jai būdai sovietinio laikotarpio Lietuvos teatre." *Menotyra* 17 (2): 124–31.

Klumbys, Valdemaras. 2008. "Lietuvos kultūrinis elitas sovietmečiu: Tarp pasipriešinimo ir prisitaikymo." *Lietuvos etnologija: Socialinės antropologijos ir etnologijos studijos* 8 (17): 137–57.

——. 2016. "Ezopo kalbos prielaidos ir formavimasis sovietinėje Lietuvoje." *Genocidas ir rezistencija* 2 (40): 68–85.

Klumbytė, Neringa. 2003. "Ethnographic Note on *Nation*: Narratives and Symbols of the Early Post-Socialist Nationalism in Lithuania." *Dialectical Anthropology* 27 (3–4): 279–95.

——. 2010. "The Soviet Sausage Renaissance." *American Anthropologist* 112 (1): 22–37.

——. 2011. "Political Intimacy: Power, Laughter, and Coexistence in Late Soviet Lithuania." *East European Politics and Societies* 25 (4): 658–77.

——. 2012. "Soviet Ethical Citizenship: Morality, the State, and Laughter in Lithuania." In *Soviet Society in the Era of Late Socialism, 1964–85*, edited by Neringa Klumbytė and Gulnaz Sharafutdinova, 91–116. Lanham, MD: Lexington Books.

——. 2014. "Of Power and Laughter: Carnivalesque Politics, Political Opposition, and Moral Citizenship in Lithuania." *American Ethnologist* 3:473–90.

Klumbytė, Neringa, and Gulnaz Sharafutdinova, eds. 2012. *Soviet Society in the Era of Late Socialism, 1964–85*. Lanham, MD: Lexington Books.

Klumbytė, Neringa, and Cristina Vatulescu. 2015. "Editors' Note." *Perspectives on Europe* 45 (1): 6–11.

Kmita, Rimantas, ed. 2015. *Nevienareikšmės situacijos. Pokalbiai apie sovietmečio literatūros lauką*. Vilnius: Lietuvių literatūros ir tautosakos institutas.

Kondratas, Benjaminas. 2021. "Algirdas Skinkys." In *Visuotinė lietuvių enciklopedija*. Vilnius: Mokslo ir enciklopedijų leidybos centras. https://www.vle.lt/straipsnis/algirdas-skinkys/.

Kotkin, Stephen. 1995. *Magnetic Mountain: Stalinism as a Civilization*. Berkeley: University of California Press.

Kozin, Alexander. 2009. "*Krokodil* in Transition: The Case of the Bureaucrat Cartoons." *Russian Journal of Communication* 2 (3/4): 215–33.

Kozlov, Denis. 2013. *The Readers of Novyi Mir: Coming to Terms with the Stalinist Past*. Cambridge, MA: Harvard University Press.

Kozlov, Vladimir A. 1997. "Denunciation and Its Functions in Soviet Governance: A Study of Denunciations and Their Bureaucratic Handling from Soviet Police Archives, 1944–1953." In *Accusatory Practices: Denunciation in Modern European History, 1789–1989*, edited by Sheila Fitzpatrick and Robert Gellately, 121–52. Chicago: University of Chicago Press.

Krakus, Anna. 2015. "Revealing the Past: The Formerly Secret Police Files in Poland and Andrzej Wajda's Counter-archive." *Perspectives on Europe* 45 (1): 53–60.

Krakus, Anna, and Cristina Vatulescu. 2019. "Foucault in Poland: A Secret Archive." *Diacritics* 47 (2): 72–105.

Krylova, Anna. 2000. "The Tenacious Liberal Subject in Soviet Studies." *Kritika* 1:119–46.

Kubik, Jan. 1994. *The Power of Symbols against the Symbols of Power: The Rise of Solidarity and the Fall of State Socialism in Poland*. University Park: Penn State University Press.

Kubilius, Vytautas. 1978. "Humoras, paradoksas, groteskas." In *Šiuolaikinės prozos problemos*, edited by Petras Bražėnas, 155–171. Vilnius: Vaga.

Kulpinskas, Steponas-Vytautas. 1966. *Kai kurios mūsų satyros ir humoro problemos*. BA thesis. Vilniaus Valstybinis V. Kapsuko universitetas.

Kundera, Milan. (1984) 2005. *The Unbearable Lightness of Being*. Translated by Michael Henry Heim. New York: Harper Perennial Modern Classics.

Lampland, Martha, and Maya Nadkarni. 2016. "'What Happened to Jokes?' The Shifting Landscape of Humor in Hungary." *East European Politics and Societies* 30 (2): 449–71.

Lankauskas, Romualdas. 1992. "Ilgas ir sunkus vieno netikusio autoriaus auklėjimas." In *Rašytojas ir cenzūra*, edited by Arvydas Sabonis and Stasys Sabonis, 102–25. Vilnius: Vaga.

Laucius, Jeronimas. 1990. *Aforizmai: Iš Perestroikos epochos*. Self-published.

Lauk, Epp. 1999. "Practice of Soviet Censorship in the Press: The Case of Estonia." http://citeseerx.ist.psu.edu/viewdoc/download?doi=10.1.1.114.9904&rep=rep1&type=pdf.

Lebow, Katherine. 2014. "Autobiography as Complaint: Polish Social Memoir between the World Wars." *Laboratorium* 6 (3): 13–26.

Ledeneva, Alena V. 1998. *Russia's Economy of Favours*. Cambridge: Cambridge University Press.

Lietuvių kalbos žodynas. 2018. "Juokas." Last modified January 1, 2018. Vilnius: Lietuvių kalbos institutas. http://www.lkz.lt/?zodis=juokas&id=16017610000.

Lietuvos dailės istorija. 2002. Vilnius: Vilniaus dailės akademijos leidykla.

Lietuvos Respublikos Baudžiamasis Kodeksas. 2020. "99. Straipsnis. Genocidas." https://www.infolex.lt/ta/66150#.

Lipstadt, Deborah E. 2011. *The Eichmann Trial*. New York: Nextbook/Schocken.

Literatūra ir menas. 1963. "'Suglaustomis gretomis': Iš E. Mieželaičio pranešimo LTSR Rašytojų sąjungos valdybos plenume." May 11.

Livshin, Ia. Aleksandr, and Igor' B. Orlov. 1998. "Revoliutsiia i sotsial'naia spravedlivost': Ozhidaniia i real'nost' (Pis'ma vo vlast' 1917–1927 godov)." *Cahiers du monde russe: Russie, Empire russe, Union soviétique, États indépendants* 39 (4): 487–513.

Lõhmus, Maarja. 2012. "Political Correctness and Political Humour in Soviet Estonia and Beyond." In *Estonia and Poland: Creativity and Change in Cultural Communication*. Vol. 1, *Jokes and Their Relations*, edited by Liisi Laineste, Dorota Brzozowska, and Władysław Chłopicki, 139–58. Tartu, Estonia: ELM Scholarly.

Lomsargytė-Pukienė, Silvija. 2004. Dita. Paralelės. Kaunas: Jotema.

Low, David. 1950. Review of *Krokodil Cartoonists*. *Soviet Studies* 2 (2): 163–70.

Lubytė, Elona. 1997. *Tylusis modernizmas Lituvoje, 1962–1982*. Vilnius: Tyto alba.

——, ed. 2019. "Ar buvo tylusis modernizmas Lietuvoje?" Special issue of *Acta Academiae Artium Vilnensis*. Vilnius: Vilniaus dailės akademijos leidykla.

Lukošienė, Mykolė. 2016. "Boring Soviet Humor: The Artificiality of International Women's Day and an Imitation of Criticism." *Darbai ir dienos* 65:163–94.

Lukša, Albertas. 1958. "'Šluotos' feljetonai." University degree thesis. Vilnius University library, unpublished manuscripts. Library record F85-Ž92.

Lunacharskii, Anatolii V. (1931) 1964. "O smekhe." In *Sobranie sochinenii v 8 tomakh*. Vol. 8. Moscow: Khudozhestvennaia literatura.

Mahmood, Saba. 2011. *Politics of Piety: The Islamic Revival and the Feminist Subject*. Princeton, NJ: Princeton University Press.

Mannheim, Karl. (1929) 1991. *Ideology and Utopia: An Introduction to the Sociology of Knowledge*. Translated by Louis Wirth and Edward Shils. San Diego: Harcourt Brace.

Marcinkevičienė, Dalia. 2007. "'Laiškas pakvietė kelionėn': Buitinių skundų praktika sovietinėje Lietuvoje." *Genocidas ir rezistencija* 2 (22): 110–23.

Marcinkevičius, Arūnas. 2020. "Amžiaus problema: Kada Rusija kompensuos okupacijos nuostolius." *Delfi*, January 12. https://www.delfi.lt/news/daily/lithuania/amziaus-problema-kada-rusija-kompensuos-okupacijos-nuostolius.d?id=82487905.

Martinaitis, Marcelijus. 2003. "Įslaptinta cenzūra." In *Lietuviškos utopijos*, 49–67. Vilnius: Tyto alba. http://www.xn--altiniai-4wb.info/files/literatura/LH00/Marcelijus_Martinaitis._%C4%AEslaptinta_cenz%C5%ABra.LHE102.pdf.

Maslauskaitė, Aušra, Vladislava Stankūnienė, Dalia Ambrozaitienė, and Rasa
    Balandienė. 2006. *Lietuvos gyventojai: Struktūra ir demografinė raida.*
    Vilnius: Lietuvos statistikos departamentas, Socialinių tyrimų institutas.
Mazzarella, William. 2013. *Censorium: Cinema and the Open Edge of Mass Publicity.*
    Durham, NC: Duke University Press.
Mbembe, Achille. 1992. "Provisional Notes on the Postcolony." *Africa: Journal of the
    International African Institute* 62 (1): 3–37.
——. 2001. *On the Postcolony.* Berkeley: University of California Press.
McLean, Hugh, ed. 1963. *"Nervous People" and Other Satires by Mikhail Zoshchenko.*
    Bloomington: Indiana University Press.
Mesropova, Olga, and Seth Graham. 2008. *Uncensored? Reinventing Humor and Satire
    in Post-Soviet Russia.* Bloomington, IN: Slavica.
Milkevičiūtė, Giedrė. 2020. "Dailininkas Kęstutis Šiaulytis: 'Humoras padeda nugalėti
    stresą.'" *Savaitė*, April 2. http://kestutis-galerija.blogspot.com/2020/04/giedre-
    milkeviciute-dailininkas.html.
Milne, Lesley. 2004. Introduction to *Reflective Laughter: Aspects of Humour in Russian
    Culture*, edited by Lesley Milne, 1–14. London: Anthem.
Misiunas, Romuald, and Rein Taagepera. 1983. *The Baltic States: Years of Dependence,
    1940–1980.* Berkeley: University of California Press.
Molé, Noelle J. 2013. "Trusted Puppets, Tarnished Politicians: Humor and Cynicism in
    Berlusconi's Italy." *American Ethnologist* 40 (2): 288–99.
Molla Nasreddin: Polemics, Caricatures and Satires. 2017. Edited by Slavs and Tatars.
    I. B. Tauris.
Naiman, Eric, and Christina Kiaer. 2006. *Everyday Life in Revolutionary Russia: Taking
    the Revolution Inside.* Bloomington: Indiana University Press.
Naudžiūnienė, Akvilė. 2021. "'Naujasis žmogus' iki pareikalavimo: Mokinys vėlyvojo
    sovietmečio (1964–1988 m.) LTSR mokyklose." *Lietuvos istorijos studijos*
    47:99–117.
Neofotistos, Vasiliki P. 2010. "Critical Engagements with Cultural Intimacy."
    Anthropological Quarterly 83 (2): 229–37.
——. 2012. *The Risk of War: Everyday Sociality in the Republic of Macedonia.*
    Philadelphia: University of Pennsylvania Press.
1934–1964 "Šluota." Karikatūros. 1964. Vilnius: LKP CK Laikraščių ir žurnalų
    leidykla.
Nobel Prize. 1990. "The Nobel Peace Prize 1990." Nobel Prize, October 15. https://
    www.nobelprize.org/prizes/peace/1990/press-release/.
Nordstrom, Carolyn. 2004. *Shadows of War: Violence, Power, and International
    Profiteering in the Twenty-First Century.* Berkeley: University of California
    Press.
Norris, Stephen. 2009. "'Laughter Is a Very Sharp Weapon': Boris Efimov and Soviet
    Visual Humor." Paper presented at the conference "Totalitarian Laughter:
    Cultures of the Comic under Socialism." Princeton University, Princeton, NJ,
    May 15–17.
——. 2013. "The Sharp Weapon of Soviet Laughter: Boris Efimov and Visual Humor."
    Russian Literature 74 (1–2): 31–62.
Official Statistics Portal. 2013. "Ethnicity, Mother Tongue and Religion." https://osp.
    stat.gov.lt/informaciniai-pranesimai?articleId=223122.
O'Keeffe, Brigid. 2013. *New Soviet Gypsies: Nationality, Performance, and Selfhood in
    the Early Soviet Union.* Toronto: University of Toronto Press.
Orwell, George. (1945) 1968. "Funny, but Not Vulgar." In *The Collected Essays,
    Journalism and Letters of George Orwell.* https://orwell.ru/library/articles/funny/
    english/e_funny.

Oushakine, Serguei A. 2011. "Laughter under Socialism: Exposing the Ocular in Soviet Jocularity." *Slavic Review* 70 (2): 247–55.

——. 2012. "'Red Laughter': On Refined Weapons of Soviet Jesters." *Social Research* 79 (1): 189–216.

——. 2014. "'Against the Cult of Things': On Soviet Productivism, Storage Economy, and Commodities with No Destination." *Russian Review* 73 (2): 198–236.

Paloff, Benjamin. 2021. "Qué ridículo! Bakhtin and the Power of Not Being in on the Joke." Paper presented at the Havighurst Colloquium, Miami University, Oxford, OH, April 5.

Papaurėlytė, Arida. 1999. "Cenzūra tarpukario Lietuvoje." *Literatūra* 37:153–68.

——. 2003. *Knygos laisvė ir kontrolė Lietuvoje 1918–1940 m.* PhD diss., Vilnius University.

Paretskaya, Anna. 2012. "A Middle Class without Capitalism? Socialist Ideology and Post-collectivist Discourse in the Late-Soviet Era." In *Soviet Society in the Era of Late Socialism, 1964–85*, edited by Neringa Klumbytė and Gulnaz Sharafutdinova, 43–66. Lanham, MD: Lexington Books.

Patico, Jennifer. *2002.* "*Chocolate and Cognac*: Gifts and the Recognition of Social Worlds in Post-Soviet Russia." *Ethnos* 67 (3): 345–68.

Pearce, Katy, and Adnan Hajizada. 2014. "No Laughing Matter: Humor as a Means of Dissent in the Digital Era; The Case of Authoritarian Azerbaijan." *Demokratizatsiya: The Journal of Post-Soviet Democratization* 22 (1): 67–85.

Pehowski, Marian. 1978. "*Krokodil*—Satire for the Soviets." *Journalism and Mass Communication Quarterly* 55 (4): 726–31.

Pelėgrinda, A., and A. Saulius. 1979. "Vieni plaukia, kiti laukia." *Šluota*, no. 11: 7.

Perechen' svedenii, zapreshchennykh k opublikavoniiu v otkrytoi pechati, peredachakh po radio i televideniiu. 1976. Moscow.

Pesmen, Dale. 2000. *Russia and Soul.* Ithaca, NY: Cornell University Press.

Petrauskaitė, Audronė. 2006. "Karininkijos dorovės problemos prieškario Lietuvoje." *Karo archyvas* 21:117–35.

Petrović, Tanja. 2018. "Political Parody and the Politics of Ambivalence." *Annual Review of Anthropology* 47:201–16.

Pirmasis Lietuvos TSR kultūros darbuotojų suvažiavimas. 1971. Vilnius: Mintis.

Pocevičius, Darius. 2018. *Istoriniai Vilniaus reliktai 1944–1990.* Vol. 1. Vilnius: Kitos knygos.

Praspaliauskienė, Rima. 2022. *Enveloped Lives: Caring and Relating in Lithuanian Health Care.* Ithaca, NY: Cornell University Press.

Propp, Vladimir. 2009. *On the Comic and Laughter.* Edited and translated by Jean-Patrick Debbèche and Paul Perron. Toronto: University of Toronto Press.

Prybyla, Jan S. 1971. "Soviet Man in the Ninth Plan." *Current History* 61 (362): 227–34, 242.

Putinaitė, Nerija. 2015. *Nugenėta Pušis. Ateizmas kaip asmeninis apsisprendimas tarybų Lietuvoje.* Vilnius: Lietuvių katalikų mokslo akademija, Naujasis Židinys-Aidai.

——. 2019. *Skambantis molis: Dainų šventės ir Justino Marcinkevičiaus trilogija kaip sovietinio lietuviškumo ramsčiai.* Vilnius: Naujasis Židinys-Aidai.

Pyanov, Aleksey, and the editors of *Krokodil* magazine. 1989. *Soviet Humor: The Best of Krokodil.* Kansas City: Andrews and McMeel, a Universal Press Syndicate Company.

Radzevičius, Bronius. (1979) 2008. *Priešaušrio vieškeliai.* Vilnius: Lietuvos rašytojų sąjungos leidykla.

Ramonaitė, Ainė, ed. 2015a. *Nematoma sovietmečio visuomenė.* Vilnius: Naujasis Židinys-Aidai.

———. 2015b. "Viešos nepaklusnumo demonstracijos: Etnokultūrinio sąjūdžio mobilizacinė galia." In *Nematoma sovietmečio visuomenė*, edited by Ainė Ramonaitė, 195–217. Vilnius: Naujasis židinys-Aidai.

Ramonaitė, Ainė, and Jūratė Kavaliauskaitė, eds. 2011. *Sąjūdžio ištakų beieškant*. Vilnius: Baltos lankos.

Ramonaitė, Ainė, Jūratė Kavaliauskaitė, and Valdemaras Klumbys, eds. 2015. *Kažkas tokio labai tikro: Nepaklusniosios sovietmečios visuomenės istorijos*. Vilnius: Aukso žuvys.

Rancière, Jacques. 2009. *Aesthetics and Its Discontents*. Translated by Steven Corcoran. Cambridge: Polity.

———. 2010. *Dissensus: On Politics and Aesthetics*. London: Bloomsbury Academic.

Rancière, Jacques, and Davide Panagia. 2000. "Dissenting Words: A Conversation with Jacques Rancière." *Diacritics* 30 (2): 113–26.

Rehak, Jana Kopelent. 2019. "Humor against Forgetting: Joking in the Space of Death." In *The Politics of Joking: Anthropological Engagements*, edited by Rehak Jana Kopelent and Susanna Trnka, 70–84. London: Routledge.

Reid, Susan E. 2005. "In the Name of the People: The Manege Affair Revisited." *Kritika: Explorations in Russian and Eurasian History* 6 (4): 673–716.

———. 2014. "Makeshift Modernity: DIY, Craft and the Virtuous Homemaker in New Soviet Housing of the 1960s." *International Journal for History, Culture and Modernity* 2 (2): 87–124.

Riaubienė, Arida. 2005. "Valstybinės cenzūros mechanizmas tarpukario Lietuvoje." *Knygotyra* 44:103–13.

Ries, Nancy. 1997. *Russian Talk: Culture and Conversation during Perestroika*. Ithaca, NY: Cornell University Press.

Rimša, Antanas. 2007. "Pasimatymai *Šluotos* redakcijoje (1972–1978)." *Alytaus naujienos*, January 12. Article no. 363.

Roberts, Steven V. 1987. "Reagan and the Russians: The Joke's on Them." *New York Times*, August 21.

Rogers, Douglas. 2009. *The Old Faith and the Russian Land: A Historical Ethnography of Ethics in the Urals*. Ithaca, NY: Cornell University Press.

Rothberg, Michael. 2019. *The Implicated Subject: Beyond Victims and Perpetrators*. Stanford, CA: Stanford University Press.

Roudakova, Natalia. 2017. *Losing Pravda: Ethics and the Press in Post-truth Russia*. Cambridge: Cambridge University Press.

Russell, Matheson, and Andrew Montin. 2015. "The Rationality of Political Disagreement: Rancière's Critique of Habermas." *Constellations* 22 (4): 543–54.

Sabonis, Stasys. 1992. "Kas dirbo Glavlite? Pokalbis su buvusia ilgamete Glavlito darbuotoja Marija Senkuviene." In *Rašytojas ir cenzūra*, edited by Arvydas Sabonis and Stasys Sabonis, 410–13. Vilnius: Vaga.

Sabonis, Arvydas, and Stasys Sabonis, eds. 1992. *Rašytojas ir cenzūra*. Vilnius: Vaga.

Sadaunykas-Sadūnas, Jonas. 1988. *Komunistai*. Vilnius: Mintis.

———. 2002. *Geltonos vanago akys*. Vilnius: Žuvėdra.

Sartwell, Crispin. 2010. *Political Aesthetics*. Ithaca, NY: Cornell University Press.

Satkauskytė, Dalia. 2018. "The Role of Aesopian Language in the Literary Field: Autonomy in Question." In *The Literary Field under Communist Rule*, edited by Aušra Jurgutienė and Dalia Satkauskytė, 18–36. Brighton: Academic Studies.

Scott, James C. 1985. *Weapons of the Weak: Everyday Forms of Peasant Resistance*. New Haven, CT: Yale University Press.

Sėdaitytė, Edita. 2017. "Sovietinės cenzūros istoriografija: Pagrindinės tyrimų kryptys ir cenzūros sampratos." *Knygotyra* 69:84–102.

Semenov, Manuil. 1982. *Krokodil'skie byli*. Moscow: Mysl'.

Senn, Alfred E. 2002. *Lithuania Awakening*. Vilnius: Mokslo ir enciklopedijų leidybos institutas.

Shabad, Theodore. 1964. "Behind the Smile on Krokodil." *New York Times*, June 7. https://www.nytimes.com/1964/06/07/archives/behind-the-smile-on-krokodil.html.

Shafir, Iakov. 1922. "Pochemu my ne umeem smeiat'sia?" *Krasnaia pechat'* 17:6–9.

Shryock, Andrew, ed. 2004. *Off State / On Display: Intimacy and Ethnography in the Age of Public Culture*. Stanford, CA: Stanford University Press.

Šiaulytis, Kęstutis. 2017. Presentation at Martynas Mažvydas National Library of Lithuania, April 28. Giedrius Subačius video. https://vimeo.com/215490915.

Siegelbaum, Lewis H. 2008. *Cars for Comrades: The Life of the Soviet Automobile*. Ithaca, NY: Cornell University Press.

Šileika, Ričardas. 2003. Interview with Kazys Kęstutis Šiaulytis, "Negalime būti tik praeiviai nereaguojantys į tai, ką mato." *Literatūra ir menas*, August 22.

Skradol, Natalia. 2009. "Exceptional Laughter." Paper presented at the conference "Totalitarian Laughter: Cultures of the Comic under Socialism," Princeton University, Princeton, NJ, May 15–17.

Šliažienė, Julija. 2005. "Žurnalistas, kolekcininkas L. A. Kiauleikis bylinėjasi su Liustracijos komisija." *Delfi*, August 23. https://www.delfi.lt/news/daily/lithuania/zurnalistas-kolekcininkas-lakiauleikis-bylinejasi-su-liustracijos-komisija.d?id=7334795#ixzz3Ov877mQS.

Slider, Darrell. 1985. "Party-Sponsored Public Opinion Research in the Soviet Union." *Journal of Politics* 47 (1): 209–27.

Šluota. 1991. "Plunksnos brolių galerija, Juozas Bulota." *Šluota*, no. 24: 3.

Šmidchens, Guntis. 2014. *The Power of Song: Nonviolent National Culture in the Baltic Singing Revolution*. Seattle: University of Washington Press.

Smolkin, Victoria. 2018. *A Sacred Space Is Never Empty: A History of Soviet Atheism*. Princeton, NJ: Princeton University Press.

Šniukas, Domas. 2004. *Juozas Olinardas Penčyla: Šaržų karalius*. Vilnius: Margi raštai.

——. 2018. "Linksmiausias iš Bulotų." In *Žurnalistikos lankose: Gairės, datos, veidai*, 294–99. Vilnius: Kriventa.

Soysal, Levent. 2010. "Intimate Engagements of the Public Kind." *Anthropological Quarterly* 83 (2): 373–99.

Ssorin-Chaikov, Nikolai V. 2003. *The Social Life of the State in Subarctic Siberia*. Stanford, CA: Stanford University Press.

Stites, Richard. 2010. *Passion and Perception: Essays on Russian Culture*. Washington, DC: New Academia.

Stokes, Gale. 1993. *Walls Came Tumbling Down: The Collapse of Communism in Eastern Europe*. Oxford: Oxford University Press.

Stravinskienė, Vitalija. 2016. "Kaimų tuštėjimas Rytų ir Pietryčių Lietuvoje XXa. septintajame—aštuntajame dešimtmetyje: Tarp provincijos gyvenvietės, miesto ir Vilniaus." *Lietuvos istorijos metraštis* 1:97–114.

Streikus, Arūnas. 2002. *Sovietų valdžios antibažnytinė politika Lietuvoje (1944–1990)*. Vilnius: Lietuvos gyventojų genocido ir rezistencijos tyrimo centras.

——. 2004. "Ideologinė cenzūra Lietuvoje 1956–1989 m." *Genocidas ir rezistencija* 1 (15): 43–67.

——. 2018. *Minties kolektyvizacija: Cenzūra sovietų Lietuvoje*. Vilnius: Naujasis Židinys-Aidai.

Suziedelis, Saulius, William J. H. Hough, Kestutis Girnius, and Asta Banionis. 1989. *History and Commemoration in the Baltic: The Nazi Soviet Pact, 1939–1989*. Chicago: Lithuanian-American Community.

Swain, Amanda. 2015. "Commemorating the 'Living Torch of Freedom': Searching for a Usable Past in Romas Kalanta's 1972 Self-Immolation." *Ab Imperio* 2:162–82.

Tamkevičius, Sigitas. 2021. "The Chronicle of the Catholic Church in Lithuania." http://www.lkbkronika.lt/index.php/en/3-the-chronicle-of-the-catholic-church-in-lithuania.html.

Tamošaitis, Mindaugas. 2010. *Didysis apakimas: Lietuvių rašytojų kairėjimas 4-ajame XX a, dešimtmetyje*. Vilnius: Gimtasis žodis.

Tarybų Lietuvos enciklopedija. 1985. Vol. 1. Vilnius: Vyriausioji enciklopedijų redakcija.

Tismaneanu, Vladimir, and Marius Stan. 2018. *Romania Confronts Its Communist Past*. New York: Cambridge University Press.

Tomkus, Vitas. 1988. *Taranas*. Vilnius: Mintis.

Truska, Liudas. 1997. "Glavlito veikla Lietuvoje 1940–1947 metais." In *Lietuvos istorijos metraštis 1996 metai*, 216–29. Vilnius: Lietuvos istorijos institutas. http://www.xn--altiniai-4wb.info/files/istorija/II00/Kult%C5%ABros_sovietizavimas_ir_cenz%C5%ABra.II2102.pdf.

Tsipursky, Gleb. 2010. "'As a Citizen, I Cannot Ignore These Facts': Whistleblowing in the Khrushchev Era." *Jahrbücher für Geschichte Osteuropas* 58 (1): 52–69.

——. 2016. *Socialist Fun: Youth, Consumption, and State-Sponsored Popular Culture* in the *Soviet Union, 1945–1970*. Pittsburgh: University of Pittsburgh Press.

Ukaz Prezidiuma Verkhovnogo Soveta SSSR. 1968. "O poriadke rassmotreniia predlozhenii, zaiavlenii i zhalob grazhdan." April 12. N 2534-VII. http://pravo.gov.ru/proxy/ips/?docbody=&nd=102080532&rdk=&backlink=1.

Vaiseta, Tomas. 2014. *Nuobodulio visuomenė: Kasdienybė ir ideologija vėlyvuoju sovietmečiu (1964–1984)*. Vilnius: Naujasis Židinys-Aidai.

——. 2018. *Vasarnamis. Vilniaus psichiatrijos ligoninės socialinė istorija 1944–1990*. Vilnius: Lapas.

Vaišnys, Andrius. 1999. *Spauda ir valstybė 1918–1940: Analizė istoriniu, teisiniu ir politiniu aspektu*. Vilnius: UAB Biznio mašinų kompanija.

Valadka, Česlavas. 1977a. "Atsargiai—žmogus!" *Šluota*, no. 13: 2–3.

——. 1977b. "Atsargiai—žmogus!" *Šluota*, no. 19: 15.

Varga-Harris, Christine. 2015. *Stories of House and Home: Soviet Apartment Life during the Khrushchev Years*. Ithaca, NY: Cornell University Press.

Varnas, Jonas. 2017. Presentation at Martynas Mažvydas National Library of Lithuania, April 28. Giedrius Subačius video. https://vimeo.com/215879279.

Vaskela, Gediminas. 2014. "Lietuvos ūkis TSRS ir Rytų Pabaltijyje XX amžiaus 5–6 dešimtmečiais." In *Stalininis režimas Lietuvoje 1944–1953 m.*, edited by Regina Laukaitytė, 225–48. Vilnius: Lietuvos istorijos instituto leidykla.

Vatulescu, Cristina. 2014. *Police Aesthetics: Literature, Film, and the Secret Police in Soviet Times*. Stanford, CA: Stanford University Press.

Važgauskaitė, Jūratė. 2019. "Anekdotai sovietmečiu—pavojingas ir smagus juokas pro ašaras." TV3, November 24. https://www.tv3.lt/naujiena/lietuva/anekdotai-sovietmeciu-pavojingas-ir-smagus-juokas-pro-asaras-n1020164.

——. 2020. Interview with Saulius Grybkauskas, "Sovietinės medžioklės ypatumai: Be svetimų ausų, bet su netikrais kiškiais." TV 3, February 23. https://www.tv3.lt/naujiena/lietuva/sovietines-medziokles-ypatumai-be-svetimu-ausu-bet-su-netikrais-kiskiais-n1030678.

Venckūnas, Valius. 2010. "Lietuviškas humoras: Kas buvo prieš pradedant juoktis iš politerotikos." *Universiteto žurnalistas*, September 30. http://www.universitetozurnalistas.kf.vu.lt/2010/09/lietuviskas-humoras-kas-buvo-pries-pradedant-juoktis-is-politerotikos/.

Venclova, Tomas. 1985. *Tekstai apie tekstus*. Chicago: A. Mackaus knygų leidimo fondas.

Verdery, Katherine. 1996. *What Was Socialism, and What Comes Next?* Princeton, NJ: Princeton University Press.

———. 2003. *The Vanishing Hectare: Property and Value in Postsocialist Transylvania.* Ithaca, NY: Cornell University Press.

———. 2011. *Peasants under Siege: The Collectivization of Romanian Agriculture, 1949–1962.* Princeton, NJ: Princeton University Press.

———. 2014. *Secrets and Truths: Ethnography in the Archive of Romania's Secret Police.* Budapest: CEU Press.

———. 2018. *My Life as a Spy: Investigations in a Secret Police File.* Durham, NC: Duke University Press.

Vidugirytė, Inga. 2012. *Juoko kultūra: Studijų knyga.* Vilnius: Vilniaus universiteto leidykla.

Wedeen, Lisa. 2019. *Authoritarian Apprehensions: Ideology, Judgment, and Mourning in Syria.* Chicago: University of Chicago Press.

White, Stephen. 1983. "Political Communications in the USSR: Letters to Party, State and Press." *Political Studies* 31 (1): 43–60.

White, Stephen, John Gardner, and George Schöpflin. 1987. *Communist Political Systems: An Introduction.* 2nd ed. New York: St. Martin's Press.

Wolf, Erika. 2017. *Aleksandr Zhitomirsky: Photomontage as a Weapon of World War II and the Cold War.* New Haven, CT: Yale University Press.

Wolfe, Thomas C. 2005. *Governing Soviet Journalism: The Press and the Socialist Person after Stalin.* Bloomington: Indiana University Press.

Yekelchyk, Serhy. 2006. "No Laughing Matter: State Regimentation of Ukrainian Humor and Satire under High Stalinism (1943–1953)." *Canadian American Slavic Studies* 40 (1): 79–99.

Yeremieieva, Kateryna. 2014. "'Kommunist-optimist? Kak izmerit' 'Bodrost' dukha' obshchestva." *Vestnik Permskogo Universiteta* 4 (27): 24–36.

Yeremieieva, Kateryna. 2018. *Byty satyroiu: Zhurnal "Perets" v sotsiokul'turnomu seredovyshchi Radians'koi Ukrainy.* Kharkiv: Rarytety Ukrainy.

Yeremieieva, Kateryna, *and Vladimir Kulikov.* 2013. "Potrebitel'skii ideal v iumoristicheskom diskurse Sovetskoi Ukrainy: Kontent-analiz sovetskikh anekdotov zhurnala 'Perets.'" *Res Historica* 36:262–77.

Young, Iris Marion. 2003. "Political Responsibility and Structural Injustice." Lindley Lecture, University of Kansas, May 5. https://kuscholarworks.ku.edu/bitstream/handle/1808/12416/Political%20Responsibility%20and%20Structural%20Injustice-2003.pdf?isAllowed=y&sequence=1.

Yurchak, Alexei. 1997. "The Cynical Reason of Late Socialism: Power, Pretense, and the Anekdot." *Public Culture* 9 (2): 161–88.

———. 2003. "Soviet Hegemony of Form: Everything Was Forever, until It Was No More." *Comparative Studies in Society and History* 45 (3): 480–510.

———. 2006. *Everything Was Forever, until It Was No More: The Last Soviet Generation.* Princeton, NJ: Princeton University Press.

Žeimantas, Vytautas. 2014. "LŽS Senjorų klubas nutarė rekomenduoti LŽS XVI suvažiavimui vėl išrinkti Dainių Radzevičių LŽS pirmininku." *Lietuvos žurnalistų sąjunga* news, November 6. http://www.lzs.lt/lt/naujienos/aktualijos_354/lzs_senjoru_klubas_nutare_rekomenduoti_lzs_xvi_suvaziavimui_vel_isrinkti_dainiu_radzeviciu_lzs_pirmininku.html.

Zhuk, Sergei. 2010. *Rock and Roll in the Rocket City: The West, Identity, and Ideology in Soviet Dnepropetrovsk.* Baltimore: Johns Hopkins University Press.

Žilinskaitė, Vytautė. 1966. "Nemirtingumo paslaptis." *Šluota*, no. 16: 4.

Zubok, Vladislav. 2009. *Zhivago's Children: The Last Russian Intelligentsia.* Cambridge, MA: Belknap Press of Harvard University Press.

Index

Boxes are indicated by letter b, figures by an f, and tables by a t.

Adzhubei, Aleksei, 244n6
Aesopian language
  dissensus and, 43
  hidden meanings and, 15, 75, 112, 146, 166
  ideological discourse and, 67
  opposition to state authority and, 142, 144, 217
  rearticulation of, 12
  satirical laughter, 226
Alaniz, Jose, 159, 253n99
al-Assad, Bashar, 227
antagonistic complicity, 10, 13–15, 31, 43, 143, 151, 165, 233
antisemitism
  in cartoons, 16, 53, 54f
  censorship of, 22
  editors views and, 18
  employment discrimination and, 238n48
  in *Krokodil*, 242n21
  post-Soviet period, 223
  post-World War II, 259n59
  in *Wooden Clog*, 46b
  Zimanas and, 239n15
Anušauskas, Arvydas, 13, 117
Aputis, Juozas, 118
Arendt, Hannah, 30–31
art-politics, 26, 118–19, 138, 141, 168
Astrauskas, Gediminas, 61, 122, 220
At the Table All Are Welcome . . .," 140
"Attorney's Speech" (Tilvytis), pseudonym of A. Brička, 192
Augustinas, J., 112
authoritarian regimes, 226–27, 234
authoritarian stigma, 14, 25, 75, 230–32
Avyžius, Jonas, 94

Bakhtin, Mikhail, 4, 11–12, 29, 242n4, 251n36
Baldišius, Rimantas, 82
Baltušis, Juozas, 240n28, 254n120
Banadienė, Ona, 209, 220
banality of evil, 30–31
banality of power, 10, 29–30, 52–53, 64, 74
banal opposition
  at *Broom*, 166, 168
  cartoons and, 151, 154

censorship and, 117, 224
  definition of, 10, 15
  establishment writers and, 166
  justification of art, 158
  political intimacy and, 16, 18, 90
  rejection of Communist ideology, 142–43
  Šiaulytis's cartoons as, 147
  US as Soviet Union, 150
Barkauskas, Antanas, 142
Basanavičius, Jonas, 44
Baužytė, J., 186
"Be Careful—a Human Being!" 170
Beresniovas, Vladimiras, 91b, 139, 231
Bilevičius, E., 98–99
"Billionaires for Bush" (Haugerud), 227
Binkis, Kazys, 43
Bittner, Stephen, 175
Blium, Vladimir, 5–7
bourgeois ideology
  aesthetics of, 126
  Broom (Šluota) and exposure of, 71b, 86, 95
  Broom (Šluota) language transformation, 130
  Broom (Šluota) rejections and, 132
  communism and, 4, 93, 195, 235n8
  entertainment and petty themes, 6, 94
  past leftover, 100, 256n58
  socialist regime and, 214
  Western culture, 131
  Western culture and, 141–42
Boyer, Dominic, 48
Brezhnev, Leonid
  Broom cartoon, 109f, 110
  in cartoons, 109f, 113
  complaint letters and, 175
  forbidden to draw, 91b
  on laughter, 5
  material welfare and, 199, 208
  speeches of, 76, 145
Broom (Šluota), 2–6, 7f, 41f, 91b
  "After the *Broom* Wrote," 197
  anti-Soviet and anti-Communist jokes in, 222–23, 234
  artist collaboration in, 8

Broom (Šluota) (*continued*)
  censoring of, 100
  censorship and, 21, 89–90, 91b, 92, 94,
    128f–29f, 130, 222
  consumer experiences, 208–9
  contextualizing images, 111-13
  contributors and rejections, 120–26, 132,
    249n3, 249n13, 249n22, 249n27
  CP ideological work, 22–23, 67–70, 73–77,
    78b–79b, 80–82, 86–87, 95, 153
  CP members, 69, 151, 244n10
  crime prevention and, 9
  destroyed Leninist issue, 106t, 107, 135,
    136f, 250n2
  editorial board and job titles, 235n4,
    236n21, 240n28
  editors and comedy performance scripts, 8,
    236n22
  editors' complicity, 31, 120
  ending of, 225
  "Following Readers' Letters" column,
    209–10
  founding, 1, 34, 44b–46b, 93, 235n2
  gifts, 36
  graphic art in, 144, 252n37
  honoraria, 47–48, 242n5, 249n3, 252n65,
    255n18
  household issues, 82, 245n43
  hunting and drinking, 58–59, 61, 79b
  ideological censorship of, 100–104
  ideological editing and, 127, 132–33
  ideological institution, 3, 235n6
  interviews, 24–25
  Lenin's one hundredth birthday, 135, 250n1
  modernist art and artists, 138, 141
  office space, 35
  political aesthetics and, 92, 119–20, 124–27,
    130, 133, 168
  political education at, 22, 73, 76–77, 141
  political intimacy and, 63–64
  popularity of, 8–9, 236n15, 236n18, 237n25
  positive and negative portrayals, 102, 119,
    127, 130–32, 139
  PPO and ambiguity, 113
  PPO assessment report, 70b–72b
  PPO meetings, 95, 114, 141, 144, 153, 242n5
  purpose and humor of, 25–26
  reasons to join, 29, 32
  "Red October" shoes, 208, 212
  reframing of experience, 12–13
  revolutionary period, 221–23
  role of satire, 81
  satirical coverage of bureaucratic language, 77

  site visits, 19
  Soviet life criticism, 224
  spinal injury case, 169–71
  topics addressed, 82–83, 84b–86b, 95
  underground origins, 45, 186
  unofficial jokes, 9, 83, 167, 216, 225–26
  See also complaint letters
Broom cartoons and illustrations, 8–9, 141
  Adventures of Smoky and Pewit, The (comic
    strip), 160, 162–63
  anti-imperialist cartoons, 147–51, 251n20
  antireligious cartoons, 152–54
  award winning cover of USSR's fiftieth
    anniversary, 140f
  Blinda—Leveler of the World
    (comic strip), 160
  cartoon exhibition, 236n20
  cats and birdhouses, 113
  consumer complaints and, 209
  current-issues cartoons, 144–47
  destroyed Leninist issue, 136f
  erotic or naked drawings, 90–91, 102, 106t,
    110, 112, 156–57, 157f, 221, 238n44
  "Expulsion from Eden," 101f, 112
  family of snowmen, 111–12
  foreign humor, 154–59
  Fred— the Wooden Leg (comic strip), 160, 163
  "Fruits of Education in the World of
    Capital," 151
  "Gentlemen, Don't Tell Me We're Going to
    Die without Fulfilling Our Dream," 109f,
    110–12
  "Go Home" signs, 150
  Heart, Knife, and Colt (comic strip), 163
  on hunting, 58
  "I'm at a meeting," 145
  Jack and Bobby (comic strip), 160–61, 163,
    164f, 165, 253n101
  "Let me Go to the Homeland," 53, 54f
  "Matryoshki" (Deltuva), 108
  "Our bus stop, the best in the district," 146f
  political cartoons, 151
  republication and awards, 142, 251n29
  revolutionary (post-Soviet) period, 222
  Russian car buying joke, 167, 254n123
  topics addressed, 86b, 144, 150–51, 252n41
  unreliable prison system, 156
  US Army portrayal, 148, 149f, 150
  women's issues, 82
  See also comic strips
Buivydas, Juozas, 40, 144, 240n28
Bulota, Andrius (brother), 33
Bulota, Andrius (uncle), 32, 239n14

Bulota, Antanas (brother), 34
Bulota, Jonas (brother), 8, 45
Bulota, Juozas
  American family, 239n17
  on antireligious topics, 153, 251n20
  apartments and summer houses, 19–20, 35
  bourgeois ideology and, 95
  on Brezhnev's book, 236n11
  Broom editor in chief, 3, 19, 33–34, 242n20,
    243n50
  Broom editors, 41f
  on Bytautas and proclamation, 50
  caution on criticism, 185
  censorship and conflict, 16, 112
  childhood and private life, 32, 36
  clay bust, 1, 2f, 19, 27, 235n1
  on comic strips, 163, 165
  complaint letters, 215, 255n13
  complaint letters and, 172, 191
  contributors and rejections, 123
  CP and, 69, 72, 151
  destroyed Leninist issue, 137–38
  drinking rituals and, 60, 62, 79b
  Glavlit and, 115
  greeting cards and gifts, 36
  hiring and dismissal orders, 34–35, 44,
    240n28
  hundredth birthday celebration, 18
  hunting and, 58, 59f
  ideological editing and, 127
  on investigative pieces, 175
  "laughter is a weapon," 81
  Lomsargytė-Pukienė denunciation and
    defense, 54
  modernist art and artists, 138, 141
  on nudity, 157
  party reprimand for "Expulsion from
    Eden," 101f
  pen names of, 242n24
  on Perestroika, 220, 253n93
  political intimacy and, 53–54, 56–57, 63
  PPO work, 74, 124
  problem cartoon and, 53
  proclamation parody, 49
  pseudonym of Jonas Bool, 160
  relatives of, 18–19
  retirement, 36, 235n3
  on satirical justice, 172
  at *Truth*, 38
  on wall newspaper content, 126, 188
  World War II and Soviet partisans,
    239nn12–13
Bulota, Juozas (son), 18, 36, 189, 235n1, 239n12

Bulotienė, Donata, 18, 34, 239n16
bureaucratic showcasing, 23, 51, 74, 77, 78b–79b,
  80, 97, 231
Bytautas, Česlovas, 47–49, 50b, 51–53, 63–64,
  242nn2–3
Bytwerk, Randall, 148

censorial indistinction, 91–92, 96, 116–17,
  119, 234
censorship
  aesthetic principles and, 119
  authors and, 119–20
  burning down, 96, 113
  censors' errors, 95–97, 246n18
  by citizens, 110
  contextualizing images, 111–14, 116, 144,
    231–32
  foreign humor and, 156, 238n44
  ideological censorship, 6, 89–93, 95–96,
    98–100, 234
  political-ideological errors, 97–98
  secrecy and, 88, 90
  Soviet takeover and, 92–93, 249n1
  state control and, 89–90, 93–94
  total control and, 92, 116
  unwritten rules, 115
  See also under Broom; Glavlit; LCP CC;
    Perechen'; political intimacy
Central Committee of the Communist Party
  (CP CC), 3, 5, 12, 110
Černiauskaitė, Vlada, 240n28
Charlie Hebdo, 26
Cheremnykh, Mikhail, 135, 250n1
Chronicle of the Lithuanian Catholic Church
  (periodical), 94–95
comic strips, 6, 25, 142, 159–65, 167, 229,
  253n99, 253n101
  See also under Broom cartoons and
    illustrations
Communist party, ideology, 44, 131, 134
Communist Party of the Soviet Union (CPSU)
  Broom and, 80–81
  communist paradise, 199
  congresses, 69, 93
  objectives of, 70–72, 91b, 244n6
  regulations of, 73, 76
  Sadaunykas case and, 60
Communist Party of the Soviet Union Central
  Committee (CPSU CC)
  cartoon scrutiny, 112
  Khrushchev speech, 199
  LCP CC and, 34
  letters to state institutions, 174, 176, 212

Communist Party (*continued*)
  resolutions of, 76, 80, 94, 254n10
  secretary position requirements, 37
  Twenty-Fifth Congress Resolutions, 71b,
    83, 84b
Communist Party Primary Organization (PPO)
  annual assessment, 70b–72b
  archives of, 21, 75–77, 151, 251n14
  CP members, 69–70, 244n7
  CPSU objectives and, 70, 71b
  documents, 23, 38, 52, 77
  meetings, 42b, 51, 57, 60, 67, 78b, 244n8,
    244n17
  performative aspect, 62, 77, 80
  reports, 48–49, 57, 76, 80
  role of satire, 81
  secret meetings, 66
  Soviet ideological language, 42b
  See also Lukša, Albertas; Tilvytis, Rytis
Communists (Sadaunykas), 38
complaint letters
  activists and, 189–91
  after independence, 225
  Broom and *Krokodil*, 254n11, 255n13
  bus and train station, 207b, 208
  dystopian world of, 198, 199f, 200–201, 203,
    204f, 205, 206f
  food and clothing complaints, 210–11
  road accidents and murders, 207
  safety in public places, 206
  small matters and, 194b–95b
  Soviet everyday life, 211–12, 259n51
  Soviet materialities and, 217–18
  staged images, 204
  target of criticism, 186, 196, 200, 257n98, 258n3
Comrades' Courts, 61, 194–95, 225, 243n46
CP CC. *See* Central Committee of the
  Communist Party
CPSU. *See* Communist Party of the Soviet Union
Creed, Gerald, 237n31
cultural intimacy, 16–17, 238n45
Cvirka, Andrius
  award winning cover, 140f
  Broom personal relationships, 64
  Bulota and, 139
  child of the monument, 31–32
  CP membership, 72
  dark humor cover and foreign humor, 159
  drinking and drunk tank, 62, 243n48
  drinking and hunting, 58–59
  drinking rituals and, 58
  Glavlit ignorance and censorship, 247n25
  Illustration Department chair, 154
  independence of, 166

interview of, 24
joins *Broom* (1967), 29, 41
Lenin's one hundredth birthday cover, 135,
  136f–37f, 138
multidirectional humor and, 144
Palčiauskas and, 165
post-independence, 225
Sąjūdis and Lithuanian revolution, 220
on subotnik, 250n4
World War II and, 28–29
Cvirka, Petras, 29, 31, 231

Dadzis (Thistle), 7f, 142, 233
Dalgis, J., 102
Davoliūtė, Violeta, 202–3
Deltuva, Andrius, 91b, 108f, 151, 229, 231
Deni, Victor Nikolaevich, 250n1
Dimitrov, Martin, 175–76
dissensus
  artists' expression of, 118
  citizen's letters and, 176, 211–12
  complicity and, 15, 40, 43, 143
  definition of, 10, 12
  editors' relation to power, 142
  multidirectional humor and, 233
  post-Soviet laughter, 227
  satirical stories and, 224
Dobužinskis, Mstislavas, 241n67
Donelaitis, Kristijonas, 99
Douglas, Mary, 11
Dovainis, 242n24
Draitser, Emil, 5, 7, 26, 172, 238n48
Drilinga, Antanas, 158
drinking and drinking rituals, 38, 57–58,
  60–62, 79b, 88, 98, 108f, 124, 191–93, 197
dystopia and utopia, 198, 211–12
  See also complaint letters

Efimov, Boris, 4, 26, 110, 148, 151
Eichmann, Adolf, 30–31
Eichmann in Jerusalem (Arendt), 30–31
Eisenstein, Sergei, 4
environmental pollution and ecology, 15, 166
Eremeev, Konstantin S., 44b, 182
Estonia, 93, 246n8
  See also Pikker
Etty, John, 11, 247n47, 251n36–52n36
Eulenspiegel, 142, 148
"Everyday Lyrics" (Valaitis), 103–4

Fehérváry, Krisztina, 217
Ferensienė, Goda, 223
Feshbach, Murray, 166
Fight for Freedom Movement, 13, 237n34

Fitzpatrick, Sheila, 10, 173
Flashlight of Komsomol, 189
Freud, Sigmund, 11
Friendly, Alfred, Jr., 166

Garey, Amy, 236n22
Gérin, Annie, 182, 235n10
Getty, Arch, 10
Gimberis, Jurgis, 225
Ginkūnienė, Angelė, 192
Glaeser, Andreas, 235n6
Glavlit (the Main Directorate for Literary and Publishing Affairs)
    ambiguity, 113
    annual reports, 97
    archives of, 22
    bourgeois propaganda and, 99
    Broom and approval, 115
    Broom censored content reports, 101–4, 104t–6t, 107, 107t, 108, 111f
    Broom editors and, 115
    censorship ending, 221
    censorship by, 6, 12, 21, 89–90, 93, 95, 97, 111f, 120, 245n1, 246n16
    censors' lack of knowledge, 247n25
    erotic cartoons, 157
    establishment and conclusion, 92, 95
    factories and houses, 88
    founding, 246n11
    Lankauskas and, 116–17
    literature and, 89
    modernist style and, 142
    political undertones, 133
    procrastination and drinking at, 98
    relationship with Moscow, 246n18
    reports, 96–98
    Šiaulytis's cartoons and, 147
    tourist maps, 89
    Žilinskaitė and, 114
    See also Broom; censorship; Gurvičius, Borisas; Slizevičius, Mykolas
Gogol, Nikolai, 5
Goldstein, Meryl, 26
Good Soldier Svejk, The (Hašek), 35
Gorbachev, Mikhail, 3, 219–20, 240n36, 259n2
Gorbačiovas, V., 209
Gordin, Michael D., 198
Gricius, A., 240n28
Grybkauskas, Saulius, 57–58
Gudaitis, Leonas, 93
Gurvičius, Borisas, 95–97, 115

Hajizada, Adnan, 226
Hall, Kira, 26

Hašek, Jaroslav, 35
Haugerud, Angelique, 227
Havel, Vaclav, 67, 89
Hemment, Julie, 227
Herzfeld, Michael, 16–17, 238n45
historical ethnography, 19, 78b, 238n49
Holocaust, 13, 28, 31, 85, 238n2
homosexuality, 63, 155, 243n54

ideological socialization, 69, 86, 234
"I'm at a meeting," 145
implicated subject, 14, 31, 230, 239nn9–10
Ingram, Matthew Bruce, 26
In search of Sąjūdis origins (Ramonaitė, Kavaliauskaitė), 224
Internal Affairs Ministry, 9, 178, 191
Irony of Fate, The (film), 23, 61
Ivanauskas, Vilius, 117, 224
Izvestiia, 244n6

Jakštas, Šarūnas, 115
Jankauskas, P., 71
Juozapavičius, J., 82
Jurašas, Jonas, 89, 116
Juršėnas, Česlovas
    Bulota's funeral and, 36
    criticism of regime, 165
    interview with, 24, 234
    on Juozas Baltušis, 254n120
    leadership role, 142
    relationship with *Broom*, 63, 101, 243n52

Kalanta, Romas, 94–95, 238n36
Kalninis, Valdimaras, 145
Karkauskaitė, Irena, 204–5
Kassof, Brian, 89
Katilius, V., 186, 209–10
"Kaunas Resident X in Vilnius, Vilnius Resident X in Kaunas." (Kunčinas), 108
Kaušinis, Vytautas, 40, 240n28
Kavaliauskaitė, Jūratė, 166, 224
Kazakauskas, A., 82
Keblytė (*Broom* editor), 57
KGB
    archives of, 21–22
    Broom collaboration and, 255n30
    Broom incident with Sadaunykas, 63–64
    complaint investigation, 213–14
    informant, 42b, 241n62
    political intimacy and, 52
    proclamation parody, 49, 242nn2–3
    See also Kiauleikis, Leonas
Khrushchev, Nikita
    anti-formalism campaign and, 141

Khrushchev, Nikita (*continued*)
  on communist paradise, 199
  de-Stalinization, 174–75
  on food shortage, 168
  liberalization of media, 34, 53, 187
  on satire, 4, 124
  Secret Speech, 93
Kiauleikis, Leonas
  Broom hire, 240n28
  censorship of, 99
  CP member, 72, 244n7
  CP member, left *Broom* (1969), 69, 77
  KGB agent, 42b, 220, 241n62
Kindziulis (*Broom* character), 9, 126, 167, 213,
    237n24, 237n26
kolkhoz (collective farms)
  in *Broom*, 16, 66, 84b, 102, 125, 146–47
  criticism of, 33
  positive portrayals, 99–100
Koltsov, Mikhail, 4
Kozlov, Denis, 235n5
Kozlov, Vladimir A., 257n69
Kranklys (Raven), 220
Krasauskas, Stasys, 32, 36, 54f, 240n28
Krikhatskii, Vladimir, 250n4
Krokodil (Crocodile)
  anti-imperialist cartoon signs, 150
  antisemitism in, 242n21
  archives of, 21–22
  Broom and, 46b, 79b, 142
  Broom and Dadzis announced, 7
  Broom imitation, 67
  censorship and, 247n47
  complaint letters, 254n11
  contextualizing images, 111
  counter-commentaries on Soviet
    orthodoxies, 251n36
  distinction of art in, 15, 41
  editing strategies, 127
  fiftieth anniversary of, 36, 163
  history of, 44b
  injustices not covered, 186
  laughter as a weapon, 81, 182–83
  Lenin's one hundredth birthday cover, 135
  political aesthetics and, 119
  political event coverage lead, 148
  popularity of, 8, 236n14, 236n17
  portrayal of capitalists, 110
  positive portrayals, 139–40
  racism and, 151
  Soviet laughter, 5–6, 172, 233
  study of, 26
  tool of threat, 189
  Žilinskaitė and, 114

Krokodil cartoons, family of snowmen, 112
Krylova, Anna, 13
Kubilinskas, Kostas, 239n8
Kubilius, Vytautas, 9
Kučaitė, Regina, 240n28
Kundera, Milan, 68, 89
Kunickis, G., 150
Kuntaplis (Wooden clog), 6, 46b
Kurklietytė Bubnienė, Elena, 32–33, 35,
    42b, 240n28

"Lady," 113–14
Lampland, Martha, 58, 226
Lankauskas, Romualdas, 42b, 90, 115–17, 229,
    246n4
Laucius, Jeronimas, 122–23, 249n11
laughter, Soviet perspective, 5, 235n10,
    237nn30–31
Lauk, Epp, 93, 246n8
LCP CC. *See* Lithuanian Communist Party
    Central Committee
Leites, Natan, 43
Lenin, Vladimir
  Broom editors and, 76, 78
  censorship and, 113
  Lenin's one hundredth birthday, 137
  modern apartment blocks, 202
  monument to, 99, 260n28
  one hundredth birthday celebration, 107,
    135–36
  Pravda founding, 44
  press mission, 4, 43
  quotes ignored, 151
  schoolchildren and, 69
  statue razed, 228f
Lenin at the First Subbotnik (Krikhatskii),
    250n4
Lewin, Moshe, 10
List, The. *See Perechen'*
Literaturnaia gazeta, 5
Lithuania, modern history of
  Act of Independence, 44
  genocide, crime of, 13, 237n35
  independence movement, 219–20, 224,
    260n5, 260n7
  inspection by censors, 15
  interwar period, 13, 246n10
  interwar period artists, 241n67
  language, 237n33
  Marxist interpretation, 119
  population of, 236n16
  post-World War II, 28–29, 92
  Soviet occupation and, 238n38
  See also Holocaust

Lithuanian Communist Party
  banning of, 75
  Broom and, 45b, 157
  higher positions at work, 72–73
  literature and, 94
  secret meetings, 66
  See also Lithuanian Communist Party
    Central Committee
Lithuanian Communist Party Central
  Committee (LCP CC)
  archives of, 21
  Broom and, 34, 70, 76, 143, 243n50
  Broom issues destroyed, 107
  Bytautas and, 50–51
  censorship and, 6, 108, 110
  Glavlit and, 97
  Goda Ferensienė and, 223
  ideological control actions, 95
  interviews, 24
  Laucius and, 122
  modernist art and artists, 142
  oversight by, 68
  political education and, 73–74
  post-Soviet history and, 75
  private regime criticism, 165
  publications of, 8, 33
  See also Propaganda and Agitation
    Department
Lithuanian Freedom Army, 37
Lithuanian Green Organization, 166
Lithuanian language, 236n10, 249n112,
  251n31, 254n2, 255n19, 255n21, 259n55
Lithuanian National Resurrection Party
  (NRP), 227
Lomsargytė-Pukienė, Dita, 242n23
  Broom editor, 31–32
  Broom personal relationships, 64
  drinking rituals and, 60
  Letters Department, 34
  mother and watermelons, 87
  Nazi occupation and, 239n3
  post-World War II, 28–29
  Truth denunciation and defense, 54b–55b
Lukša, Albertas
  "After the *Broom* wrote" and, 179
  background, 65–66
  Broom editor, 41f
  Broom editor in chief, 261n1
  Broom hire (1959), 33, 35, 40, 66, 241n53
  Broom PPO secretary, 22, 66, 66f, 67, 69–70,
    74–76, 78b
  on Bulota, 124
  Bytautas's accusation, 49
  on Bytautas and proclamation, 51

college thesis, 5
complaint letters and, 189, 191
copyeditor at *Truth*, 39
CP ideological work, 68
CP member, 23
on homosexuality, 243n54
ideological editing and, 127
injustices not covered, 186
investigative journalism and, 80
justice for the people, 179b
KGB and, 213–14
museum of defective items, 258n29
political education and, 73
on political intimacy, 63, 243n50
political intimacy and, 57
post-World War II, 39, 241n50
PPO meetings, 175, 244n7
proclamation meeting, 50b
Sadaunykas case, 60
Sąjūdis and Lithuanian revolution, 220
Šepetys accusation, 243n50
university thesis and laughter, 183
"Vanished Laughter" and, 229
Lukšienė, Stasė, 50b, 65, 70b
Lunacharsky, Anatoly, 4–5, 182, 235n9

Mačinskas, Vytautas, 240n28
Malaia zemlia (Small Land*)* (Brezhnev), 5
Manege Affair, 93–94, 116
Mannheim, Karl, 198
Mansurov, N. S., 159
Marcinkevičienė, Dalia, 186
Marcinkevičius, Justinas, 35
Martinaitis, Marcelijus, 89, 113, 117, 119
Marx, Karl, 5, 108, 212
Marxism-Leninism, 5–6, 12, 73, 99, 119,
  173, 226
"Matryoshki" (Deltuva), 108f
Mazzarella, William, 111, 114
Mbembe, Achille, 29–30, 52
"Meeting in a Sauna, A" (Sadaunykas), 108
Mieželaitis, Eduardas, 35, 115
Miłosz, Czesław, 89
"Miniature Cake, A," 121
Mirror of Shame, 189
modernism, 7, 15, 43, 77, 138, 141–42, 144,
  147, 166
Moriak Litvy (Lithuanian sailor), 99
Motuza, Boleslovas, 45b, 185
multidirectional humor, 2–3, 6
  ambiguity and, 7, 150
  authoritarian regimes and, 227, 233
  Broom editing and, 131, 133, 230–31
  Broom success and, 8, 18

multidirectional humor (*continued*)
cartoons and, 110, 146–47
cats and birdhouses example, 113
censorial indistinction, 117
definition, 11–12
dissensus and, 118
embedded messages, 143–44
global examples, 260n26
grotesque and, 150
ideological discourse and everyday life, 217
independence movement, 224
Jack and Bobby example, 165
political intimacy and, 16, 64
post-authoritarian laughter, 221
stiob and, 61
US Army portrayal, 149
Žilinskaitė's feuilleton, 216
"Mummies" (Dalgis), 102

Nadkarni, Maya, 226
Naudžiūnienė, Akvilė, 125, 249n27
Niunka, Vladas, 142
Nobel Peace Prize, 259n2
Nordstrom, Carolyn, 87
Norris, Stephen, 148

On the Postcolony (Mbembe), 29
Orwell, George, 26
"Our bus stop, the best in the district," 146
Oushakine, Serguei, 5–6, 150

Pabijūnas, Algimantas, 103, 240n28
Pakalnis, Antanas, 61, 138–39, 231, 240n28, 251n14
Pakalnis, Arvydas, 72, 111, 145–46, 151, 220–22, 251n29
Palčiauskas, Romas, 41f, 59, 160, 161f, 163–65, 229, 253n100, 261n1
Paškevičienė, Liudmila, 191–92, 257n86
Pažūsis, LCP CC representative, 51
Pearce, Katy, 226
Peasants Visit Lenin (painting), 135
Pehowski, Marian, 43, 236n14, 236n17, 254n11
People's Courts, 9, 178
Perechen' ("The List"), 90, 97, 246n7
Perets (Pepper), 8, 156, 216, 236n13, 236n14
Pesmen, Dale, 17
Petrović, Tanja, 110
Petrulis, N., 240n28
Pikker (magazine), 32, 142, 144, 233, 261n2
Pimenov, Iurii, 202–3, 211
Playboy (magazine), 33, 158
political aesthetics, 134, 139, 165–66, 223

See also under Broom
political intimacy
censors and cultural elites, 97–98
censorship and, 89–90, 117
conflicts and, 57, 115–16, 189, 191
definition of, 10, 15
hunting and drinking, 58–60, 62, 243n35, 243n40
interdependence, 17–18
internal resolution, 57, 64
Lomsargytė-Pukienė incident, 54–55
ordinary people and, 77
PPO and, 79b
proclamation accusation and, 49, 52–53
recognition and loyalty, 16, 56, 238n44
relationality, 92
sociality and, 57
Soviet authoritarianism and, 233
svoi (one of us), 17
unequal distribution, 63
Žilinskaitė and, 114
"Political Intimacy: Power, Laughter, and Coexistence in Late Soviet Lithuania" (Klumbytė), 17
post-Soviet laughter, 18, 25, 226–27
post-Soviet predicament, 230
post-Stalin period, 4, 21, 44, 93, 119, 182, 246n13
"Power of Pedagogy, The," 123–24
PPO. *See* Communist Party Primary Organization
Prakash, Gyan, 198
Pravda (Truth), 6, 44b, 174, 236n17
Propaganda and Agitation Department (LCP CC)
Bulota on complaint letters, 255n13
Bulota on investigative pieces, 175
Bulota on working conditions piece, 185
censorship by, 108
Juršėnas at Bulota funeral, 36
Juršėnas LCP CC, 142
Juršėnas on *Broom* discipline, 101
Juršėnas on criticism of regime, 166, 234
political intimacy and, 63
replacement of chair and editors, 95
reports, 35, 236n17
Žeimantas on meetings, 42, 217
Propp, Vladimir, 148
publications, humor in, 8, 237n24
Puchalski, Juliusz, 222
Pukis, Povilas, 240n28

Radvilavičius, Algirdas, 64, 91b, 110, 113–14, 149–50, 152–54, 229, 238n44
Ramonaitė, Ainė, 224
Ranciere, Jacques, 10–12, 200, 237n30
Raščius, Pranas, 108, 123
Reagan, Ronald, 254n123
Red Genocide, 15, 219–20
Reform Movement of Lithuania. *See* Sąjūdis and Sąjūdis era
Reid, Susan, 93, 202, 217
revisionist and post-revisionist scholarship, 9–10, 237nn27–28, 238n36
Rimša, Antanas, 34, 43–44, 61
Rothberg, Michael, 14, 31, 33, 239n9
Rudzinskas, Antanas, 50b, 244n7
Ryazanov, Eldar, 61

Sadaunykas, Jonas
autobiographical novel, 33, 37–39, 53, 56, 60, 64, 240n20, 241n40
background, 37–38
Broom editors, 41f
Broom executive secretary, 33, 37
Broom hire, 240n28
on Bytautas and proclamation, 49
censorship, 108, 113
on comic strips, 164
and Communism, 38
CP member, 69
drinking case, 60–62, 243n48
KGB and, 63
on Kiauleikis's ambition, 42b
Lukša hired for *Broom*, 35
modernism and, 138
political cartoons, 154
political prisoner, 241n41
PPO and, 70b
proclamation meeting, 50b
socialist realism and, 141
Truth employment, 38
Sąjūdis and Sąjūdis era, 36, 38, 40, 75, 222, 224, 240n36, 259n4, 260n6
Sakharov, Andrei, 89
Saltykov-Shchedrin, Mikhail, 5
Samukas, Fridrikas, 40, 144, 220–21, 230–31
Sartwell, Crispin, 118
satire and humor magazines, Eastern European, 142, 160, 252n78
satire and humor magazines, Western, 154
Satire in the Battle for Peace, 251n29
satirical justice
authoritarian governance and, 172, 176, 183, 188, 233

Broom and, 173, 177, 182, 184, 188–89, 193, 197
definition of, 171
discontinuation at *Broom*, 196, 222, 225
fear of criticism, 187–94, 196, 257n69
ideologically correct requirement, 184, 256n60
prevention and propaganda, 191–97
preventive function, 191
Soviet institution, 182
spinal injury case, 171, 254n2
"Secret of Immortality, A" (Žilinskaitė), 214–15
Semenov, Ivan, 140, 189
Semenov, Manuil, 119, 182, 189
Šepetys, Lionginas, 63, 142, 243n50
Serov, Vladimir, 135
Shafir, Iakov, 5
Šiaulytis, Kęstutis
Broom popularity, 8
on *Broom* popularity, 237n25
bust of Lenin, 43
Bytautas case, 51
citizen's complaint to KGB, 110–13
on comic strips, 165
Glavlit censorship and, 115
hidden meanings and, 133
ideological campaigns, 82
kolkhoz cartoon, 146–47
Krokodil and foreign policy, 148, 156
Krokodil imitation, 67
in *Last Supper* cartoon, 231
on LCP membership, 72
modernist artist, 139
opposition to state authority and, 15, 117, 143, 222
post-Soviet laughter and, 226
PPO meetings and, 66
proclamation accusation, 52
on Sadaunykas, 38
Sąjūdis and Lithuanian revolution, 220
US as Soviet Union, 150
at "Vanished Laughter," 229, 261nn1–2
younger generation, 41, 225
Šiekštelė, Algirdas, 40, 150, 240n28
Siudikaitė, Julijona, 169–72, 176–77, 191, 254n1
Skinkys, Algirdas, 239n8
Slizevičius, Mykolas, 95–96, 99, 102–4, 114–15
Šluotos kalendorius (*Broom* calendar), 8, 237n24
Smetona, Antanas, 45b–46b, 55b, 246n10
Sniečkus, Antanas, 34, 93–94, 115, 157
Šniukas, Domas, 8, 33–34, 229, 261n1
socialist realism, 93–95, 141–42, 166
Solzhenitsyn, Aleksandr, 89, 94

"Soviet Hegemony of Form" (Yurchak), 80
Soviet journalism, 185, 256n59
Soviet literature, 235n5
Soviet materialities, 19, 21, 200, 202–3, 210, 213–14, 215f, 216–18
Soviet predicament, 10, 31, 38, 67–68, 72, 86–87
Soviet presence, 42–43
Soviet satire, 5, 10, 24–25, 43
    See also Broom; Krokodil; Kuntaplis
Soviet Union
    collapse of, 223–24
    print media censorship, 249n1
    right to complain to the state, 174, 254n9
Soviet Woman (magazine), 77
Sri Lanka and watermelon, 87
Stalin, Joseph, 4, 6, 32, 113, 241n45
    See also post-Stalin period
Stalin's cap, 38, 241n45
Šteinys, Zenonas, 41, 231, 232f
stiob (parody)
    on drinking, 61
    proclamation, 47–49, 242nn1–4
    proclamation meeting, 50b
    Sadaunykas drinking explanation, 61
    See also Bytautas, Česlovas
Stites, Richard, 139
Stokes, Gale, 67
Streikus, Arūnas, 94, 246n19
Subačius, Adomas, 88–90
Suchockis, Vitalijus, 40, 221
Survila, Gintautas, 222

Taranas (Tomkus), 256n65
text boxes, 241n58
Thurston, Robert, 10
Tiesa (Truth). See Truth
Tilley, Helen, 198
Tiltas į jūrą (A bridge to the sea) (Lankauskas), 116
Tilvytis, Rytis
    Broom associate editor, 49
    Broom editors, 41f
    Broom hire, 35, 40, 240n28
    complaint letters and, 191
    CP member, 69, 244n7
    hired as a literary editor, 40
    Lankauskas parody, 116
    letters to Broom as tool of threat, 189
    macabre cover discussion, 159
    on political cartoons, 154
    PPO meetings, 244n17
    PPO secretary, 40, 57, 71b–72b, 74, 178, 189
    proclamation meeting, 50b
    Sąjūdis and Lithuanian revolution, 220

Tilvytis, Teofilis, 40, 240n28
Tomkus, Vitas, 185–86, 256n65
Truth (Tiesa), 8, 33, 39, 42, 54–55, 63, 67, 91b, 186, 217
Tvardovsky, Aleksandr, 94

Unbearable Lightness of Being, The (Kundera), 68

Vaigauskas, H., 209
Vaiseta, Tomas, 184, 188–89, 256n60
Valadka, Česlovas, 41f, 48, 52, 64, 160, 161f, 170, 180b, 220
Valaitis, L., 103, 108
Valk, Heinz, 144
"Vanished Laughter, The," 25, 228–30, 261n1
Varnas, Jonas
    antireligious cartoons, 153
    banality of opposition and, 143
    cats and birdhouses, 113
    censorship and, 16, 90
    Glavlit censors and, 98
    in Last Supper cartoon, 231
    Lenin monument and, 228
    modernism and, 40
    post-Soviet era, 225
    public exhibitions, 97, 236n20
    Sąjūdis reform movement, 220
    self-censorship, 115
    "Vanished Laughter, The," 229–30, 261n1
Vatulescu, Cristina, 76
Veblauskas, Vytautas, 145, 166
Venclova, Tomas, 89
Vileišytė, Donata, 33
"Vilnius is ours," 213, 259n56
Vitulskis, Aleksandras, 240n28
Voice of America, 167
Vorobjovas, Leonidas, 187
"Vyriausioji sąžinė" (Highest conscience) (Pabijūnas), 102

Wedding on Tomorrow Street (Pimenov), 202–3
Wedeen, Lisa, 226
Western aesthetic, 43
Western culture, 15, 19, 93, 116, 141, 143–44, 154–56, 253n83, 253n93
    See also modernism
"What Happened to Jokes?" (Lampland, Nadkarni), 226
Wolfe, Thomas C., 155
Wooden Clog, 40, 46b
World War II and postwar, 44, 239n3
    watermelons for starving Lithuanians, 87
    World War II and Soviet partisans, 239nn12–13

Yellow Eyes of a Hawk, The
    (Sadaunykas), 37
Yeremieieva, Kateryna, 156, 216
Yurchak, Alexei, 17, 43, 48, 80, 86, 155, 189,
    216, 223, 242n4

Žeimantas, Vytautas, 42–43, 63, 67,
    75–76, 217

Žekonis, Bronius, 46b
Zhuk, Sergei I., 155
Žilinskaitė, Vytautė, 114–15, 186, 214–16,
    259n61
Zimanas, Genrikas, 33, 39, 142, 239n15
Zoshchenko, Mikhail, 131
Žukas, Stepas, 46b
Zurbienė, Laima, 42b

Printed in the USA
CPSIA information can be obtained
at www.ICGtesting.com
CBHW032132090424
6682CB00002B/75